Mikhail Glinka

Glinka in 1852. Portrait by G. Kordik

Mikhail Glinka

A Biographical and Critical Study

DAVID BROWN

LONDON
OXFORD UNIVERSITY PRESS
NEW YORK   TORONTO
1974

Oxford University Press, Ely House, London W.1

GLASGOW NEW YORK TORONTO MELBOURNE WELLINGTON CAPE TOWN
IBADAN NAIROBI DAR ES SALAAM LUSAKA ADDIS ABABA DELHI BOMBAY
CALCUTTA MADRAS KARACHI LAHORE DACCA KUALA LUMPUR SINGAPORE
HONG KONG TOKYO

ISBN 0 19 315311 4

Printed in Great Britain
by W & J Mackay Limited, Chatham

Contents

List of plates   vii

Preface   1

Note on transliteration, translations, dates, and musical
   examples   6

1. Childhood   7

2. The St. Petersburg dilettante   23

3. Italy and Berlin   56

4. First opera   75

5. *A Life for the Tsar:* process of composition   91

6. *A Life for the Tsar:* the music   111

7. Problems and responsibilities: Imperial Kapellmeister   137

8. Second opera   155

9. *Ruslan and Lyudmila:* process of composition   183

10. *Ruslan and Lyudmila:* the music   198

11. Paris and Spain   237

12. Smolensk and Warsaw   257

13. Last years   278

14. Conclusion   300

   Appendix:

      Glinka, *Biographical note*   305

      Berlioz, *A Life for the Tsar* [and] *Ruslan and Lyudmila*   310

   Bibliographical note and selected bibliography   316

   List and index of works   321

   Index of persons   335

List of Plates

Frontispiece   Glinka in 1852. Portrait by G. Kordik.

Plate I   Glinka, his mother, and sister, Pelageya, in 1817.
Miniature by an unknown artist.   Facing p. 24

Plate II   Glinka as a young man (1826). Portrait by an unknown
artist.   Facing p. 56

Plate III   Glinka and his servant, Yakov. Drawing by
N. A. Stepanov.   Facing p. 216

Plate IV   Glinka and his sister, Lyudmila Shestakova, in 1852.
Daguerreotype.   Facing p. 248

Plate V   Glinka in 1853. Caricature by V. Samoilov.
Facing p. 280

Plate VI   Glinka in 1856.   Facing p. 312

To Gerald Abraham

Preface

'Glinka. An unprecedented, astonishing phenomenon in the sphere of art. A dilettante who played the violin and piano a little; having composed completely insipid quadrilles, fantasias upon popular Italian tunes, having also tried his hand at serious musical forms (quartet, sextet) and at songs, but not having written anything except banalities after the taste of the thirties, suddenly in his thirty-fourth year[1] creates an opera which for genius, sweep, originality and irreproachable technique stands beside the greatest and most profound in musical art!
. . . How came Glinka, who had long been an insipid dilettante, suddenly in a single stride to stand alongside (yes! alongside!) Mozart, Beethoven, and whomsoever you will? . . . Almost fifty years have passed since then; many Russian symphonic works have been composed; it can be said that there is a real Russian symphonic school. Well? It's all in [the orchestral scherzo] *Kamarinskaya*, just as the whole oak is in the acorn. And for a long time Russian composers will draw from this rich source, for it will need much time and much strength to exhaust all its wealth. Yes! Glinka is a real creative genius!'[2]

Tchaikovsky, like Russian musicians in general, became immoderate as soon as he started to write about Glinka, and his comparisons with Mozart and Beethoven are too absurd to require argued refutation. Yet in other respects he could be very balanced in his view of his predecessor, for he saw clearly and was constantly troubled by the personal triviality of the man who could produce such remarkable music. Nevertheless there is one hard fact in Tchaikovsky's evaluation which he was in a position to know as well as anyone: without Glinka, Russian music would have taken a very different course. All the important late nineteenth-century Russian composers—Balakirev,

---

[1] In fact Glinka was thirty-two.

[2] From Tchaikovsky's diary: entry for 27 June/9 July 1888. Quoted in *Dni i godui P. I. Chaikovskovo* (edited by A. Orlova and others) (Moscow/Leningrad, 1940), pp. 449–50.

Mussorgsky, Borodin, Rimsky-Korsakov, Tchaikovsky himself—owed a gigantic debt to this man who, single-handed, had laid the foundation for a Russian musical tradition. Today, of course, our music history books dutifully repeat this fact, yet how much do we actually know of the music of this nonentity of genius? Neither of his operas has been given professionally in England for many years. *Ruslan and Lyudmila* is, admittedly, a lost cause in the opera house, but does its music deserve the complete neglect we accord to most of it? We all know the captivating overture from numerous concert performances, broadcasts, and recordings, but for most English listeners knowledge ceases abruptly even before the curtain has risen. Yet what musical riches lie buried in this score! *Kamarinskaya* and the Valse-Fantaisie are occasionally heard, the Spanish Overtures more rarely. But what of the *Prince Kholmsky* music? What of the many songs? Although most of these last works are of no great importance, the fact remains that some of them are splendid pieces which could greatly enrich our recital repertoire.

There is therefore no need to apologize for attempting a full-length study of Glinka in English in the hope that this will stimulate both a reappraisal and a wider investigation of his music. No such study has ever appeared in print, for the slim volume by M. Montagu-Nathan, which is now over fifty years old, is no more than a general introduction. In 1916 Montagu-Nathan would have found it virtually impossible to write a really comprehensive study, even had he wished to, for some of Glinka's music had not yet been printed, and other pieces which had been published long since would have been difficult to come by. Now, however, these difficulties have been removed by the arrival from the Soviet Union of an eighteen-volume complete edition of Glinka's music. Since the Second World War, too, Soviet musicology has given us not only a new two-volume edition of Glinka's literary legacy, but also a host of research studies on aspects of Glinka's life, work, and environment. Thus the scholar of the 1970s has a new and unprecedented base upon which to found his own study of Glinka.

But there are problems, too. The complete edition is *not* complete, for it prudishly omits Glinka's church music. Admittedly this would not have added very much to our knowledge, but since the editors have seen fit to print every little fragment, no matter how small, that seems to have come from his pen (including some 135 pages of technical exercises which Glinka worked with Dehn), they cannot plead that his church music has been excluded because it was not important enough.

The reason for its omission is obvious; since the texts used are ideologically unacceptable to the Soviet authorities, and since it was quite impracticable to substitute other words, its existence was simply not recognized. The problem of 'incorrect' sentiments in the words of some of Glinka's other vocal pieces has been solved by the provision of new texts. Mostly this does not matter very much, though if the piece concerned has never been printed before, it means that it is virtually impossible to find out what the original text was. The one really serious case of text substitution is the wholesale re-writing of the libretto of *A Life for the Tsar* (which, not surprisingly, is now known by its original title, *Ivan Susanin*). Fortunately there exist earlier editions of this which contain the original words. Yet the most serious of all the criticisms of this new edition concerns its level of accuracy, which is sometimes roughly comparable to a first set of uncorrected proofs. Its standard would be quite unacceptable in the West. In general it is easy enough to see where many of the errors lie and to make reliable guesses at the correct readings; nevertheless, these patent mistakes must raise fears that there are other more fundamental imperfections which are not detectable without consultation of the original sources. Nor is the level of accuracy as consistently high as it should be in the presentation of some of the literary studies of Glinka's work. All this is the more regrettable since many of the scholars who have worked on the edition and the various studies appear to be well trained, diligent men and women, whose editorial work is often as invaluable as it is elaborate. It is they who must regret more than anyone that their work should sometimes be presented to the world in imperfect forms.

After Glinka's compositions the most important sources for this present book have been his literary remains and the numerous recollections of him written by relatives and friends. Glinka's *Memoirs* are fundamental, though he often shows poor discrimination in deciding what is worthy of record. They have recently appeared in an English translation, but this is sometimes inaccurate, even on rather elementary points. Beside the *Memoirs* must be set Glinka's letters. These at least were current writings and problems of memory did not arise, but unfortunately the surviving ones are spread so unevenly over his life that some important phases are barely documented at all in them. The first biography of Glinka was written by Vladimir Stasov, and appeared in the year after Glinka's death. It is of prime importance, though Stasov, who knew Glinka well in his last years, is very partisan, and inclined to overemphasize the national side of Glinka's art. The first publication of the *Memoirs* in 1870 seems to have been the signal for a succession of reminiscences concerning the composer, which continued to appear until after the end of the century. Their worth is variable, for most were written after Glinka had become something of a classic. Thus their objectivity is often seriously suspect, and the passage of time between Glinka's death and their writing has obviously not improved their factual accuracy. Of these reminiscences the most important are those of Lyudmila Shestakova, Glinka's sister. Her trouble is that she is too aware of her close position to her exalted brother, and excessively anxious to emphasize just what she did for him, and how emotionally dependent he was upon her in his later years. Her memory for facts, especially dates, is not infallible. The composer, Aleksandr Serov, also wrote important reminiscences, though he is idiosyncratic—too full of admiration for the songs, and wearisome both in this and in pressing the point that *Ruslan and Lyudmila* was a dramatic misconception, even though freely admitting the beauties of the score. Like Shestakova, Serov is not always secure in his facts, despite the relatively early date at which he was writing (1860). Among the others, Aleksandr Strugov-shchikov gossips, and Feofil Tolstoi rambles, romanticizes, trivializes, and digresses. The recollections of Pyotr Stepanov seem as trustworthy as any; conversely the voluminous diary of Nestor Kukolnik is the most unreliable of all. Fortunately before the nineteenth century was out Nikolai Findeizen brought a splendidly scholarly approach to the study of Glinka, preparing a comprehensive catalogue of the composer's manuscript and other remains in the St. Petersburg Public Library, and publishing the first collected edition of Glinka's letters in 1907. Unfortunately his detailed biographical study of the composer did not get beyond the first thirty-six pages.

The reader will realize that there has been no dearth of material for this book. On the other hand there have been at times great problems in establishing factual accuracy because of the conflicting evidence and subjective views of some of the primary sources, and the uncertain accuracy of some later ones. I have endeavoured, using as wide a range of materials as are available in this country, to establish the facts as best I can and to present them here. Original sources have been used where accessible; where irreconcilable differences have emerged in secondary sources I have tried, by examining as wide a range of these as possible, to establish the true facts. It is not practicable to set out the reasons for a particular conclusion in all such instances, for the text would become impossibly cluttered, though I have thought it advisable in some cases to point out where a statement in this book is at variance with the evidence of an important source like Glinka's *Memoirs*. I have quoted liberally from source material, partly to enable the reader to get as close as possible to the basic evidence, but also so that he may gauge for himself something of its reliability from its tone and terms. As for the critical opinions expressed in this study, I must take full responsibility for these. Little guidance in such matters is to be found in Soviet writings, for the heavy political conditioning to which the Soviet scholar is subjected often leads him to partial, even strange judgements, and sometimes to conclusions which an objective examination of the facts would find untenable. The best critical writing on Glinka is still to be found in the studies which Gerald Abraham published during the 1930s; it was these, indeed, which first led the present writer to turn his attention seriously to Russian music.

Help in writing a book like this is contributed by many people in many different ways. My first debt is to Dr. Abraham, who really started it all for me, and who has aided my investigations of Russian music by his unstinting advice, encouragement, and practical assistance, in this instance by lending me some invaluable material from his own library, and by reading the final typescript, making supplementations and suggestions. Dr. Anthea Baird, Music Librarian of London University, and Mr. A. Helliwell of the library of the School of Slavonic and East European Studies of London University both gave prolonged assistance with books and scores. My mother, casting aside the burden of mid-septuagenarian years, typed most of the book. Finally my wife not only made the translation of the Berlioz article in the Appendix, but also helped with the final checking. To these and all the others who have helped in various ways, my warmest thanks.

University of Southampton   DAVID BROWN
December 1971

Note on Transliteration, Translations, Dates, and Musical Examples

Russian names have, of course, been transliterated. Sometimes a Western equivalent exists (Alexander for Aleksandr, Nicholas for Nikolai), but in order that consistency may be maintained, these equivalents have not been used. Only where a name is not really Russian at all, but clearly of Western origin, has the original Western spelling been adopted. All Russians have their own name followed by a patronymic —that is, the name of their father with the suffix '-ovich' or '-evich' for boys, and '-ovna' or '-evna' for girls. Patronymics are omitted from the main text of this book, but are given in the index, together with dates of birth and death where known.

Although the titles and texts of works in Western languages have been retained in their original tongue, all Russian titles and texts have been translated into English. The English titles of Glinka's vocal works and of Russian folk-songs are not intended as the first lines of singing translations, but simply as labels to identify each piece. In musical illustrations the Russian text has been transliterated, and a rough, sometimes summary English translation provided below.

In Glinka's lifetime the Russian calendar was twelve days behind the Western. Dates are given in both versions, of which the second is the Western. In the case of less precise chronological references, the time has been adjusted to a Western equivalent (e.g. 'at the end of May' has been changed to 'at the beginning of June', 'in the middle of July' to 'at the end of July').

In musical examples from orchestral scores, all instruments play at the written pitch.

I / *Childhood*

On 3/15 June 1854, Glinka started to write his autobiography. He worked steadily over a period of some ten months, rising early each morning and writing until about 10 o'clock, after which he took the day's work to his sister, Lyudmila, for her scrutiny. He was not recording his life, he said, because he thought he would one day be the subject of a biography: 'I am writing these reminiscences without any attempt at stylistic beauty, but am recording simply what happened and how it happened in chronological order, excluding everything that did not have a direct or indirect relationship to my artistic life,' he wrote to his friend, Nestor Kukolnik.[1] Yet these *Memoirs* are not only the most useful source of information on his biography but also on his personality, for his surviving letters afford only spasmodic help. The sizeable quantity written during his Italian journey (1830–3) were destroyed as not being of special interest; indeed, over half his surviving correspondence dates from the last six years of his life, when he had virtually ceased to compose. These *Memoirs* are long-range reminiscences, and therefore must naturally be approached with some caution. His last important composition had been written six years before, and the writing of his first opera, *A Life for the Tsar*, was an event nearly twenty years away in the past. But however much the passage of time may have blurred Glinka's memory, his *Memoirs* still contain a wealth of invaluable information. They are also quite attractive simply as reminiscences, for Glinka did not confine himself strictly to matters related to his artistic life. Admittedly there is a great deal of triviality in them, and Glinka the hypochondriac becomes wearisome. He goes to considerable length to justify himself in the failure of his marriage, though he is disingenuous in the account of his own probity and in his affected shock at his

[1] GLN2, p. 502.

wife's infidelity. They show that he was a social animal, liking bright if not flashy company, vain in personal matters, enormously pleased when the Tsar took notice of him in public, and proud of his attractiveness to women. All this is in the sharpest contrast to his humility where his own musical achievements were concerned. Intellectual studies without imaginative features had little interest for him. He was very good at drawing, but lost interest in this at school when he was set to copy objects slavishly. He excelled at languages, learning English, French, German, Latin, and Persian, and later becoming proficient in Italian and Spanish, though English and Persian he soon forgot for want of practice. He had a great liking for the natural sciences, but disliked mathematics when it came to analytics. Roman and criminal law he loathed, and he confessed to having no aptitude for either dancing or fencing. The man who emerges from these *Memoirs* is an extrovert—trivial, vain, and shallow in many ways—yet gifted with an abundant imagination, and a very precise observation of the world around him.

Glinka's earliest biographer, Vladimir Stasov, asserted that 'it would have been useless for Glinka to have wished to smother his constant urge to write exclusively national music'.[1] Stasov, however, was writing too soon to be able to see the composer in perspective, and today it is no longer possible to subscribe to his idealized view of Glinka as the pre-ordained apostle of Russian musical nationalism who could have done nothing if he had strayed from his predestined path. Composers are born and then made, and it is their making which determines their musical character. In fact, Stasov's image of Glinka as the unwavering pursuer of musical nationalism is factually false. Although Glinka did sometimes use folk material and manners in his earliest compositions, he was nearly thirty before he consciously aimed to write really Russian music, and in his subsequent works he easily slipped back into a Western European manner. He was, as it happens, a right man in a right place, though it is perfectly possible to envisage a composer who could have established a Russian musical style more efficiently and thoroughly than he. In any case, Glinka's Russianness was not a matter of course, for the Glinkas seem to have been Polish in origin, though a branch of the family was already firmly established in the Smolensk region by 1654, when this area was finally wrested from the Poles by the Russian Tsar. Yakov Glinka, the head of the family, declined the offer of repatriation which the Tsar made, and was

[1] SG, p. 527.

rewarded by him with more lands. The family in the Smolensk region grew in size and became thoroughly Russianized, with a strong tradition of service to the Tsar.

By the time of the composer's birth some of the Glinkas were also pursuing cultural interests. For instance, among the composer's more distant relatives, there was Grigory Glinka, who was the first occupant of the Chair of Russian language and literature in the newly founded University of Dorpat (now called Tartu) in Estonia. Grigory established himself as a scholar, original writer, and translator. Significantly perhaps, in view of the composer's later nationalism, Grigory was one of the first Russians to apply his energies to investigating the history and culture of the Slavs. His younger brother, Vladimir, was a friend of Pushkin, as was also Fyodor Glinka, soldier, author, and a poet of sufficient stature to gain honourable mention in histories of Russian literature. Fyodor had a strong interest in Russian folk-song, would readily provide texts of his own for Russian folk tunes, and advocated that Russian music should become a reflection of Russian national life. Fyodor's elder brother, Sergei, published a journal, *The Russian Messenger*, in which his hatred of Napoleon was vented so forcefully that Napoleon himself instructed the French Embassy in St. Petersburg to make representations to the Russian authorities about it. Sergei was both a dramatist and a librettist. His play, *Minin*, enjoyed an enormous success in 1812 because of its topicality, and he provided two opera libretti for the minor Russian composer, Daniil Kashin. Like his brother he had a strong interest in Russian folk-song. Later his two sons were also to be active in the literary and journalistic fields.

The clan into which the composer was born had therefore a strong tradition of loyalty and service to the Tsar, and some members of it had acquired a lively interest in culture, ideas, and contemporary events. They were landowners, secure if not rich. The composer's father, Ivan Glinka, retired from the army with the rank of captain when he married his second cousin, Yevgeniya Glinka, in 1802. The bride's elder brother, Afanasy, who was also her guardian, opposed the match on the grounds of their affinity, and the marriage finally took place only after the bride had been romantically abducted.[1] The newly-weds were

[1] The laws concerning the marriage of individuals in any way related to each other were very strict in Russia at this time. The bridegroom's father obtained a clearance for the marriage from the authorities, but Afanasy was still not satisfied that this solved all the difficulties, and continued to oppose the match. Hence the elopement.

installed in the bridegroom's house at Novospasskoye, some five or six miles from Shmakovo, the bride's former home. Fortunately good relations with the guardian were soon restored, and the Shmakovo establishment was to play an important part in the earlier musical education of the future composer. The inclinations of the composer's father were more for the things of the eye than of the ear. On his own father's death in 1806, Ivan built a new two-storey house modelled on his bride's former home at Shmakovo, and furnished it with taste and lavishness, surrounding it with a splendidly planned garden. This obviously required money, but he was energetic and a good business man, whose interests entailed frequent visits to St. Petersburg, thus fostering cultural contacts between Novospasskoye and the outside world. He loved the poetry of Zhukovsky, and named his daughter Lyudmila after the heroine of Zhukovsky's ballad. He engaged an architect, too— a very unusual step for a provincial Russian. This architect was to be the composer's first drawing master.

Yet initially this world was to be almost entirely closed to the future composer. Mikhail Ivanovich Glinka's earliest childhood was extraordinary, and Stasov was unquestionably right in attaching a fundamental importance to it. Mikhail was the Glinkas' oldest surviving child,[1] and he tells of these first years in his *Memoirs*:

I was born at dawn on 20 May/1 June 1804 in the village of Novospasskoye [now called Glinka] which belonged to my father, Ivan Nikolayevich Glinka, a retired army captain. The estate is situated fourteen miles from the town of Yelnya [or Elna] in the Smolensk district; it lies along the River Desna (near its source), and is closely encircled by impenetrable woods which are joined to the famous woods of Bryansk. Soon after my birth my mother, Yevgeniya Andreyevna (née Glinka), was forced to leave my initial upbringing[2] to my grand-

[1] The Glinkas had ten children:
  Aleksei (1803: died in infancy)
  Mikhail (1804–57): the composer
  Pelageya (1805–28): married Y. M. Sobolevsky
  Natalya (1809–?): married N. D. Gedeonov
  Yelizaveta (1810–50): married V. I. Fleri
  Mariya (1813–?): married D. S. Stuneyev
  Yevgeny (1815–34)
  Lyudmila (1816–1906): married V. I. Shestakov
  Andrei (1823–39)
  Olga (1825–60): married N. A. Izmailov.

[2] The original version reads more strongly: 'to give up her rights over me', and Lyudmila Shestakova recalled that her parents 'had to surrender him into the complete command of the old lady his grandmother' (SB. Quoted in GVS, p. 32.). It has been suggested

mother, Fekla Aleksandrovna (my father's mother) who, having gained control of me, bore me off to her own room. I spent about three or four years with her as my nurse and provider, seeing my parents very infrequently. I was a child with a weak constitution, very scrofulous, and of a very nervous disposition; my grandmother, a woman of advanced years, was almost always ill, and as a result the temperature in her room (where I lived) was at the very least 77° fahrenheit. Despite this I always wore a fur coat; at nights and often during the day I was given tea with cream, with a lot of sugar, knot-shaped biscuits, and baked dough rings of various sorts. I was very rarely let out into the fresh air, and only in warm weather. There is no doubt that this initial upbringing had a strong effect upon the development of my physique, and explains my irrepressible longing for warm climates—and now, when I am already 50 years old, I can say emphatically that I find it better to live in the south, and suffer less there than in the north.

My grandmother spoiled me to an incredible degree—I was refused nothing. Despite this I was a gentle and well-behaved child, and only when I was disturbed while I was busy did I become *touchy* (like a mimosa), which sometimes still happens to this day. One of my favourite occupations was to crawl about the floor drawing trees and churches with chalk. I was very devout, and religious ceremonies, especially on major holy days, filled my soul with the liveliest poetic rapture. Having learned to read when I was exceedingly young, I often stirred the tender emotions of my grandmother and others of her age through my readings of sacred books. My musical talent expressed itself at this time in a *passion* for bell sounds (*peals*); I listened greedily to these sharp sounds, and was able to imitate the bellringers skilfully on two copper basins. When I was ill they brought little bells into the room to amuse me.

I already had weak nerves from my earliest years. For several days before my grandmother's death they treated her with an evil smelling poultice. But no power could force me to go in to her, and I was not present when she died, even though I loved her very much.[1]

But his grandmother unwittingly did more for Glinka than simply undermine his naturally delicate constitution, and confirm him as a hypochondriac. By this incarceration she efficiently cut him off from almost all music, except for that which he might hear in church, and folk-song. Her husband, Glinka's grandfather—'a quiet, gentle, and very devout man', according to Lyudmila Shestakova[2]—was devoted to

---

that Glinka's domineering grandmother took this course because Glinka's elder brother had died in infancy, and she wished to ensure that the second son, the head of the next generation, should be preserved.

[1] GLN1, pp. 61 and 63.
[2] SB. Quoted in GVS, p. 29.

church singing, and had often made pilgrimages through the northern parts of Russia to hear church music, which had preserved its older forms more perfectly in these outlying regions. He was mainly responsible for the musical tradition of the church at Novospasskoye, and fostered not only singing but bell music. The Smolensk district was noted for its bell music, and the Novospasskoye peal was famed throughout the region. It boasted six bells, sufficiently sonorous to be heard in Shmakovo on a calm day. Five of these were cast by order of Glinka's grandfather in 1791, and in 1812 Glinka's father added another, tuned to a low B flat. The tuning of these six bells was thus (Ex. 1a):

Ex.1.

In 1904 transcriptions were published of some of the musical patterns which were played on them (Ex. 1b).[1] However approximate these transcriptions, and however much later than Glinka's own time they may be, they afford a clear idea of the brilliant and 'strident' (as Glinka called them) sounds to which his ear was accustomed from its earliest years.

Then there were folk-songs. These he heard from his nurse, Avdotya Ivanovna, 'a young, cheerful woman . . . [who] knew many different tales and songs'.[2] When his grandmother noted that Mikhail was bored or off colour, she would immediately cry: 'Avdotya, tell some tales, and sing.'[3] Avdotya fed his fancy with fairy stories, and nourished his musical needs on folk-song. Apart from bell music and the music heard in church, folk-song was the only other contact Glinka had with music

[1] Quoted in KNG1, p. 38. These transcriptions are drawn from the periodical *Niva*, No. 90 (1904), p. 368.

[2] SB. Quoted in GVS, p. 32.

[3] ibid.

for the first six years of his life.[1] From his nurse he could, of course, hear only folk melodies, but these he experienced in abundance, absorbing their characteristic shapes, rhythms and modes, and laying up that store of knowledge and understanding upon which he was able to draw many years later in his own compositions.

There was another very important brand of folk-song from which the cloistered life imposed by his grandmother's regime may have excluded him, but which he must have heard frequently in the freer life he led after her death. This was the performance by peasant choirs using the special *podgolosnaya* technique to which the Russians habitually treated their songs in ensemble performance. This technique, as it survived into the early twentieth century, has been described and defined by Alfred Swan. He found that the peasant choirs were usually of eight to fourteen voices, nearly always women's. After an initial phrase sung by the leader, the whole choir joined in and sang unbroken melody to the end. This technique was closer to heterophony than polyphony, and Swan described it thus: 'A principal melody improvised simultaneously by several singers, retaining its main outline in each voice, yet showing enough independence to result in places in 2- and 3- and 4-part harmony.'[2] Swan's investigations revealed a practice stemming from the contrapuntal instinct in the Russian musical mentality—but an instinct that is for a form of decorative rather than organic counterpoint. Ex. 2[3] is a sample of this technique as noted down by a Russian scholar in the first years of this century. For Glinka acquaintance with this style must have been of immense importance, for, with its starker and freer use of dissonance, it would have accustomed him to accept a harmonic and contrapuntal style emancipated from the smooth progressions and logically organized dissonance of Western music.

'After my grandmother's death my way of life changed somewhat,' wrote Glinka. 'My mother spoiled me less, and even tried to accustom

---

[1] E. Kann-Novikova attempts to demonstrate the similarities between certain folk-songs of the Smolensk region and themes in Glinka's *A Life for the Tsar*. In this she is perhaps over-enthusiastic, for V. Protopopov convincingly demonstrates equally close parallels with folk-songs from other regions. Nevertheless, Kann-Novikova's researches into the background to, and early phases of, Glinka's life are very thorough, and the material she sets out is valuable, even if some of her conclusions must be accepted with reservations.

[2] A. J. Swan, 'The Nature of Russian folk-song' (*The Musical Quarterly*, vol. 29 (1943), p. 509).

[3] Quoted from A. M. Listopadov, *Pesni donskikh kazakov* (first edition, 1906: re-published in Moscow, 1949).

Ex.2.

me to fresh air, but these ventures for the most part had no success.'[1] Glinka's education had been initiated by the local priest, Johann Stabrovsky, and now the architect his father had engaged tried to develop his ability with the pencil. He showed Glinka how to draw ears, eyes, noses, and so on, but demanded a mechanical imitation which Glinka found distasteful, though he managed the task well enough. He found far more imaginative rewards in the frequent visits of a distant relative, Aleksandr Kipriyanov. 'He loved to tell me of distant lands, of wild peoples, of the climates and products of tropical countries—and, seeing how eagerly I listened to him, he brought me a book called *A History of travels in general*, published in the reign of Yekaterina [Catherine] II. I set about reading this book voraciously.'[2] Here already are signs of Glinka's love of exotic and faraway places which was to find musical expression in his oriental and Spanish stylizations. But at this time his musical activities were still restricted to producing bell sounds on his copper basins: 'my feeling for music still remained crude and undeveloped. Even in my eighth[3] year, when we escaped from the French advance to Orel, I listened to the sounds of the bells with my former eagerness, distinguished the peal of each church, and diligently imitated it on my copper basins.'[4]

When Napoleon advanced on Moscow in 1812 the Glinka family was evacuated from Novospasskoye. This proved to be a wise precaution, for it was attacked by a detachment of seventy French troops. The inhabitants had taken refuge in the church, the defence of which was organized so successfully by Stabrovsky that the French withdrew and wrecked buildings on the estate instead. It is difficult to believe that

[1] GLN1, pp. 63–64.   [2] GLN1, pp. 64–65.
[3] In fact this happened in his ninth year.   [4] GLN1, p. 65.

this personal contact with a threat to his country, with the damage done to his own home by invading troops,[1] and with the subsequent defeat of Napoleon, should not have stirred a patriotic awareness in the future composer of *A Life for the Tsar*.

Yet, surrounded as he was largely by women, and being by nature quiet and gentle, it is not likely that at this time such events would have made more than a passing impression. It was not the advance of Napoleon's armies but the performance of a clarinet quartet by the now forgotten Finnish composer, Bernhard Crusell, which had the greater significance for Glinka. This happened when Glinka was ten or eleven years old, and the experience was afforded by musicians from the Shmakovo establishment, which had figured prominently in his cultural experiences ever since his grandmother's death. The Glinkas at Shmakovo were distinguished by their leanings towards the fine arts. Here presided Glinka's uncle, Afanasy, the guardian who had so stoutly opposed his younger sister's wedding. This uncle was 'an educated and well-bred man'[2] with a taste for all types of culture. When young he had kept a troupe of actors, and to the end of his life he maintained an orchestra of his own serfs.[3] The Shmakovo orchestra, with its up-to-date repertoire, was to prove invaluable to Glinka. There were no resident musicians at Novospasskoye, and when music was required the Shmakovo establishment was borrowed, the musicians staying sometimes for several days, playing for dancing, as well as performing other pieces after the guests had departed.

Once (I remember it was in 1814 or 1815 . . .) [wrote Glinka] they played a clarinet quartet by Crusell. This music produced an incomprehensible, new, and delightful impression upon me. Thereafter I remained for the whole day in a sort of feverish condition, was submerged in an inexplicable, sweetly lethargic state, and next day during my drawing lesson I was inattentive. In the course of the next lesson my inattentiveness had become even greater, and the teacher, noticing that I was not now drawing with enough care, repeatedly reproved me. Finally, however, having guessed what was the matter, he told me that he noticed I was thinking all the time only of music. 'What can I do about it?' I replied: 'Music is my soul.' And, indeed, from that time I passionately loved music.[4]

---

[1] One source states that Glinka's own home was pillaged (see KNG1, p. 95).

[2] SB. Quoted in GVS, p. 30.

[3] Such orchestras were common in Russia at this period; contemporary records reveal the existence of over 300, and there must have been many more unrecorded (see LPG1, p. 29).

[4] GLN1, pp. 65–66.

His uncle's orchestra offered Glinka the opportunity of hearing Western dances—écossaises, quadrilles, and waltzes—and Glinka, sitting alongside the orchestra, would take a violin or piccolo and join in on the tonics and dominants, a practice which sometimes led his father to accuse him of unsociability with the guests. In addition Glinka recalled that

during supper they usually played Russian songs arranged for two flutes, two clarinets, two horns, and two bassoons. I loved exceedingly these sadly gentle, but to me completely acceptable sounds (I found it difficult to bear harsh sounds— even the low notes of horns when they were played loudly), and perhaps these songs which I heard in my childhood were the prime reason why I later began to cultivate mainly Russian folk music.[1]

Yet the real root of Glinka's attraction to, and understanding of Russian folk music may be traced further back. His earliest musical knowledge had been of the Russian folk-songs in his nurse's repertoire— unaccompanied, sung quite certainly in just intonation, modal, and employing a rhythmic manner substantially different from that of Western music. However much he may later have succumbed to the attractions of the latter, these earliest and basic experiences afforded a style which he had thoroughly assimilated, and upon which he could draw much later when his interest in the possibility of writing a truly Russian music was awakened. Perhaps we may gauge the over-whelming strength of these fundamental experiences by the four- or five-year delay which ensued before Glinka's love of Western music was suddenly aroused. His ear was especially sensitive to sound and sound quality, and a major adjustment would have been called for when passing from the folk melos into a highly professional music founded upon equal temperament, with melody conditioned and sometimes dictated by a harmonic system based on the triad, the whole of which was disciplined into a regular metrical scheme.

After the impact of Crusell's quartet Glinka's interests seem to have shifted primarily to cultivated music, for this was a new territory, far wider than folk music, with infinite bounds to explore. In 1815 a governess, Varvara Klammer, was summoned from St. Petersburg for the older Glinka children, and she undertook their general education in a thoroughly efficient, if unimaginative manner. This mechanical approach extended to her music lessons and piano method, though such

[1] GLN1, pp. 66–67.

systematic discipline did Glinka no harm, and he made very good progress. Violin lessons were started with a member of his uncle's orchestra, but these were less beneficial, since Glinka caught his teacher's stiff bowing habits. Glinka's piano technique developed sufficiently well for him to play movements from sonatas by Daniel Steibelt, notably the rondo, *L'Orage*. But orchestral music was still his greatest love—above all the arrangements of Russian folk-songs. His other favourites were three overtures: Boïeldieu's *Ma tante Aurore*, Kreutzer's *Lodoïska*, and Méhul's *Les deux aveugles*. He played the last two of these in piano transcriptions.

At the beginning of the winter of 1817[1] Glinka was taken to St. Petersburg to be enrolled in the Blagorodny Boarding School attached to the Chief Pedagogical Institute. He fully appreciated the magnitude of this move. During the whole journey he assured his sister that they were going to discover a new country, new lands: 'For Columbus discovered America, and I shall discover some country, they will write about me in books, and in these new lands I shall establish various concerts, orchestras, music, and many good musicians.'[2]

The imposing buildings of St. Petersburg deeply impressed the young Glinka, for he had never before seen anything as grand. On 2/14 February 1818, he started his studies, sharing quarters with three other students, a special tutor, Wilhelm Küchelbecker, with whom he was distantly connected (though Küchelbecker's main ancestry was German), a fine, newly installed Tischner grand piano, and various breeds of pigeons and rabbits. Küchelbecker, a poet and critic with an honourable place in Russian literature, was a distinguished mind, and at the time of Glinka's entry the school was on the whole an excellent establishment. There were about 120 pupils, and some very well qualified senior staff, many of whom had finished their studies at German universities, and who were not only academically well educated but also thoroughly acquainted with the currents of thought in Western Europe. Russia itself was at this time seething with new ideas. The Russian officers who

---

[1] It has been suggested that Glinka in fact started school in St. Petersburg nearly two years earlier, initially entering another school, the Blagorodny Boarding School of the Tsarskoselsky Lyceum, on 4/16 March 1816 (see A. Orlova, *Godui ucheniya Glinki* in OG, pp. 74–75). This is supported by some substantial evidence, including the testimony of Glinka's sister, Lyudmila, that he started school in 1816. Nevertheless, V. Bogdanov-Berezovsky offers evidence which contradicts this (see GLN1, p. 403). The matter remains therefore uncertain.

[2] SB. Quoted in GVS, p. 34.

had pursued Napoleon into Europe, and who stayed on in the army of occupation, had been brought into contact with the ideals and consequences of the French Revolution. They had begun to question the system of Russian serfdom, and more and more attention was being focused on the plight of the peasant by the growing tendency of Russian literature to concern itself with the lives and experiences of ordinary men and women. Secret societies were formed to discuss these new ideas and how they might be implemented, and some teachers at the Blagorodny Boarding School were deeply involved in such discussions. Thus Glinka lived in a world of vigorous and progressive thought. Love of one's country, and the primacy of people over government, were preached, and ideas were actively propagated against the social system in Russia, against serfdom and despotism.

For Glinka the close contact with Küchelbecker was particularly fortunate, since Küchelbecker was even more interested in Russian culture than in social and political ideas, although finally his zeal in the cause of reform led him to participate in the Decembrist rising of 1825, as a result of which he spent the last twenty years of his life in Siberia. He was a great enthusiast for Russian literature and the Russian language, 'of which there is not the like in Europe'.[1] Even Goethe experienced Küchelbecker's evangelism on behalf of his native tongue and literature, and close contact with such a man must have had a part in rousing Glinka's awareness of the worth of Russian culture, however long it may have taken him to realize this finally for himself.[2] Küchelbecker discussed literature and politics with his pupils, and read with them forbidden verses by Pushkin, who in 1820 was exiled to the south of Russia. One of Glinka's fellow students records that Glinka participated in such discussions, showing that he was 'a good judge of poetry as well as of music, and in no way sympathized with any Bourbon'.[3] Küchelbecker's Pushkin sympathies were to precipitate his dismissal in 1820 after he had publicly read verses in honour of the banished poet. Among Küchelbecker's pupils was Pushkin's brother, Lev, and a 'disorder' led by the latter in support of the dismissed master resulted not merely in his own expulsion, but in the resignation or dismissal of other members of the staff. The school declined badly, and Glinka wrote home

[1] Quoted in GLN1, p. 404.

[2] Küchelbecker had very real musical interests. He played the violin, and even wrote a libretto for Verstovsky, *Love unto the grave*, or *The Moors of Granada*. He also undertook to revise the text of Haydn's *Il ritorno di Tobia*.

[3] N. Markevich, *Memoirs*. Quoted in KNG2, p. 22.

to his parents lamenting the fact. This is the only comment on the school itself anywhere in his writings, and it is significant that he makes no more than a passing reference to the more distinguished, progressive teachers. What he did remember of those days were certain of the junior members of staff, and his *Memoirs* contain sketches of some of these individuals—including an Englishman, Mr. Bitton, evidently a former sea captain, whose passion for rice pudding led him, when this delicacy was served for dinner, to engineer pretexts for confiscating a number of portions in order that he might devour them himself.

In general Glinka did well at school, and he seems to have been reasonably happy there until his last year. Although politics featured in his discussions, one suspects that his lack of sympathy for 'any Bourbon' was purely theoretical. There is nothing to suggest that he was actively interested in contemporary politics, and he certainly never participated in them. He claimed that he was, at least until his final year, a model student, behaving himself, and well liked by his fellows and teachers. Each year he was awarded a prize, and he ended his school days second in his class. But a notable omission in his *Memoirs* is of any reference to musical activities in the school. In fact, although singing was part of the curriculum, other music lessons had to be paid for, and the school does not appear to have been prepared to allocate many of its resources to music, even though Catterino Cavos was the inspector (years later it was Cavos who was to conduct the first performance of Glinka's *A Life for the Tsar*). Almost the only glimpse we have of Glinka musically occupied at school is afforded in the very romanticized account of Nikolai Melgunov, one of his closest friends, who wrote that Glinka spent a great deal of time improvising on his piano: 'At that time he [Glinka] still occupied himself little with the theory of music; but it was then, in the long winter nights, in the summer twilight of St. Petersburg . . . [that] he would abandon himself to a flight of free improvisation . . . In these sounds, trembling with rapture, he expressed his childhood dreams, his languid sorrow, and his lively joys.'[1] The evidence of other friends also suggests that Glinka's musical talents during his school years manifested themselves primarily in improvisation. Another of Glinka's younger contemporaries, Aleksandr Strugovshchikov, described him vividly, but more objectively, as he remembered him from 1823, the year after Glinka had left school: 'His serious

---

[1] MG, p. 714. The value of Melgunov's essay is diminished by its excessively ecstatic posture.

face with its dark southern complexion, with its squinting or, more precisely, short-sighted stare, was constantly alive during conversation— and if his black frock-coat stood out sharply against our "regulation" coats, he was set even further apart from us by the peculiar liveliness of his movements, by his resonant voice and bold, energetic speech. Sometimes his abrupt, as it were, convulsive movements struck you unexpectedly. Or he would suddenly stop, clasp the waist now of one, now of another companion, or stand on tiptoe and urgently whisper something in the ear of each of them in turn, as intense people often do. His stature was a little more than short, but rather below average; his figure was, in the main, proportioned and reasonably well shaped.'[1]

It is not surprising that a vivacious person, such as Glinka clearly was, should have sought social contacts outside the narrow confines of his school, and it is clear that he found all the musical tuition and experience he wanted in St. Petersburg itself. He was fortunate in having there another uncle, Ivan Glinka, who was a keen music-lover and a good pianist—and also a great lover of cage-birds, just like his own brother, Afanasy, and his composer nephew. Glinka spent much of his leisure time in his uncle's house, and it was through the offices of Ivan that he was able to gain access to certain musical circles and to some eminent musicians—men like John Field, who had made Russia his home since 1803, and who had gained a great reputation as composer, performer, and teacher. Glinka had three lessons from him, but Field's departure for Moscow unfortunately forestalled a longer association. Glinka rated Field highly as a pianist, and knew his piano music well; he mentions learning Field's Second Divertimento with the composer himself, receiving warm approval from Field for his performance. He also studied Field's First Piano Concerto with his subsequent teacher, V. Aumann (himself a Field pupil). Through his Shmakovo uncle, Afanasy, Glinka also met Hummel when the latter was visiting Russia. Glinka played the first solo passage of Hummel's Piano Concerto in A minor, and Hummel, who was evidently favourably impressed, returned the compliment by improvising: 'he played gently, precisely, as though he had already composed the piece and learned it thoroughly by heart,' Glinka wrote.[2] In 1822, on the day he left the Blagorodny Boarding School, Glinka performed publicly the piano part of this same concerto. At this time he was still mainly interested in instrumental performances, both solo and orchestral, and he particularly recalled

[1] SGV, pp. 698–99.   [2] GLNi, p. 78.

hearing Lvov's violin playing: 'the gentle sounds of Aleksei Fedoro-vich's sweet violin engraved themselves deeply in my memory'.[1] Later Lvov was to be a close associate of his in the Imperial Chapel. His own progress on the violin was less worthy of recall; his teacher, Franz Boehm, not only on the staff of the Blagorodny School, but also the leading violinist in the St. Petersburg theatre world, was a good per-former himself, 'but did not, however, have the gift for communicating his skills to others, and when I wielded my bow badly, he would say: "Messieur Klinka, fous ne chouerez chamais du fiolon"'.[2]

Nor were Glinka's theoretical studies any more successful. After his lessons with Aumann, he continued with Karl Zeuner who certainly helped him improve his piano technique and style, but failed to fire him with his teaching of intervals and their inversions. Again it was the mechanical learning and the absence of any scope for the imagination which irked Glinka, and he transferred to Charles Mayer, another former pupil of Field. Mayer was to become a firm friend, and in the next few years he was to do more than anyone to help Glinka develop his musical talents.

During his school vacations Glinka returned home and was able to play in his uncle's orchestra, which had been augmented with several boys whom his father had had trained so that he might have his own resident musicians for dancing. A governess had been engaged for Glinka's younger sisters, and her husband, Karl Hempel, a musician of German extraction, shared with Glinka his musical activities. Rossini's overtures especially pleased Glinka, and that to *Cenerentola* so delighted him that he and Hempel arranged it for piano duet and often played it together. But he had far less enthusiasm for the talents of an Italian singing teacher, Todi, who was living at Novospasskoye at this time.

Back in St. Petersburg, Glinka visited various households in his round of musical activities. At Uncle Ivan's he played piano duets both with his uncle Ivan and with his cousin Sofya, who was the same age as he. Together they performed arrangements of overtures by Cherubini, Méhul, Mozart, Righini, Spontini, Paer, and Rossini. A serf orchestra belonging to another amateur, Pyotr Yushkov, afforded Glinka a weekly opportunity of hearing playing and singing. In the early spring of 1822, at the home of another family, he experienced the pangs of love. Here lived a young harpist with a delightful soprano voice, and while Glinka and his uncle were playing duets, she would sit alongside the

[1] GLN1, p. 77.   [2] GLN1, p. 76.

piano, joining in vocally during her favourite passages. The result was Glinka's first attempt at composition—a set of variations on her favourite theme from the opera, *The Swiss Family*, by Weigl. Next came some variations for harp or piano on a theme of Mozart, and then an original waltz in F major for piano. Only the variations on the Mozart theme[1] have survived, and the two sources both date from the end of Glinka's life when he was writing out, often from memory (and in this case from his sister Lyudmila's memory), his earlier compositions. Just how grammatical the original was we can therefore never know, but the variations are certainly no better than tinkling salon music. Glinka's romantic attachment came to nothing, but the incident revealed to him the beauties of the harp when used properly.

Glinka must have been very glad when his own schooldays ended in 1822. Not only had some of the best teachers left, but, as a result of the disorder which Lev Pushkin had led the previous year, over half the pupils had gone. Glinka's best friends were no longer there, and during his last year he made every excuse to get away from the place. Still, it had given him a good formal education, had brought him close and extended contact with persons who commended to him the worth of Russia's own culture and heritage, and had provided him with a number of acquaintances who were to become lifelong friends. On leaving school he briefly visited his parents, and then returned to St. Petersburg to take up residence near his former school inspector, Lindquist, with whom he arranged to have breakfast and dinner. His father wished him to enter the Foreign Service, but Glinka was unenthusiastic. Music was the only activity which really interested him, and now he intended to devote himself to as much enjoyment of it as he could.

[1] The theme is Papageno's bell tune in G major from the finale to Act 1 of *Die Zauberflöte*.

2/ The St. Petersburg Dilettante

We have from Glinka's sister, Lyudmila, a revealing account of her brother's relations with the peasants at Novospasskoye. 'It is true,' she wrote, 'that my late brother loved the Russian people passionately and understood them. He knew how to talk to them; the peasants trusted him, obeyed him, and respected him. During his childhood in the country, up to his thirteenth year, he often had to observe and hear their views, and afterwards when he arrived in the country for the summer (and he sometimes even spent the winters there), he would often call the peasants and servants together and would give them good times, entertaining them and arranging dances and such-like amusements for them. His one thought, his one wish, was that the people should be free, but unfortunately he did not live to see his cherished idea fulfilled.'[1]

Glinka's own father had been popular with his serfs, and there is no reason to doubt the essential truth of this account of his son's attitude, for other sources confirm his social activities with the peasants on the family estate. Yet this is almost the only precise record of Glinka's personal attitude towards the plight of the Russian peasants, and certainly nothing to be recorded in the next three chapters gives the slightest hint of this side of his life, nor any suggestion of the direction his mature work was to take. Yet in the knowledge of this attitude, *A Life for the Tsar* becomes less surprising, since a natural liking for, and understanding of the Russian peasant was bound to be of far greater help in presenting this type on the stage than any doctrinaire view of the plight and destiny of an impersonal peasant class. Such considerations did not interest him either at school or afterwards, when he threw him-

[1] From notes on Ivan Panayev, *Literary recollections*, cited in P. Weimarn, *M. I. Glinka: biografichesky ocherk* (Moscow, 1892), p. 17. Quoted in LPG1, p. 45.

self into the far wider society of St. Petersburg. He had already encountered Pushkin while still at school, and he had enjoyed the constant
guidance of Küchelbecker; now he met Vasily Zhukovsky, next to
Pushkin the greatest Russian poet of his time, and the man who was
later to give Glinka the subject for his first opera, and even to provide
some lines for it. Behind Pushkin and Zhukovsky was a host of lesser
but still exceedingly talented men—like the lazy, good-natured Anton
Delvig, who was one of Glinka's companions on a trip to Finland in
1828, the brilliant romantic, Pyotr Vyazemsky, who with Pushkin and
Zhukovsky was to contribute to the laudatory poem to Glinka after the
première of *A Life for the Tsar*, and Aleksandr Griboyedov, who was so
tragically killed on a diplomatic mission to Persia, and whose comedy,
Woe from wit, is the first great play in the Russian language. These names,
and those of other men of letters, appear in the pages of Glinka's
Memoirs. He knew them, he enjoyed their society, sometimes he set
their poems; yet he never seems to have had any real personal interest
in their art, let alone in the ideas about society, religion, justice, and so
on, which exercised many of them so much. They were simply good
social companions, useful as poets only when he felt like writing a song.
Many of them were to be implicated in the Decembrist rising of 1825.
As was noted earlier, Küchelbecker's participation cost him exile to
Siberia for the last twenty years of his life; Griboyedov was arrested as
a result of it, and Pushkin, who had already experienced official dis-
grace, was known to be sympathetic to the insurgents. Not Glinka; he
said nothing, was alarmed when it seemed that he might suffer in the
aftermath of the rising, and retired to the country until the affair had
blown over. Despite the fact that he lived through the richest period of
Russian poetry and knew all the leading figures of the literary world, he
seems to have been quite unaffected by it all. As for music, all he now
wanted from it was the pleasure of enjoying it to the full in a thoroughly
dilettante manner.

And certainly there was an enormous amount of music to be heard.
In the early years of the nineteenth century St. Petersburg was much
like any large Western European city with a vigorous musical life
well acquainted with the current trends of European music. The national
element was growing stronger, but had not succeeded in shaking the
ascendancy of Italian and French genres. Public concerts, at which the
best European performers were to be heard, were expanding out of
the confines of the Lenten period into a second season in the late

Glinka, his mother, and sister, Pelageya, in 1817. Miniature by an unknown artist

PLATE I

autumn, but the dominating feature of St. Petersburg's musical life was still opera, and the new operatic successes of the West were quickly heard there. 1817, the year of Glinka's arrival in St. Petersburg, also saw the first performance there of *Tancredi*, and this marked the beginning of Rossini's domination of Russian opera; Glinka lived in the capital during the time of his ascendancy, maintaining a curiously ambivalent attitude towards the Italian master. Mozart was known as early as 1797 through performances of *Don Giovanni* and *Die Zauberflöte*, but it was the visit in 1806 of a German company performing the former which marked the beginning of the cult of Mozart which is a notable feature of nineteenth-century Russian musical life.

French opera had a large following, too. The established idols were Boïeldieu and the Maltese, Isouard; Glinka specially mentions seeing the former's *Le petit chaperon rouge*, and the latter's *Joconde*. Nor did St. Petersburg neglect the more serious representatives of the French school, Cherubini and Méhul, and Glinka records having seen both Méhul's *Joseph* and Cherubini's *Les deux journées* during his schooldays. We may get some measure of St. Petersburg's capacity for appreciating serious opera when we note that, while *Joseph* was very popular, Cherubini's *Médée* was never produced in Russia. Glinka himself, when he saw *Médée* in Frankfurt in 1830, confessed to understanding nothing of the music except the overture, which had been a favourite of his since his St. Petersburg days. Doubtless his compatriots would not have succeeded any better where Glinka failed. *Joseph*, though serious and dignified, is uncomplicated in expression, simple and effective in its musical drama. Its acceptance in St. Petersburg is sufficient to exonerate the musical public of that city from charges that its tastes were exclusively frivolous. Later, Weber was to make an impact when *Der Freischütz*, of which Glinka spoke enthusiastically, was produced in St. Petersburg in 1824.

Parallel to the imported European opera there also ran a stream of indigenous musico-dramatic productions, founded upon Western musical techniques and forms, but introducing folk-songs and other national elements which added a mild regional sauce to an otherwise cosmopolitan dish. But however worthy may have been their aims, and however national their intention, none of these works was sufficiently compelling to propagate a national tradition. Clearly Glinka paid no serious attention to them, since neither in his *Memoirs* nor in his surviving letters is any mention made of a single composer of such pieces

—of men like Davuidov, Titov, and Kozlowski. Verstovsky is not mentioned until 1838, two years after the first production of *A Life for the Tsar*, and Cavos, the inspector at the Blagorodny Boarding School and first conductor of *A Life for the Tsar*, is named only as a performer and director. In 1833 Glinka did perpetrate a set of variations on a song, *The Nightingale*, by Alyabyev, but that is his only compositional connection with them. Jealousy can hardly be the explanation, for he was on good terms with them. Their work simply made no impression on him. What they did do was to create a cultural situation into which a national work of genius could fit and be accepted when the time came for it to be born.

But opera was not all that St. Petersburg offered him. There were also the concerts of the St. Petersburg Philharmonic Society, founded in 1802. Financially its aims were charitable; musically it became the means for familiarizing the city with the larger works of the choral repertoire. Its orchestra was made up of professionals and outstanding amateurs, while its chorus was drawn from the Imperial Chapel Choir. Some of the best Russian singers appeared as soloists. To these forces was joined the Imperial Horn Band, a body of some forty players performing upon special horns, each of which could play only one note.[1] The horn band took the role of organ—with remarkable success, to judge from Spohr's account of a performance he heard on his Russian visit in 1803.[2] In the first concert Spohr attended, the orchestra consisted of 36 violins, 20 bass strings, and a double set of wind; in addition to the horn band, there was a 50-strong chorus of men and boys from the Imperial Chapel. At a performance of Haydn's oratorio, *The Seasons*, Spohr describes the orchestra as the largest he had ever seen—70 violins, 30 bass strings, and a double set of wind. The performance was well attended, a sign of Haydn's unrivalled popularity as a composer of choral and instrumental music in Russia during the first years of the nineteenth century. However, Haydn's supremacy in the affections of Russian music lovers was soon challenged by Mozart and Beethoven, and it is a sign of highly developed taste and remarkable expertise that

---

[1] A number of these horn bands existed in Russia at this time, and the skill they attained in ensemble was sometimes very remarkable. Their repertoires included overtures by Rossini, Méhul, Boïeldieu, and Cherubini, as well as symphonies and overtures by Mozart. Glinka had a great liking for them, and deplored their disbandment following the introduction of keyed trumpets. Spohr wrote in dazed admiration of their agility.

[2] See L. Spohr, *The Musical journeys of Louis Spohr*, translated and edited by Henry Pleasants (Norman: Oklahoma, 1961), pp. 33–34.

the Society could rise in 1824 to delivering the first complete performance anywhere of Beethoven's *Missa Solemnis in D.*

As for instrumental music, the symphonies and quartets of Haydn
and Mozart were well known during Glinka's early years in St.
Petersburg, and Beethoven's symphonies were performed. His three
Razumovsky quartets, Op. 59, were played there in 1812. Later, Beethoven's cause in Russia was fostered by Ignaz Schuppanzigh, the Austrian violinist whose quartet had been particularly associated with the
performance of Beethoven's quartets in Vienna, and who spent much
time in Russia from 1816 to 1823. In the less public musical world
Russian society followed the practice of Western cities. At the upper
end of the social scale were the fashionable salons, meeting regularly
with a fairly steady membership, and drawing into their company
foreign artists who were visiting Russia. Glinka's own musical life was
to become a vivid reflection of the dilettante activities of leisured St.
Petersburg amateurs. In domestic music-making the guitar occupied
a special place. Its popularity, like that of the lute in the sixteenth century, may be attributed to its self-sufficiency as an instrument, coupled
with its comparative cheapness. An interesting difference existed, so we
are told, between the playing styles of St. Petersburg and Moscow, the
former favouring a classical strictness of approach, while the latter
cultivated a more cantabile and fiery style. At all levels folk-songs were
performed, though often in arrangements that did gross violence to the
original. Likewise romances, in Russia very much the equivalent of the
drawing-room ballad, were very popular. Their melodic style was
simple, direct and sentimental, embodying emotions familiar to all.
They were expressively declaimed 'from the heart', *con rubato*, to an
accompaniment of piano, harp, or guitar.

This extended sketch establishes the breadth of the musical experiences St. Petersburg offered Glinka for the thirteen years between
his arrival in 1817 and his departure for Italy in 1830. During these
years he was able to absorb all aspects of Western music, hearing recent
operas and the best singers, making the acquaintance of fine, large-
scale choral works through the concerts of the Philharmonic Society,
and absorbing the instrumental music of Western Europe, including a
selection of symphonic masterpieces of Haydn, Mozart, and Beethoven.
Glinka never missed the chance of attending a concert, and was thrown
into 'indescribable rapture' when taken to the theatre to see opera or
ballet while he was still at school. 'At that time the Russian theatre was

not in as grievous a condition as it is now [1854] from the constant incursions of Italians. These Italian songsters, ignorant yet inflated with their own imagined worthiness, had not then flooded the capitals of Europe like pirates. Fortunately for me there were none of them in St. Petersburg then, and so the repertoire was varied,' observed Glinka.[1] Thus, on leaving school, he plunged into a round of musical activities, and his studies with Mayer and even with Boehm went ahead profitably. It was about this time that he took some lessons with a musical theorist, J.-L. Fuchs, but still nothing like a systematic professional training was attempted.

At the earliest opportunity he determined to travel. He had a convenient, if curious excuse; once, during his school holidays, a married cousin had, in a state of trance, made the remarkable disclosure that the mineral waters of the Caucasus would be beneficial to Glinka. While there can be no doubt that his constant pre-occupation with his health did commend to him the healing properties of Caucasian spas, we can be equally certain that the attractions of the place also weighed with him. At this time a trip to the Caucasus was very much an adventure, for it was still remote, with the romantic attractiveness of a relatively unknown region. Pushkin's *A Prisoner of the Caucasus*, published in 1822, had brought its allurements before the Russian reader, and when this was produced as a ballet in January 1823 it had a tremendous success. Perhaps it was the impact of this ballet which settled the matter for Glinka. In March his father gave his approval, since from Kharkov Glinka could travel with one of his father's acquaintances, as well as with a doctor. Glinka hurried off to Novospasskoye to make provision for the journey. Travelling thither proved difficult, though this was to produce a pleasant diversion for him and his travelling companions, Uncle Ivan and two cousins. After journeying about 250 miles they became stuck in slush, but a local wealthy landowner, a certain Zherebtsov, not only sent out to fetch them to his own house, but insisted upon them staying for several days to enjoy his lavish hospitality. Zherebtsov had his own theatre, and among Glinka's entertainments were some hilarious rehearsals of Ferdinand Kauer's opera, *Lesta, the Dnieper water nymph*,[2] in which the actors were servants.

At the beginning of May, Glinka, accompanied by a servant and

[1] GLN1, pp. 76–77.
[2] This was a Russian version, with additional music by Cavos and Davuidov, of Kauer's *Das Donauweibchen*.

cook, left Novospasskoye for the Caucasus. The weather had already improved, and 'a few days later near Orel, the warm breath of spring began to blow—and when I had crossed the River Oka, I found I was already in a different southern region that was new to me. Oak groves replaced our beeches; along the ravines, pear, apple, and cherry trees in blossom began to appear instead of bare shoots. The appearance of the fields and villages, with bleached clay-walled huts instead of black timbered cabins, irregularly but picturesquely scattered about—all this rejoiced the eye by day, and at night the clear sky, studded with brightly glittering stars, enraptured me.'[1] On 10/22 May they arrived in Kharkov. Glinka's sociable inclinations did not permit him to waste time while waiting for his remaining travelling companions to arrive; he therefore introduced himself to a certain Ivan Vitkovsky,[2] a violinist who had a first-rate music shop, played the first solo passage of Hummel's A minor concerto, and was promptly borne off to the bosom of the proprietor's family to pass the time in profitable musical recreation.

Glinka was deeply impressed by the new vistas that opened to him. Admittedly he found the steppes that they had to cross unattractive, though he felt pleased with himself for having at last reached Asia after they had crossed the Don at Oksaya. But when they reached their destination, Pyatigorsk, he was thrilled. The town 'was completely wild but majestic . . . the range of the snow-covered Caucasus mountains stretched away majestically, and the River Podkumok twisted across the plain like a ribbon, while eagles in great numbers soared about the clear sky.'[3]

It would have been uncharacteristic of Glinka to have tolerated any personal discomfort, however splendid the scenic compensations. His companion had come well furnished with books, they ate and drank excellently—and Glinka kept goats. The cure proved less fortunate. His companion derived great benefit from taking sulphur baths, but Glinka found being 'boiled' in them upset his 'weak nervous constitution'. After a few trials of the sulphur baths, they moved up the mountains to try the iron springs. These were even less successful, though the magnificent scenery again impressed Glinka. They moved to Kislovodsk, where the effect of the waters was disastrous. Glinka was now thoroughly

[1] GLNi, p. 81.
[2] Vitkovsky, who claimed to be a pupil of Haydn, was an important figure in Kharkov's musical life in the early nineteenth century. Among his pupils was Gogol's mother to whom he gave free piano lessons.
[3] GLNi, p. 82.

upset, and thirty years later he could still tenderly recall all the details of what he suffered on the return journey. A suspicion that a basic malady had been cured proved to be a false alarm. In the middle of September he arrived back in Novospasskoye.

The importance of this Caucasian expedition to Glinka, though difficult to gauge precisely, was clearly immense. Not only had he responded readily to the scenic wonders afforded to his impressionable mind, but he had also 'seen the dance of the Circassian women, [and] the games and races of the Circassian men'.[1] This would have been the festival of Bairan which each year attracted people who were visiting the Caucasus. The festival started with music and dancing, the dancers forming themselves round a musician playing on a bowed instrument like a gudok. The first dance, the *denona*, was danced mostly by the women, and the whole performance ended with a wild, elemental warriors' dance. The games and races were the climax of the festival, and included various kinds of tournaments, shooting matches on horseback, and so on. As night approached, the festivities became wilder and noisier. Such sights and sounds must have imprinted themselves deeply into Glinka's mind; here, surely, is one original source of that orientalism which was to appear many years later in *Ruslan and Lyudmila*.

Back in Novospasskoye, Glinka allowed himself a rest to recover from the cure, and then applied himself eagerly to music. In his *Memoirs*, he stated that he had been much occupied with folk music during this period, and we have the testimony of some of the peasants on the estate concerning this. Often Glinka 'would send one of the servants into the village to summon to his house peasant women and girls, whom he would ask to sing songs to him'.[2] Glinka would improvise an accompaniment on the piano during this, and would then write it down. We know nothing of the nature of these accompaniments, though we may reasonably suppose that they represented Glinka's earliest efforts at solving a problem which occupied him greatly—and most profitably— in some of his later compositions: namely, the problem of devising a characterful accompaniment which did no violence to, and maybe even enhanced, the folk tune to which it was fitted. During the next months he was also to gain especially valuable knowledge of the craft of orchestration. His uncle's musicians paid about two visits a month to Novospasskoye, staying up to a week, and each time Glinka would take the less accomplished players aside and go through their parts

[1] GLN1, p. 82.   [2] Quoted in GG, p. 364.

individually until they were note perfect. Afterwards he observed the general effect of the ensemble. Thus for some six months he was able to study the craft of orchestration in a way few composers are ever lucky enough to enjoy. The benefits of this may be gauged from Glinka's own compositions, for no matter what criticism may be levelled at other aspects of his work, no one ever denies his skill in handling the orchestra. The Shmakovo orchestra's repertoire consisted mainly of overtures and symphonies, though sometimes concertos were tackled. In his *Memoirs* Glinka listed the works they played:

OVERTURES.	Cherubini:	*Médée*
		L'Hôtellerie portugaise
		Faniska
		Lodoïska
		Les deux journées

(the first two were Glinka's favourites)

	Méhul:	*Joseph*
		Le trésor supposé
		L'Irato
	Mozart:	*Don Giovanni*
		Die Zauberflöte
		La Clemenza di Tito
		Le Nozze di Figaro
	Beethoven:	*Fidelio*
	Bernhard Romberg:	[Overture in] E flat
	Maurer:	[Overture in] E flat

(As the viola part was missing from this last one, Glinka spread out the other parts on chairs and, by comparing them, reconstructed the missing line without making any mistakes, as far as he could remember.)

SYMPHONIES.	Haydn:	Symphony in B flat
	Mozart:	Symphony in G minor
	Beethoven:	Symphony No. 2 in D

(Glinka liked the last especially.)

Conspicuously absent from the above list are overtures by Rossini, and Glinka explained this as the result of the considerable improvement which Mayer had effected in his taste before the Caucasian trip. The value of Mayer's lucidly intelligent approach to music was readily acknowledged by Glinka. Mayer had made him play the piano naturally and without affectation, and had helped him to make considered judgements about music for himself. On returning to St. Petersburg in March or April 1824 Glinka resumed his sessions with Mayer, who now refused to take him as a pupil: 'You have too much talent for me to give you lessons. Come every day as a friend, and we'll make music together.'[1] With Mayer Glinka studied much music, including compositions by Mayer himself, though more often works by Hummel. Despite the fact that he still had no systematic grounding at all in the technique of composition, he had started on a Septet and then on an Andante Cantabile[2] and Rondo for orchestra. Mayer did his best to correct such efforts, always setting them against the background of composers like Mozart, Cherubini, and Beethoven, who represented 'the highest degree of perfection'.[3] Looking back in 1854, Glinka still felt that this sort of enlightened but very general guidance was what he needed: 'the noted contrapuntist [Heinrich] Müller was in St. Petersburg at that time, but somehow I never managed to meet him. Who knows, perhaps it was for the best. Strict German counterpoint does not always agree with glowing fantasy.'[4]

Both the Septet and the Andante Cantabile and Rondo reflect the sort of music Glinka had been occupied with at Novospasskoye and with Mayer, and the same is true of the two overtures (in D major and G minor) which he also composed at about this time. Despite his distrust of 'strict German counterpoint', Glinka employed some very deliberate contrapuntal working in the developments of both overtures; so, too, in the first movement of the Septet there are some simple but effective contrapuntal dovetailings of the themes and motifs which are worked quite tightly to produce a movement that is facile but neat. Glinka had no more ability than most other Russian composers for evolving his thought in organic counterpoint, but he liked devising contrapuntal combinations, and he had a positive flair for decorative counterpoint. In view of the rich melodic gifts he later displayed, the melodic poverty of many passages in his early compositions is the more surprising. It is not merely that their melodies are thoroughly uncharacteristic; it is that Glinka will provide a deplorably weak answer to an initial phrase, or round off a paragraph with the most lame of conclusions. The slow movement of this Septet is feeble throughout, and the minuet and trio, and incomplete rondo finale are unmemorable, though Glinka must be given credit in general for handling his medium well throughout the

---

[1] GLN1, p. 86. [2] In his *Memoirs* Glinka described this as an Adagio.
[3] ibid. [4] GLN1, pp. 86–87.

work. The Andante Cantabile and Rondo are expressively more ambitious. The Andante is a substantial, rather laboured piece with a
determined motivic concentration which shows Glinka doggedly pursuing classical models, while the Rondo is pleasant but commonplace.
One clear hint of the mature composer is the liberal use of the clarinet as
a solo instrument. Another work which must also date from this period
is the Symphony in B flat, of which only two fragments survive. As a
piece of composition it is too juvenile to warrant comment, but it is of
documentary interest because Glinka used three folk-songs as its main
thematic material. Unfortunately the remains of the allegro that follows
the adagio introduction are too imperfect to indicate clearly whether
Glinka was intending to evolve a sonata structure or simply some sort
of pot-pourri; what is definite and prophetic is the extended variation
treatment of the folk-tune that appears just before the allegro breaks off.[1]
Altogether there are some five consecutive statements of the tune, and
all but the last are varied. An equally definite second group of variations
on another folk-tune make up most of the other allegro fragment that
survives from this symphony; here the first statement of the tune 'In the
garden, in the vegetable patch' is followed by three variations. Glinka
is already using the technique that was to prove his most favoured and
successful way of treating a folk-tune in an extended movement. Nevertheless the variations themselves are unenterprising, even crude, and
Glinka later observed of all these early compositions that they could
only serve 'as an indication of my musical illiteracy at that time'.[2]

So far Glinka had avoided taking employment, but now his father
asserted that he was finding it difficult to pay for his language and music
lessons. Glinka resigned himself unenthusiastically to the inevitable.
Through the agency of a distant relative a suitable post was found, and
on 7/19 May he started work as an under-secretary in the office of the
Council of Communications at a salary of 1,000 roubles a year. Fortunately the job involved no more than five or six hours' work a day,
and the new musical contacts which he made through this post were
compensation for his official labours. The senior member of the Council,
Count Sivers, was an intelligent man and a real music-lover, at whose
house Glinka was able to participate in homely performances of operas,

---

[1] The tune, *Hoi, do not go, Gritsyu*, became well known in England during the Second
World War when set to the words 'Mother, may I go out dancing? Yes, my darling
daughter'.
[2] GLN1, p. 86.

himself sometimes singing a part, usually with Mayer at the piano. Glinka specially recalled performing Antonio in the finale to Act 1 of Cherubini's *Les deux journées*, and hearing there the piano and wind quintets in E flat by Mozart and Beethoven. He continued composing— so intensively that the relative with whom he was then living tried to dissuade him from this 'pernicious inclination' that would bring him only envy and sorrow. Later Glinka admitted that there had been some truth in this prediction.

In fact, he was not really progressing at all as a composer. He tried his hand at a string quartet in D, but felt it was no advance upon his earlier works. He was quite right; it is a student exercise in a classical manner. His Variations on an Original Theme ('dedicated to whom I shall not say') for piano shows a nice grasp of Field's nocturne style in its third (minor key) variation, and in the preceding two variations Glinka does essay a less trite ornamentation; but the slow introduction is clumsy, and the end no better than any other salon music. A first move- ment of a sonata for viola and piano was tidier, Glinka felt, and he thought well enough of it to have it performed. Later, in 1828, he added an adagio, though the projected rondo finale came to nothing.[1] This sonata is certainly a more interesting piece than the quartet, more up-to- date, with some Hummelian brilliance in the piano writing of the first movement, and a greater, if still conventional, warmth. As a piece of organic structure the first movement could not be taken seriously; some parts positively creak, the development is rudimentary, and the passage work that erupts whenever a transition or codetta is required is empty. But the melodic incidents, especially the second subject, contain some passages of genuine beauty which show that a real composer, and not just a note spinner, is at work (Ex. 3). An intriguing feature of this ex- ample is the curiously Schumannesque premonition in some of the chromatic and dissonant touches. Clearly this was a type of music much closer to Glinka's heart than the frigid pseudo-classicism of the quartet, and he expressed himself well pleased with the later slow movement. Before the end of 1824 he had attempted vocal composition, writing a

---

[1] He later used the Russian-style theme intended for this in his Children's Polka for piano. He revised the other two movements in the 1850s when he was putting his musical affairs in order. The version published in the USSR is based upon what appears to be the last of the three surviving sources, and probably represents Glinka's version of the 1850s. It is substantially different from the versions in the other two extant sources, and is there- fore unreliable as evidence of Glinka's first effort. This source gives the date of composition as 1825. All three sources are printed in GPSS4.

Ex. 3. Allegro moderato

romance (unsuccessfully, he confessed), 'My harp'.[1] The text of this was by Konstantin Bakhturin, son of the head of the office in which Glinka worked, and the author of a number of plays which enjoyed some popularity in their day; it was a compressed paraphrase of one of Edmund's songs from Walter Scott's *Rokeby*, which had been published in Russia the year before (1823). Scott was enjoying a great vogue in Russia, and it is very possible that this romance was part of an opera that Glinka was planning to compose on this subject. But such an enterprise would have been still quite beyond him, and only a few tiny fragments of the music survive. Romances were comparatively easy to produce, and another, written early in 1825, 'Do not tempt me needlessly', was in Glinka's opinion a success. Twenty years later he was to look back and judge this song to have marked the beginning of his career as a composer. Certainly it had an immediate success, becoming well known in St. Petersburg circles, where its pallid passion probably seemed quite monumental against the background of the average drawing-room romance. This work at least foretold that Glinka's greatest single strength would lie in his melodic gifts; harmonically it is thoroughly unenterprising.

Glinka now started singing lessons with a good teacher, Belloli, who taught him to sing *buffo* parts well, and Glinka found the performance of such roles a good way of entertaining his friends. Yet despite all these musical activities, he was still a thoroughly undirected dilettante. He flitted about, repeatedly changing his lodgings, and accepting a constant round of social engagements which his natural sociability and musical attributes readily gained for him. Towards the end of his life, he recalled the protracted visits to his friend, Princess Khovanskaya, as 'the happiest days of my youth',[2] and doubtless he derived some benefit from playing duet versions of Haydn and Mozart symphonies, Haydn quartets, and pieces by Beethoven with a young Viennese lady called Ligle, but this was not really helping his development as a composer. The trouble was that Glinka was only too ready to indulge in the pleasures of St. Petersburg society. It accords well with his life at that time that his first work ever to be performed in public was a French quadrille, composed for a ball at Princess Khovanskaya's. Needless to

---

[1] As the original MS. had been lost, this was among the works Glinka wrote out from memory in 1855. The song was 'antediluvian', that is, composed before 7/19 November 1824, when St. Petersburg suffered a very severe flood. Glinka described the excitement of that day in his *Memoirs*.

[2] In a letter of 17/29 October 1853. Quoted in GLN2, p. 465.

say, no one really listened to it, for the dancers were far too busy chattering with their partners. Nevertheless, it was reported that Glinka was very satisfied. He was flattered by the admiration of his musical talents by women, and he preferred their company to that of men. To increase his social attainments, he took dancing lessons over some two years. Late in 1825 he met an old school friend, Mikhail Glebov, who, Glinka records, 'reproached me because I had given up serious occupations to waste valuable time on what he called idle amusements. I remember that I replied to the effect that I would make a success later on, but that now I thought it proper to consider my own inclinations and my age.'[1] Glinka noted—with some evident satisfaction—that the friend was very soon to pay for his own 'thoughtlessness', for after participating in the Decembrist rising, Glebov was deprived of his rank and nobility, and exiled to Siberia.

Glinka's own easy-going life was itself about to be disturbed in the aftermath of the revolt. The Decembrist rising was the open eruption of some of the ideas and tensions which had been exercising Russian intellectuals and aspiring reformers for many years. During Glinka's schooldays the regime of Aleksandr I had been growing more reactionary; academic freedom had been progressively more cramped, the press had been increasingly muzzled, and in this condition of growing repression it was inevitable that tension should mount. Aleksandr died on 6/18 December 1825, leaving the position of the succession utterly different from what it appeared to be. His heir apparent was his next brother, Konstantin, but nearly four years earlier Konstantin had secretly agreed with Aleksandr to abdicate his right, though this was not to be disclosed until after Aleksandr's death. Nikolai, the next brother, to whom the succession now passed, was therefore quite unaware of his position. In the confused days that followed the Tsar's death, the Guard acted. On 14/26 December, 2,000 soldiers filled the square outside the palace, roaring for 'Konstantin and a Constitution'. After an effort to negotiate, Nikolai reluctantly ordered loyal troops to open fire. The rebellion collapsed; five of the ringleaders were executed, and many others were exiled.

Glinka was to record his own memories of the rising. He had gone to the square early in the morning with Lindquist's son, and had seen Nikolai come out of his palace, walk calmly into the crowd, and tell them to disperse. Glinka had never seen the Tsar before, and the sight

[1] GLN1, p. 93.

deeply moved him. They stayed several hours, but then Glinka felt hungry and decided to go to Bakhturin's. He asserted this may have saved his life, for soon afterwards the bullets began to fly. But this was not the end of the matter for him. A few days later he was rudely awakened in the middle of the night, and summoned to appear forthwith before the authorities. He was petrified—but fortunately all turned out well. It emerged that Glinka's old tutor, Küchelbecker, had taken a leading part in the uprising. When it had been put down, he had fled, and it was suspected that he was hiding with two of his nephews, Dmitri and Boris Glinka. Glinka's account of the affair offers no explanation of exactly why he should have become involved, but he was able to give sufficient assurance of his own innocence to secure his immediate release.

An excuse to get away from St. Petersburg must have been very welcome after such an alarming experience, and this was afforded by the betrothal and marriage of his sister, Pelageya, to their Novospasskoye neighbour, Yakov Sobolevsky. Glinka coupled attendance at these events with a visit to Smolensk to stay with another relative, Aleksei Ushakov. Ushakov had an 18-year-old daughter, Yelizaveta, who was not only a good pianist, but pretty. Glinka liked her very much and it seemed she was drawn to him, but if ever there was any romance, nothing came of it, for in 1828 she married another. On this visit there was much music-making, of course, and Glinka composed for Yelizaveta a set of piano variations on 'Benedetta sia la madre', an Italian romance that was currently very popular. Later, after Mayer had made a few corrections, it was published—the first of Glinka's works to be printed. In fact, the merit of certain of Mayer's revisions is very questionable; in variation 3, where he laid his hand most heavily upon Glinka's work, he merely reduced the original to something more conventional. The real composer was already stirring, and by now Glinka was writing this sort of music very well; the variations are quite beautifully turned and thoroughly acceptable, without ever passing beyond the confines of the salon. A second set, written at about the same time, on the folk-song, 'Among the gentle valleys', only emphasizes how far Glinka was from devising a musical treatment which did not completely annihilate the national characteristics of his material.

A more enterprising composition came from Glinka's association with another Smolensk family, that of a retired General Apukhtin. The general was a sociable man and, since official mourning forbade dancing, he decided to have a musical event, and asked Glinka to compose a *Prologue* on the death of Alexsandr and the accession of Nikolai. A French text was provided by the French tutor to the general's household, and Glinka composed a C minor chorus (with a central unaccompanied terzetto), and an aria with final triumphal chorus in B flat. The accompaniment was for piano and double bass. Glinka's old musical associate from Novospasskoye, Karl Hempel, played the piano and sang the tenor solo in the opening chorus, and the aria was sung by Glinka himself, dressed up as a spirit. 'Despite some gaucheries and the incongruity of the keys of C minor and B flat, I consider this cantata my first successful attempt at a larger-scale piece of vocal music.'[1] The stylistic root of this piece is French, especially in the opening chorus which echoes the *tombeau* tradition of the French opera. Glinka had had plenty of opportunities to acquaint himself with the choral manners of French opera; to a modern English listener this opening chorus would perhaps most readily recall Gluck. The music has more dignity than the attitudinizing plaints and fulsome flattery of Olidor's text. The best compliment that can be paid to Glinka's contribution is to concede that it is thoroughly worthy of the occasion.

Glinka stayed at home until May, living in unashamed idleness. Surrounded by the sixteen cage-birds he had collected, he surrendered himself to the spell of Zhukovsky's sentimental poetry, and dreamed away the evenings at the piano. He composed two melancholy romances, 'Consolation' ('The moon shines over the cemetery') and 'The poor singer', but otherwise accomplished very little that he could remember. 'The poor singer' is the better of the songs. It never really breaks out of the musical simplicities of the drawing room, but it is a touching little piece that just skirts the melodically predictable, enriching the second of its two verses with a six-bar interpolation that nicely broadens the original. Ex. 4 might have fathered a phrase which Glinka was later to use in Gorislava's lament in *Ruslan and Lyudmila* (see Ex. 62).

In May Glinka returned to St. Petersburg but promptly requested an extension of leave, pleading illness. That autumn he visited his old school friend, Melgunov, in Moscow, where Pushkin, who had just returned from exile, was giving private readings of *Boris Godunov* and of his recently completed prologue to *Ruslan and Lyudmila*. Glinka already knew the poet from his schooldays when he had come to visit

[1] GLN1, p. 96.

Ex.4.

(My deceived soul expected happiness. My dreams are finished, everything has perished.)

his brother, Lev, and it is possible that he again encountered him during his Moscow visit. At the end of the year business brought his father to St. Petersburg, and he stayed with his son until the early spring. Glinka always got on particularly well with his father and was very glad of his company, even moving to a larger flat so that they could live together. This move brought a good fortune as great as it was unexpected, and which was to make Glinka's life more easy financially than it would otherwise have been. Opposite their new flat lived a state councillor, Pogodin, who, having satisfied himself of the good character of Glinka's father, offered to take a half-interest in a new venture he was projecting. With the half million roubles which Pogodin invested, the enterprise proved so successful that it was possible to clear all the debts on the Glinka estate. But an affair of the heart turned out less well for the son. Glinka had fallen for a certain Katinka who had been introduced to him by a lady friend of Aleksandr Rimsky-Korsakov,[1] a former school friend with whom he had shared his lodgings for the last two years. But there was no hope; 'her heart belonged to another, and all my efforts

---

1 Glinka habitually referred to him as Rimsky-Korsak, presumably on account of his pseudonym as a writer, A. Korsak.

and *wicked artifices* to arouse a like feeling in her remained unavailing.'[1] Glinka vented his feelings in a romance, '"I love" was your assurance' (later, with a French text, known as 'Le baiser').

During the summer of 1827 Glinka participated in an enterprise which epitomizes the whole character and aim of his musical activities before the composition of *A Life for the Tsar*. Among his many friends was Prince Sergei Golitsuin, a knowledgeable musician and bass singer, whom Glinka credited with an important part in the development of his musical talents. At the end of August, Glinka and some other young people decided to entertain the public with a serenade. A similar corporate event had been organized some six months earlier[2] at the house of Count Kochubei, the then president of the Council of State, when a group of some sixteen performers had presented an entertainment with full orchestra, and Mayer at the piano. Among the delights of this occasion had been Glinka, in a white dress and red wig, singing the part of Donna Anna in the introduction to Act 1 of Mozart's *Don Giovanni*; he had also improvised. Such events caught on, and were to be repeated elsewhere. Some of Glinka's compositions were performed at these, including his couplets with chorus, 'Lila in the black mantle'. The soloist in the couplets was Nikolai Ivanov, a tenor in the Imperial Chapel, whose 'gentle and resonant voice'[3] struck Glinka—though he decided he could extend Ivanov's range for him and, to that end, took him in hand, and in a very short time had him singing up to top B flat. Ivanov was to be Glinka's companion during most of his Italian journey. On another of these musical occasions Glinka played Figaro in excerpts from Rossini's *Il barbiere di Siviglia*.

The serenade which was now projected was to take place in boats on the river for the entertainment of a wider public. Rehearsals were held at the house of Prince Vasily Golitsuin, and attracted a large number of eavesdroppers. For the performance two barges were used, in one of which were Glinka and his friends, and in the other the trumpeters of the Horse Guards regiment. A third vessel followed with the fireworks. Glinka conducted and accompanied on the piano. The programme included a Venetian barcarolle and the opening chorus from Boïeldieu's *La Dame blanche* ('Sonnez, sonnez, cors et musette!'), while

---

[1] GLN1, p. 98.

[2] In his *Memoirs*, Glinka stated that this performance was a result of the success of the public serenade on the Black River which he ascribed to 1828, but other contemporary sources indicate that the order was different from that which Glinka remembered.

[3] GLN1, p. 110.

the trumpets played a specially composed mazurka. The scene was described in the *Northern Bee* of 27 August/8 September 1827:

At 9 p.m. pinnace[s], festooned with lighted lanterns, appeared on the quiet waters of the Black River . . . Russian songs, French romances, and operatic arias were sung in turn by a choir with piano accompaniment. In the breaks between the singing the sounds of the trumpets rang out, and at the same time, Roman candles, firework fountains, Catherine wheels, and rockets lit up the groups of listeners . . . The serenade continued until midnight.[1]

Glinka especially recalled the natural trumpets, and in his *Memoirs* he lamented that they had now fallen into general disuse:

Instruments with valves had then not yet been invented. Musical ears did not suffer as they do now from the untrue, offensive sounds to which we are mercilessly treated . . . I wrote the march and finale of my opera, *A Life for the Tsar*, specifically for natural trumpets, and if it were now possible to find a battery of trumpets like those which participated on that occasion in our serenade, there is no doubt that the finale of the opera would produce significantly more effect.[2]

Glinka had an exceptionally sensitive ear. Elsewhere in his *Memoirs*, he was to enthuse over a horn band he had heard playing on the River Neva, and was to bewail the disbandment of this 'fantastic orchestra' in favour of a group using 'repulsive valve trumpets'.[3] Some years later, in Milan, he met a clarinettist, Ivan Müller, who had invented a clarinet with a complex key system which enabled him to play freely in any key. Glinka loathed it, characterizing its sounds as 'harsh tones, like the screech of a goose; yet the inventor was proud of his invention. Fortunately for lovers of good music, this clarinet was not introduced into the orchestra. . . .'[4]

Afflictions other than aural ones were now besetting him, for his health was beginning to cause him trouble; at least, he was to be much occupied in the next year or two with various attempts to cure his ills. The first, prescribed by a certain Dr. Brailov, was a particularly revolting medicine of which, Glinka was assured, he would have to drink thirty or more bottles to be completely cured. The effect was drastic—a violent purging, aches, pains, and insomnia. Glinka stoically finished all the bottles, and then allowed his health to recover to its former state. Despite all these discomforts, he continued composing, producing several operatic movements, including a recitative and duet in A major

---

[1] Quoted in GLN1, p. 414.   [2] GLN1, p. 109.
[3] GLN1, p. 112.   [4] GLN1, pp. 138–9.

for tenor and bass, a chorus in C minor on the death of a hero, an aria in A flat for baritone, and a Prayer in F, scored for three voices. These were Glinka's very first attempts at writing music for the stage, and he found part of one of these worth preserving in another context, since the adagio of the baritone aria was to be used for the canon in the finale to Act I of *Ruslan and Lyudmila* (unfortunately the original aria is lost). He was fortunate in being able to test the effect of some at least of these pieces, for through an acquaintance, Count Dever, who was both a very good violinist and regimental adjutant in the Horse Guards, Glinka could recruit wind players quite easily. There was no great difficulty about getting strings either, and with the help of the composer and singing teacher, Aleksandr Varlamov, who both mustered singers for the chorus and sang bass himself, Glinka was able to marshall sufficient forces to try through his works. Years later he was to declare to the composer, Aleksandr Serov, just how valuable these diverse experiments in operatic composition were to prove for him. If, he said, he had straightway attempted to set a whole libretto, his experience would have been restricted to the music demanded by the situations of that libretto. By choosing to set separate scenes and ensembles, he could treat a far wider range of dramatic situations and gain that far broader experience which he felt he needed at this time. His passion for composition had now crowded out any sustained efforts to improve his instrumental ability—a fact he rather regretted, since he had met a violin teacher, Rémi, who was in a few lessons able to correct his longstanding bowing faults.

All this time Glinka kept up a full round of social activities, attending dinners and parties of all sorts, at which his performing talents were constantly in demand. Vladimir Sollogub, who was later to be a candidate as librettist of *A Life for the Tsar*, recorded his memories of Glinka on such occasions. 'Often he would sit down at the piano and submerge himself completely in his playing, neither seeing nor knowing what was going on around him.' As for Glinka's singing, 'his voice was dull, weak, unpleasant. On starting to sing he whispered as though speaking with shades of expression, [a manner] which I, of course, began to understand only afterwards: then, becoming livelier bit by bit, he passed almost into a state of frenzy, and yelled out the high notes with effort, fury, even pain. Then he would get up from his seat, would let out a child-like laugh, and having stuck a finger into his waistcoat and thrown back his head, would start to walk about the room, asking:

"How was that chesty B flat?". It seems to me that from that time J began to perceive tacitly that genius and personality are two quite different conceptions, completely independent of each other. Genius can burn in a man along with, even in spite of, his personality. The man who heard Glinka perceived that it was possible to be a grand and stupendous singer, [though] not possessing any physical resources for this.'[1] Concerning Glinka's great potential as a singer, Sollogub was perhaps being wise after the event, for we have it from Glinka himself that his voice changed suddenly some years later in Italy as the result of illness, and his greatest successes as a singer date from after this strange event. Glinka himself reported of his own voice in the 1820s that it was 'husky, rather nasal, and undefined, i.e., neither tenor nor baritone'.[2] Nevertheless, even if Glinka was a rough, imperfect vocalist at this period, he evidently could still command an audience by the sheer character in his performance. His natural sociability made him popular, and his social circle continued to widen. Visits from a Tolstoi family proved very pleasant; Feofil Tolstoi had already delighted Glinka with his tenor voice during the river serenade. Inspired by the joint literary activities of Rimsky-Korsakov and a school friend, Nikolai Lukyanovich, he tried his hand at poetry, and his poem, *Alsand*, was actually published in that year, 1828. He was also visited by the assistant inspector at the Blagorodny Boarding School, Ivan Kolmakov, of whose idiosyncrasies, foibles, friendliness, and engaging enthusiasms Glinka wrote at affectionate length in his *Memoirs*. These convivial occasions provided relief from his physical sufferings, to which an eye affliction was now added. In March 1828 he again visited Novospasskoye, seeing for the last time his sister Pelageya, who had been his close companion in childhood; she died that summer.

At the beginning of May, he set out for Moscow to visit Melgunov. Most of Glinka's friends provided him with acceptable social diversions or pleasant partners in music-making; Melgunov may have given him more. By 1828 Melgunov had arrived at a view of what Russian national opera might be—a conception remarkably close to that which Glinka was to embody in *A Life for the Tsar*. In this year Melgunov was one of a number of writers who compiled an article for the *Moscow Messenger* on Verstovsky's new opera, *Pan Twardovski*. In this article the following passage, contributed by Melgunov, occurred: 'An opera made up of folk melodies is always more like a vaudeville than a purely

[1] SVos, p. 330.   [2] GLN1, p. 89.

artistic, individual creation. The person who can write a Russian opera is one who, having saturated himself sufficiently in our folk melodies, will transmute them within himself, and then in their spirit will write his own music, which will be national not because it will remind us of melodies we already know, but because it will conform to our musical demands and feeling.'[1] This can hardly have been a reflection of Glinka's own view at the time, for the orientation of his interests was towards Western styles in general and Italian opera in particular. But a friend who put such views into Glinka's head was doing him an incalculable service, though neither may have realized it at the time. On this occasion Glinka could pay only a short visit. Nevertheless, he managed to write the adagio of his Viola Sonata ('there was some quite skilful counterpoint in this piece, I remember').[2] His leave was up on 9/21 May, but since this was Melgunov's name-day, he stayed till that very morning so that he might celebrate it with him. Glinka had an obvious respect as well as liking for Melgunov and his parents, and Glinka's father had been sufficiently taken with the family to have considered letting his son travel abroad with them, though in the end he had decided against it. He had no wish to see his son become a Frenchman, and in any case felt that the tenth class civil service grade for which Glinka had qualified on leaving school made it worth while pursuing a career at home.

In fact, Glinka's brief days in the civil service were already drawing to a close. When he first joined the Council for Communications he had had regular contacts with the family of one of the generals of the council, Gorgoli. Glinka had frequently accompanied and sung duets with one of the daughters, Poliksena, but his visits had become less frequent as his own circle of acquaintances had widened. In any case, he found the general's family provincial in their habits, and especially detested their practice of all talking together at the tops of their voices so that no one else in the room (not even the general) could make themselves heard. The growing infrequency of Glinka's visits caused anger, and the general started to find fault with the punctuation in his reports at work. When Glinka ceased his visits altogether, the fault-finding increased. Glinka promptly resigned, 'because of a comma', as he later wrote.

Yet this was obviously not the sole reason behind his resignation.

[1] Quoted in KNG2, p. 39.
[2] GLN1, p. 104. See footnote on p. 34.

The drudgery of work was uncongenial to him, he was prone to physical suffering—and he was probably already turning his attention in the direction of Italy. In 1828 productions of Italian operas sung by Italian singers were resumed in St. Petersburg after a long break. No fewer that eleven operas by Rossini were included in the repertoire, and this may have stimulated Glinka's interest. He started taking Italian lessons with a certain Marochetti, though he enjoyed even more those given by the daughter of the Italian singer, Luigi Zamboni. His progress in the language was characteristically rapid. With Zamboni's son he studied composition. A more academic element entered into these lessons, for the young Zamboni included exercises in two-part fugue. Glinka already knew Bach's *Das wohltemperierte Clavier*, and he took little pride in his own efforts. Zamboni also made him write recitatives, arias, and so on, to Italian texts. The result was an increasing number of such works from Glinka's pen, including two vocal quartets, 'Come di gloria al nome', and 'Sogna chi crede d'esser felice', both with string accompaniment; in addition there were 'O mia dolce, mia carina' (a serenade on words which his friend, Feofil Tolstoi, chose for him; this piece was well liked at the time), and at least eleven songs or arias for voice and piano. These Italian pieces range from the efficient to the banal, and the triteness of their melodies and the frequent clumsiness in the accompaniments reveal all too clearly how far Glinka was from commanding the smooth assurance with which a Bellini or Donizetti handled the materials and procedures of contemporary Italian opera. Perhaps the most worthy of these pieces is the quartet, 'Sogna chi crede d'esser felice'. Having larger forces to control, Glinka was less able to fall into the easy melodic note-spinning which he was beginning to command. But facility has now been replaced by stiffness. Good Italian ensemble writing never sounds like counterpoint; sometimes Glinka's does, and his harmony then acquires a Teutonic tread. He had much to learn in this line, and fortunately he was well aware of this. He was much more successful in two romances, 'Pour un moment' and 'Heart's memory', the latter for Aleksei Stuneyev, whose brother, Dmitri, was to marry Glinka's sister, Mariya. Though Glinka and Aleksei were on very good terms, Glinka asserted that he was the cause of several of his life's ills (it was at Aleksei's flat that he was to meet Mariya Ivanova, Aleksei's sister-in-law, to whom he was to be unhappily married). The current misfortune was a course of treatment with a certain army doctor, Gasovsky, who had a passion for prescribing mighty doses of medicine, his favourites being mercury, sulphur, quinine, and opium. Later Gasovsky was to confess that his methods had made him 'an enemy of the human race'.[1] Without examining Glinka, he condemned him to treatment with the first of these remedies; after a month's incarceration in a stuffy room, he was ordered to take sulphur baths. The results were surprisingly mild—merely a slight irritation in the solar plexus, and a false appetite. In the context of Glinka's normal post-treatment experiences, this might be considered a success.

Glinka's own recollection of the order of his life's events over the next two years is vague, though since they were mostly as trivial as the majority of the happenings already recorded, this lack of precision is no great loss. His constant social rounds continued, and his circle of acquaintances widened. He met the Polish pianist, Maria Szymanowska, and through her was introduced to the great Polish poet, Adam Mickiewicz. Among other men of letters were Delvig, who adapted his own song, 'O thou black night', for Glinka's music (Glinka set Delvig's 'The maids once told me, grandfather'), and Griboyedov, also a keen amateur pianist and musician. Griboyedov furnished Glinka with the theme of a Georgian song which he used for a romance, and to which Pushkin added the words, 'Sing not, thou beauty, in my presence'. Another amateur musician who was to die young was Yevgeny Shterich, a dilettante composer and pianist, whom Glinka described as 'an *élégant* in the full sense of that word',[2] who loved to shine in salons, but who had other more serious qualities. In addition there was Anna Kern, whom he had first met in 1826, and with whose daughter he was many years later to have a serious love affair. In June 1829 Glinka was one of a party including Anna Kern and the Delvigs which visited the waterfall of Imatra on the other side of the Finnish border.[3] Anna Kern later recorded a little incident that was to have material results in Glinka's subsequent work: 'Having arrived at one station, we noticed that he [Glinka], with a pencil in his hand and a sheet of paper, was standing behind a half-ruined shed, writing something, while his coachman was in front of him singing some song.'[4] What Glinka was noting down was the tune he was later to use for Finn's Ballad in *Ruslan and Lyudmila*. Meanwhile he was so taken with the tune that he used it for a piano composition on returning from Imatra. This tiny piece, one of the

---

[1] GLN1, p. 105.   [2] GLN1, p. 108.

[3] In his *Memoirs* Glinka assigned this expedition to June 1828.

[4] Quoted in OG, p. 188.

slenderest of his early piano compositions, is also the most interesting of them. Glinka was content to provide the very simplest of accompaniments, but already his imagination is stirred to provide something other than a conventional treatment of its end. Ex. 5 contains the entire

Ex.5. Allegretto

second half of the composition, and in 1838 he still felt this was good enough to be transferred into his far more elaborate deployment of the tune in Finn's Ballad. For a brief moment Glinka had liberated himself from the pianistic manners of the salon. In the autumn of that year he acquired yet another song which he was to use in *Ruslan and Lyudmila*. This time it was a Persian song sung by a secretary to the Persian envoy, Khozrev-Mirza;[1] Glinka used this for the Persian Chorus at the opening of Act III.

In 1828 Glinka and Sergei Golitsuin decided to publish a *Lyrical Album* consisting of eight vocal pieces and nine piano pieces by various composers. Glinka contributed his two romances, 'Heart's memory' and

---

[1] Glinka expressed this unclearly, apparently naming Khozrev-Mirza 'Minister of Foreign Affairs'. He was in fact nephew to the Shah of Persia, and had arrived in St. Petersburg as ambassador on 4/16 August 1829 to make peace with the Tsar after the murder of Griboyedov in Tehran.

'Tell me why', an Italian duet for contralto and tenor, 'Mio ben, ricordati', and three piano pieces, a cotillon, a mazurka, and a contredanse. The collection appeared early in 1829 under the names of Glinka and Nikolai Pavlishchev, who was Pushkin's brother-in-law, and an amateur musician as well as a literary man—and the one who, Glinka admitted, was really responsible for getting the volume into print at all. Among other compositions of this period are three of his most worthwhile early works, the romance, 'Disenchantment', and the two Russian songs, 'O gentle autumn night' and 'Not the frequent autumn shower', the latter for tenor and men's chorus. Glinka was to adapt the verse part of this last piece for Antonida's Romance in *A Life for the Tsar*.

In the three years following the composition of 'The poor singer' and 'Consolation' in 1826, Glinka wrote some fourteen romances or folk-song stylizations, and these include what were his most important compositions of the 1820s. It would be a great mistake to dismiss all the romances out of hand as being of interest solely as evidence of Glinka's career as a composer. Admittedly 'Tell me why' and '"I love" was your assurance' are undistinguished, but both 'Heart's memory', with its wide-ranging melody, and the brief but touching strophes of 'Pour un moment' achieve a more intense lyricism with some strangely Schumannesque premonitions, especially in the former (Ex. 6). Such premonitions have already been noted in the Viola Sonata (see Ex. 3), and

Ex.6. Moderato

(O heart's memory! Thou art stronger than reason's sad memory, and often with thy fascination thou captivatest me in a distant land.)

they also occur in the striking 'Disenchantment', with its very effective echo of the piano introduction at the end of both verses, and with its ensuing chromatic descent as accompaniment to the disintegrated vocal line. In this song Glinka started to move beyond the confines of the drawing-room romance. 'Shall I forget?' is a serious song too, but the only peer to 'Disenchantment' is 'A voice from the other world', written, according to Lyudmila Shestakova, for Yakov Sobolevsky after the death of Pelageya, his wife (and Glinka's sister), in 1828. The lyric, which Zhukovsky translated from the words sung by Thekla's spirit to Max in Schiller's *Wallenstein*, obviously stirred Glinka as strongly as they must have moved the bereaved husband, for nowhere in his early music did he ever achieve such a depth of feeling. This poignant little song, though still scented with the aroma of the drawing room, is a most beautiful little piece (Ex. 7).

Glinka's six surviving folk-song stylizations from the 1820s could almost all be taken for arrangements of the genuine article as readily as his one arrangement of a genuine folk-song, the Georgian tune to which Pushkin set the words 'Sing not, thou beauty, in my presence'; only occasionally, as in the touch of chromaticism at the end of 'O thou

(Do not enquire whither I have bent my course, into what realm I have crossed out of the world. O beloved, I have fulfilled all earthly things; on earth I have lived and loved.)

black night', does it become apparent that a more sophisticated composer is creating the material as well as the dressing. Ex. 8 is one entire song—a mixolydian tune treated with that economy which is essential if the character of the tune is not to be betrayed by the harmonization. Such tiny pieces are worth more than all the elaborate tinsel of the piano variations, or the second-hand dramatic posturing of the Italian scenas.

Glinka was being more and more troubled by his health. His *Memoirs* recount the various treatments his body suffered in the search for a cure; indeed, a cynic might be forgiven for supposing that he must have had an iron constitution to have survived so many medicinal assaults. In October 1829, in response to a full account of his sufferings, his mother and sister Natalya had taken him back from St. Petersburg to Novospasskoye. Here, in the intervals between bouts of illness, he played the piano part in a number of performances of Hummel's Septet, and set about improving his technique with studies by Cramer and Moscheles. Sometimes he played Bach. In 1830 he composed a string quartet in F

Ex.8. Andante sostenuto

1. Noch o-sen - nya - ya, lyu-bez-na-ya, noch o-sen-nya - ya, khot glaz ko-li.

O spa-si - bo te-be, no-chen-ka, noch o - sen - - nya - ya.

(Beloved autumn night, darkest autumn night. O thanks be unto thee, O night, O autumn night.)

major, but was dissatisfied with it when he heard it performed, feeling that it reflected his bad state of health at the time. It is possible that Glinka's discontent derived from his general musical condition rather than from the actual accomplishment of this quartet, for it is a notably smoother work than the earlier one in D major, with melody that is at least efficient if not distinctive, and with a cleaner technique. Glinka the craftsman had come a long way, but the substance is still no more than dull pastiche, and by now this line of evolution held no more interest for him. In fact, the Quartet in F marked the end of what might be labelled Glinka's classical symphonic apprenticeship. We may gauge how little value he attached to these instrumental pieces by the fact that, though he could still write out from memory some of his earliest songs during the last years of his life, he quite failed even to recognize as his own work one of his quartets when a performance of it was arranged by Vassily Engelhardt in the 1850s.

The truth is that it was not only Glinka's health that was troubling him; he was deeply restless, urgently needing to move on to a new stage which would offer new experiences. He diverted himself by writing seven elaborate contralto studies for his sister, Natalya, teaching Lyudmila geography and music, and building his younger brothers and sisters a slide which they might descend sitting in copper basins. But in his mind was already rooted a wish to get away from Russia. It had been there before he was brought from St. Petersburg. 'This wish, awakened by the hope of being rid of my suffering and of perfecting myself in music, was subsequently made even stronger from reading about travels. I remember that before my actual departure for the country I had read about a journey to Spain, and from that very time dreamed of that interesting country.'[1] He had hoped to get his father's permission to go abroad, but was bitterly disappointed when this was firmly refused. His father knew perfectly well that Glinka was intending to immerse himself in Italian opera, and he was stoutly opposed to his son's devoting himself entirely to music. However, Glinka's wish was to be granted. That winter they were visited by an army doctor named Spindler, who was an old and respected friend of Glinka's father. After examining Glinka's case, the doctor pronounced that only a term of at least three years in a warmer climate could possibly cure him of his numerous ailments. Thus it was decided that he should go abroad to Italy via Germany. A travelling companion was needed and, as Glinka himself was too ill to go to St. Petersburg, his father kindly undertook everything, finally persuading Ivanov to go with him, and arranging with Fyodor Lvov that Ivanov should get a two-year leave from the Imperial Chapel; he also agreed to subsidize the assistance which the Imperial Chapel gave Ivanov for the trip. In early May, Ivanov arrived in Novospasskoye, ready to start for Western Europe.

And so, just before his 26th birthday, Glinka set off for Italy. He was a typical young Russian with time on his hands, going abroad to recover his health, pursue a hobby, and enjoy himself. So far his whole life had been quite purposeless. He had had no musical education which could in any way equip him to be a real professional. He had written some music, but the great majority of his compositions were of no real importance, and some were better forgotten. If Glinka's friends had been told that this gifted dilettante, whose enthusiasm for Italian opera was about to be indulged in a three-year tour of Italy, would give them a mere six years hence a Russian national opera of genius, after which Russian music could never be quite the same—or that this social butterfly, who enlivened their gatherings with his performing gifts, and who

[1] GLNi, p. 114.

turned out mostly undemanding salon music, would twelve years hence present them with a second opera which would contain some of the most original music, and some of the most novel and influential sounds of the whole nineteenth century, they would have been incredulous. Yet this is precisely what did happen.

3/Italy and Berlin

On 25 April/7 May 1830, Glinka and Ivanov set out for Europe. They travelled through Smolensk, Brest-Litovsk, and Warsaw to Dresden, where Glinka consulted a fashionable doctor who prescribed the waters of Ems and Aachen. From Dresden they proceeded via Leipzig to Frankfurt-am-Main. Initially Glinka had found the journey exhausting, but by now he was feeling much more himself, and where possible each stop was spent in musical diversions with Ivanov and a travelling companion who sang bass. With this vocal trio and a piano they amused not only themselves but also the local inhabitants at their various stopping places with bits of opera; Glinka recalled that their performances of the trio and chorus from Act 1 of Weber's *Der Freischütz* had a particular success. Having reached the Rhine at Mainz, they continued their journey by boat. Just before Koblenz they disembarked, and walked thence to Ems. They stayed there three weeks, but the waters affected Glinka adversely.[1] At Aachen they were more beneficial, though Glinka considered the degree of treatment was overprescribed. Here he heard *Der Freischütz,* Spohr's *Faust* and Beethoven's *Fidelio:* 'Ivanov and I did not understand *Fidelio* the first time; the second performance reduced us to tears,' he wrote.[2]

After a brief stay in Ems to meet his old friend, Shterich, Glinka set out via Schlangenbad to Frankfurt. By now it was August. Here he saw Cherubini's *Médée,* of which he confessed to understanding nothing except the overture. The passage across Switzerland was enough for him to be enthralled by that country's scenery. He and Ivanov stayed in Basel, and proceeded through Solothurn, Bern, and Lausanne to Geneva.

---

1 The effect must apparently have been drastic, for during August rumours that he had died reached some of his friends then living in Italy.

2 GLN1, p. 118.

Glinka as a young man (1826). Portrait by an unknown artist

PLATE II

The last stage of their journey to Milan took them over the Simplon Pass, where it was misty, drizzly, and cold, and then through the d'Ossola Valley to Baveno on Lake Maggiore, where the weather was once again perfect. At the Simplon Pass Glinka experienced an instance of English eccentricity which he still remembered a quarter of a century later. They had got out of the carriage to walk the last and steepest part to the top of the pass and, on arriving at the top, they noticed that one of their fellow-travellers, a young Englishman, had disappeared. A search finally revealed him sitting on a rock overhanging an awesome precipice:

'What are you doing, sir?' cried the driver.
'I am experiencing the sensation of danger,' replied the islander coldly.
'But don't you see that you risk falling down the precipice?' said the driver.
'It is because of this risk that I am getting a real sensation of danger,' said the Englishman, and resumed his seat.[1]

Glinka was delighted with Milan, its cathedral, and the dark-eyed Milanese girls in their mantillas. Shterich had come to Milan too, though he had to go on to Turin, where he was to take up a diplomatic appointment. Glinka and Ivanov found satisfactory lodgings, and then followed Shterich to Turin. Though Glinka was delighted with the production he saw there of Fioravanti's opera buffa, *Le cantatrici villane,* he found Turin 'dead'. But back in Milan in early November he was thoroughly happy, and had already made up his mind to stay there before going to Naples for a long stay the next autumn. The competition between the La Scala and Carcano theatres ensured first-rate singers, and on 24 November/6 December he could write to his old school friend, Sergei Sobolevsky, who was in Turin: 'Italy is in all respects a second homeland to me. Here, after such protracted suffering, I am for the first time beginning to recover.'[2]

On the other hand, the first direct attempts to continue his musical education were not so fortunate. As a composition teacher he had been recommended to take Basili, the director of the Milan Conservatoire, whose main claim to fame is that he rejected the young Verdi when he wanted to enter this institution as a student. Basili set Glinka to work on strict counterpoint which, not surprisingly, proved utterly uncongenial to him, and the lessons were soon discontinued. Needless to say, however, Glinka very soon had his social musical activities well organized. He made friends not only with some of the more important people in

[1] GLN1, p. 119.   [2] GLN2, p. 59.

Milan—men like the Russian envoy to the Sardinian Court at Turin, Count Vorontsov-Dashkov, who let Glinka use his box in the Carcano theatre, and invited him to dine—but also with a whole host of second- and third-rate musicians and singers, some of whom would gather at Glinka's lodgings of an evening to pass the time in various enjoyable activities. Glinka also found other diversions in the society of a young dancer, Adelaide (known also as Didina), who lived in the same house.

The opening of the new opera season on the day following Christmas introduced him to fresh delights. It was the smaller Carcano theatre which offered the richer pleasures. Here Rubini, Pasta, and other leading singers performed, while Bellini and Donizetti appeared as conductors. Glinka attended the first performance of Donizetti's *Anna Bolena* with a star cast: 'I wallowed in rapture, the more so since at that time I was still not indifferent to virtuosity as I am now.'[1] He also saw Rossini's *Semiramide,* Zingarelli's *Giulietta e Romeo,* and Donizetti's *Gianni di Calais.* But the climax of the season was the première of Bellini's *La Sonnambula,* presented by the singers with as much emotional enthusiasm as it was received by the audience. 'Shterich and I, embracing each other in the ambassador's box, likewise shed a copious flood of tears of emotion and rapture.'[2] Returning home after each opera, he and Ivanov relived their favourite moments by picking them out on the piano, and then performing them, to the surprised delight of their landlady, friends, and neighbours.

The winter weather brought Glinka some health troubles. Easter 1831 was spent in Turin with Shterich, who was deeply involved in an emotional entanglement with a young dancer called Colombi, against growing opposition from his mother. Glinka remembered Shterich weeping on his breast about this during a performance in Milan of Meyerbeer's *Il crociato in Egitto,* 'the music of which I already knew in St. Petersburg, and which I never liked'.[3] But while in Milan Glinka was generally in high spirits. The spring had come, and he and Ivanov had achieved a certain fame there, where they were now known as the 'two *maestri Russi,* of whom one sings, and the other plays the piano'.[4] To ensure that this slight fame was preserved, Glinka again turned to composition. Feeling that he was still not master of all the arts and refinements of vocal writing, he decided upon piano pieces, producing his variations on a theme from Donizetti's *Anna Bolena,* variations on two

[1] GLN1, p. 123.   [2] ibid.
[3] GLN1, p. 125.   [4] ibid.

themes from *Chao-Kang* (a ballet compiled from music by Rossini and Spontini), and a 'rondino brillante' on a theme from Bellini's *I Capuletti e i Montecchi*. Glinka certainly manufactured musical tinsel very efficiently, but these trifles, together with all the piano music he wrote in Italy, may now be profitably forgotten. His whole life at this time was one of aimless though very pleasant diversion. He walked through Milan, enjoyed trips to the surrounding countryside, and each evening was enchanted by the opera, dined out, or was diverted by a gathering of his musical acquaintances. His visit to Shterich in June was troubled by the continuing consequences of the latter's affair with Colombi, and he found the increasing summer heat of Milan and Turin oppressive, but he was able to escape from this by visiting the lakes or mountains. On medical advice he tried the waters at Trescore near Bergamo, but the results were disastrous. He also tried another cure, 'l'eau de M. Pollin', described as 'antisyphilitique'; obviously not all Glinka's relationships had been platonic. 'M. Pollin' was, in fact, Francesco Pollini, the very distinguished pianist, pupil of Mozart and friend of Rossini, of whom Glinka wrote that 'to him and to no other belongs the invention of the new method of playing the piano; Liszt also agrees with this'.[1] Quite apart from the virtues of Pollini's 'eau' (though Glinka himself had to discontinue the cure because of violent side effects), Glinka admired Pollini both as pianist and composer. At about this time he was introduced to Mendelssohn. It seems to have been an uncomfortable meeting. Glinka recalled: 'I was ill, and he, I suppose because of the not fully merited reputation I had gained for being an excellent pianist, adopted a somewhat derisive tone towards me. I did not play, but he, after much persuasion, played a rondo of a light variety, from which it was impossible for me to assess the dimensions of his talent.'[2]

In September 1831, Glinka and Ivanov decided to go to Naples. Shterich was due to return to Russia, and he accompanied them to Genoa. Here they parted; it was the last time Glinka was to see Shterich, who died early the next year. Glinka and Ivanov continued their journey to Rome by steamboat, calling in at Leghorn and Civitavecchia. In Rome they stayed for about two weeks with the Princess Zinaida Volkonskaya, a lady of very wide cultural interests and abilities, who had once been a pupil of Boïeldieu. They saw the sights of the city, but Glinka was not unreserved in his praises: 'I could not convince myself of the worth of St. Peter's, probably because to this very day I prefer

[1] ibid. [2] GLN1, p. 128.

Gothic and Byzantine churches to all others.'[1] The most noteworthy event for him was really his meeting with Berlioz, then in the Italian capital as a holder of the Prix de Rome. It is surprising that Glinka did not recount this meeting in his *Memoirs,* but Berlioz did record it. Fourteen years later he recalled that Ivanov had sung some of Glinka's songs excellently: '[these songs] struck me greatly with their ravishing melodic turn of phrase, so completely different from what I had heard up to then.'[2]

Glinka's initial impressions of Naples, where they arrived on 20 October/1 November, were much more favourable. The journey thither, through regions with palms and cacti, reawakened his childhood visions of exotic tropical lands, especially Africa. As for Naples itself, 'I was completely enraptured, and I could not admire enough the unusual majestic beauty of its situation; the clearness of the air, the bright festive world—all this was new and ravishingly beautiful to me.'[3] The view of Capri and Sorrento across the bay enchanted him, and he deeply regretted that he never actually visited these places. Still, he did explore the Bay of Baiae with the Sybil's grotto, and one day in December set off to see the lava stream from Vesuvius. But unfortunately the weather deteriorated, and finally turned into a thoroughly Russian snowstorm. They were forced to turn back—luckily with a group of French tourists —though, in descending the mountain, the wind blew out their torches, and they finally had to grope their way down in the dark. Then the carriage that was taking them the last part of the journey broke down, and they had to complete their return on foot. Inevitably Glinka was ill after this; nevertheless he was sufficiently fascinated to return with Ivanov to see the sight when the weather was better.

Glinka visited the opera houses, liking best the little San Carlino theatre. Among the operas he saw in Naples were Rossini's *Il Turco in Italia,* and a comic opera in Neapolitan dialect, *Il ventaglio,* by Raimondi, which he judged to be poor. The visit to Naples turned out particularly well for Ivanov, who studied with Andrea Nozzari, a very noted singer who must have been deeply impressed with him, for he gave him free lessons. With help also from Joséphine Fodor-Mainvielle, another opera singer who was the daughter of a French violinist and who had spent her childhood in St. Petersburg, Ivanov improved so much that he earned the praise of Rubini, and was finally to make his début in Naples in Donizetti's *Anna Bolena.* Glinka later acknowledged that he himself was

[1] ibid.   [2] See Appendix p. 311   [3] GLN1, p. 129.

indebted to Nozzari and Joséphine Fodor-Mainvielle more than to any others for his own knowledge of singing. As Ivanov's leave was almost up, Glinka advised him to go back to Russia for a year, and then to resign and return to Italy. But Ivanov decided not to return to Russia at all. In Naples he and Glinka parted, and on Glinka's side there were no regrets—except that he was later to experience some official displeasure in Russia at his failure to ensure Ivanov's return. As for Ivanov himself, the Tsar decreed that he should never more be mentioned in the Russian press.

Yet, for all its operatic delights, and for all the immeasurable benefits of Nozzari's and Mme. Fodor-Mainvielle's teaching, Glinka's feelings about Naples were divided. Within ten days of his arrival he was reporting that 'Naples, despite the wonderful beauty of its situation, is antipathetic to me, partly because of a certain similarity to St. Petersburg, which I hate, and partly because I find little in it that is Italian'.[1] At this stage he still thought the climate was good for him, but he soon changed his mind. 'So far I have not been able to accustom myself to the local electric-sulphureous air. It affects my nerves so strongly that I have slept scarcely a single night since I arrived here.'[2] At the beginning of March 1832 a very weary Glinka returned to Rome and, after a short stay, headed for Milan by way of Bologna, Parma, Modena, and Piacenza. In Milan he was warmly welcomed back to his old quarters by his landlady and Adelaide, and his former empty life was resumed. On themes from Bellini's *La Sonnambula* he composed a Divertimento brillante for piano and string quintet, which he heard well performed in July, and he started work on a Serenade for piano, harp, and four other instruments on themes from Donizetti's *Anna Bolena*. Women figured more and more in his life: indeed, he had written both these serenades for lady pianists. His doctor, de Filippi, had a married daughter living in a village between Lakes Como and Maggiore, and Glinka's acquaintance with this lady had to be firmly broken by her father because of the gossip it was exciting, though not before this lady's pianistic abilities had fired him to start work on a *Gran sestetto* for piano and strings. The end of the affair was marked by a romance, 'Il desiderio' ('Oh, se tu fossi meco'). At Varese, at the villa of de Filippi's friend, Dr. Branca, Glinka again met his niece, Emilia Branca, who was a competent harpist and who had been one of the feminine inspirations for his *Anna Bolena* serenade; now he enjoyed a second pleasant interlude with her which encouraged him to complete this confection. But the consequences were

[1] GLN2, p. 60.   [2] GLN2, p. 62.

less happy when some time later he endeavoured to oblige a prima donna called Tosi with a special cavatina which she might interpolate into Donizetti's *Faust* when she sang in it at La Scala (her complaint was that Donizetti had not provided her with a good entrance); Glinka could not satisfy the lady, even when he made alterations, and he vowed never to write any further pieces for Italian prima donnas.

The fact is that by now the process of Glinka's disenchantment with Italy was well under way, and his thoughts were turning slowly but surely towards Russian music. Towards the end of 1832 Feofil Tolstoi visited him in Milan, and nearly forty years later remembered that Glinka had 'set out in detail a plan which he had conceived for a grand five-act opera . . . The proposed subject was completely national with a strongly patriotic colouring, and was rather gloomy . . . He was already playing . . . the melody, "When my mother was killed" [later to be the Orphan's Song in *A Life for the Tsar*], and lovingly pointed out the counterpoint on "My Vanya is singing to himself all about a fledgeling".'[1] At that time there was no talk about the words, but the idea of decorating a simple native melody with, as he put it, all the artifices of musical wisdom had already fully matured in Glinka's head: '"The themes will remain as they were . . . and the presentation of them will remain national; but as far as other ornamentation is concerned—there I shall pay my compliments! On this matter I shall not stint myself."'[2] Tolstoi could not remember what the subject of this opera was, and Glinka remembered things quite differently, claiming that 'When my mother was killed' was composed in Berlin in 1833 or 1834. Yet even as early as the Symphony in B flat, Glinka had exposed folk-song to variation treatment, and there are further experiments pointing in the direction of the changing-background technique in the Symphony on two Russian themes and the Capriccio on Russian themes, both of 1834. The essential truth of Tolstoi's recollections is substantiated by the contents of a letter from Sergei Sobolevsky in the autumn of 1832 (Sobolevsky was living in Milan at this time, and saw a good deal of Glinka)— and we have Glinka's own word for it that the idea of writing in a Russian manner grew upon him gradually during his stay in Italy.

There is no point in listing further Glinka's circle of acquaintances in Italy, nor the trivial details of his various visits. He was never at a loss for offers of hospitality, always seemed to find it easy to get invited as a house guest whenever he wanted to escape from Milan, and was always

---

[1] These are the words of Susanin's first vocal entry in this act.   [2] TVG, pp. 430-1.

happy when the situation offered a young lady with whom he might dally. In Milan he kept up a constant musical acquaintance both with Pollini and Bellini, frequently attending the opera, and applying a sharply critical ear to every eminent voice that he heard. He specially recalled performances of Bellini's *Norma* and Rossini's *Otello*, and was reduced to tears by the playing of the eighty-year-old Alessandro Rolla, principal viola of the La Scala orchestra, when he participated in a performance of Glinka's *Anna Bolena* serenade in Milan. Glinka's compositions continued to be mainly trivia based upon opera tunes, though in the Trio Pathétique for clarinet, bassoon, and piano he attempted something different. He had been undergoing a course of treatment which had made him feel very ill: 'I was deprived of appetite [and] sleep, and I fell into the cruellest despair which I expressed in the above-mentioned trio.'[1] Nevertheless, the possibility that the despair also had its origins in an unhappy love affair is suggested by Glinka's note on the autograph: 'I have only known love through the punishments that it causes.'

At the beginning of March 1833 he set out for Venice in the hope that a change of scenery would, as usual, do him good. But it was not to be. The pleasantly feminine reception for which he had hoped from a certain Ninetta Zampo was a disappointment, the climate proved unfavourable, and he had the added disappointment of witnessing the failure of his friend Bellini's new opera, *Beatrice di Tenda*. Finally, another cure applied by a local doctor had such a devastating effect that Glinka had to rush back to Milan. Fortunately he was in the same coach as his friend and publisher, Giovanni Ricordi, who had already issued several of Glinka's Milanese compositions. It is a proof of the high assessment of Glinka by contemporary Italians, that Ricordi could write that he considered Glinka the equal of Bellini and Donizetti, 'but more learned than them in counterpoint'.[2] Ricordi and a lady companion looked after him on the journey, and back in Milan he was dutifully nursed for some six weeks by his landlady and Adelaide. Glinka later recalled the effect this illness had upon his musical activities: 'In the intervals between the attacks my sufferings became less; I sat at the piano and involuntarily drew out fantastic sounds in which were expressed the fantastic feelings that were agitating me.'[3] Also, to his amazement, his voice suddenly changed into a strong and resonant high tenor.

[1] GLNi, p. 141.   [2] From a letter to Sergei Sobolevsky, quoted in KNG3, p. 50.
[3] GLNi, p. 143.

Glinka's days in Italy were nearing their end. At the beginning of May, de Filippi sent him to Dr. Branca at Varese, who made Glinka take exercise. He visited other friends, but by now he was becoming utterly out of love with Italy. His sufferings prevented him composing. Weakened by his illness, he became melancholy, then homesick. Finally the moment of decision arrived. His sister, Natalya Gedeonova, was in Berlin with her husband. Glinka immediately felt an urge to join them there. At the beginning of August he left Italy for good.

In his *Memoirs* Glinka summarized what those three years in Italy had meant for him: 'I suffered much, but there were many happy and truly poetic moments. Frequent contact with second- [and] first-class singers, both professional and amateur, afforded me practical acquaintance with the capricious and difficult art of controlling the voice and writing skilfully for it . . .

'My labours at composition I consider less successful. It cost me no little effort to counterfeit the Italian *sentimento brillante,* as they call the sense of well-being which is the result of an organism being happily placed beneath the influence of the beneficent southern sun. We, the inhabitants of the North, feel differently: impressions either do not touch us at all, or else penetrate our souls deeply. With us it is either frantic jollity or bitter tears. With us love, that delightful feeling that creates a universe, is always joined to sadness. There is no doubt that our mournful Russian song is a child of the North, and perhaps owes something to the inhabitants of the East . . . All the pieces written by me to please the inhabitants of Milan, and very neatly published by Giovanni Ricordi, only served to convince me that I was not following my own path, and that I could not sincerely be an Italian. A longing for my own country led me gradually to the idea of writing in a Russian manner.'[1]

The works Glinka had written in Italy were nearly all instrumental, for despite his absorption in Italian opera, he had almost completely eschewed setting Italian texts. It is an odd fact that it is in his one essay in Italian operatic composition of the time, the aria, 'L'iniquo voto', that there appears a momentary anticipation of a thoroughly individual harmonic progression (Ex. 9) which recurs in his later works, often in the coda (Glinka recalls this progression in the coda of this aria). Otherwise 'L'iniquo voto' (which is quite certainly the cavatina, 'Beatrice di Tenda', which Glinka wrote for Luiggia Giulini, daughter of

[1] GLN1, pp. 144–5.

Ex.9. Moderato

a retired Milanese merchant, in the summer of 1832) shows how efficiently he can now challenge the Italians on their own ground, and the
romance, 'Il desiderio', likewise reveals an easy command of Bellinian
cantilena. He had treated his own language no more liberally. In Milan
in 1832 a friend had drawn his attention to two lyrics by Zhukovsky,
and this had resulted forthwith in 'The Conqueror', set as a swaggering
polonaise,[1] and 'Venetian night', which is as Italianate as its title suggests;
but this was all. His solo piano pieces, as noted earlier, are profitably
forgotten. The most substantial of his Italian works are those for piano
and instrumental ensemble, all composed, it seems, in 1832. Not one of
these is of any real importance. The Divertimento Brillante on *La
Sonnambula* themes is no more than a pot-pourri, thoroughly unpreten-
tious, thoroughly effective, and thoroughly negligible. The strings fare
better against the piano in the Gran Sestetto, and the first movement
shows how consummately Glinka can fabricate an efficient sonata pattern
of absolute predictability—except for the re-introduction of the re-
capitulated second subject in the submediant, a device he repeats exactly,
though at greater length, in the finale. The second movement is a completely Italianate serenade, attractive but insignificant; indeed, the whole
work might be described as a most distinguished example of musical
mediocrity. Nor, despite Glinka's declaration of deeper motivations,
does the Trio Pathétique really rise to a higher level. Ex. 10, the opening of

---

[1] In one source, however, it is described as a 'Spanish romance', and might therefore
be intended as a bolero. Glinka's compositions in polonaise and bolero manners are often
indistinguishable.

the first movement, is a worthy sample of its content. The first four bars are a rhetorical gesture, bars one and two anticipating the first 'allegro energico' of the Liszt Piano Sonata; yet it is only necessary to observe how Liszt allows his motif to initiate a series of incidents in

which tension and thrust are maintained, in order to perceive the limp-
ness of Glinka's continuation in bars three and four. As for the cantabile
tune that follows, it has all the facility of Mendelssohn, but the movement that ensues lacks the spacious melodic flow and easy redeploy-
ment of material which the German composer could successfully
substitute for really organic evolution (as, for instance, in *his* D minor
Trio, Op. 49). None of the melodic material of Glinka's first movement
is of any distinction. The scherzo has some genuine musical wit, though
the trio is commonplace. The third movement adapts Italian operatic
melody to the individualities of the clarinet and bassoon, and the finale[1]
endeavours to draw some earlier threads together by using material
from the first and third movements. In fact, the Trio Pathétique does get
an occasional performance in the West, but there is really no reason why
we should remember it more than any of Glinka's other Italian compositions. The one positive quality shared by all these works is the easy
mastery of the chosen instrumental medium. By this time Glinka himself had fully realized the limitations of such pieces. He had mastered
their undemanding procedures, and had developed a ready melodic
facility, but everything was borrowed, secondhand. He knew that none
of this music really mattered, and he knew that if he were at last to
create an extended piece that was really individual, really representative,
he would need a stretch of sustained application devoted to enlarging his
technique and expanding his expressive range. Thus it was inevitable
that he should now wish to flee Italy just as eagerly as three years earlier
he had come to taste of her delights.

His first objective on leaving Italy was Vienna. He travelled thither
by way of Como, Varenna, Sondrio, and the Stelvio Pass to Innsbruck,
and thence through Salzburg and Linz. He was fortunate in being able
to engage the services of Dr. Branca, who took him to an anatomical
wax museum in Vienna where, by explaining everything that was
connected with Glinka's own ills, he was actually able to relieve the
patient's mind of a lot of fears. In Vienna Glinka often heard with pleasure the orchestras of Strauss and Lanner. A cure at Baden was prescribed,
and after Dr. Branca had left and Glinka had been placed under the
supervision of a local doctor, over-treatment had the expected calami-
tous effects. But deliverance was at hand. Glinka's new valet took him
to a priest who possessed a piano, and the priest, struck by the melancholy

---

[1] Glinka may have viewed this as the allegro conclusion to a conventional bipartite
aria, of which the slow movement formed the first part.

of Glinka's improvisations, was apprised of his illness; whereupon he recommended homoeopathic treatment. Glinka was sceptical, but when his condition had deteriorated so much that his valet and his wife had to bear him off to their apartment in Vienna, Glinka decided to try the doctor he had been recommended. The first day after the treatment there was already an improvement, and soon he was able to resume his usual activities. He read Schiller, hired a piano, and wrote the theme he was to use in the *krakowiak* in *A Life for the Tsar* (see Ex. 14). In September he was visited by his cousin, Natalya Ruindina, and her husband, and by his old friends, Pavel and Sofiya Engelhardt. Glinka still seems to have been incapable of organizing anything for himself, but the arrival of Fyodor Gedeonov, his sister Natalya's brother-in-law, proved most timely. Gedeonov made the necessary arrangements, and in October shepherded Glinka off to Prague, and thence to Berlin.

The reunion with his sister Natalya and his brother-in-law worked wonders. Continued treatment with a homoeopath kept his health in reasonable order, and he had Chirkov, an old flat-mate from St. Petersburg, as company too. But he was to find especial pleasure in the society of Maria, a beautiful Jewish girl of about 17 or 18, tall, and who 'rather resembled a madonna'.[1] This proved to be the beginning of Glinka's first really serious love affair. He started to teach her singing, and wrote six vocal studies for her, one of which he later used for the 'Hebrew Song' in the incidental music to *Prince Kholmsky*.

Yet Glinka's most important contact in Berlin was with Siegfried Dehn. Dehn was a teacher whose systematic approach was just what Glinka now desperately needed. He realized it himself, and for five months he applied himself diligently to sketching fugues or sections of fugues on themes by well-known composers, and working chorale harmonizations. Yet Dehn could evidently combine imaginative stimulus with systematic disciplined teaching. 'He put my theoretical knowledge in order, and wrote out for me in his own hand *The science of Harmony or General bass, The science of Melody or Counterpoint,* and *Instrumentation*—all this in four small notebooks. I wanted to have them printed, but Dehn would not consent to this.

'There is no doubt that I am more indebted to Dehn than to all my other teachers. He . . . not only put my knowledge in order, but also my ideas on art in general—and after his teaching I began to work clearheadedly, not gropingly.'[2]

[1] GLN1, p. 148.   [2] GLN1, pp. 148–9.

Nevertheless, for all his awareness of how necessary this teaching was for him, Glinka was still restless. He wrote a few pieces—two romances, 'The leafy grove howls' and 'Say not that love will pass' (the first in particular now shows him as firmly in a German style as formerly he had been in an Italian), a set of variations on Alyabyev's 'The Nightingale', and a capriccio for piano duet on Russian themes. In the last Glinka confessed to a contrapuntal bias, while a symphony on two Russian themes was quite deliberately written in a German style. Yet, despite this, both these last two works already contain a great deal of music that seems characteristic of Glinka, and represent a radical shift from the style of the pieces he had written in Italy. There is no mistaking his contrapuntal preoccupations (and problems) in the allegro of the symphony, which becomes progressively more conventional—as was so often to happen even in his later works when he resorted to Western procedures. The andante introduction is far more interesting. Here a simple statement of the first Russian tune is followed by two variations, which pass into a free section which derives from the theme and which leads into the allegro, where the second of his Russian themes is introduced as the first subject. Again Glinka is initially content to repeat it with simple but effective new accompaniments, and at the recapitulation he provides new backgrounds for further repetitions (Ex. 11a), though not as yet revealing any of the imagination which he displayed in some of his later works, for the hand of German counterpoint lies heavily upon this section. Nevertheless, this was a further stage in the road

Ex. 11.

towards a treatment of a folk tune which was to reach its apogee fourteen years later in *Kamarinskaya,* where Glinka was to found a whole
instrumental piece upon the principle of the changing background, the
tune remaining intact (or almost so), while the accompaniment is con-

stantly varied. This principle was to create an ideal situation for his contrapuntal gifts, for it allowed his counterpoint to be decorative without demanding the sort of extension which leads in this symphony to congested textures and tediously repetitive or sequential writing. The symphony is in every way an experimental piece, insecure in style (when the first subject theme is turned into the second subject, it is presented in such a guise that its Russian genesis is completely obscured (Ex. 11b)), but fascinating because of the liveliness of the mind behind it. The capriccio for piano duet is really no more than a pot-pourri (this is how Glinka himself described it in his *Memoirs*), though in the later stages Glinka recalls some of his earlier themes, sometimes rubbing them roughly against one another (Ex. 12). His attempt at a more formal fugue is mercifully very brief. As in the symphony, the first two tunes are treated with simple variations in which the meretricious tinsel of the piano variations has gone. Often the accompaniments are very simple, and if there is brilliance, there is also some genuine musical invention in it. One of the later tunes is given a strong drone accompaniment, which ideally suits it. The capriccio is in fact a bolder piece than the symphony, as effective—and as new—as it is crudely wrought. For the first time in an extended piece Glinka has really managed to maintain his own,

Ex.12.

albeit rough-hewn, image (despite the brief lapse into a more salonish manner in the section 'agitato ed amoroso con molto passione').

Glinka's mind, however, was already turning to a much bigger Russian project. While he was still working with Dehn he wrote to a friend,[1] revealing a good deal of what he was feeling and planning at this time. 'I left that cheerful country [Italy] without any particular regret . . . That merry, playful and noisy daily life began at length to pall on me . . . [Now] I occupy myself with Dehn each day, spending the greater part of my time in making good use of his counsels . . . But here also in Berlin, if I tell you the *whole* truth, I do not feel—and this is the most important—calm and contented with myself. I work, work, work—but often ask myself to what purpose. I shall not remain here long, and I await impatiently that minute when I shall embrace you. I have a project in my head, an idea . . . but I do not want to say too much about it; perhaps if I told you all, I fear you would look at me with a disbelieving smile.

'But, still, perhaps you yourself, when you embrace me in the near future, will notice some change in me; perhaps you will find more in me than you could have imagined or suspected before my departure from St. Petersburg.

'Shall I confess all to you? It seems to me that I, too, should be able to give our theatre a work worthy of her. It won't be a masterpiece—I am the first to agree about that—but all the same, it won't be so bad.

'What do you think about this?

'The main thing is the choice of subject. In any case, I want everything to be national: above all, the subject—and the music likewise—so much so that my dear compatriots will feel they are at home, and so that abroad I shall not be considered a braggart or a crow who seeks to deck himself in borrowed plumes . . . Who knows whether I shall be able to fulfil the promise I have made myself.'[2]

Although the evidence of Tolstoi and Sobolevsky shows that Glinka was already thinking of the possibility of writing a really Russian opera as early as 1832, Glinka recollected in his *Memoirs* that it was while he was with Dehn that 'the idea of a national music (I do not say that it was yet operatic) became more and more clear. I composed the theme, "When my mother was killed" [which Tolstoi asserted was composed by 1832]

---

[1] The friend was probably Sergei Sobolevsky. This important letter is known only through Italian and French translations, published in 1874 and 1880 respectively. The addressee in the Italian print is designated as 'Sereno Tobolski'. This makes no sense, since there was no Tobolski among Glinka's known acquaintances, nor does the word 'sereno' make sense here. Clearly this was a faulty transliteration, and E. Kann-Novikova has suggested that the addressee was Sobolevsky, supporting the hypothesis with a good deal of convincing evidence.

[2] GLN2, pp. 77–79.

. . . and the first theme of the overture's allegro.'[1] At this time, however, Glinka certainly had no idea of using the story of Ivan Susanin. It was not until he returned to Russia that he at last hit on a possible, though quite different, subject.

It is perhaps a sign of Glinka's increasing preoccupation with the formation of his own musical style and technique that he did not go to hear much other music while he was in Berlin. He saw Weber's *Der Freischütz* and remembered hearing Méhul's *Une folie,* but this seems to have been all. He met some of the local musical celebrities, but otherwise lived quietly and contentedly in the society of his sister, her husband, Chirkov, and Maria. This happiness was about to be cruelly shattered, however, for on 4/16 March 1834 his father died. Glinka was the more shocked by the news because it was quite unexpected. Since the treatment for which his sister had come to Berlin had been of no avail, they all decided to return to Russia.

Thus in April they left Berlin, taking along a new servant, a young girl called Luisa, who was to be the unwitting cause of a very important event in Glinka's life. Travelling through Poznan, Kaliningrad (Königsberg), Vilnius, Minsk, and Smolensk, they reached Novospasskoye at the beginning of May.

[1] GLNI, p. 150.

4/First Opera

GLINKA spent the first month after his return to Russia with his family at Novospasskoye; then, in June, he set off to Moscow to visit Melgunov. Being anxious to impress with what he had done in Italy, he entertained the Melgunovs and their circle with his performances and compositions. Glinka was obviously in his element on such occasions, and thoroughly enjoyed himself. Living in the same building as the Melgunovs was the poet, Nikolai Pavlov, who gave Glinka one of his poems which he forthwith set, with Pavlov standing by him. This was 'Call her not heavenly', whose charming, easy invention shows Glinka purveying drawing-room romances as effortlessly as ever. Yet, for all its undemanding amiability, this song marks a step forward. Up to now all Glinka's songs on Russian texts had been either straightforward ternary structures or, more likely, strophic pieces. Very occasionally the scheme had been slightly varied (as in the vocal coda attached to the end of the three-strophe 'Tell me why'), and in 'The poor singer' and 'Disenchantment' he had introduced modifications and even interpolations into the second strophe; but in 'Call her not heavenly' he set the first six lines of three of the four strophes differently, employing the same music only for the concluding couplet common to each verse. Glinka was now showing a concern for making a song more of an evolving organism, and this was to become one of the most pronounced trends of his last songs. By the end 'Call her not heavenly' has made a weightier impression than its opening would seem to promise.

It was while he was in Moscow that Glinka at last came upon an idea which might prove suitable for a Russian opera. This was Zhukovsky's *Marina Grove*. The project proved abortive, but Glinka composed several bits for it at the piano, later incorporating these into *A Life for the Tsar*. However, another enterprise was soon to be carried through (though in the end it proved as disastrous as *A Life for the Tsar* was to be successful); at last Glinka started courting the girl he was to marry. For Glinka's visit Melgunov had found him rooms of which he had jokingly said that 'all who live in them inevitably get married'.[1] At this time Glinka was still thinking of Maria, and was anxious to get back to Berlin. On returning to Novospasskoye he applied for, and was granted a passport. His mother was strongly opposed to any idea of marriage with this foreign girl, though other more urgent matters were to distract her attention, for it was reported that another of her sons, Yevgeny, was mortally ill in St. Petersburg, and she hurried thither with her daughter, Yelizaveta. Meanwhile it was agreed that Glinka should take Luisa back to Berlin, and at the beginning of September he set out, stopping with his sister, Mariya Stuneyeva, in Smolensk, and then proceeding to Vilnius. Here, however, they encountered a technical difficulty with Luisa's passport; it had not been dealt with properly when she had entered Russia, and now it would be necessary to go to St. Petersburg to get it regularized before she could leave the country again. Glinka had no wish to delay his journey, but felt duty bound not to leave Luisa. He hurried to St. Petersburg, hoping to be able to complete the journey to Berlin while the weather remained good. Fate decreed otherwise.

On arriving in St. Petersburg, Glinka stayed with Aleksei Stuneyev, now the brother-in-law of his sister Mariya. In his *Memoirs* Glinka related what happened at Stuneyev's flat: 'The first persons I encountered on my arrival were Luisa and a pretty girl, whose hair she was combing. This was Mariya Petrovna Ivanova, the sister of Sofya Petrovna, wife of Aleksei Stuneyev. In Berlin my sister Natalya and my brother-in-law had said that my late father had sometimes jokingly called her his daughter-in-law. Insensibly I began to be attracted by Mariya Petrovna's prettiness and by a certain innate grace which she possessed, and I did not hasten my departure, although my mother had bought me a carriage so that I might avoid the autumn dampness on the journey. The German girl was jealous of Mariya Petrovna because of me, and everything asserted that I would end up marrying her.'[2] And so he did. Glinka lingered on till 1/13 October, when snow fell and travelling proved impossible. Thus an infuriated Luisa had to resign herself to a winter in St. Petersburg.

Glinka settled down with the Stuneyevs. For this he had to endure Aleksei's continued enthusiasm for introducing him to doctors who

[1] GLN1, p. 151. [2] GLN1, p. 153.

might offer him a new cure, including one who pronounced Glinka to be in a 'magnetic condition', and who proposed to demagnetize him. Needless to say, Glinka's nerves were unable to stand the treatment, and it was discontinued in favour of homoeopathy. But to offset these tribulations there were the charms of Mariya Petrovna. Aleksei had a passion for singing romances, relentlessly proceeding through every verse, and Glinka admitted his sensitive ear found the result uningratiating ('he sang mercilessly through his nose, and pronounced the words clumsily'),[1] but he encouraged these protracted and increasingly impassioned performances so that he might pursue his whispered courtship on the sofa. He expressed his own feelings in a romance, 'I had but recognized you', which is as tender as it is brief. A second romance, 'I am here, Inezilla', foretold a second love that was to blossom after the first had withered, for Glinka, fired by Pushkin's serenade of a Sevillian lover,[2] responded with an infectious Spanish stylization. Ten years later Glinka was to be drawn to Spain as strongly as he had formerly been attracted to Italy.

Glinka was now slipping back into that purposeless activity (or inactivity) which came to him so readily. His Berlin Maria was forgotten in the increasing attraction he felt for his St. Petersburg Mariya. She knew nothing of music, and he later recalled the conversation he had with her after he had attended a particularly splendid performance of Beethoven's Seventh Symphony. He had been deeply moved but 'when I arrived home,' Glinka recorded, 'Mariya Petrovna asked me with a look of concern: "What's the matter with you, Michel?"'

'"Beethoven," I replied.'

'"What's he done to you?" she continued . . .'[3]

Nevertheless Glinka was undeterred by this deficiency, and tried to rectify it by teaching her singing. Other singers began to visit the flat, and pleasant musical activities resulted. Among his visitors was 'a small man in a blue frock coat and a red waistcoat, who talked in a high-pitched soprano'.[4] This was the young Aleksandr Dargomuizhsky, the composer who was to be second only to Glinka as a founder-father of nineteenth century Russian music. 'I played duets with him a great deal,' Dargomuizhsky recorded in his autobiography, 'and [we] studied Beethoven's symphonies and Mendelssohn's overtures in score.' Glinka

---

[1] GLNı, p. 154.
[2] Pushkin based his lyric upon a poem by the Englishman, Barry Cornwall.
[3] GLNı, p. 157.   [4] GLNı, pp. 155–6.

also lent Dargomuizhsky Dehn's notebooks so that he too might benefit from the German pedagogue's guidance. Glinka's attitude to the music of other countries still seems to have been ambivalent, however much he may have wanted to write Russian music. 'A Life for the Tsar was already half written,' recorded Dargomuizhsky. 'I was delighted with it, and could not understand his current passion for Italian music. Of the French repertoire he esteemed only Cherubini's operas, and even considered them exemplary works . . . Of German music he only recognized symphonic works.'[1]

The charms of Mariya Petrovna tended to keep Glinka indoors, but he did attend the weekly meetings at Zhukovsky's of a group of poets, writers, and people interested in the arts—a group which also included Pushkin and Gogol. Sometimes there would be music (on such occasions ladies might be invited), but more often there were readings; Glinka recalled once hearing Gogol read his *Marriage*. It was at one of these meetings that Glinka mentioned to Zhukovsky his plans to write a Russian opera. Zhukovsky applauded the idea, and suggested as a subject the story of Ivan Susanin, the Russian peasant who in 1612 or 1613 had saved Mikhail, the first of the Romanovs, by leading the Polish troops who were pursuing the Tsar away into a forest and there perishing with them. Glinka was enthusiastic. The scene in the forest immediately caught his imagination, as did the whole national character of the subject. Initially it was intended that Zhukovsky himself should be the librettist, but the pressure of other commitments prevented him doing this except in part. Finally the work was to be done by a variety of other people as well—by Vladimir Sollogub, Nestor Kukolnik, but mostly by Baron Georgy Rosen, 'an assiduous writer of German extraction, who was at that time Secretary to H.R.H. the Tsarevich'.[2] Glinka proved to be a disorderly, impulsive composer. He described his own compositional processes thus: 'many themes and even details of their workings flashed into my head at once. I began to work, but completely haphazardly—to wit, I began with the overture with which others finish.'[3] Fortunately Rosen was good at fitting words to music—an indispensable gift, it proved, since Glinka's exuberant imagination often ran ahead of his librettist.

The next two years were intensively occupied with the composition, rehearsals, and performances of *A Life for the Tsar*. We will not go into the details of composition here, since the whole complicated matter of

[1] Quoted in GVS, p. 165.   [2] GLN1, p. 156.   [3] ibid.

the conception of the opera, and the stages in which it was realized are better left to the next chapter. Suffice it to say here that the facts as re-collected by Glinka in his *Memoirs* are not always in accordance with more direct documentary evidence.

Now that Glinka had fixed upon Ivan Susanin as a subject, his imagination burst into brilliant and prolonged flame. His contentment was further increased by his developing relationship with Mariya Petrovna. He proposed, was accepted, and in the middle of March 1835 wrote to his mother asking her blessing on the marriage. She gave it, and Glinka was in ecstasy. He wished the marriage to take place soon so that he could leave for the country, where he planned to settle in Sukhoi Pochinok, another of the Glinkas' estates alongside Novospasskoye. He was now seeking an appointment in the court theatre, but the matter was proceeding slowly, and since Glinka was in no hurry to be burdened with official duties or to be tied to St. Petersburg, he was prepared to let the affair take its leisurely course. On 26 April/8 May he and Mariya were wed, and Glinka imagined himself married to a paragon of all wifely virtues. Others were already well aware of Mariya Petrovna's shortcomings. As Pushkin's sister, Olga Pavlishcheva, wrote to her eminent brother shortly after the marriage: 'Michel Glinka has married the Ivanova girl, a young thing quite without fortune or education . . . who, moreover, hates music.'[1] However, for the present Glinka was happy, and five days later he wrote to his mother that among his bride's qualities were 'order and thrift . . . Above all, despite her youth and liveliness of character, she is very reasonable, and exceedingly moderate in her wishes',[2] so much so that it was difficult for him to know what she wanted. Yet already in this same letter there are signs of that shortage of funds which was to drive Glinka to ask his mother repeatedly for money —and, as for Mariya's thrift, he was soon to be disabused about that. Nevertheless, for the moment his happiness was complete, and he was working well: 'My muse has arisen again, and for all this I am beholden to my angel Mariya.'[3]

In the middle of May, Glinka, his wife—and mother-in-law—set out for Moscow to visit his wife's relations, and then directed themselves to Novospasskoye. Here Glinka settled into intensive work. He was by no means a 'private' composer, and he recalled that the Bridal Chorus in *A Life for the Tsar* had suddenly come to him when he was in the carriage near Novgorod on the way from St. Petersburg to Moscow. He

[1] Quoted in KNG3, p. 127.   [2] GLN2, p. 86.   [3] GLN2, p. 87.

described his way of working at Novospasskoye thus: 'I worked assiduously—that is, I got down in score what was already done, and planned
ahead. Each morning I sat at the table in our large and cheerful drawing
room in our house at Novospasskoye. This was our favourite room; my
sisters, my mother, my wife—in a word, the whole family swarmed
there, and the more lively their chatter and laughter, the quicker went
my work. It was a wonderful time.'[1] Karl Hempel paid an extended
visit, and gave him some practical assistance as a copyist. In August
Glinka returned to St. Petersburg and settled into his new house.
Mariya's mother was soon allowed to join them—a disastrous decision,
as he was later to discover. But for the present he was too absorbed in
his work to perceive the danger. 'Each morning I sat at the table and
wrote some six pages of close-packed score . . . In the evenings,
sitting on the sofa in the circle of my family and sometimes of a few
good friends, I took little part in all that was going on around me; I was
completely immersed in my work, and though much was already
written, there still remained a good deal to think about, and these
deliberations took a lot of attention. Everything had to be fitted together
so that it made an harmonious whole. In the winter I wrote the scene of
Susanin in the wood with the Poles; before I began writing, I often read
the scene aloud with feeling, and placed myself in the hero's situation so
vividly that my very hair stood on end, and it made my flesh creep.'[2]

Work was now sufficiently far advanced for rehearsals to begin.
During the winter of 1835–6 Glinka made the acquaintance of a number
of singers, including Osip Petrov, who was to sing Susanin in the first
performance, and Anna Vorobyeva (who later married Petrov), who
created the part of Vanya. Nearly fifty years later, the latter recalled her
first meeting with Glinka. He had started by asserting his hostility to all
Italian music, pointing out that he had not once attended the opera in
St. Petersburg, 'even though I know that you recently put on [Rossini's]
Semiramide very successfully'.[3] He demanded naturalness in performance, and could make clear to his singers in a very few words exactly
what he wanted. Clearly he very quickly won their support, and rehearsals
went well—though he aroused the wrath of the theatre director, Aleksandr Gedeonov, who accused him of spoiling his singers' voices by
making them sing in rooms filled with tobacco smoke.

On 1/13 February 1836 Glinka was able to try over the first act with
Prince Yusupov's orchestra, singing some of the vocal parts himself,

[1] GLN1, p. 160.   [2] GLN1, pp. 161–2.   [3] VVG, p. 613.

with two other good amateurs, Praskovya Barteneva and Nikolai Volkov, helping in the other roles. Glinka declared himself satisfied with
the orchestrations, and on 10/22 March Count Mikhail Wielhorski made
his house available for a full rehearsal of Act 1. Gedeonov attended the
rehearsal, and it went very well. Glinka's friends made some suggestions
for improvements, and he confessed himself especially indebted not only
to Wielhorski, but also to Prince Vladimir Odoyevsky and his old
friend, Mayer, who gave particular assistance with problems of orchestration, especially in handling tutti. It seems that, although Glinka's mother
attended the rehearsal, his wife did not. When Glinka had started work
on *A Life for the Tsar*, she had complained to his aunt that he was spending money on manuscript paper. To her Glinka's opera was a rival.
Pyotr Stepanov remembered calling at the Glinka home one morning
and finding Mariya Petrovna in tears.

'What are you crying about?' Stepanov asked.

'I am unhappy. Glinka doesn't love me.'

'Mariya Petrovna, what are you saying? No-one has ever loved you
or will love you as he does.'

'No, no, he has betrayed me.'

'For what, please tell me?'

'For her . . . for his hateful opera. He is only concerned with that,
and he has deserted me, left me all alone.'[1]

By now, Mariya Petrovna was thoroughly resentful of her husband's
preoccupation with his new opera, and during the spring she and her
mother took themselves off to Peterhof to stay with Mariya's married
brother. Glinka visited them infrequently, pleading that sea air did not
suit him. In any case, the opera had to be completed, and the preparations for getting it staged were absorbing all his time. But not quite all;
he still found time to complete an aria with chorus for a drama, *The
Moldavian girl and the gipsy girl* (or *Gold and the dagger*), by his friend,
Konstantin Bakhturin. The play was given—unsuccessfully—on 8/20
April and Glinka's contribution was for some unknown reason performed only at the première. Vorobyeva was the soloist, and Glinka's
wish to introduce some local colour may have inclined him a little
towards that oriental languor he was to create so much more thoroughly
and compellingly for the same Vorobyeva in Ratmir's music in *Ruslan
and Lyudmila*. The chromatic flattened sixth is already in evidence. Much
more important than this aria was the setting which he made at this same

---

[1] StVG, p. 41.

time of Zhukovsky's as yet unpublished translation of J. C. von Sedlitz's ballad, 'The midnight review'. The poet brought it to Glinka who forthwith set it, singing it that very same evening to both Zhukovsky and Pushkin. One wonders what sort of impact this extraordinarily novel and powerful song had upon the two poets. Glinka treated the narration of the dead leader's midnight review of his phantom troops as a stark, sinister 'fantasia' which could hardly have been further removed from the cushioned sentimentalities of his romances. Unlike his earlier songs it is not carried by its melodic invention, for the voice part is deliberately constricted into a simple, inexorably repeated rhythm; instead the expressive character stems from the measured, relentless rhythmic tread through consonance and dissonance which may be produced by auxiliaries (the E natural in Ex. 13a, which leans strongly against the sustained F minor chord), by appoggiaturas which make seventh chords spring out of nowhere (Ex. 13b), or by gravely-moving passing notes, or by pedals, sometimes inverted or internal (Ex. 13c). Nothing in Glinka's earlier work had given the slightest hint of the sinister strength of this

(At midnight.)

(And in the dark graves a drum wakens the mighty infantry.)

(At midnight the leader rises from his grave. He wears a frock coat over his uniform, with a small hat and a sword. On his old war steed he slowly goes along the line, and his marshals follow him.)

ballad, and it had no successor among his compositions. It was to be in the work of Mussorgsky (and not only in 'Field Marshal Death', for which this song is the obvious precedent) that the harmonic suggestions of this song were to be further developed. Many of Glinka's most striking works seem to have been the result of a brilliantly charged and quite impulsive response to some outside stimulus. 'The midnight review' is one of the first fruits of such a response, and the first of Glinka's compositions to suggest that his great talent had something of original genius in it.[1]

Glinka now encountered those gossipings and intrigues which almost inevitably surround the production of a new opera by an untried composer. On the 8/20 April he petitioned Gedeonov to accept the work. At this stage Glinka suspected that Catterino Cavos, the conductor of the theatre, was doing his best to prevent it from being accepted, for in 1815 Cavos had himself composed a successful opera on the story of Ivan Susanin, and might not unreasonably have been reluctant to let it be challenged by another work on the same subject. Glinka's suspicions turned out to be groundless, however, for whereas Gedeonov had no wish to mount Glinka's work, Cavos proved to be its strongest supporter. Having assured its acceptance, he was both vigorous and thorough in his preparation of the orchestra, though Glinka found him lacking in attention to dynamics, and not very perceptive about tempi. The opera was duly accepted, but only on condition that Glinka would require no payment for it—and the ballet master, Antoine Titus, also required some of the dances to be re-written. It was left to Glinka to rehearse the soloists and chorus, and to consult with the stage manager, Andrei Roller, about the mounting of the opera. Here Glinka acknowledged the great assistance he had from Zhukovsky, who sometimes attended these meetings, and provided very useful counsel and ideas.

Glinka was fortunate in catching the interest of the Tsar in his opera. On 1/13 May he wrote to his mother: 'three weeks ago I was at a soirée at the Empress's, and I cannot describe to you just how charming and gracious she was. The Emperor himself turned to me twice and enquired about my opera. Fortunately that evening I was in good voice and sang successfully, and I was told afterwards that my singing was liked by Her Majesty.'[2] But his personal life had its difficulties during these months.

---

[1] In his *Memoirs* Glinka stated that he wrote this towards the end of the winter of 1836–7, but other documentary evidence shows clearly that he remembered wrongly.

[2] GLN2, p. 94.

Back at the beginning of the year he was already behind with the rent, and his wife was ill. This and other expenses had drained his exchequer, and he had to turn to his friends for money. In the spring his mother sent him 500 roubles. By now his wife was getting better, but he himself was ailing. The tensions and frictions involved in getting *A Life for the Tsar* mounted produced times of depression. After telling his mother of the interest of the royal family in his opera, the mood of the above-quoted letter changes. Admittedly Glinka was always inclined to become pathetic in tone when writing to his mother, especially when he was after money; yet there is probably some quite genuine feeling behind the next part of his begging note: 'All these escapades have reduced me so that music and the opera have become hateful to me, and I only wish to get it off my hands very quickly, and to quit St. Petersburg, which for expensiveness is too much for my purse. We are constantly in want.'[1]

Still, Glinka's excitement must have increased as the première approached. The orchestra, which Glinka found uneven but generally good with some really excellent players, had joined the soloists in their enthusiasm, and at rehearsal had warmly applauded the D major polonaise and the C major chorus where the pizzicato strings imitate balalaikas. Glinka was deeply touched by this: 'I admit that this approval gave me more satisfaction than all the expressions of pleasure from the general public.'[2] The Tsar himself attended one of the final rehearsals, and after Vorobyeva and Petrov had performed the E flat duet near the beginning of Act III, he spoke with Glinka. Up till now the opera had been known by the name of the hero, but after this royal visit, 'through Gedeonov's good offices, I received permission to dedicate my opera to the Tsar and, instead of *Ivan Susanin*, it was called *A Life for the Tsar*'.[3] The change certainly had a political significance. Nikolai I was a thorough autocrat, ruling firmly, exercising a rigorous censorship, yet constantly fearing the challenges that might still come from discontented subjects. From his point of view the chance of emphasizing Susanin's loyalty to his Tsar, the founder of Nikolai's own dynasty, was an opportunity too good to be missed.

The final rehearsals had their problems. One produced an amusing little incident which Vorobyeva later recalled. Leonov,[4] the tenor who

---

[1] ibid.   [2] GLN1, p. 166.
[3] GLN1, p. 169. Initially the revised title appears to have been *A Death for the Tsar*
[4] The illegitimate son of John Field.

was to sing the part of Sobinin, was indisposed, and Glinka offered to deputize for him. But disaster was to follow. When it came to Sobinin's Act I entrance 'Glinka approached the footlights very boldly, opened his mouth to sing the first phrase: "Unbounded happiness," but, pronouncing the first syllable "Un . . .", he stopped. The orchestra also fell silent; everyone looks at him in bewilderment. We all said to him: "Mikhail Ivanovich, what's up with you? Carry on." But he replied in confusion: "I can't. I feel scared." '[1] Fortunately, Glinka's distress at his own embarrassment was outweighed by the amusement of the singers. But if such an incident helped to relieve some of the strain in the last stages of preparation, the conditions in the theatre itself did not. The boxes of the Bolshoi theatre were being reconstructed, and the continual noise of the workmen's hammers made the last rehearsals difficult. Odoyevsky recalled the effect upon Glinka: 'Outwardly Glinka showed great composure towards this and much else, but inwardly he was deeply distressed by such disregard both for art in general, and for himself personally.'[2] The strain finally proved too much, and he was unable to attend the last rehearsal, though Odoyevsky assured him that the opera was going to be a success. The interest of the public was intense, and Gedeonov, despite his earlier unfriendly attitude, made sure that the opera was lavishly produced. On 27 November/9 December, in the presence of the Tsar and the royal family, the première took place. Glinka recalled the evening in his *Memoirs*:

It is impossible to describe my feelings on that day, particularly before the performance began. I had a box in the second tier; the first was occupied entirely by members of the court and high officials with their families. My wife and relations were in the box; I do not know for sure whether my mother was there.

The first act went well, and the well-known trio was warmly applauded. During the Polish scene, from the polonaise to the mazurka and final chorus, a deep silence reigned. I went on to the stage, being deeply distressed by the audience's silence—and Ivan Cavos, the son of the *Kapellmeister* who was conducting the orchestra, assured me in vain that this was because the actors were playing Poles. I remained bewildered.[3]

The appearance of Vorobyeva dispelled all my doubts about success; the orphan's song, the duet of Vorobyeva and Petrov, the quartet, the G major scene with the Poles, and other numbers in this act were done with great success.

---

[1] VVG, p. 611.   [2] Quoted in GLN1, p. 429.

[3] Vorobyeva offered an alternative explanation for this: 'If an audience of that time was watching dances, they paid no attention to the music, [and these] dances were abominably produced.' (VVG, p. 616.)

In the fourth act the chorus who were playing the Poles fell upon Petrov so furiously at the end of the scene in the wood that they tore his shirt, and he had to defend himself from them in earnest.

The magnificent spectacle of the Epilogue, depicting the rejoicing of the people in the Kremlin, struck even me; Vorobyeva, as always, excelled herself in the trio with chorus.

The opera's success was complete. I was in a daze, and now I simply do not remember what happened when the curtain fell. Immediately after this I was summoned to the Tsar's box at the side of the theatre. First the Tsar thanked me for my opera, observing that it was bad that Susanin was killed on the stage. I explained to His Majesty that, not having been at the dress rehearsal because of illness, I could not know how it had been arranged, and that according to my plan, when the Poles were falling upon Susanin, the curtain should immediately fall. Susanin's actual death is reported by the orphan in the Epilogue. After the Tsar, the Empress thanked me, and then the other royalty who were in the theatre.

Very soon afterwards I received a gift from the Tsar for the opera—a ring worth 4000 roubles, consisting of a topaz surrounded by three rows of the finest brilliants. I forthwith gave this to my wife.

Even before the première Kukolnik had helped me sell the copyright of the opera to Snegirev; the sales went very well, especially at first, and I received some profit.[1]

However Glinka was satisfied neither with the general quality of Snegirev's piano arrangements, nor with the quality of the actual publications, nor with the speed at which they were issued. As for critical reaction, he was clearly stung by the *Northern Bee* when it issued two articles by Faddei Bulgarin—nor was he altogether gratified by the judgment of some aristocrats that *A Life for the Tsar* was 'music for coachmen'[2]—though he noted tartly in the margin of the copy of his *Memoirs* that 'this is good and even just, for coachmen are more sensible than gentlemen'.[3] It must seem surprising today that some intelligent, cultured people found the opera a little difficult, but even Pyotr Vyazemsky wrote to a friend: 'About [Glinka's] opera we'll talk another time, when I've heard it two or three times. In general there are no effective moments; nothing impresses at once either the spirit or the ears of our fraternity of ignoramuses as in the operas of Rossini, Bellini, Meyerbeer, and such like. Consequently it is necessary to listen attentively and to become closely acquainted with the music in order to assess it.'[4] In

[1] GLNi, pp. 170–1.   [2] GLNi, p. 171.   [3] ibid.   [4] Quoted in GLZ, p. 117.

fact the first audiences do seem to have found the piece over-long, and Cavos induced Glinka to make some cuts.[1] Nevertheless the opera was, on balance, a huge success, and most of the printed critical reaction was unreservedly favourable. In another article in the *Northern Bee*, Odoyevsky wrote that 'with this opera is settled the question that is important for art in general, and for Russian art in particular, namely, the existence of Russian opera, of Russian music . . . With Glinka's opera there appears what they have long sought but not found in Europe—a new element in art, and there begins a new period in its history—the period of Russian music. Such an exploit . . . is a matter not merely of talent but of genius.'[2] Yanuary Neverov, writing for the *Moscow Observer*, endorsed Odoyevsky's observations on the Russianness of the opera: 'Never before has any piece for the theatre aroused such lively, complete enthusiasm among us as *A Life for the Tsar* . . . Mr. Glinka has fully deserved this attention. To create a national opera—that is such an exploit as will impress his name for ever on the annals of our country's art.'[3] The great Nikolai Gogol, writing in the journal *The Contemporary*, was even more ecstatic on this point: 'What an opera you can make out of our national tunes! Show me a people who have more songs! . . . Glinka's opera is only a beautiful beginning. He has managed to fuse felicitously all strains of Slavonic music in his creation. You hear where the Russian is speaking, where the Pole; the one breathes the expansive motif of a Russian song, the other the precipitate motif of a Polish mazurka.'[4] Melgunov, who years before had envisaged the character of a true, viable Russian opera, saw his vision embodied in Glinka's work: 'He has understood the meaning of the words "Russian music, Russian opera" differently from his predecessors. He has not confined himself to a more or less close imitation of folk-song; no, he has studied deeply the repertoire of Russian songs, the actual performance of them by the people—their exclamations, their sharp transitions from the grand to the lively, from the loud to the quiet, their chiaro-

---

1 The subsequent history of the opera on the Russian stage makes reading that is sometimes deplorable. It was first given in Moscow on 7/19 September 1842, and within a year something like a third of it had been cut. These cuts even included Susanin's aria in Act IV, while the overture was replaced by a new composition of the theatre's conductor, Johannes! Glinka was to bewail repeatedly the philistinism of Russian operatic circles.

2 Quoted in GLN1, p. 430.

3 ibid.

4 Quoted in GLN1, p. 431. Gogol must have attended the early rehearsals of the opera, and must have been writing on the evidence of these, for he left Russia in June 1836.

scuro, unexpectednesses of every kind, lastly [he has studied deeply] their particular harmony, based on no accepted rules, and the development of their musical sentence: in a word, he has opened up a whole system of Russian melody and harmony, founded upon the very music of the people, and in no way resembling the music of any prevailing schools. His first great effort, his opera *Ivan Susanin*, will show to what degree he has fulfilled his idea and his dream.'[1] It is worth noting also that some critics perceived the special dramatic nature of the opera. '*A Life for the Tsar* is not a drama but a canvas,' Neverov asserted,[2] and Filipp Vigel wrote to Vladimir Odoyevsky, praising the music highly, but observing 'this opera can rather be considered as an oratorio with set[s] and costumes'.[3] Thus it was that *A Life for the Tsar* established the stage-picture tradition which was to dominate subsequent Russian opera.[4]

A Life for the Tsar had a brilliant success in the theatre, and tunes from it quickly became popular songs. Glinka was famous, and thoroughly enjoyed the experience. After six performances he could write to his mother of the rewards the opera had brought him. Besides the Tsar's ring, he had gained 'Fame. I am unanimously recognized by all as the first composer in Russia and, according to the experts, in no way inferior to the best composers.'[5] On 13/25 December, at a dinner in his honour, four stanzas were improvised on him, two by Zhukovsky, and the last by Pushkin himself; these were forthwith published with a musical setting by Glinka and Odoyevsky. Glinka must surely have been well content with the seal set upon his achievement by Pushkin:

---

[1] MG, p. 719. This article was not published until 1874, when Strugovshchikov incorporated it into his reminiscences of Glinka (SGV). Melgunov was abroad, and wrote the article in anticipation of the first performance (hence the future tense of the last sentence), intending it to appear before the première. He sent it to Glinka to look through, and then to send on to the *Moscow Observer*. It is not known why Glinka held on to it instead, though he may have been embarrassed by Melgunov's over-enthusiastic, sometimes fulsome tone. Despite its ecstatic expression, this article contains some intelligent observations on the character and the whole problem of musical nationalism.

[2] Quoted in LPG2, p. 210.

[3] Quoted in OG, p. 265.

[4] Similar comments were to be made about *Ruslan and Lyudmila*. As a certain S.K. was to write in *Repertoire and Pantheon* of 1843 (No. 5): 'Some assert that one should not look upon the music of *Ruslan and Lyudmila* as upon an opera, but rather as though it were an oratorio performed on the stage with costumes and with sets.' (Quoted in OG, p. 155.) This was also the view of Fyodor Koni: 'it is more a large fantastic oratorio, performed on the stage in costumes and with sets.' (*Literary Gazette* (15/27 December 1842). Quoted in LPOK, vol. 1, part 1, p. 275.)

[5] GLN2, p. 98.

'Hearing the new creation
Let envy, darkened with spiteful lust,
Rail—but yet it cannot
Trample our Glinka in the dust.'[1]

[1] The whole *Comic canon* is quoted in GLN1, p. 432. The last line evidently contains a pun on Glinka's name; 'Glina' in Russian means 'clay' or 'loam'.

5/A Life for the Tsar: Process of composition

FOR some two centuries the story of Ivan Susanin seems to have been largely forgotten in Russia. Interest in his exploit revived during the first two decades of the nineteenth century, partly through the growing consciousness among Russians of their national identity, and partly through the strong upsurge of patriotism provoked by Napoleon's assault of 1812. Three years after Napoleon's incursion, Cavos had composed an opera on the subject (to which his librettist, Aleksandr Shakhovsky, gave a happy ending), and in 1823 the poet, Kondraty Ruileyev, used it for a ballad which is likely to have been the source from which Glinka drew some inspiration while writing his opera.[1] The story was a special favourite of Zhukovsky, and in 1830 he had tried hard but unsuccessfully to persuade his friend, Mikhail Zagoskin, to write a novel based upon it. It must therefore have been a special satisfaction to Zhukovsky when four years later he persuaded Glinka to take up the subject.

The plot of the opera in its final form of four acts and an epilogue is, very briefly, as follows. Act I opens in the village Domnino, where a crowd of peasants is waiting to welcome back Sobinin, who has been to the wars. With them is Susanin and Antonida, Susanin's daughter, whom Sobinin is to marry. Susanin warns, however, that a Polish army is advancing on Moscow, and that any thought of the wedding must be put away until the security of Russia has been provided for by the election of a new Tsar. But after his triumphal entry and dismay at the postponement of his marriage, Sobinin announces that this election has

---

[1] Glinka recalled how, before working on the scene of Susanin with the Poles in the wood, he had 'often read the scene aloud' (GLN1, p. 162), but since it seems that the libretto for this scene was written after the music had been composed, he must have been reading from some already existing text.

taken place, and Susanin gives his blessing to the wedding. Act II takes place in the fortress of the Polish commander, where a splendid ball is in progress. The confidence of the Poles is shaken when a messenger reports that a Polish army has been defeated, and that a new Tsar has been elected. A plan is laid to capture the new Tsar in the monastery where he is living, and the dancing is resumed. The action of Act III returns to Domnino where Susanin and Vanya, his adopted son (the 'Orphan'), join with Antonida, Sobinin, and the peasants in preparations for the wedding, despite the disturbing news that the Poles are searching for the Tsar. In the middle of their preparations a detachment of Polish troops enters and tries to force Susanin to disclose the Tsar's where-abouts. Susanin instructs Vanya to warn the Tsar while he (Susanin) decoys the Polish troops. Antonida re-enters as her father is preparing to leave with the Poles. She is distraught, and when Sobinin arrives she tells him of her father's apparent plight. Sobinin gathers a group of peasants and sets off to rescue Susanin. Act IV opens with two quite separate scenes. In the first Sobinin is seen in his search for Susanin, bolstering the morale of his followers with his own determination; in the second Vanya appears at the gates of the monastery and warns the inhabitants of the Tsar's danger. In the final scene of the act Susanin has led the Poles deep into the forest. He proudly admits his stratagem, and faces death at the hands of his captors. The Epilogue shows Moscow excitedly preparing to receive the Tsar. Antonida, Sobinin, and Vanya enter and relate Susanin's deed and death. The soldiers share their grief, and then the crowd turns to hail the Tsar.

Glinka's first intentions were much less ambitious than the final result. According to Odoyevsky, he had originally envisaged some-thing in the nature of stage tableaux, or even an oratorio: 'he wanted to restrict himself to only three tableaux; the village scene, the Polish scene [almost certainly the scene of Susanin with the Poles in the wood, not the ballroom scene], and the final triumph . . . without linking recitatives, and even almost without choruses.'[1] Glinka had already

---

[1] From a letter to Stasov, quoted in PISG, p. 22. Protopopov notes that it is possible that this scheme was derived from the historical note which Pavel Stroyev published along-side Ruileyev's ballad. Protopopov's book is an invaluable source of information about this opera. Much of this present chapter's factual information has been sifted from this study, except where such information is afforded by the score as published in GPSS12, or by GLN1 or 2. Protopopov also undertook a very thorough investigation of the relationship of Glinka's opera to indigenous Russian music, though unfortunately he is sometimes over-enthusiastic in detecting relationships between folk-song and Glinka's melodic material.

either written or at least planned all the music for this, and had played it over to Odoyevsky, but he was quickly persuaded to expand the project into an opera of four acts with an epilogue—though, as noted earlier, a good deal of the original oratorio character was to remain in the finished opera. The earliest known evidence for this elaborated scheme is the so-called *Initial Plan*, written, it seems, at the end of 1834.[1] This plan gives a detailed account of the proposed content of the individual numbers, and was clearly a guide to a librettist. Unfortunately the only part of this scheme to survive is that covering the first three acts, but by a careful examination of the autograph score, it has been possible to pro-duce very convincing suggestions for the original structure of Act IV and the Epilogue. Since the process by which *A Life for the Tsar* grew to its final dramatic form is complicated, it will be useful to trace this first, before even considering the muddled matter of the librettists. As for the work's progress to its final musical form, this will be left until later still.

The heading of the *Initial Plan* reads: 'National heroic-tragic opera in five acts or parts'. The way in which Glinka planned to open the first act remained essentially the same in the final version:

From a distance is heard first a male chorus—then, from the opposite side, a female chorus—which, coming together, merge as one. This chorus, unfolding as a fugue, must express the strength and light-hearted fearlessness of the Russian people, must be written in a Russian metre.[2]

But after this Glinka originally intended that the act should proceed very differently:

The men go out first, the women quickly follow them, and when the voices, and then the orchestra, have little by little grown quiet, there enters along the river a boat with rowers, who sing a sustained unison song (tenors only) . . . When the boat has arrived in the middle of the stage and the choir has reached *ff*, the orchestra will strike up a dance which, getting more vigorous, will

---

[1] The fact that the Bridal Chorus in Act III is designated as in $\frac{5}{4}$ has led Protopopov to suggest that the *Initial Plan* was not written earlier than May 1835. Against this it might be pointed out that Glinka stipulated in the *Initial Plan* that 'in the middle of the third verse it is suddenly broken off', whereas in the final version at least of the Bridal Chorus, the third verse is completed. The time signature could very well have been a statement of intention. Certainly the *Initial Plan* must have been written before Glinka returned to St. Petersburg in August 1835 since the Trio in Act I, which is not provided for in the plan, was composed before then.

[2] GLN1, p. 306.

gradually drown the singers, and then the [dancers participating in this] round dance will go out to this dance, and then the prima donna will make her entry.[1]

The prima donna (Antonida) was to have an Andante and Rondo, after which Susanin was to appear. However, Glinka probably felt that it would be better to alternate or even mingle solo and choral elements throughout the act rather than have a massive choral scene at the beginning, followed by a succession of largely solo items, and so in the final version he split this huge opening chorus into two, bringing Antonida and Susanin on to the stage at the very beginning of the act, and inserting their initial solos (Antonida's cavatina and rondo, and Susanin's brief scena with chorus) before proceeding with the second part of the chorus (the Chorus of Rowers). Since the first chorus now ended with a *ff* perfect cadence in G major, the contrast with Antonida's ensuing cavatina was too great, and after the first general rehearsal of Act I on 10/22 March 1836 Count Wielhorski persuaded Glinka to add the quiet orchestral coda, during which the chorus might disperse, and which would lead gently into Antonida's cavatina. It was also at Wielhorski's suggestion that the Chorus of Rowers was used to make a triumphal preparation for the entry of Sobinin. Glinka had evidently gone back on his original intention, and now planned to keep the chorus offstage, but Wielhorski suggested they should enter while singing, and finish *ff*. Glinka was delighted with the idea: 'through this the entry of the bridegroom was made incomparably more triumphal'.[2] The orchestral dance disappeared completely from the scheme, and a good deal of the projected content of Susanin's first scene (including a part for Antonida) was also cut in the final version. To end the act there was to be 'either a finale or, better still in my opinion, a tenor aria'.[3] This intention was changed, and in the final version the tenor aria became the trio, followed by a finale.

The second act, the Polish ballroom scene, remained essentially the same as in the *Initial Plan*. After the Polonaise and the Krakowiak, Glinka noted that there would be a '*Pas de trois, Pas de cinq*, and such-like, all ad libitum'.[4] In fact, he did complete two dances which did not go into the final version. These were a *Passo a tre* in E minor/major (with a solo violin part specially composed for Boehm) after the Krakowiak, and a *Passo a due* in C major with obbligato parts for oboe and cello to follow the Waltz (*Passo a quatro*). Act III was to open with Vanya's

---

[1] ibid.   [2] GLN1, p. 163.   [3] GLN1, p. 308.   [4] GLN1, p. 310.

song;[1] it was to be 'naïve—like the character of the orphan himself'.[2] During the last verse Susanin, Antonida and Sobinin were to enter, and join with Vanya in a quartet 'expressing the calm and sweet feelings of family happiness. [It] must certainly be written in a Russian metre in imitation of old songs. In the music itself I shall endeavour to produce a rounded piece, consisting of a canonic adagio and an allegro.'[3] But the quartet was to work out very differently in the end, and was to be divided from Vanya's song by a considerable quantity of other music— namely, a duet for Vanya and Susanin, and a chorus. In the stretch that followed the quartet the final version adheres in general to the *Initial Plan*. From the beginning Glinka had very clear ideas about how this should be approached dramatically: 'I beg you most earnestly to keep this number as short as possible, and in general to write Susanin's part as simply as you can, for it is now necessary that the strength should come from the [dramatic] situation itself. His [Susanin's] replies to the Poles must be (in my opinion) short and strong—and the shorter they are, the better it will be for the music, which will not be recitative but characterized song without formal melody. I shall say more of this (in my opinion) most difficult number—that it may be divided up into sections in the following manner:

a. Susanin and his family prepare the room for the wedding—until the appearance of the Poles.

b. The appearance of the Poles—contrast. They sing in $\frac{3}{4}$ (polonaise and mazurka), and become angry. Susanin sings in $\frac{2}{4}$ or $\frac{4}{4}$.

c. The Poles' anger continues to smoulder, and Susanin hatches the idea of deceiving them.

d. Antonida guesses the danger.'[4]

The Bridal Chorus and Antonida's romance with chorus were to follow in the same form as they were to take in the final version (except that in the Bridal Chorus the music was to break off in the middle of the third verse instead of completing it, as in the final version), but the last stages of the finale were ultimately to be much expanded beyond the original scheme.[5]

[1] In the *Initial Plan*, Vanya was called Andrei.
[2] ibid.
[3] ibid.
[4] GLN1, pp. 312 and 314.
[5] Odoyevsky recalled that Glinka had originally intended to finish this act with a quartet, and claimed that it was he who persuaded Glinka to use choruses in *A Life for the*

The autograph score reveals that Act IV was also very much shorter initially than it was to become. Not only did it omit the scene of Vanya at the gates of the monastery (Glinka added this in 1837), but also the opening scene of Sobinin with the peasants in the wood. Thus, after the entr'acte, the act proceeded straight to the scene of Susanin with the Poles. But at this earlier stage the brevity of this act was compensated by the Epilogue which was linked to it by an orchestral interlude. The Epilogue itself was likewise much shorter at first, being only a single choral scene (the *Slavsya* chorus). Later, after he had added Sobinin's scena with chorus at the beginning of Act IV, and had inserted the trio with chorus into the epilogue (thus splitting the *Slavsya* chorus in two), Glinka detached the Epilogue from the fourth act, using the end of the original orchestral link as part of the new entr'acte which ushers in the Epilogue. Some of this must have been done at a very late stage, for the libretto passed by the censor only six weeks before the première still shows the Epilogue as consisting of a single scene. The opera was now recognizably in the five divisions we know, but for the first performance it was described as being in three acts with epilogue, thus:

Act I: i. In Domnino (now Act I)
         ii. In the fortress of the Polish leader (now Act II)
Act II: In Susanin's cottage (now Act III)
Act III: i. Sobinin and the peasants in the wood ⎫
         ii. Susanin and the Poles in the wood   ⎬ (now Act IV)
                                                  ⎭
Epilogue: i. The approaches to Moscow
         ii. The Red Square in Moscow

It is therefore clear that from the very beginning the form of *A Life for the Tsar* was constantly changing. It could not very well have been otherwise when so many people had a hand in it, either as librettists or as friendly advisers—and, from comparing the copy of the score which Glinka had made for himself at the time of the première[1] with his autograph score in which he incorporated later changes, it is also clear that revising continued after the first performance. Zhukovsky soon

---

Tsar. Glinka, said Odoyevsky, still viewed the chorus as superfluous decoration, and intended to make it a soloists' opera. It would be unwise to discount Odoyevsky's evidence completely, but he was writing immediately after Glinka's death, and was probably anxious that his own role in Glinka's creative evolution should appear as great as possible.

[1] Now usually known as the 'Balakirev' copy, since it was later to pass into Balakirev's hands, and to be used by him as the basis for his own editions of *A Life for the Tsar*.

found that he was unable to write the libretto himself, but not until he had completed the whole Epilogue[1] (though, while composing this, Glinka was to revise Zhukovsky's text heavily). The trouble was that Glinka had already written too much of the music, and Zhukovsky, who worked very slowly when making singing translations, knew that the similar labour of fitting words to existing music for a big opera would take an enormous amount of time, far more than he was able (or prepared) to give. The next person to be approached was Vladimir Sollogub, but this collaboration was short-lived. Sollogub was evidently introduced to Glinka by Odoyevsky after the scenario and a good deal of the music had been completed. This was not to Sollogub's liking; he considered the task 'unflattering', though he recollected later that he was pleased to be associated with the man who was considered 'the hope of Russian music . . . I wrote the first two choruses very badly,' he recalled, 'and then Antonida's aria, and Glinka observed: "Write what you like, only always see that high notes are given 'a' or 'ee'." . . . However the collaboration with Glinka did not last long. We parted over the second act. When I asked what it was to consist of, Glinka replied that it would contain a polonaise, mazurka, krakowiak, and chorus. "Excuse me," I observed, "this is not an act but a divertissement." '[2] Sollogub wanted some action, but he asserted that Glinka only laughed at the suggestion. Wounded, he withdrew from the collaboration before the end of 1834.

Glinka next approached Nestor Kukolnik, and it is very possible that the *Initial Plan* was written as a guide for him, since it was found among his papers. Then in the middle of January 1835 Kukolnik moved to Moscow, 'whence he sent me a sample of one scene,' Glinka recalled, 'from which I saw that it would be impossible to work by correspondence, especially since the greater part of the music was ready, and it would be necessary to fabricate verses for it'.[3] But his fourth librettist, Baron Rosen, proved to be an adept at this sort of fabrication. Rosen's daughter later recorded that it was the Tsar himself who suggested to Zhukovsky that her father was the man to be Glinka's collaborator. Certainly it was Zhukovsky who had effected the introduction, and Glinka had good cause to be grateful for it. Sollogub's work was rejected, and 'in March and April [1835], he [Rosen] prepared the words of the first and second acts in accordance with my plan. This presented

---

[1] Not just the trio, as Glinka implies in his *Memoirs*.
[2] Quoted in PISG, p. 27.   [3] GLNi, p. 165.

him with no small labour. The greater part not only of the themes but also of the working-out of the movements had been completed, and he had to invent words for music which sometimes demanded the most strange metres. Baron Rosen did this splendidly; you would order so many lines of such-and-such a metre, two- or three-syllable—even something quite unprecedented; it was all the same to him. A day later it was all completed. Zhukovsky and others used to say jokingly that Rosen had lines already written and distributed among his pockets, and that all I had to do was to say what metre I needed, and how many lines, and he would take out as many of each sort as were required—each variety from a particular pocket.'[1] On occasions Odoyevsky rendered invaluable service as an intermediary, for sometimes it was he who would take Glinka's vocal part and, 'in accordance with his [Glinka's] intentions, would mark the accents on the notes, trying to give the metre a viable form. In accordance with the metres and the concept expressed by the music, Rosen wrote the greater part of the verses.'[2]

From the one fragment of Rosen's libretto which survives with Glinka's annotations,[3] and from the differences between the published libretto and the text in the opera, it is clear that Glinka substantially revised Rosen's text, excising where Rosen was prolix, expanding where he felt more action or weight was needed, and requesting re-working of the text where his librettist's lines did not accord properly with his music. The partnership was not untroubled. Glinka related in his *Memoirs* that Rosen could at times be quite intractable in defence of his lines, and the differences between the published libretto and that of the opera suggest that Rosen was determined to preserve some of his rejected lines for the public's admiration. Critical reaction to his work was mixed.[4] Despite Glinka's tribute to him in his *Memoirs*, it is likely that relations were strained by the time of the première. It is perhaps significant that when, in 1837, Glinka added the scene of Vanya at the gates of the monastery, the text was provided by Kukolnik, with whom he had still remained on good terms after their earlier partnership had proved unworkable.

[1] GLN1, pp. 157–8.

[2] From a letter to Vladimir Stasov. Quoted in GLN1, p. 425.

[3] This is part of the scene with the Poles in the wood after Susanin has sung his aria— a scene which, Glinka specifically stated, was worked out by Rosen in accordance with his (Glinka's) own plan.

[4] Rosen's text has now been suppressed in the U.S.S.R., and the opera has been furnished with a new (and ideologically acceptable) libretto by S. Gorodetsky.

Unfortunately many of the sources which would prove invaluable to a study of Glinka's compositional processes in bringing *A Life for the Tsar* to its final form have now disappeared—like the notebook of 'themes for various parts of the opera, often with their contrapuntal working-out',[1] to which he alludes in his *Memoirs*. When he set to work upon his opera he already had a certain amount of material available, quite apart from the unspecified relics from the abortive *Marina Grove*. The two main themes of the Overture's vivace had been composed in Berlin in 1833 or 1834 (but see above, p. 62). The very first phrase that Susanin sings in Act I had been taken down by Glinka from a Luga coachman, and a theme from the middle of the Krakowiak in Act II (Ex. 14) had been composed in Vienna in 1833 after hearing the

Ex.14.

orchestras of Strauss and Lanner. Antonida's romance with chorus in Act III was based on Glinka's own song with chorus, 'Not the frequent autumn shower', composed in 1829. Having decided upon this subject for his opera, Glinka set straight to work upon the Overture, 'which,' he asserted, 'I wrote for piano duet, with indications of the scoring.'[2] Glinka's memory must have played him false, for while there does exist a piano duet score of the Overture as we know it with the scoring indicated,[3] there also survives a full score which is very substantially different, and which must be earlier. This score shows that there was

[1] GLN1, p. 157. Glinka was no more systematic in the preservation of his manuscripts than in his process of composition. Works composed for other people were often dispatched without any care being taken to keep a copy, and Glinka's valet, Yakov Netoyev, who had charge of his manuscripts, was very casual about his care of them. In his *Memoirs* Glinka acknowledged that it was Vasily Engelhardt who later took upon himself to act as the custodian of his manuscripts, and to whom posterity must be grateful that the losses were not even greater (Vasily was the son of Glinka's friend, Pavel Engelhardt). But quite apart from the casualties of time, other parts of the original manuscript of *A Life for the Tsar* have been lost quite simply because, when Glinka had to rewrite a page in the course of the revision, he just inserted a new sheet in the manuscript, throwing the old one away. Fortunately on other occasions he pasted his revision over the rejected portion, and sometimes it is possible to uncover the original. However, the number of revisions must have been much larger than those we can still detect, and in other instances where we know a revision was made, we shall never know what the new version replaced.

[2] GLN1, p. 156.

[3] A few of these indications differ from the final scoring. Presumably, therefore, Glinka was making revisions of his orchestration right up to the last moment.

originally no slow introduction, and that the vivace opened with only four bars of dominant crescendo, not eight as in the final version. Glinka then added a fourteen-bar introduction (Ex. 15a), founded upon the melody of the opening chorus, and he expanded the dominant D at the opening of the vivace to eight bars, as in the final version. But this introduction still did not satisfy him, and in the third and final version he greatly expanded it, incorporating a substantial extract from the trio in the Epilogue,[1] four bars taken from the quartet in Act III, and another four bars extracted from the finale to Act II; he now prefaced these with the opening theme of Act I, reduced to a laconic group of chords (Ex. 15b). Since the trio of the Epilogue was one of the last pieces of the opera to be composed, it seems certain that this definitive version must likewise have been a late conception.

Glinka also had second thoughts about the vivace of the Overture. Certain sections could be made more concise, and he was not happy about the way he had made the recapitulation occur out-of-key (in A minor instead of G minor). In the final version the vivace was reduced by one-sixth, largely through two related cuts in the codettas to the exposition and recapitulation. Glinka excised some thirty bars from each and also the first thirty bars of the development; though he retained the next section, he abbreviated the string parts.[2] Even allowing for substituted material, the Overture lost fifty-six bars through these changes. Glinka left the next section (the contrapuntal development of the first subject) unchanged, except that by starting it a tone lower (in E minor), he ensured that the recapitulation arrived in the tonic. It was now necessary to recast the transition to the second subject, and again Glinka used this as an opportunity to compress a little. Originally he had ended the Overture with nine bars of dominant, thus projecting it straight into the first act. He removed these bars so that it finished conclusively on the tonic.

The vast majority of the revisions in *A Life for the Tsar* are minor ones such as might be expected of a keen-eared composer who had heard his work rehearsed. To take just a few of the many examples in Act I: in the Introduction, during the G minor version of the opening theme, the tenors' ending (Ex. 16a) had originally been the same as the

[1] According to Darya Leonova, Glinka obtained the opening phrase of the trio from a coachman near Smolensk. (See footnote on p. 112.)

[2] Glinka removed from them the phrases which still survive in modified form in the last eighteen bars of the entr'acte to Act III.

Ex.15.

(May I have glory in holy Russia.)

orchestral codetta that follows it, but Glinka removed the crotchet triplets in favour of a simpler version (Ex. 16b), perhaps to gain extra resonance and to make a precise performance on stage more easy. It is clear that the trombones were an afterthought in Antonida's rondo, for their parts were added at the bottom of the score. Glinka revised the link leading into the Chorus of Rowers, rightly rejecting the simple parallel sixths as too feeble (Ex. 17). His original intention had been to

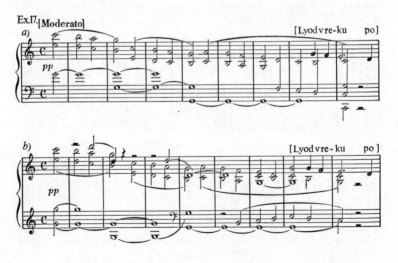

restrict the Chorus of Rowers to high tenors, but he subsequently added altos to this line (the chorus altos were boys, not women), doubtless to avoid any sense of strain at the opening. Yet it is noteworthy that Glinka's alterations of scoring consist quite as much of additions as of subtractions; unlike many young composers, Glinka tended to under- rather than over-orchestrate. As for the major alterations in Act I, we are indebted to Glinka's *Memoirs* for the knowledge that he had origin- ally composed the trio in $\frac{2}{4}$ and in A minor, but that, having decided there had been too much duple time already, he resolved to transform it into a $\frac{6}{8}$ metre and to transpose it into B flat minor. Glinka also con- fessed his own deep emotional involvement in this trio, which he composed in the country during the summer of 1835 as 'the result of my current insane love'.[1] Nevertheless, however love-laden the original version may have been, he felt these changes 'indisputably expressed the languor of love better'.[2] A particularly illuminating modification was also made during Susanin's first solo.[3] The first version of bars 16 to 22 (Ex. 18a) was decidedly crude—almost as though Glinka was trying to give something of a *podgolosnaya* roughness to this treat- ment of a genuine folk-song. But he was dissatisfied, performed a com- plete volte-face, allowed the song an independent bass which behaves in a thoroughly Western fashion, and at the end completely falsified the mode by replacing the modal final C with a D so as to close with a cadence in G minor (Ex. 18b).[4] This mixture of a Western harmonic language with a Russian melodic manner is a microcosm of Glinka's style in *A Life for the Tsar*.

The changes in Act II suggest a tussle between composer and ballet master. The excision of two whole dances has already been noted. Although this act provided the expected element of ballet in the opera, with these two dances it would have been even more inordinately long. The *Passo a tre* was poor stuff, anyway—a vapid showpiece for Boehm's

---

[1] GLN1, p. 158.

[2] GLN1, p. 160.

[3] There is some uncertainty here. In the Complete Edition this variant appears in a piano reduction by Protopopov at the end of the vocal score of *A Life for the Tsar*. Never- theless, in the supplementary volume of variants to the full score in this edition, only the cadence of this first version is printed, and this includes an inner cello part not in the piano reduction. To add greater confusion to the matter, the version of this cadence printed in PISG contains yet more differences. Nevertheless, there is nothing to contradict the essential truth of what is written above.

[4] One wonders whether the F sharp in the middle of the tune really existed in the original folk tune.

Ex.18. [Moderato]

(Our town is uneasy, Russia is dark. The king has moved threateningly on Moscow.)

violin—but the other with solo oboe and cello parts has some passages of charm which Glinka decided to rescue for one of the ballets in *Ruslan and Lyudmila*. According to Vorobyeva's testimony, Glinka also removed the Waltz after a few performances, and this excision was still being observed at the time she was writing (1879). This was done on Cavos's advice. Otherwise Glinka appears to have made no changes of substance in this act except to shorten some of the dances by the wholesale removal of repetitions. Most of these repetitions were subsequently restored, so it appears that the cuts were made for the first performances only, and were then dropped. This was probably done in 1837 when the opera was first performed in the five divisions as we know it, for the length of these dances would have been more tolerable when Act II was separately performed than when it was still an appendage to Act I. Glinka hardly made any alterations to the opening Polonaise, but he re-scored a few places in the Krakowiak. He recalled in his *Memoirs* that it was to Charles Mayer that he owed the Mazurka's accompaniment figure (Ex. 19) which 'is repeated in various keys with different scoring, and produces rather a good effect'.[1]

Ex.19. Tempo di mazurka

In Act III Glinka was evidently worried that the Peasants' chorus would prove too small, and he developed the choral parts beyond those envisaged by Rosen. He was then also worried that it would be too static, and not only himself supplemented the text Rosen had provided for Susanin, but also added parts for Vanya and Sobinin. According to Vorobyeva, these solo additions were made after the première 'as an experiment',[2] but it seems the experiment did not satisfy Glinka, and he rejected them. The vivace in the quartet was clearly longer in its first than it its final form, and in the following scena and chorus (which Glinka had evidently composed before August 1835) he decided to delay Vanya's exit to the end of the movement instead of dispatching him in the middle. He also felt he could improve the effect of Antonida's

[1] GLN1, p. 165.
[2] According to the Preface to Balakirev's edition of *A Life for the Tsar*, quoted in PISG, p. 117. There is some doubt about the truth of Vorobyeva's assertion.

fearful cry just before her exit, and removed the stormy orchestral accompaniment in favour of a bar's utter silence. But in the Bridal Chorus he did not alter a single note—not surprisingly, perhaps, since this is surely the most perfect conception in the whole opera. It had been born in happy circumstances, for it had come to him quite suddenly in May 1835 while near Novgorod on a carriage journey to Moscow where he was to visit his wife's relatives immediately after his marriage. Likewise the touchingly beautiful romance with chorus for Antonida is free of all alterations. But Glinka made a substantial change at the end of the finale to the act, which Rosen had wanted to end rather intimately with a women's chorus consoling Antonida. Not only did Glinka hold to his intention of a grand, forceful conclusion but even, it appears, reinforced its impact beyond what he himself had originally intended, for the last fifty or so bars before the final orchestral passage appear to be an addition to the final version.[1] After five or six performances Cavos persuaded Glinka to excise the duet for Antonida and Sobinin from the finale, and the cut became customary.

If the changes in Act III were mainly slight, those in Act IV were far-reaching. The entr'acte certainly existed in an earlier form, though it seems probable that this only differed from the final form in the orchestration, not in substance.[2] In the scene which opens the act Glinka made a small excision in the middle of Sobinin's adagio, and also provided a version of this central section transposed a minor lower third (B flat instead of D flat), thus relieving the tenor of his top Cs and D flat. In fact, Cavos talked Glinka into excising the whole of this scene at the same time as he dropped the Antonida/Sobinin duet in Act III, and the scene of Vanya at the gates of the monastery, added in 1837, was to fill the gap. But by far the most drastic musical revision in the whole opera occurred in Susanin's aria, for the first attempt bore no relationship either in words or music to the definitive version. Unfortunately only the end of the earlier aria has survived, but it is enough to disclose just how different it was from Glinka's second thoughts (Ex. 20). In the finale, Glinka confessed that at the meno mosso he had in mind the brigands' song 'Down by Mother Volga', 'employing its beginning in diminution as the accompaniment'[3] (Ex. 21). The recollection of the

---

[1] The vocal parts may originally have ended with a slightly extended version of the perfect cadence in bars 438–9.

[2] Only the last five bars of the first version have survived.

[3] GLN1, p. 164.

(victory over fire and the sword and over unmeasured torment)

(I say to you in reply:)

Luga coachman's song which occurs a few bars later was incorporated at the suggestion of Odoyevsky, who liked the tune very much.

Originally Glinka had provided an orchestral interlude to join Act IV to the Epilogue. Ex. 22 sets out the first part of this;[1] the remaining

[1] The anticipation of the 'Tristan' chord in bar 11 is purely coincidental.

Ex.22. [Vivace]

This extract begins six bars from the end of Act IV in the published score.

twenty-three bars of the surviving fragment follow exactly the course of the development of the first subject in the overture (bars 199ff.), transposed up a tone. Though the middle of this interlude is lost, the end of it quite certainly survives as the last half of the entr'acte to the Epilogue.[1] It is clear that this interlude was to accompany a scenic transformation, and this intention is clearly described in a surviving copy of the libretto with Glinka's stage directions written in:

They seize Susanin, and with a wild cry bear him off-stage. The stage is empty; the orchestra expresses the dying torments of the martyr. The noises die away. At that moment Sobinin rushes in with his levy, listens, and hearing Susanin's last groan, noisily hastens thither. There is a battle behind the scenes, expressed in music. Clouds descend upon the stage.[2]

[1] From the meno mosso in bar 43.

[2] GLN2, p. 692. Rosen's copy of the libretto contains similar stage directions. The autograph score of the entr'acte to the Epilogue still has stage directions relating to its old function as an interlude, for above bar 72 is struck through the direction 'the clouds clear',

Then the clouds were to clear slowly, the scene would change to Moscow, and the *Slavsya* Chorus would follow forthwith.[1] Glinka recalled that the trio with chorus was written at the end of the summer of 1836 with special attention to Vorobyeva's talents[2]—and in far from private circumstances. The event happened at Kukolnik's apartments: 'I remember as though it were now that some fifteen people had gathered; Petrov (the actor) was also there, and I wrote, or rather composed, this affecting scene surrounded by the noise and chatter of my feasting friends.'[3] It was Odoyevsky who suggested to Glinka the *divisi* violin scoring at the opening of the scena preceding the trio, and who also suggested that Glinka should replace his viola/cello/double bass accompaniment to the trio with a scoring for five cellos *divisi*, supported by two unison double basses.[4] His first intention had been to join the trio with chorus to the resumption of the *Slavsya* Chorus, but he subsequently suppressed this link. It appears, from the pagination of the autograph, that the first sixteen bars of the resumed *Slavsya* Chorus were not in the original.

Such was the casual, unsystematic, back-to-front way in which the first memorable piece of Russian music came to be composed. It would be easy to attribute this disordered process solely to Glinka's lack of professionalism, and it does indeed reflect the dilettante at work. But to a Russian such a way of creating was not so very unnatural, and it certainly does not indicate a lack of concern for the quality of the finished work. The *Initial Plan* is quite enough to show that Glinka was very clear-headed at an early stage about the outlines of the scenario, and his concern that every detail in the opera should tell is reflected clearly in his decision to set the text throughout in developed recitative, instead of using spoken dialogue to link the musical numbers, as had been done in all previous Russian operas. *A Life for the Tsar* certainly cannot be

---

while at the end is decipherable the rubric 'the clouds, having cleared, reveal a view of Moscow'.

[1] It is perhaps worth recording that at the opening of the *Slavsya* Chorus Glinka clearly specified the balance between the three choirs. Choirs 1 and 2, placed on the left and the right of the stage, were each to contain twenty singers, and Choir 3, in the centre, was to be thirty strong.

[2] Zhukovsky had assigned the narration of Susanin's death to Antonida; it was Glinka who transferred it to Vanya, the role Vorobyeva was to sing.

[3] GLN1, p. 167.

[4] In his *Memoirs* Glinka stated that the suggested scoring was for 'four solo cellos and one double bass' (GLN1, p. 168). Protopopov unaccountably does not comment upon the discrepancy between this and Glinka's actual scoring.

classified as an example of Russian realism in the way that Dargo-muizhsky and Mussorgsky were to understand it, but by using continuous music to make every moment as alive as possible, Glinka was certainly moving towards a more intense and constant audience involvement in the story. Since he kept to the pattern of set pieces (arias, choruses, etc.) as used in contemporary Western operas, he could not, of course, follow each turn of the libretto with absolutely apt music, but by using self-contained numbers, each concerned with an explicit situation or feeling, he was able to run ahead of his librettist, leaving the latter to fit matching words at a later stage. This may not be an ideal order of events, but *A Life for the Tsar* shows that it was not unworkable. Nor may the haphazard order in which the parts of the opera were composed have been the best way of ensuring coherence in the final result, but since it seems to have been a typically Russian procedure to build a work by pasting together a number of self-contained pieces rather than by letting it grow organically through continuous evolution, it was not so very unnatural for Glinka to start wherever he liked in the scheme, and to assemble the finished pieces in the right order. It was not only Russian operas that were to be written this way; Balakirev certainly composed *Tamar* episodically. If the making of *A Life for the Tsar* was a disordered process, it was nothing compared to the chaotic way in which Borodin was to compose *Prince Igor*—a work which he left unfinished after seventeen years without even having bothered to write down a proper scenario. As it was, Glinka was very aware that special care would have to be taken if an overall unity was to be ensured, and not the least remarkable thing about *A Life for the Tsar* is that so coherent a work should have come out of such disordered labour.

6/A Life for the Tsar: The Music

DESPITE his three-year exposure to Italian opera in its native land, Glinka's *A Life for the Tsar* is quite as much in the French operatic tradition as in the Italian. Glinka attributed his knowledge of how to handle the human voice to his Italian interlude, and it is in the solo vocal music that his debt to the Italian operatic style is most apparent, but *A Life for the Tsar* has also the spectacular choral scenes and the elaborate ballet which belong much more to the French tradition. The opera shows therefore a characteristically Russian eclecticism in its combination of different operatic lines. But disentangling the French and Italian operatic traits is relatively easy compared with the task of isolating the Russian elements which Glinka deliberately added. It is not surprising therefore that the strength of the nationalism in *A Life for the Tsar* has always been a contentious matter. César Cui went so far as to assert that 'in the whole opera there is perhaps not a single musical phrase having closer affinity with the music of Western Europe than with that of the Slavs'.[1] The Soviet writer, Protopopov, has brought a much more scholarly Russian view to the subject, though even he is over-zealous in his endeavours to relate the opera to indigenous Russian music. Any Russian view must obviously be treated with respect, for Russian ears are naturally more sensitive to such matters than ours, though the Russian temper has been naturally disposed to find similarities and to over-emphasize them. In the West Gerald Abraham has been able to take a more balanced view, rejecting Cui's verdict as 'gross exaggeration'.[2] Yet all writers do seem to agree that it is in the opera's melodic content that its nationalism is to be found, despite the fact that, except for the Luga coachman's song and the derivative from 'Down by

---

[1] César Cui, *La Musique en Russie* (Paris, 1880), p. 23.   [2] AORM, p. 6.

Mother Volga', all the melodic material is Glinka's own invention.[1]
The remarks of Melgunov at the time of the première have already
been noted; to these should be added Odoyevsky's observation that

Ex.23.

A Life for the Tsar demonstrated how 'Russian melody, by nature now
mournful, now gay, now bold, could be elevated to a tragic style'.[2]

Yet the most revealing record of public reaction to the opera, and
certainly the most penetrating contemporary analysis of Glinka's
achievement, came from Neverov, who examined the problem of
composing a genuinely national opera by comparing *A Life for the Tsar*
with earlier operas by Verstovsky:

Mr. Verstovsky, an intelligent composer of true, though not, however, of
dramatic talent, has attempted to transfer Russian song to the stage. But he has
not succeeded in this because he thought to create an opera sometimes by borrowing folk tunes in their entirety, and sometimes by imitating them. Because there
is nothing dramatic in the words or the music of our folk-songs, operas put
together from them have had the same disjointed, lyrical character. Mr. Verstovsky's best compositions, such as *Vadim* and *Askold's Tomb,* are essentially nothing
more than a collection of, for the most part, delightful Russian tunes joined
together by German choruses, quartets, and Italian recitatives . . . Here there
was no nationalism, and at the same time the thing had lost all shapeleness, and
the opera seemed to be an arbitrary mixture of arias, duets, and trios of all

[1] According to Darya Leonova, the oboe theme of the Overture's introduction and of
the Epilogue's trio (Ex. 23b) was likewise based upon a coachman's song. She asserted
that Glinka himself had told her how 'he was once returning home, and near Smolensk
his coachman began to sing it [his song]. In the opera, *A Life for the Tsar*, there is a tune . . .
"Ah, not to me, poor wretch." Mikhail Ivanovich took this straight from the coachman
who, on the word "Akh", sang [here Leonova used solmization syllables: see Ex. 23a].
This was enough for M. I. Glinka to compose such a massive piece as the Overture to the
opera, *A Life for the Tsar*, and the trio.' (Quoted in LV, pp. 340–1.) Protopopov has
drawn attention to another parallel between this oboe theme and the song, 'Down by
Mother Volga', used by Glinka in Act IV (Ex. 23c).

[2] Quoted in PISG, p. 163.

styles and all peoples in which the listener sought in vain for any unity or dominating idea. Mr. Glinka has set about it differently; he has looked deeply into the character of our folk music, has observed all its characteristics, has studied and assimilated it—and then has given full freedom to his own fantasy which has taken images which are purely Russian, native. Many who heard his opera noticed something familiar in it, tried to recall from which Russian song this or that motif was taken, and could not discover the original. This is high praise to our maestro; in fact, in his opera there is not one borrowed phrase,[1] but they are all clear, comprehensible, familiar to us simply because they breathe a pure nationalism, because we hear in them native sounds.[2]

Neverov had hit on the real secret of Glinka's nationalism. What Glinka did was to draw upon characteristics of all the varieties of indigenous Russian music he had heard from his earliest years, not with the condescension of the sophisticate who wants to be 'folksy', but with the perfectly natural ease of a musician for whom folk-song was as deeply rooted and as valid an experience as more cultivated music. To the student of Glinka this poses great problems, for the subject of Russian folk music is as vast as Russia itself. Not only were there very marked differences between the folk music of the various regions and peoples of the country, but since the early eighteenth century there had appeared a deep dichotomy between the music which continued to evolve in the country areas and the new popular music that was developing in the towns and cities. Peter the Great had deliberately opened the doors of Russia to the West, and the new town music of the eighteenth century was an amalgam of the indigenous tradition with the techniques and styles of Western music. The lyrics of the new town songs were regularly metrical and therefore fostered tunes which had regular barring as opposed to the more flexible rhythms of the country songs. Waltz and march rhythms became particularly common. The wide melodic range of these town songs, rarely less than an octave, contrasted sharply with the more restricted tessitura of many country songs, and large melodic leaps became more frequent. Country songs had made

---

[1] This is not quite true; see above, pp. 99, 106, and 112.

[2] Quoted in LPG2, p. 213. Neverov's article appeared in the issue of October 1836 of the *Moscow Observer*, the publication of which was much delayed, evidently by the censor. Neverov's article was only dispatched to Moscow on 11/23 December. Fyodor Koni reinforced Neverov's point about the novelty of Glinka's work. Again comparing Glinka to Verstovsky, he observed: 'Mr. Verstovsky often took folk songs and turned them into operatic motifs—and they perished. Mr. Glinka has created Russian motifs, and they have turned into folk songs.' (From the *Northern Bee*, 17/29 April 1837. Quoted in LPG1, p. 206.)

much use of repetitions of tiny melodic cells, but the practice of sequence which now appeared in town songs was caught from Western music. There was a pronounced shift away from the modes to major and minor scales; above all, town songs showed the influence of Western harmonic practices, with the primary triads exercising an especially strong influence upon their formation. The typical town song was conceived with a Western-rooted harmonic accompaniment in mind, and was usually performed as a solo song with instrumental accompaniment (often provided by a guitar), though simple three-voice harmonizations were also popular. Naturally these harmonizations followed Western harmonic practices, and bore no relation to *podgolosnaya* methods.

The town tradition was, of course, a thoroughly contaminated one; nevertheless, despite all the Western elements in it, it still did have much that was essentially Russian in character, and the continuing interaction between it and the country tradition was an additional guarantee that this Russianness would be maintained. What must be emphasized here is that, for all Glinka's childhood acquaintance with the purer country line, it was really the town music that was to prove of as great, if not greater importance to him. Nowhere in his work is there anything as utterly and consistently Russian, for instance, as Stravinsky's *The Wedding*, which is rooted firmly in a village milieu.[1] And it was perfectly natural that Glinka should draw upon this town line, for, since it was already a mixture of Russian and Western elements, it offered him an excellent basis for his own more ambitious and elaborate attempts to fashion a music founded upon Western techniques, but filled with Russian character. Perhaps the Western scholar may be forgiven a passing regret that this was so, for if Glinka had drawn more heavily upon the pure country tradition, he would find his task of assessing the national element in Glinka's work far easier. As it is, Russian town music sounds to the Western ear already more than half Western, though to a Russian who is naturally more sensitive to those inflections which stem from his own indigenous tradition, its Russianness may appear much stronger (hence, perhaps, Cui's assertion of the overwhelming Russianness of the melodic content of *A Life for the Tsar*). But the problem of disentangling Russian and Western elements is further complicated by the additional Italian and French operatic factors which the composition

---

[1] Despite the fact that Stravinsky's borrowed material in this work is from town material.

of *A Life for the Tsar* obviously involved. The fact is that Russia and Western Europe are often quite inextricably mixed in Glinka's music. For instance, he employs the modes that we associate with Russian folk-song, but will modulate in a way quite foreign to folk music. What sometimes takes his modulations out of a thoroughly Western musical world is that they are made to keys which would not so readily be expected of a Western composer. It is often the non-Western features of the melody which prompt such modulations; thus the oboe theme of the Overture's introduction (see Ex. 15b), clearly starting in G minor, arrives in its fifth and sixth bars on F, and Glinka accordingly cadences on the flattened leading note. It would probably be truer to say, rather limply, that the effect is more non-Western than positively Russian. It is because of this complex interaction of different musical cultures in Glinka's music that so many different views have been expressed about its Russianness. The subject requires a separate book, and all that can be done here is to point out a little later some more obvious features which some of Glinka's own melodies share with Russian folk music.

Glinka's melodic nationalism seems effortless and was, one suspects, quite artless. It is important to emphasize this, for an examination of *A Life for the Tsar* reveals all sorts of small but very real similarities between quite separate tunes. Now, Glinka was very concerned, as he himself said and as we shall later see, to ensure that the opera made 'an harmonious whole', and he set about this by creating many substantial cross-references between its component parts. Therefore might not a concern to tighten the structure have led him to fabricate these smaller thematic similarities? To take just two examples: the flute phrase in the coda to the Introduction in Act I (Ex. 24b), itself related to the opening theme of the first act (Ex. 24a), clearly leads to the arabesque at the opening of Antonida's cavatina (Ex. 24c), while this in turn is mirrored in the opening melody of the following rondo (Ex. 24d). Secondly, at the other end of the opera, this same flute phrase from the Introduction's coda seems to have generated a conspicuous vocal counterpoint near the end of the *Slavsya* Chorus, and the opening theme of the Introduction is also briefly echoed in the *Slavsya* Chorus.[1] Since the relationships between at least three of these examples (Ex. 24 b, c, and d) are evidently deliberate, the possibility that other smaller thematic connections were also consciously contrived cannot be completely discounted. What seems more plausible, however, is that Glinka, by

[1] See the passage following bar 29.

Ex.24.

(I look upon the empty field.)

focusing upon a smaller range of melodic types with certain traits in common 'for the range of melody in *A Life for the Tsar* is much smaller than that in *Ruslan and Lyudmila*), made the opera more of a piece than it would otherwise have been. It is certainly true that a number of easily recognizable features of Russian folk melody recur in Glinka's tunes. For instance, there is the plagalism which is conspicuous in certain folk-songs, especially those of an heroic character. Although they may have been conceived entirely without any conscious harmonic background, these tunes very naturally harmonize with a tonic-subdominant-tonic progression (this is true of the one Russian folk-song every Englishman knows, the so-called 'Song of the Volga boatmen'). The subdominant is usually relatively unaccented, and sometimes the first tonic is omitted. In addition, in many folk-songs a certain fundamental contour may be traced in the melodic line (Ex. 25; the bracketed notes are sometimes

Ex.25.

omitted). The treble notes of Ex. 25b are (with an E flat) the opening notes of the Overture and opening chorus, while the complete line of Ex. 25a sets out the very notes used by Glinka to open Lyudmila's cavatina in the first act of *Ruslan and Lyudmila*. These contours appear in both the main themes of the opening Chorus of *A Life for the Tsar* (Ex. 26d and e); the folk-song quoted in Ex. 26f[1] had been used by

(I am not grieving, my friends, because I regret [the loss of my maiden] freedom.)

(You are coming, O my dawn! I look into your face.)

---

[1] Taken from N. Afanasyev, *64 russkiye pesni* (Moscow, 1866). Quoted in PISG, p. 179.

Glinka for the capriccio for piano duet, composed just before he started work on *A Life for the Tsar*. A similar plagalism also appears in the opening of Antonida's romance in Act III (Ex. 26a), which takes its departure from Sobinin's spirited phrase at the opening of the last section of the quartet (Ex. 26b; this phrase is quoted in the brief recitative just before Antonida's Romance); so, too, plagalism appears at the beginning of Susanin's aria in Act IV (Ex. 26c), which is really a distant variant of the Introduction's first theme (Ex. 26d).

While the Western dominant, the fifth, is prominent in some Russian folk-songs, others acquire a markedly non-Western character by making the supertonic assume the role of the dominant,[1] and Glinka uses this same supertonic emphasis in the theme of the Chorus of Rowers in Act I (Ex. 27). This chorus also employs the rapid concluding descent

Ex. 27.
[Moderato]

through five notes from the 'dominant' to the 'tonic' which is a common ending in Russian folk song (it is often preceded or, as here, followed by an octave rise). This ending was frequently used by Glinka (see, for instance, Exs. 24c, 29a, and 32). In the chorus theme in Ex. 26e,

---

[1] One wonders whether the instinct to feel the supertonic as a particularly strong related centre was behind Glinka's original decision to begin the recapitulation of the Overture in A minor.

Glinka emphasizes the supertonic by the thoroughly Western device of a passing modulation to this degree. Yet, on the whole, harmony contributes very little to the national character of *A Life for the Tsar*. Despite the fertility and vitality of Glinka's melodic invention in this opera, his harmonic language remained disappointingly conventional. This is also true of the rhythmic element in the opera; except for the notable vigour of a few pieces like the Overture, the *Slavsya* Chorus, and the unusual five-beat pulse of the Bridal Chorus, there is nothing which one might set down as characteristically Russian about its rhythmic life. Real harmonic and rhythmic enterprise had to wait until *Ruslan and Lyudmila*.

In any case, regarding harmony, there was the danger that attaching a harmonization to any tune of a genuinely Russian character might compromise or even destroy that character. But since there existed, of course, a strong tradition of unaccompanied performance in Russian native music, Glinka's refusal to provide an accompaniment was not necessarily begging the question. Thus when, after the bright, effective Overture, in which the variable duple and triple metres consciously symbolize the impending clash of Susanin and the Poles, Glinka opened the opera with a solo voice (see Ex. 24a) and brought the chorus in on the second phrase, he was only using a very common practice of Russian choral folk-singing. Vorobyeva testified to the power of Glinka's national—and dramatic—instincts in the introduction: 'The realism of this chorus struck me forcefully; while the calm melody of the men's voices is being sung, a group of peasant women gossip like chatterboxes. After Italian music this was so novel and natural that my breath was taken away in my excitement.'[1] The next movement, Antonida's very striking cavatina, carries the monodic principle even further, for over half is unaccompanied cantilena, and elsewhere the accompaniment is skeletal. The arabesque, the tonal ambivalence (is it F minor or A flat?), and the seven-bar phrase structure of the opening (see Ex. 24c) are the sort of things that contribute further towards removing it from a Western musical milieu. But the ensuing rondo is only mildly and intermittently Russian, and a phrase like that in Ex. 28 could easily have escaped from an Italian opera. After Susanin's entry with the Luga coachman's song (see vocal part of Ex. 18a), there follows the Chorus of Rowers, and again unaccompanied melody is prominent, for the first two verses of this very Russian tune (see Ex. 27) are virtually unharmonized; when an accompaniment is added, it is a derivative of the

[1] VVG, p. 615.

Ex.28. **Allegro** *scherzando*

Moi su - zhe - nuy pri - dyot. Voz - go - vo - rit: zdo - ro - vo.

tenute
pp

(My betrothed is coming. He will greet me.)

women's chorus theme from the Introduction (see Ex. 26e),[1] delivered this time by pizzicato strings in imitation of balalaikas—a brilliant stroke which deservedly won applause from the orchestra at rehearsals (see above, p. 85), for it is one of the most imaginative passages in the whole opera. The sentimentality of the following trio won it immediate popularity, though it has a pathos which prevents it becoming saccharine, and is an excellent movement of its type.

Throughout this act Glinka reveals himself to be a composer inclined to build a movement through melodic extension and variation, often involving simple but effective counterpoint. Much of the effect both of the Introduction and of the Chorus of Rowers comes from rubbing two tunes together, while in the trio each of the successive statements of the sixteen-bar theme acquires an extra freely evolving melodic line as accompaniment. Thus though this movement is initially a strophic conception, the thematic recurrences are converted into very simple variations through the addition of contrapuntal decoration. Obviously the Chorus of Rowers is likewise a strophic piece—but so, too, is the preceding scene of Susanin's entry, for here everything centres round four freely varied statements of the Luga coachman's song. Even the fugue of the Introduction splits into a number of clear sections of which the first three are each a simple fugal exposition founded upon the men's tune, followed by a clear conclusion based on the end of the women's tune; thus is created another series of free variations. Here is fresh confirmation that variation procedures of

---

[1] This invention was probably a legacy of the time when the Introduction and this chorus were one movement (see above, pp. 93–4).

various kinds were Glinka's most favoured and most successful way of extending a movement beyond an initial melodic proposition.

It is easy enough to perceive the limitations of Glinka's technical skill in *A Life for the Tsar*, but some caution is needed before all such apparent limitations are interpreted as liabilities. The strength of this opera lies in its combination of melodic inventiveness with an instinct for simple yet strong drama. It is important to remember that this is music for the theatre, and that Glinka had a sure sense of what would be musically effective on the stage, even though on paper it may appear rough or even simple-minded. His strokes are direct, sometimes very functional (as in the choral interjections in the recitatives), but are almost always at least serviceable dramatically, and sometimes very telling. Thus the fugue of the Introduction may look crude in the score, but the bluff entries of the subject convey a robust simplicity which is admirably apt for a peasant crowd, where a more sophisticated musical organism would probably have failed. Nor was Glinka incapable of organizing a good broad design, for Act I is very well proportioned, with the two most static movements, Antonida's cavatina and rondo and the trio, placed symmetrically near either end. And the pace is good—which underlines what is probably, in fact, the most truly remarkable feature of the opera: the handling of the dialogue. Though there were precedents for recitative in Russian melodrama and oratorio, *A Life for the Tsar* was the very first Russian opera to be set entirely to music without spoken dialogue. On hearing it, the perceptive Neverov wrote that Glinka had created 'a completely individual type of recitative . . . His recitatives are like neither German nor Italian ones; they combine the expressiveness and dramatic flexibility of the former with the melodiousness of the latter, and in them it seems that you hear the intonation of Russian speech.'[1] The Western listener has to take the last statement on trust, but what he will repeatedly observe are the well-formed, characterful phrases, the firm simple accompaniments, and the tautly constructed sections. These features are admirably shown after Sobinin's entry (Ex. 29a). The importance of this recitative style for later Russian composers was enormous: already, for example, passages like those in Exs. 29b and 30a foreshadow the solemn manner of sections of Mussorgsky's *Boris Godunov*.

Glinka's evident concern at the lack of dramatic interest in Act II has already been noted. Being entirely concerned with the Poles, it could not

[1] Quoted in PISG, p. 215.

be expected to contain any elements of Russian nationalism, but little of it is even really Polish in character. It opens well enough with a choral-orchestral Polonaise, a ternary structure which very effectively contrives to integrate the melody of the central section into the return of the first part. But beyond this the music is markedly light-weight. Glinka had a natural facility for inconsequential, if charming melody,

-da zhe s po - lya che - sti Rus-sky vo - in u- -da- loi, Bez u -

(*Sobinin*: Unbounded happiness! Is it you, my soul, my dear bright sun!
Susanin: Tell us, what news do you bring us?
Chorus: Fine fellow, tell us good news!
Sobinin: Ah, when has a bold Russian warrior [returned home] from the field of honour without [brave good news]?)

b) **Allegro deciso [più lento]**
SUSANIN
[*p*] Do - ro- gob da - li___ chto- bui v po - lon po- i- -mat.___

VANYA   **Tempo I**
Kak bui syu - da ne pri - shli?___ Ruish-chut vez- de po Ru-

Tempo I

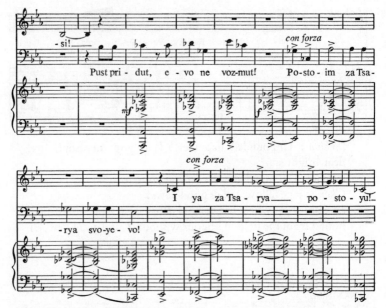

(*Susanin*: They would pay dearly to take him prisoner.
Vanya: How is it they have not come here? They are scouring all Russia.
Susanin: Let them come! They won't take him! We shall stand by our Tsar!
Vanya: And I shall stand by my Tsar!)

and it is evident in this ballet music, which outstays its welcome. Nor, when the dancers are disturbed by the entry of the messenger, is the level restored. The ballet music lingers on, and the dialogue is far less inventive than that in Act I.

If the earlier part of Act III, though musically more weighty, is dramatically slack, Glinka himself was at least partly to blame. Had he kept to his original scheme as set out in the *Initial Plan*, all might have been well. He made very clear to Vorobyeva his dramatic view of the Orphan's Song with which the act opens: 'Mlle. Vorobyeva, . . . everyone tells me that you are a true contralto with a depth of feeling. In view of this, I beg you to sing this song from my opera . . . without any feeling . . . The Orphan, who lives at Susanin's, is sitting alone in his hut at some trivial work, and is singing the song to himself, giving the words no significance, but devoting more attention to his work.'[1] This is sure testimony of Glinka's values in this song, and the dialogue between Vanya and Susanin, which he inserted after the Orphan's Song, maintains the dramatic level (see Ex. 29b). However, with the duet, the more formal set piece takes over. Both this duet and the quartet are too long, even though Glinka shortened the latter by pruning Rosen's libretto. But, in addition, a quite unnecessary, if very pleasant Peasants' Chorus was interpolated between the duet and quartet. Having decided upon this chorus, Glinka himself was responsible for expanding it, though he certainly became aware subsequently of its dramatic inertia, and tried to enliven it with exchanges for Susanin, Vanya, and Sobinin (see above, p. 105). These, however, could only be palliatives. Nor is the Western listener likely to feel that these movements are more than intermittently Russian. So often in *A Life for the Tsar* the national flavour tends to be strongest near the beginnings of movements or sections, to weaken as the extending processes begin (especially when modulations set in), and to disappear completely when the final cadencing is reached. Towards the end of his life Glinka himself was to tell Feofil Tolstoi of his own disapproval of this duet's structure and character, especially of the allegro vivace and coda: 'the form recalls Italian [fashions]. Is it possible that such a man as Susanin would have taken it into his head to repeat word for word a fifth lower the naïve outpouring of the orphan, Vanya? Why didn't you [this addressed to Tolstoi] point out to me the unsuitability of the coda? . . . How it reeks of Italianism!'[2] This was in 1854, when much had changed in Glinka's attitudes, and by which time he could look more dispassionately on his 'old woman', as he came to describe *A Life for the Tsar*. But in 1843, only seven years after the première, he expounded to Serov ideas which also implicitly criticize this duet: 'As I understand it, every duet must be as one person singing; it must consist of the melody or thought A, then of thought B, and finally of the sum of A and B, which must again be something other than A or B, and all must be based on contrasts (but in normal Italian operas one singer sings A, the other sings A, and then together they sing the very same A in thirds or sixths). According to this theory, a quartet must be A+B+C+D and so on.'[3]

---

[1] VVG, pp. 612–13.

[2] TVG, p. 453.

[3] Reported by Serov to Vladimir Stasov in a letter published in *Russkaya Starina*, December 1876, p. 792. Quoted in PISG, p. 316.

The musical inequalities of the centre of Act III are even greater. Glinka chose to present the marauding Poles largely with their music from Act II —certainly a precocious use of leitmotif for 1836, but inept, for this decorative ballet music cannot convey their menace here any more than similar music is capable of reflecting their wrath in Act IV. Nevertheless this central section opens very beautifully, and prophetically, too, for since Susanin's and Antonida's parts in this scena and chorus are initially laid out against five statements of the opening sixteen-bar theme, it is yet another foreshadowing of the changing-background technique which was to emerge fully formed in *Ruslan and Lyudmila*. Glinka's deliberate intention of setting the Poles' triple time against Susanin's duple metre led him to devise one brief passage in which six bars of Susanin's music in $\frac{4}{4}$ are counterpointed to eight bars of Polish music in $\frac{3}{4}$. Nevertheless this scene is not memorable for such contrivances; what really do linger are some of Susanin's utterances, like the quiet passage which anticipates the splendid theme of the Epilogue (Ex. 30a), his bold defiance of the Poles which draws upon the chorus with which the opera had opened, or (most of all) the tender farewell to his daughter (Ex. 30b). Fortunately the latter stages of this Act

Ex.30.
a) Maestoso

Vui - sok i svyat nash Tsar-sky___ dom, i

kre - post Bo - zhi - ya kru - gom; Pod

ne - - yu si - la Ru - si tse - la.

(The Tsar's abode is high and holy, and a fortress encircled by
God. Under it the strength of Russia is intact.)

Ya ne mo-gu tak sko-ro vo-ro-tit-sya. Sui-

-grai-te va-shu svad-bu bez me-nya. Lyu-

(Do not grieve, my child—cry not, my beloved child. May
God bless your life. I cannot return very soon. Celebrate
your wedding without me.)

are on a more consistently high level, not so much in the finale, which
has some dull stretches,[1] as in the preceding romance with chorus for
Antonida (see Ex. 26a), a most touchingly pathetic plaint whose Russian
complexion is unmistakable. Yet the real jewel of this Act—indeed, of
the whole opera— is the Bridal Chorus (Ex. 31a), whose innocent charm
is the more affecting for following immediately upon the troubled exit

Ex.31.
a)
Con moto
Chorus of girls (behind the scenes)

Raz-gu-lya-la-sya, raz-li-va-la-sya vo-da vesh-nya-ya

[1] The customary excision of the farewell duet for Antonida and Sobinin has been
noticed earlier (see above, p. 106).

po — lu-gam. Ra - zui-gra-li - sya, ras-plya-sa - lis kras-nui de-vi-tsui v te - re - mu. Kak od-na si - dit, ne i - gra - yet, pod-go-ryu-ni-las, slyo - zui lyot, ___ slyo-zui gor - - ki - ye! ___

(Raging, the spring floods pour out over the meadows. With increasing abandon, fair maidens dance in the tower, while she sits alone and does not play; sorrowing, she weeps bitter tears.)

of Susanin with the Poles. This chorus, composed quite impulsively just after Glinka's marriage (see above, p. 79), is not only the most perfect but, with its unusual $\frac{5}{4}$ rhythm, virtual pentatonicism, modal cadences, and unharmonized cantilena in the second half, is also the most thoroughly national piece in the whole opera. Its affinity with the genuine article (Ex. 31b and c)[1] is easy to perceive.

Glinka's orchestration is the one feature of his work which all critics seem united in praising. It is seen to much more striking advantage in *Ruslan and Lyudmila,* but already in *A Life for the Tsar* there is a pronounced clarity of texture, and the Entr'acte to Act IV is notable for some of its sharply defined, even stark sounds (Ex. 32)—lean, uncluttered timbres which contrast strongly with the more blended, romantically warm palette of German instrumentation. Glinka is already laying the

Ex.32. **Allegro con spirito**

[1] Ex. 31b is taken from KNG1, p. 57, and 31c from PISG, p. 195.

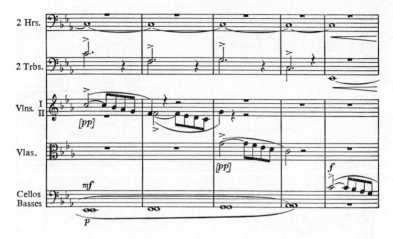

foundations of an approach to orchestral sound which characterizes much nineteenth century Russian music, and which still rings out clearly in our century in the works of Prokofiev and Stravinsky. There is also something a little prophetic in Sobinin's adagio amoroso in the first scene of the following act (Ex. 33), for here is heard something of that more individual lyricism which Glinka developed further in *Ruslan and Lyudmila*. The melting progress of the lines beneath the singer's top F and the lightly romantic chromatic touch already breathe a lyricism which can readily be associated with the Russian musical tradition; the chromatic flattened sixth (F flat) in the voice part was to become a very characteristic fingerprint of Glinka and his successors (it is also to be found in the Bridal Chorus (see Ex. 31a, bar 3)). As recorded earlier, the two scenes at the beginning of this act were afterthoughts. Both scenes (Sobinin exhorting his followers in their search for Susanin, and Vanya at the gates of the monastery) are efficient, and musically quite independent of the rest of the opera. In this latter respect they contrast sharply with what follows, for one of the most important—and original— features of *A Life for the Tsar* is its system of musical cross-references. Glinka well understood the great emotional potential in the recollection, during the later stages of a work, of music heard earlier, and he has rightly been acclaimed as a pioneer in the use of Leitmotif. But he also saw their usefulness in drawing the musical web of the whole opera more tightly into the 'harmonious whole' he wished to achieve. Thus

Ex. 33.

(We will find your father, we will bring him home.)

there is little of the Overture that does not recur in the main body of the opera;[1] the entr'actes to Acts III and IV both anticipate music used in the ensuing acts; the opening phrase of the opera (see Ex. 26d) reappears in Susanin's part in Act III, and much more extensively still in the Entr'acte to the Epilogue. The ballet music of Act II accompanies the Poles in

[1] And even more was repeated when the interlude between Act IV and the Epilogue was still in existence (see above, pp. 107–8).

Acts III and IV, and the *Slavsya* Chorus is clearly anticipated in one of Susanin's utterances in Act III (see Ex. 30a); the music of his farewell to his daughter (see Ex. 30b) recurs in the middle of the Epilogue. There are over forty such cross-references scattered throughout the opera, over half the quotations of earlier material occurring during the second half of Act IV and the Epilogue. And so, quite apart from the strong emotional impact of some of these recollections, there is also in these last ones a sense of a final drawing together of musical threads.

This deeply moving scene of Susanin with the Poles is the emotional climax of the opera. It is night, and the Poles are asleep around him. To the accompaniment of harp arpeggios (which may be intended to suggest the folk instrument, the gusli) Susanin unburdens himself in an aria of noble simplicity and strength thoroughly worthy of the situation (see Ex. 26c), and then reflects upon his family in a recitative into which are incorporated no less than eight recollections of earlier music associated with Antonida, Vanya, and Sobinin, thus adding extra emotional associations to this already powerful situation. It seems, however, that the novelty of this procedure was too much for the first audiences, and only later was its full dramatic impact felt. After the Poles have awakened, the Luga coachman's song reappears, and much use is made of the coda to the Overture (the earlier part of the coda had appeared during Susanin's exchanges with the Poles before his aria and recitative). In the course of the orchestral interlude during which the Poles awaken, fragments of Antonida's duple-time rondo from Act I are flung with striking effect against the Poles' triple-time music drawn from the Overture's coda; this is one of the few moments when the Poles are made to sound really menacing. Susanin dies, hurling defiance at his captors, and the Entr'acte to the Epilogue symbolizes his last struggle with them—with a final sure ascendancy of his music over that of the marauders, thus nicely complementing the dualism of the Overture. The Epilogue acts as a glorification both of the Tsar and of Susanin—a short act in the stage-picture manner which was to become important in later Russian opera (this scene is the obvious model, for instance, for the Coronation Scene in Mussorgsky's *Boris Godunov,* which is cast in the same ternary form with large choral flanks). The *Slavsya* Chorus, like the opening of the central section of Act III, is another foreshadowing of the changing-background technique, for its two halves are together largely made up of seven simple statements of the chorus theme (Ex. 34), each time further enriched or adorned with new accompaniments. Later this splendid

Ex.34.

Slavsya tune was to become almost a second national hymn.[1] Vladimir Stasov was enraptured with its national qualities, stating that it

> consists of a number of plagal cadences following one another in unbroken succession . . . We have here a melody composed entirely in the character of our ancient Russian and Greek church melodies, harmonized with the plagal cadence of the middle ages.[2]

Stasov's historical view of harmony was clearly shaky, and as for the melodic affinities with church music, we must take these on trust, though they are clearly exaggerated. What may really puzzle the Western listener about this statement is Stasov's assertion of plagalism. Doesn't the harmony sound like a good deal of C major tonic and dominant at the beginning, with a final swing to the dominant? Paradoxically, both views are equally defensible. The point is that the tune, taken by itself, could be in the mixolydian mode; thus G would be the final, and the opening C major chord would be a subdominant. Presumably Stasov really heard it this way, but the Western listener is equally justified in

---

[1] After the 1917 Revolution the tune of the *Slavsya* Chorus was seriously suggested as a new national anthem.

[2] SG, p. 600 (footnote).

taking it as C major, especially since Glinka confirms this impression of C as the tonic by ending the whole chorus unequivocally in that key. Thus the opera ends with a demonstration of the Western-Russian ambivalence which has pervaded the whole work.

For all its inequalities and obvious shortcomings, *A Life for the Tsar* is really quite an extraordinary achievement. Considering the composer's background, his quite sensational lack of professional musical schooling, and the hair-raising disorderliness of the actual process of composition, such an enterprise would have appeared to be doomed to disaster. As it was, the impossible happened, and even today, a century and a half later, *A Life for the Tsar* can still provide an experience which is both stirring and moving. It was the first really important work ever to have been written by a Russian composer, but it only went part of the way towards establishing a truly Russian dialect in European music. Any composer who wanted to write good national music—that is, not just folky pastiches, but major works that could take their place alongside the products of the mainstreams of European music—had to establish a whole new relationship with these mainstreams in which their musical techniques had been adjusted to a way of thinking which was natural for a man born and bred in different cultural surroundings, and inheriting different racial characteristics and attitudes. Chopin, who was wrestling with the problem at the same time, adopted the very opposite approach to Glinka's, for his evolving musical nationalism shows basically simple musical forms being enriched with the more sophisticated procedures of Western music. Thus his early mazurkas are little more than refined examples of the genuine folk article, but as the series progresses, so the harmonic resource increases, the structures become broader and more elaborate, and the expressive range within a single work expands, so as finally to produce compositions which can challenge in importance Chopin's other large-scale works.[1] Chopin started with national forms and then increasingly incorporated Western techniques; Glinka started with thoroughly Western manners and forms, and then enriched

---

[1] Though the process is less pronounced in Chopin's polonaises, which are from the beginning larger compositions, and which retain their square ternary structure even in the middle-period examples, yet in his last works in this form there is a notable shift towards a more subtly organic structure. This is most evident in the boldly imagined *Polonaise-Fantaisie*, which unfolds a structure which is still compartmentalized in a typically Slav fashion, yet which evolves, through Chopin's technique of haunting otherwise unrelated sections with certain melodic, harmonic and rhythmic nuclei, into one of his most organic compositions.

them with national elements. Despite the assertion in his *Memoirs* that 'in my youth, that is, soon after leaving school, I worked a lot on Russian themes',[1] it seems that such materials were still very much a subsidiary interest with him at that stage; certainly in his compositions of the 1820s there is not much really self-aware nationalism. His Italian expedition had been a pilgrimage to worship at the shrines of Italian opera, and in *A Life for the Tsar* he relied upon his experience of Western opera, and upon the practical compositional skill he had for the most part haphazardly acquired in his contact with Western music. As he grew further away from *A Life for the Tsar*, Glinka himself became more aware of its Western roots. We have already noted the unfavourable remarks he made in 1854 about the duet for Susanin and Vanya (see above, p. 125), and Dargomuizhsky recorded his further reaction to Tolstoi's fulsome compliment that *A Life for the Tsar* was faultless: 'the whole opera is riddled with cadences which weary the listener until he faints!' retorted Glinka.[2] And so, although it represented a remarkable achievement, it was not really so very novel. It was, as Gerald Abraham has described it, 'rather . . . an end, a summing-up, the best and about the last blossom produced by a rather sickly plant'.[3] Indeed, if it had been all that new, it is doubtful whether it could have enjoyed such a remarkable success. The national elements which Glinka grafted on to this Western form were enough to excite his contemporaries, but not too strong to trouble them; when, six years later, he explored a much deeper Russianness in *Ruslan and Lyudmila*, his Russian contemporaries found it more difficult to take, and the work was a comparative failure.

[1] GLN1, p. 150.   [2] Quoted in PISG, p. 337.   [3] AORM, pp. 1–2.

7/Problems and Responsibilities: Imperial Kapellmeister

I T is not surprising that Glinka hoped to use the great success of *A Life for the Tsar* to improve his material position. While composing it he already had his eye on an appointment of some sort in the Imperial Theatre, despite Gedeonov's patent opposition; now he hoped that Gedeonov would not be able to resist any longer. Initially the position would be without salary, although 'afterwards there shouldn't be any trouble about that', he confided to his mother.[1] But he was looking even more keenly for a place within the musical establishment of the Imperial Chapel, since this would carry with it not only a salary but also free accommodation and other gratuities. From his point of view, therefore, the death of the director, Fyodor Lvov, less than three weeks after the première of *A Life for the Tsar* could hardly have been more timely. Not that Glinka intended to be burdened with administrative chores and responsibilities such as Lvov had shouldered; what he wanted was control of the musical affairs of the Chapel while some other person ran the institution. Fortified with the glory of his opera, he pressed his case, and through the good offices of two friends, Prince Grigory Volkonsky and Count Wielhorski (who ten years before had composed a mazurka for Glinka's serenade on the Black River), the matter was arranged; on 1/13 January 1837 Glinka was appointed Kapellmeister at a salary of 2,500 roubles, with an allowance of 1,000 roubles for board— and with an understanding that some other acceptable person should succeed to the more mundane responsibilities of the directorship. What Glinka did not know was that, even before Fyodor Lvov's death, his son, Aleksei, had been designated as the new director. Evidently the authorities knew something of the strained relations between Glinka and Lvov senior. When the two had first met, Fyodor's bearing towards

[1] GLN2, p. 102.

Glinka had been very cordial, but had then inexplicably cooled. Glinka therefore heard the news of Aleksei's appointment with some dismay, for he feared an uneasy relationship. Nevertheless, his first meeting with Aleksei was reassuring, and the Tsar himself, when he encountered Glinka on the stage of the Imperial Theatre on the day of the appointment, inflamed his zeal for the position: 'Glinka, I have a request to make of you, and I hope you will not refuse me. My singers are known throughout all Europe, and it is consequently worth your while to be involved with them. Only I beg of you not to turn them into Italians.'[1] Glinka was so overcome with pleasurable confusion that words failed him, and he could only reply with a few respectful bows.

Glinka also found that the success of *A Life for the Tsar* seemed to have a mysterious power to expedite another matter. Since 1834 he had been engaged with his mother in trying to exact payment of compensation for losses which his father had sustained some twenty years earlier as a result of the French invasion. Now he found that an affair that had dragged on for three years could approach a solution in as many days, for only three days after the première of his opera, he received an intimation from the Senate that he might consider the matter settled in his favour, and that the case would be cleared up by February. In fact it was not to be settled that soon, and it was two years before the Tsar finally ratified the State Council's decision in Glinka's favour, but the affair henceforth proceeded less slowly than it might otherwise have done.

Despite the new security of the Kapellmeistership, Glinka's existence was still troubled by debts, and by the end of 1837 he was begging his mother for help to pay off the 10,000 roubles he owed his friends. To this was added the deteriorating relationship with his wife. In March 1837 she nearly died of pneumonia, and her capricious behaviour on her recovery finally shattered any faith he had in marital bliss. He tried to assert his authority in his own house, but he had his mother-in-law to contend with, too, and his personality was not the sort which naturally commanded obedience, though he liked to believe that he acted with masterly dignity. When domestic scenes erupted, as they frequently did, his wife would dissolve in tears, his mother-in-law would become abusive until the rising power of her emotions reduced her utterances to a 'samovar-like hissing . . . but I', claimed Glinka,

made it a rule to preserve a deep silence, to pace up and down the room with measured steps and, leaning on my right leg, at each turn to describe carefully a

[1] GLN1, p. 174.

semicircle with the toe of the left, an action which enraged my mother-in-law unspeakably, though it quickly silenced her. Then I would turn to her and ask whether she had said all she had to say. Naturally she again became enraged, but not for long; exhaustion silenced her, and I would slowly draw on my gloves, take my hat and, bowing politely to my womenfolk, would go off to my friends, where I would sometimes stay several days, depending upon what sort of domestic scene it had been.[1]

This self-portrait, so unwittingly ridiculous, makes it abundantly clear that Glinka did nothing but exacerbate the situation with a show of infuriating pomposity. His wife was uneducated, he declared: 'Her understanding of music was bad—or, rather, she understood absolutely nothing except light romances. Everything that was elevated or poetic was quite beyond her.'[2] In fact, she cannot have been entirely without accomplishment as a singer, for at parties she could bear a soprano part in vocal quartets with her husband, Vorobyeva, and Petrov. The real trouble was that she and Glinka were quite incompatible. With the added handicap of an ever-present mother-in-law, the marriage was doomed. As for Glinka himself, he seems to have been quite incapable of seeing his own blame in the matter. Before long he was seeking consolation elsewhere, and his confession of a flirtation with Karolina Kolkovskaya, a fourteen-year-old singing pupil at the theatre school where he was now doing some teaching, would be outrageous if it were not so naïvely open. He revelled in the adulation poured upon him by Karolina and the other young girls. 'Sometimes I would play and sing; then my dear pupil's face would show unfeigned delight. The other pupils listened to me eagerly; even the very young girls would flock to the doors and listened breathlessly to my singing,' he recalled.[3] Karolina was a contralto, and early in 1838 he was inspired to compose for her a romance, 'Doubt', with harp and violin accompaniment. Serov recalled hearing Glinka and Vorobyeva perform this romance in its alternative version for voice and piano at a soirée in St. Petersburg a little after this. The song was quite new to him and he was deeply impressed: 'in the smooth, plastic, expressive melody [there was] a certain blending of Italian voluptuousness with a gloom, weariness, and sadness that was purely Slav,' he observed.[4] The main musical influence is unmistakably Bellini, but Serov's testimony to the Slavonic element in music which may sound to us so like simple Italian operatic pastiche should not be overlooked.

[1] GLNi, p. 176.　　[2] GLNi, p. 180.　　[3] GLNi, p. 181.　　[4] SVG, pp. 131–2.

The fact is that Glinka was incapable of coping with the emotional and practical problems of ordinary adult existence, and in personal matters he remained a child all his life. Nevertheless, the final break with his wife was still to come. Before Easter 1837 they had moved into an official flat in the choir building, and Glinka was quickly absorbed by a commission from the Smolensk nobility for a choral polonaise to be performed at a ball in honour of the Tsarevich, who was passing through the city. Glinka felt no great enthusiasm for the work, and he substituted a text by Sollogub for the one prescribed by the commissioners. Nevertheless, he discharged the task efficiently, and the Smolensk nobility must have been well satisfied with the effect of the music. The Tsarevich was obviously impressed, though possibly Glinka himself was a little galled that it was his wife who received the official acknowledgement of this compliment to royalty—namely, a ring sent to her through Zhukovsky. However, he had the satisfaction of a personal triumph when the Trio from Act I of *A Life for the Tsar* was very successfully performed at a patriotic concert in the middle of April. The Tsar was there and joined in the ovation, and his royal words were reported to Glinka by Aleksei Stuneyev: 'Glinka is a great master. It will be a pity if we are left with only this one opera.'[1]

In addition to financial and marital problems, Glinka's health was bad—or so he pleaded to Lvov, who agreed to give him three months' leave in which to recover his strength. Thus in May the Glinkas moved to a dacha between the Black River and the Viborg Way. Sometimes they invited friends to dinner to keep up the appearance of domestic harmony, but more often Glinka went out visiting alone—to the Odoyevskys, for instance, who were also in residence. Evidently the Princess Odoyevskaya had divined the situation in the Glinka household, but Glinka was grateful that she said nothing. He also often went into town to visit the Kukolniks, enjoying there the company of the Brotherhood, a motley and very numerous collection of musicians, writers, editors, teachers, actors, publishers, and so on, in whose company he found both praise and escape. During the next year or two the Brotherhood was to figure prominently in Glinka's social life, and in his *Memoirs* he wrote at some length of his happy times there. It was at the Kukolniks early in 1838 that he was deeply impressed by performances of the late Beethoven quartets led by the eminent Polish violinist, Lipinski, who was visiting the Russian capital. Aleksei Lvov, too, offered him

[1] GLN1, p. 177.

hospitality at his home; here, to the pleasure of his host's excellent performances of Haydn and Mozart, were joined the rare delights of his wine cellar.

During 1837 Glinka composed a duet, 'Adieu, petit réduit', evidently at the special request of two of the Tsar's daughters, the Grand Duchesses Mariya and Olga Nikolayevna, who gave him the French text which Pavel Dubrovsky later rendered into Russian. Glinka's music is exactly what a commission from such exalted personages might be expected to prompt. He obviously took some care over it, and the result is thoroughly pleasing, well oiled vocally, but of no real distinction. More important are his settings of Pushkin's 'Where is our rose?' and 'The night zephyr', written a year later. Little else came from that period, for his professional duties now left rather less time for composition. After the première of *A Life for the Tsar* he had a period of very close relations with the theatre director, Gedeonov, and he taught at the theatre school until early in 1838, when he quarrelled with Gedeonov over some misunderstanding. He also fell out with Carlo-Evazio Soliva, the school's teacher of singing and theory, for whom Glinka's respect was surprising, considering that Soliva was an Italian. He even thought of taking a course in 'the strict style' from Soliva. The rupture intervened before this could be started, but not until after Soliva had given Glinka the idea for a bass fragment in the new scene (Vanya at the gates of the monastery) which Glinka added to *A Life for the Tsar* in September 1837 (Ex. 35). This scene was

Ex.35. Andante moderato

requested for Vorobyeva by her husband, Petrov, who wanted to stage *A Life for the Tsar* for his benefit performance, but who knew that he could not count on a good audience unless there was some new piece of music to be heard in it. Kukolnik supplied the words, and both Petrov and Vorobyeva recalled that Glinka had composed the entire scene in one day, though Glinka himself confessed that he could not remember whether this was so.

Most of Glinka's professional time was naturally to be absorbed by his duties with the choir of the Imperial Chapel. On his appointment,

Aleksei Lvov had made a thorough examination of the capabilities of the choir, and had uncovered a deplorable state of affairs. Many of the men were so bad that he was for having them sacked, but Glinka determined to take them in hand himself. Some could not even read music or sing properly in tune. To correct these deficiences Glinka instituted a course in basic rudiments. At first some singers remained aloof, but according to Glinka, his determination and zeal paid off, and before many lessons were past, nearly all the men were attending. He was more than satisfied with the progress made; he soon had them competent enough to give a very successful performance of a double fugue by Sarti, and was spurred on to make his own first attempt at composing church music. The result was a 'Cherubim's Song' in C major, a trifle reflecting the traditional slow, resonant solemnity of the Orthodox church music tradition, making much use of sustained passing, auxiliary, or suspended dissonance. He also tried his hand at a choral fugue, but not surprisingly this was a failure.

Ever since his appointment Glinka had been expecting to be sent to the Ukraine to recruit new singers, but it was a year before this happened. On 4/16 April 1838 the commission was issued, and on 28 April/10 May he set out with two colleagues from the choir and two servants. In Smolensk he renewed acquintance with his old school-friend, Aleksandr Rimsky-Korsakov. Glinka was missing Karolina, and he asked Rimsky-Korsakov to write a romance expressing his longing. His friend obliged:

> Always, everywhere you are with me,
> Like an unseen companion,

—and Glinka forthwith set these lines to music and dispatched them to Karolina (later he was, a little ungallantly, to substitute verses by Pushkin, 'A fire of longing burns in my blood'). After making a detour to his old home at Novospasskoye, where he spent a blissful eight days with his family, he set out for the Ukraine on 14/26 May. Passing through Chernigov, Glinka and his colleagues recruited a number of moderately able boys, but their main base was to be Kachanovka, the estate of a landowning friend of Glinka, Grigory Tarnovsky. From here Glinka found himself strategically placed for an assault upon Pereyaslavl, where Gedeon, Bishop of Poltava, had a good choir. Glinka's arrival on Saturday evening caused great consternation to the town governor, who thought he was some government official on an enquiry. Next morning Glinka's two companions went to Mass, masquerading as two merchants who liked church music. After Mass they breakfasted with the unsuspecting bishop, heard the choir again, and made their final selection. Until this operation was completed, Glinka felt it wise not to undeceive the governor, and remained incommunicado. When he finally admitted him, he clearly enjoyed the governor's expressions of deference. Needless to say, the latter was filled with relief when he discovered the truth, and promised to help, since he disliked the bishop; as for Gedeon, his choir was so decimated as the result of this visit that for a long time he went about making open complaints to his friends about Glinka.

Having deposited his youthful spoils from Gedeon's choir at Kachanovka, Glinka and his companions set off for Kiev, where they made a magnificent catch in the person and voice of Semyon Gulak-Artemovsky, who was later to become one of the most noted interpreters of the hero's role in *Ruslan and Lyudmila*. Several young boys were also recruited from Poltava, Kharkov, and Akhtuirka. By now Glinka had enlisted nineteen boys and three men. His job was done, and he could have returned to St. Petersburg, but he was in no hurry. He had recovered from the depression that had afflicted him on leaving Novospasskoye, and he and his companions could get on with training their new charges just as well at Kachanovka. There was indeed much to make the place very attractive. Tarnovsky had very broad cultural interests, possessing his own serf theatre company and orchestra (from these a choir was drawn to sing in the church on Sundays), and he also boasted a fine collection of pictures. Kachanovka seems to have been a place to which artists and writers from the surrounding area frequently came. There was good company, therefore, and Glinka could continue the study of church music which he had set himself. As for Tarnovsky, he was delighted to have imperial singers performing with his own choir in his own church. Glinka was evidently not much impressed by some features of the rather rigorous existence of his host, being enthusiastic neither about the cooking nor about Tarnovsky's meticulous observation of midnight as the deadline for his social amusements. After the official bedtime some of the more sociable members of the party would sometimes repair to the orangery where Glinka had his quarters, and continue playing Russian and Ukrainian folk-songs until three or four in the morning, evidently to the disapproval of their host. But Tarnovsky was not otherwise unsociable, and afforded them plenty of entertainments like dancing and expeditions into the surrounding country and estates. Glinka's stay was obviously very pleasant. Among the acquaintances he made at Kachanovka were Vasily Sternberg, a talented painter who presented Glinka with a picture as a memento of his stay, and the Ukrainian poet, Viktor Zabella, two of whose poems ('The wind blows' and 'Sing not, O Nightingale') he set as folk-song stylizations of little musical value in themselves, but evidently close enough to the genuine article for the tune of 'The wind blows' to acquire some wide currency and to be mistaken some years later for the real thing.[1] At Kachanovka Glinka also had the pleasure of renewing acquaintance with another old school friend, Nikolai Markevich, an historian and keen amateur musician whom he visited for three days in mid-August. Markevich provided the text for a cantata, *Hymn to the master,* in honour of Tarnovsky, which Glinka set to music. But the greatest blessing for Glinka at Kachanovka proved to be the orchestra. Though small, it was not bad, even if some of the wind were out-of-tune and the leader-cum-director was hard of hearing. They were competent enough to play entr'actes from Beethoven's music to *Egmont* very respectably, and their performance of *Clärchen's death* moved Glinka so much that at the end he felt his pulse to see whether it was still beating! Yet the most useful service afforded by the orchestra was the first opportunity of hearing some of the pieces he had composed for his new opera, *Ruslan and Lyudmila,* based on Pushkin's poem.

It is not known exactly when Glinka started work on what was to prove his most important composition. A few months before the première of *A Life for the Tsar* Pushkin had said that 'he would like to see a lyric opera in which were united all the wonders of choreographic, musical, and decorative art,'[2] but the suggestion of *Ruslan and Lyudmila* as a subject for Glinka was made by the playwright, Shakhovsky, who thought that Vorobyeva should sing the part of Chernomor. Glinka heard Pushkin say of his own *Ruslan and Lyudmila* that there were things

---

[1] This was reported by Pavel Dubrovsky in his recollections of Glinka. 'It was in St. Petersburg in the winter of 1854. At a social gathering, a music lover whom I knew . . . began to talk about Mikhail Ivanovich's works somewhat equivocally, and even observed that his music to the song "The wind blows", etc., had been appropriated in its entirety from a Ukrainian folktune, and that he had credited himself with another's work. Knowing that this piece was an original work, I wanted to expose this great expert in music and foul Zoilus. Forthwith I wrote to Mikhail Ivanovich asking him about it, explaining to him what was up, and I quickly received from him the following reply: "Indeed the music of the song, 'The wind blows' (words by Zabella), was composed by me, and if it resembles a Ukrainian folk tune, it's not my fault."' (Quoted in GPSS10, pp. xxiii–iv.)

[2] Quoted by GLN1, p. 435.

in it that he would like to alter; tragically, however, only two months after the première of *A Life for the Tsar* Pushkin was killed in a duel, and Glinka never found out what these were. Whether there was any concrete proposal that they should collaborate as librettist and composer is not known. The process whereby Glinka's second opera came to be composed was as disorderly as that which had produced his first, and we will leave a full account of this to a later chapter. Suffice it to say here that after Pushkin's death Glinka may have abandoned the idea, for in June 1837 it was reported that he was thinking of setting some piece by Vladimir Sokolovsky, a young writer who had just been released from prison after serving a two-year sentence for writing a satire on the death of Aleksandr I and the accession of Nikolai I. The projected work was not an opera but an oratorio. The subject is not known, but on 26 July/ 7 August Sokolovsky reported that he had finished the libretto of the final part for Glinka. But nothing came of this project, and Glinka must quickly have reverted to his old scheme, for on 28 August/9 September it was disclosed in the St. Petersburg press that he was setting about composing *Ruslan and Lyudmila,* and before the end of the month he had already performed some pieces from it. What these pieces were is not recorded, but by the end of the year Glinka was thoroughly distracted by the undertaking: 'all my thoughts are fixed on the new opera I am writing,' he informed his mother.[1] Indeed, the project had become sufficiently public knowledge for the Tsar to enquire of Glinka how work was progressing. According to Glinka's *Memoirs,* the plan of *Ruslan and Lyudmila* was undertaken by Bakhturin who worked it out in a quarter of an hour while drunk. Towards the end of 1837 Glinka met the officer and poet, Valerian Shirkov, whom he remembered as 'a very educated and talented man; he drew splendidly and wrote verses with great facility'.[2] Shirkov wrote the words for Lyudmila's and Gorislava's cavatinas to see whether he would make a satisfactory librettist for Glinka. The latter was more than satisfied with the results, and Lyudmila's cavatina was publicly performed in St. Petersburg on 23 March/ 4 April 1838.[3] It was successful, but not as much as Glinka had hoped, though he was delighted by Lipinski's warm approval: 'How truly Russian this music is!' the Polish violinist had exclaimed.[4] Glinka could not recall when he had written the Persian Chorus and Chernomor's March, though it seems certain that the latter at least was composed at

---

[1] GLN2, p. 109.   [2] GLN1, p. 194.
[3] In his *Memoirs* Glinka stated that this had taken place in 1839.   [4] GLN1, p. 194.

Kachanovka.[1] Glinka was able to try out both there (with the bell part played on wine glasses), and it was during this visit that he composed Finn's Ballad which he then sang many times with Tarnovsky's players.

At the end of August Glinka had to prepare to return to St. Petersburg. Having arranged for transport and suitable clothing for his singers, he set out, enjoying some pleasant interludes on the way. He stopped for several days with Pyotr Skoropadsky, a cultivated amateur whom he had met at Kachanovka; Glinka and his company ate—and drank— their host out of house and home. At Orel the deputy governor entertained them splendidly, and a certain General Krasovsky provided them with ample excellent wine which made the journey to Moscow more tolerable. But the trip had its misfortunes. Some of the singers had eye trouble from the dust on the road, and were not ready for immediate presentation to the Tsar when they reached St. Petersburg on 1/13 September. Nevertheless, when this little ceremony finally took place, the Emperor expressed himself well satisfied with Glinka's finds, and in due course made him a gift of 1,500 roubles for his pains.[2]

This money was more than welcome, though Glinka admitted that he squandered it on dinners and weekly musical parties instead of applying it to more necessary purposes. He therefore had only himself to blame that he had to divert his creative attentions away from *Ruslan and Lyudmila* towards compiling a collection of musical pieces from which he hoped to gain some material profit. He met his mother immediately on his return, but it appears that she was taking a rather stronger line with his entreaties (he was even considering the purchase of an estate in the Ukraine with which he had been very much taken). A fortnight after his return he unburdened himself to his old friend, Markevich :'My conference with my mother did not have the hoped-for success . . . I am

---

[1] A. Orlova and E. Kann-Novikova have unearthed a curious circumstance that may be connected with the inspiration for this march. Writing to Sergei Sobolevsky, Markevich included the following: 'I have conferred the Crocus-mastership upon my candidate Zabella. You don't know what an important rank a Crocus-master holds . . . ask Glinka [about it]. He knows and understands it all, and has even composed a Crocus-master march, which you will all hear during his opera, *Ruslan and Lyudmila*.' (Quoted in KNG2, pp. 88–9.) There seems to be no doubt that Markevich had in mind one of the old musicians' guilds of the Ukraine, with the 'crocus-master' as its supposed head. These guilds held processions, usually on 6/18 January and 1/13 August. It seems possible, therefore, that some light-hearted recollections of these old guild processions may have been in Glinka's mind when writing Chernomor's March.

[2] In a letter to his mother of 29 November/11 December 1838 Glinka stated that these 1,500 roubles were a 'yearly allowance' (GLN2, p. 120).

now applying myself to the album about which I told you before in the Ukraine. In it will be twelve of my compositions. Ten are already prepared, and I hope the matter will not be delayed by the others. Meanwhile, one of the newly-composed romances appears to me to have succeeded. This new romance, which is also a little in the Spanish vein, is on words by Pushkin, "The night zephyr" . . . These slight, apparently innocuous works have hindered me from continuing with *Ruslan,* and I won't hide from you that I am often pensive and melancholy when I reflect that I must employ my poor muse as a means of existence.'[1]

The album, *A Collection of musical pieces compiled by M. Glinka,* appeared in five issues during 1839. Seventeen composers were represented, including Alyabyev, Verstovsky, Dargomuizhsky, and Aleksei Lvov. There were thirty-three compositions in all; of these Glinka contributed six piano pieces and six songs. Initially he was very crestfallen because he had trouble in finding a publisher, but when they were finally taken up, he was paid 1,000 roubles. The press received it favourably, and it was twice reprinted before the year was out. The piano pieces which Glinka contributed included two of his sets of variations composed some thirteen years earlier (the set on the Russian folk-song, 'Among the gentle valleys', and the Cherubini *Faniska* set), to which he added four new dances—namely, two waltzes, a galopade, and a set of five contredanses, all of which are as vacuous as anything in Glinka's piano output. The songs, all relatively recent, are a very different proposition, though they are unequal. There was the Bellinian 'Doubt', which he had composed for Karolina, and two Pushkin settings, 'The fire of longing burns in my blood', for which Karolina had again been responsible (Liszt was later to express a particular liking for this song),

Ex.36. [Moderato]

Vot is-pan- ka mo- lo-da-ya o - per- la-sya na— bal-kon.

(There is a young Spanish girl, leaning on the balcony.)

[1] GLN2, p. 118.

and the more characterful 'The night zephyr', not nearly as much in the
Spanish vein as some of the orchestral music that was to be elicited by
his stay in that country some six years later, though already exploiting
that juxtaposition of contrasting atmospheres which was to be employed
so much more elaborately in the Second Spanish Overture, *Recollection of a Summer Night in Madrid*. The harmonic language of Ex. 36 is
thoroughly characteristic of Glinka. But the real gem among these songs
is 'Where is our rose?', a simple piece which completely eclipses the very
ordinary Zabella folk-song stylizations, 'Sing not, O Nightingale' and
'The wind blows,' which complete Glinka's contribution to this collection. Something in Pushkin's tiny lyric must have touched Glinka
deeply:

> Where is our rose?
>   Tell me, my friends;
> Dead is our rose,
>   And beauty ends.
> But say not yet:
>   Joy passes by.
> Repeat not yet:
>   Thus youth will die.
> Sighing, recall
>   Faded joys sadly—
> And on the lily
>   Let thy gaze fall.

Glinka's response was as swift and intense as the original poem;
'Where is our rose?' is as perfect an epigram as you will find anywhere
in music. Glinka himself must have been pleased with it, for no less than
four autographs of it are known, though one of these has now disappeared.
One transposes the piece into G major, makes minor alterations to the
accompaniment, and adds two superfluous bars of tonic at the end.
Another autograph does added violence by prefiguring the opening
phrase with a two-bar piano introduction, and thickens the piano coda
with sixths in the right hand and a modified left hand part, all transposed
down an octave. But with epigrams like this, economy is perhaps even
more crucial than in larger pieces. The remaining extant version appears
to be the original; if so, it demonstrates that, as with Mussorgsky in his
songs, Glinka's first thoughts are the best. No apology is needed for
quoting it in its entirety (Ex. 37).
  Glinka's time in the next year or two was to be taken up with his

Ex.37. Con moto

increasing preoccupation with the composition of *Ruslan and Lyudmila,* with his decreasing interest in his post in the Imperial Chapel, and the perpetual problem of his deteriorating marital state. And there was, of course, the non-stop round of social engagements and contacts. There is no need to particularize these. With Glinka such things could be taken for granted, but the detailed recollections in his *Memoirs* of many of the people whose company he enjoyed is enough to show just how much these things meant to him at this troubled period of his life. In particular he found pleasure in 'the ample freedom of the dear, good, and talented Brotherhood'. He recalled how this fraternity would spend a typical day: 'in the mornings we all took tea, after which each provided for himself the rest of the day. I often visited my sister, Mariya Ivanovna. In the evening we gathered together and told incredible stories. Sometimes we had supper, and then it was a festival, not because of the viands and wine (we could not afford to be gourmets), but because of the varied and lively conversation. Most of the Brotherhood were regular members, but outsiders came too, though people who also were gifted.'[1] The picture he painted of his wife at this period is far less attractive. '[In the mornings] after she had got up, she would put on one of my dressing gowns. Unwashed, bleary-eyed, with her hair uncombed, with slippers on her bare feet, with a chibouque [a long tobacco pipe] between her teeth and curses on her tongue (when she dealt with the servants), she slopped from room to room and issued her orders.'[2] Having penned this uningratiating description, even Glinka confessed that he was going beyond the bounds of objective reportage. But he recalled with obvious pride an instance of his wife's discomfiture. Once she had scornfully observed in public that all poets and artists came to a bad end, like Pushkin, who was killed in a duel. 'Although I do not think myself cleverer than Pushkin, yet I shall not get a bullet through my head because of my wife,' Glinka had replied firmly—and plainly felt he had made a withering retort.[3]

In May 1839 the Glinkas moved to a new dacha. Glinka was now staying with his wife infrequently. He pleaded that his Chapel work kept him in the city, and he frequently visited his sister, Mariya, whose husband, Dmitri Stuneyev, had an appointment at the Smolny Monastery, which was now a girls' school. This institution had a small and very bad orchestra, but Glinka gave it some of his time, imposed a kind of order, and composed a Waltz in G to suit its capabilities. It was a fairly extended piece, attractive in its commonplace fashion, and was given its première at a ball in the Winter Palace on 4/16 July 1839. A Polonaise in E and a contredanse called *La Couventine,* which seem to have grown out of the same circumstances, were likewise first heard in public at another ball two days earlier. The latter piece is designed in five sections, each

[1] GLN1, pp. 198–9. [2] GLN1, p. 198. [3] GLN1, p. 197.

reflecting one humour (*la gaité, la naïveté, la vivacité, la sentimentalité,* and *la tendresse*), but the music suggests that Glinka's novice, doubtless not a genuine religious one, but an imaginary pupil of the Smolny 'Monastery', was no more than an empty-headed flibbertigibbet. Glinka also found consolation in another affair, for Karolina was replaced by Yekaterina Kern, the daughter of Anna Kern, whom he had long known. He first met Yekaterina at Easter at his sister's. Glinka was in an agitated, nervous condition when he arrived. When his eyes first lighted upon Yekaterina, he saw that she was not well—'there was even an element of suffering apparent in her pale face. As I was pacing up and down my glance came to rest upon her involuntarily; her clear expressive eyes, her unusually well-shaped figure (*élancé*), and a charm and dignity of a special kind emanating from her whole being attracted me more and more.'[1] His spirits revived; before the evening was out he was satisfied that he had made his feelings unmistakably apparent, and before long Yekaterina responded fully.

Glinka seems to have made no secret of the affair, which makes his expressions of wounded pride over his wife's infidelity sound not only unreasonable but positively hypocritical. Glinka was simply incapable of seeing his wife's failings reflected in his own behaviour. He had for some time suspected her of misconduct, but when his brother-in-law, Yakov Sobolevsky, told him bluntly of his wife's infidelity, his anger was unbounded. It was intolerable that people should know he was a cuckold, and immediately he wanted to be rid of Mariya Petrovna. Before 1839 was out he had the evidence he needed. For three years now he had been supervising the arrangements for the education of his youngest brother, Andrei, and the care and affection with which he discharged this duty is one of the more attractive threads in his life at this time. Then, on 25 August/6 September 1839, Andrei suddenly died. Glinka, who was superstitious, later recalled that there had been omens of an impending disaster. He was greatly distressed by Andrei's death, obtained a month's leave from the Chapel, and set off for Novospasskoye. It was here that Sobolevsky gave him the first open suggestion of Mariya Petrovna's infidelity. Glinka's pride was badly stung. Goaded by Sobolevsky's assertion that he would still do nothing about it, he exploded angrily and returned to St. Petersburg, hoping to catch his wife unawares. Evidently she had been forewarned, and the scheme failed—but four weeks later he had the evidence he wanted. 'Once I fell asleep in the

[1] GLNi, p. 196.

room in which my wife and mother-in-law were. I can sleep soundly through noise and banging, but a whisper or a light rustle will suddenly wake me—which is what happened then. The old Finnish woman, my mother-in-law's servant, entered and going up to her, began to whisper quietly in German. I feigned sleep, and even pretended to snore, meanwhile endeavouring to catch every word of their secret conversation. At last I heard with my own ears how my mother-in-law, together with the old woman, was arranging a meeting between her daughter and her lover. This was enough for me; without saying a word about it, I said farewell to my wife next morning and went off to Nikolai Stepanov, who knew all about my intentions at that time.'[1]

On the evening of 6/18 November Glinka wrote to his wife informing her of his decision:

Suspicion which has crept into my heart, and reasons for which I am not bound to render account to anyone, forbid me to live with you any longer. Mutual trust—the foundation of marital bliss—has long ceased to exist between us. We must part, but part as befits honourable people, without quarrels, noise, and mutual reproaches. I pray Providence to protect you from new misfortunes. And I, on my side, will take all measures to provide as far as possible for your future state. But know that tears, explanations, regrets, questions, the intercessions of relatives and people who have power in society will not shake my intention, and the more insistent your attempts at a reconciliation, the quicker will I break the last bond that fate has made between us.[2]

Mariya Petrovna was not greatly disturbed by this insufferably stuffy letter. Glinka was disappointed, but when the next day he sent for certain personal possessions, she realized that he was serious. 'Then she cried in real earnest; they say that it even spoiled her appearance,' he noted maliciously.[3] A few days later an attempt to persuade him to return to his wife was made by a certain Sumarokov, a member of the Senate, who was very fond of Glinka and Mariya Petrovna. Sumarokov engineered a meeting with the priest who had both taught and married him, but Glinka claimed he was able to confound all their arguments. In fact, he felt thoroughly self-righteous about his own position. He straightway wrote home to his mother reporting what he had done (quoting the letter to his wife in full), and the reading of this makes an even more distasteful impression than the preceding account, taken from his *Memoirs*.

[1] GLN1, p. 202.   [2] GLN2, p. 128.   [3] GLN1, p. 203.

I decided to act swiftly, discreetly, and as a Christian and an honourable man ought. God help me; having chosen an opportune time, I sent a letter, and on my side everything proceeded quietly, discreetly and honourably. But the reckless conduct of my mother-in-law and, I admit, the cunning of Mariya Petrovna served as a fresh proof that I had acted on just grounds, and that I had nothing with which to reproach myself.[1]

However, if Glinka thought himself blameless, feminine society in St. Petersburg did not. Outraged womanhood rallied behind Mariya Petrovna so effectively that Glinka felt compelled to stay indoors to avoid trouble. He spent this time with Nikolai Stepanov, whiling away the time with visits from trusted friends, with musical activities (Pyotr Stepanov particularly recalled Glinka's delight in Bach fugues during this period), and with drawing (especially trees). Glinka recalled a room in Stepanov's apartment 'covered all over with drawings of devils and caricatures done by Nikolai Stepanov himself on the chequered black and white background.'[2] A less attractive memory was Stepanov's bulldog which disgraced itself every night so that the room had to be cleaned out in the morning. A month later he wrote to his mother to say that he was still avoiding society. The content of these letters home at this time is a mixture of starchy self-righteousness, fulsome filial noises, plaintive appeals to his mother to come to St. Petersburg and comfort him—and urgent requests for money. She sent him 1,000 roubles, but it was not enough. Finally in early January she arrived in the capital, stayed a month, and then bore him off to Novospasskoye for three months while the scandal died down.

Nor were his marriage affairs the only thing that came to a crisis at this time. Soon after returning from the Ukraine in September 1838 his interest in the musical affairs of the Chapel had declined. True, two months after his return he had gone to the church in the Anichkinsky Palace to attend Aleksei Lvov's wedding, and returned there frequently after this to hear the services, but one suspects that this was less enthusiasm for church music than a wish that the Tsar, who likewise attended these services, should notice him. The beginning of 1839 was a very hectic time for Glinka. He resented that he was now completely distracted

[1] GLN2, p. 128. The break with Mariya Petrovna came as no surprise to Glinka's mother: 'I did not expect a better end to it, though I did not think it would have come so soon,' she wrote to one of her daughters. (Quoted in KNG3, p. 127.)

[2] GLN1, p. 204. Stepanov's substantial gifts as a caricaturist can be seen from the example reproduced in this book. They are selected from his humorous series of watercolours of incidents from Glinka's life.

from his work on *Ruslan and Lyudmila*. He recalled what used to happen at the time when he was working on Gorislava's cavatina.[1]

I always composed only in the morning, after taking tea, and I was constantly torn away from this cavatina. I would not manage to write one or two pages before a servant would appear—an N.C.O. who would stand to attention, and respectfully report: "Your worship! The singers have assembled and are waiting for you." Who was waiting? Who had sent the servant? To this day I do not know; all I know is that sometimes when I got to the rehearsal room, I would also find that Lvov was already there, who would offer me his hand in a friendly way.[2]

Lvov certainly noticed his waning enthusiasm after his return from the Ukraine, and when Glinka fell ill in 1839 he visited him and suggested, very politely, that he was not attending carefully to his service. Glinka said nothing, but admitted that after he had recovered, he 'began to visit the singers *less frequently than before*'.[3] By October Lvov was threatening to send him on another recruiting trip to the Ukraine in the following spring. Finally, overburdened by the aftermath of his rupture with his wife, Glinka told Lvov he wished to resign on the grounds of ill-health. Lvov persuaded him to stay on until 18/30 December so that he might fulfil the time qualification for him to retire with the rank of collegiate assessor. Having done this, Glinka promptly left the service.

[1] Though in his *Memoirs* Glinka assigned these events to the period after his return from the Ukraine, it is possible that they may have happened a year earlier, when he first enlisted Shirkov as a possible librettist, since Gorislava's cavatina was the movement upon which the two started their collaboration.

[2] GLN1, pp. 193–4.

[3] GLN1, p. 196.

8/Second Opera

GLINKA was now wifeless and jobless, and the beginning of 1840 found him in the lowest of spirits. Yet in the end the release from his professional duties at the Imperial Chapel and from the tensions and turmoils of his domestic situation was to create the conditions under which he could once again hope to settle down to the major task of completing an opera. First, however, he needed to recover from the strains of the last three years, and other compositional projects were to intervene before work on *Ruslan and Lyudmila* could start again in earnest. While he was in 'retirement' following the break with his wife Yekaterina became seriously ill, but this was kept from him to spare him another burden of worry. He had already composed the Valse-Fantaisie for her, and when she recovered he also wrote for her the orchestral Waltz in B flat, and set the romance, 'I recall a wonderful moment', a poem which Pushkin had written some fifteen years earlier for Yekaterina's mother. Glinka's setting marks a return to the most overtly sentimental manner of some of his earlier romances, a manner from which he had largely retreated since working on *A Life for the Tsar*. Our hardbitten age finds it difficult to do justice to songs of this type. We fly from anything that savours of sentimentality, and it cannot be denied that this sort of song is essentially soft-centred and thus restricted in its expressive potential. Yet Glinka handled songs like this excellently. He meant every note of it; take it on its own stylistic terms, and it reveals it-self as a most sensitive and worthy response to Pushkin's poem. Ex. 38 sets out the conclusion of the middle section and the return of the open-ing with its former tonic-pedal bass now replaced by a more mobile line. Though basically a ternary structure, Glinka was not content to round off the song with a straightforward repetition of the first section. Instead, he brought back only the first half of the song's opening section,

(In a lonely place, in the darkness of imprisonment, my days
have dragged themselves out quietly, without a god, without
inspiration, without tears, life, or love. My love has begun to
awaken, and you have appeared once again here, like a
fleeting vision, like a genius of rare beauty.)

then allowing the music to follow a new course beyond this so that the
emotional experience might grow to the very end.

Glinka's fleeting setting of Koltsov's 'If I shall meet you', which
Yekaterina had selected for him, is a less notable achievement than 'I
recall a wonderful moment', but still rather touching. During 1839,
he also composed a nocturne in F minor, *La séparation*, for his sister
Yelizaveta; a second nocturne, *Le regret*, remained unfinished, and he
used its melody in 1840 for the romance, 'To Molly'. 1839 also saw the
composition of the songs, 'Wedding song' (or 'The North Star') and
'The bird-cherry tree is blossoming', both of which, it appears, were
composed at Vladimir Odoyevsky's request for a charity concert—
though it is possible, if a note in the autograph is to be believed, that the
former was written on the occasion of the wedding of H.R.H. the
Grand Duchess Mariya Nikolayevna which took place in that year, and
which Glinka attended ex officio. This is credible enough, for Glinka used
a traditional wedding tune, 'From behind the mountains, the high mountains', the same that he was to apply again with far greater stylistic

assurance in *Kamarinskaya*. 'The bird-cherry tree' is an innocuous piece that comes close to Glinka's folk-song stylizations. Yet, with the exception of the Valse-Fantaisie, and 'I recall a wonderful moment', none of these compositions is of any real permanent value, and the instrumental pieces are mostly banal. It was not that he was diverting his major creative energies into *Ruslan and Lyudmila,* for not a stroke of work was done on the new opera throughout the whole of 1839. The three months he was to spend at Novospasskoye in early 1840 were troubled ones, during which he read much but neglected his music completely. Hempel had to accompany him when he returned to St. Petersburg early in May. Soon he installed himself with his sister, Mariya, and spent a good deal of time studying water-colour painting with his librettist, Shirkov—without much success, he admitted. He was even less successful when, at Shirkov's suggestion, he attempted to use the *Kamarinskaya* tune as the basis of a piece for piano, three hands, and he tore it up. But at least he was now doing a little composing, and while out walking on 21 May/ 2 June, the theme of a bolero suddenly came to him. He used it as the point of departure for a piano piece, which came to the ears of Herman, who directed the orchestra at the Pavlovsk pleasure grounds. Herman orchestrated the Bolero along with Glinka's Valse-Fantaisie, and performed both pieces very successfully. The bolero tune also found service in another guise, for Nestor Kukolnik fitted words to it, 'O my beautiful maid', and then offered to provide further lyrics for Glinka to set. As a result, Platon Kukolnik suggested that Nestor and Glinka should publish a collection of songs. If we may believe the gossipy Strugovshchikov, Platon was an opportunist and unscrupulous exploiter of others. 'Even now I cannot recall without a bitter smile to what subterfuges Platon Kukolnik resorted in order to make his brother, Nestor, write several romances each week, and Glinka set them to music.'[1] Be this as it may, Nestor and Glinka worked quickly, and thus was born the set of twelve romances, *A Farewell to St. Petersburg*—a title prompted by Glinka's own wish to get away from the capital. As Glinka had some spare melodies to hand he was able to produce the complete volume without much difficulty in six weeks.

A Farewell to St. Petersburg contains nothing that represents Glinka at his very best, nor anything which shows him at his worst. It is all second-class stuff, with tunes distinctive enough to linger in the memory, but not so demanding as to prevent them appealing to a wide public.

[1] SGV, p. 708.

Its success was not surprising. Kukolnik proved a good partner to Glinka in this enterprise, for though he may have been a poor playwright (as we shall see a little later), he could measure up to the relatively undemanding task of fitting words to existing music. In fact it is not always clear which came first, the music or the text, for although in five cases (Nos. 1, 7, 9, 11, and 12) Kukolnik's texts already existed before ever Glinka set to work on this collection, Glinka also used material from an existing piece of his own to set the penultimate of these. Unfortunately the original, a piano nocturne, *Le Regret*, has disappeared, so we have no way of knowing how much, if at all, he altered his original. Likewise the melody of the plangent 'Hebrew Song' (No. 2) was based upon one of the studies which Glinka composed in 1833 for his Berlin Jewess, Maria. The volume was rounded off with a *pièce d'occasion*, a 'Song of farewell', which is almost certainly the one Glinka performed at the party his friends gave him on 9/21 August, before he left St. Petersburg.[1] In addition in this motley assortment of pieces there is the Bolero (No. 3) which isn't really at all Spanish, and could almost as easily have been labelled a Polonaise (it is very like his song of 1832, 'The Conqueror'), and an impressive dramatic ballad (No. 7), called 'Fantasia', which contains not a hint of Spanish stylization, despite the Spanish locale of the text (this piece gains an extra overall tension by finishing out-of-key (F major instead of A major)). Other pieces have Italianate musical roots—the Barcarolle (No. 8) and the Cavatina (No. 4), in which, as even more in 'To Molly' (No. 11), Glinka mines that vein of Bellinian cantilena to which he turned all too readily. Opera buffa provides the main root of the railway song (No. 6), an infectious patter piece cast in ABABA form, in which the eager anticipation of the traveller in the verse sections (B) alternates with the rattling of the train (A). The only piece with some Russianness in it is 'The Lark' (No. 10), though even here it is very diluted. This proved to be the most popular piece in the volume; doubtless its dutiful ornithological twitterings scored a quick success with an audience that responded readily to the prettily picturesque, but the tune is really

---

[1] The evidence bearing upon the order of composition of text and music is sometimes confused, even where it exists at all. According to an article which Kukolnik published in *The Artistic Gazette* of 1/13 September 1840, and which Stasov quoted in his biography of Glinka (SG, pp. 593–5), he (Kukolnik) added words to existing music in the case of Nos. 4, 5, and 6, but the evidence of his diary suggests that he did this for Nos. 5, 6, 8, 9, and 10. Kukolnik's diary is notoriously unreliable, and since it is known that the text of No. 9 was certainly in existence before Glinka started his musical settings of these texts, the validity of this evidence is in doubt. *A Farewell to St. Petersburg* was to have included 'Ilinishna's Song' from *Prince Kholmsky*, but this was finally omitted.

rather undistinguished, more so than the tremulously fleeting setting of the romance from Kukolnik's longer poem, 'David Rizzio' (No. 1). One of the most attractive pieces in the collection is the Cradle Song (No. 5), which starts ordinarily enough, but which introduces a nice modal turn at bar five, and then unwinds for a further dozen bars beyond the end of Ex. 39 to produce an admirably broad melody. For

Ex.39.

(Sleep, my angel, do not open your clear eyes. Lulla, lullaby.
If you do not sleep, time flies away.)

verse two Glinka moves into the major to devise a new but related twenty-bar tune. It is a similar melodic expansiveness that turns the rum-ti-tum melodies of Nos. 9 and 12 into distinctive paragraphs. Glinka possessed something of Verdi's ability to write a good public tune. Ex. 40 opens ordinarily enough, but the simple chromaticism of

(Farewell, dear friends! Life will scatter us in all directions; everything is like this. But wherever I may be, I shall remember you and feel melancholy. Nowhere are days bright for ever; everywhere is melancholy, everywhere languor.)

bar three adds an extra interest, and the melody gains in character, aided by the simple but positive harmonic direction. Ex. 40 contains only the first half of the tune; by the end the whole has added up to something quite substantial, which skirts pomposity without ever achieving real nobility.

It is melody, too, that is the lifeblood of the Valse-Fantaisie. This was Glinka's first complete, purely instrumental work of any real importance, and he thought well enough of it to include it in his Paris concert of 1845, though he considered that none of the pieces in this concert was among his most important works. Quite certainly he must have orchestrated it himself for this concert, and he certainly scored it again in the last year of his life. Like the larger Chopin waltzes, it is simply a series of self-contained sections, structural coherence being achieved by the recurrence of some sections, and also by the incorporation of the introduction's five-quaver figure (sometimes inverted) into later passages. The attractiveness of the Valse-Fantaisie lies especially in the variety of phrase structure, as when the twelve-bar sentence of the main theme (basically organized in three-bar groups) loses a bar on its repetition (Ex. 41a), or when the eight-bar phrase of a later section (Ex. 41b) refuses to be neatly divided in the middle. Sustained inner-part melodies, which contrast with the more mobile waltz-theme, are a constant attractive feature of the piece.[1] The engaging freshness of Glinka's tunes, coupled with the clear orchestration in which he finally presented them, makes what is essentially popular music well worth a hearing in the concert hall. The importance of such music for Tchaikovsky, the composer of ballets, can hardly be overestimated.

Glinka's health problems were not confined to himself alone. Yekaterina, though now much better, was far from well. A doctor diagnosed incipient tuberculosis, and prescribed a warmer, more healthy climate. Glinka wanted above all to go abroad with Yekaterina, but his mother, after expressing (rather surprisingly) some initial approval, then strongly opposed this scheme. The Kerns were in some financial difficulty, and Glinka, abandoning the idea of travelling to Europe, obtained money from his mother so that they (the Kerns) might go to the south of Russia, where they had relatives. The money was paid through Sobolevsky to forestall any attempt by Mariya Petrovna to claim half of it. Equipping the Kerns—and himself—with carriages, he was ready to leave by mid-August. He was still not happy: 'I wasn't

---

[1] These are not present in Glinka's original piano version from which Ex. 41 is taken.

exactly ill, nor exactly well,' he remembered. 'There was a heavy burden of grief on my heart, and gloomy undefined thoughts involuntarily crowded into my mind.'[1] Yekaterina was becoming jealous (we are not told why) and was burdening him with reproaches. Still, the Brotherhood prepared an elaborate and secret farewell party, including a three-act 'Ceremony of Send-off', in which Glinka found himself the leading performer. On the next day, 10/22 August,[2] he left St. Petersburg, met the Kerns at Gatchina, and went with them to Katezhna. During the journey he gave his companions audible proof of his new preoccupation with *Ruslan and Lyudmila*, for he delighted them by singing extracts from his opera. Only the day before he had written to Shirkov, enclosing the scheme for Act IV, adding: 'My muse is gaining strength. I have never written so much, and have never before felt such inspiration.'[3] At Katezhna he parted from the Kerns. They set off for Vitebsk, while he directed himself to Novospasskoye.

And now he really tried to apply himself seriously to composing *Ruslan and Lyudmila*. His new and strong creative urges swamped his regrets that he had not been able to travel to Europe with Yekaterina. He decided it would take about two months to write out what he had already sketched, and then he would need Act V from Shirkov. His health began to recover. In late September he returned to the capital, caught a chill, and settled in with the Kukolniks.

No sooner had he installed himself, than work on *Ruslan and Lyudmila* was again interrupted. Nestor wanted incidental music for his play, *Prince Kholmsky*, and between 19 September/1 October and 15/27 October Glinka composed an overture, four entr'actes, and two songs to add to the *Hebrew Song* he had already done to Kukolnik's words. It was the most intensive period of creative activity in the whole of his life, but it was another year before the play reached the stage. Glinka's overture and entr'actes were to be first heard at a concert in March 1841, and Kukolnik's play was at last given on 30 September/12 October 1841. It was a failure and was withdrawn after three performances. Glinka's music seems hardly to have been noticed and fell into oblivion with the play, never to be performed again in the composer's lifetime.

Kukolnik was a playwright whose popular success with his romantic historical dramas in the 1830s and 1840s was too large for any present-day historian of Russian literature to be able to avoid noticing him,

---

[1] GLN1, p. 206.　　[2] Not 11/23, as stated in the *Memoirs*.　　[3] GLN2, p. 138.

however unflattering may be the judgements he is impelled to pass. Some of the characters and events in *Prince Kholmsky* were based upon fact. In 1470 a certain Zachariah, a learned Jew and astrologer, had arrived in Novgorod and initiated there the so-called Heresy of the Judaists. Kukolnik transferred Zachariah's activities to Pskov, and provided him with a daughter, Rachel, who falls secretly in love with the other main historical figure of the play, Prince Daniil Kholmsky, whom Tsar Ivan III sent on a campaign against the Livonian Knights. During this campaign Kholmsky compromised himself through his uncertain loyalty, and was restored to grace only after he had given a written pledge of fidelity to the Tsar. Kukolnik's drama is set in 1474. At the start the Livonian Order are menacing Pskov, the inhabitants have sent to Moscow for help, and Kholmsky has been despatched with 50,000 men. The Order is weak and the stars have foretold its end (astrology plays a large part in Kukolnik's concoction); what it needs above all is to divert or, at least, to delay Kholmsky's attack. Schlummermaus, a baron of the Order and a ruthless intriguer, has a sister, Adelheid, who combines the warlike attainments of an Amazon with staggering feminine charms. Adelheid loves Knyazhich, a merchant of Pskov, and engineers her own capture by Kholmsky's forces so that she may see her beloved. When she is brought before Kholmsky he falls desperately in love with her, and Schlummermaus, who heads the delegation sent to parley with Kholmsky, forces her to feign love for Kholmsky in order to buy time for his side. Zachariah, who is also in Schlummermaus's power, is drawn into the conspiracy to persuade the besotted Kholmsky to desert the Tsar in favour of a joint rulership (with the Order's Master) of the Baltic States, and the city republics Novgorod and Pskov; this will create conditions in which Kholmsky may marry Adelheid. The plan is foiled by the refusal of the citizens of Pskov to turn traitor to the Tsar. In the last of the five acts Sereda, whose role is like that of the Shakespearian fool, tries to comfort the dejected Kholmsky, and tells him how Rachel, in the desperation of her secret love, has cast herself into an icy river (after all the correct show of wild distraction). Her body is borne off by the Judaists, and Kholmsky is so overwhelmed at the thought of this secret devotion that he swears he will recover her corpse. This series of events has been contorted into a creaking plot (the preceding summary does less than justice to the side-alleys of the tale), with dramatic posturing, implausible happenings, and characters who are either faceless or ridiculous. Nevertheless, Kukolnik's greatest riches are still in store. Kholmsky thinks that he has Adelheid, and she is being prepared for the wedding. Schlummermaus no longer supports him as her bridegroom, but he also reveals his violent opposition to Knyazhich as a brother-in-law, not because Knyazhich is a merchant (Adelheid scotches that one by revealing that their own great-grand-father had been a sailor from Hamburg, and that their own title had been bought for them), but because Knyazhich, far from being a mere merchant, had once defeated Schlummermaus in battle. Schlummer-maus had fled, and Adelheid had rushed up to save her brother, only to fall instantly in love with his assailant. Kholmsky overhears enough to know where Adelheid's true love is placed, and to realize how she has been deceiving him. When Schlummermaus turns to Knyazhich and accuses him of being a secret Judaist, Kholmsky sees his chance, and urges that Knyazhich should be killed; the play's climax has arrived:

'We will die . . . united in a kiss. Farewell for a moment!' cries Adelheid. But Kholmsky is unrelenting.

'Prince! I am yours! . . . I am prepared to suffer anything in return for his life.' Kholmsky remains inexorable.

'Mercy!' screams Adelheid, clutching his knees.

'Stop!' commands Sereda: 'He is not a Judaist!'

'Not a Judaist?' exclaims the whole assembled company.

No; it is Schlummermaus who is the real Judaist, and his devilish plot is revealed.

'God Almighty!' ejaculates Adelheid.

'I cannot live without Adelheid,' declares Knyazhich, 'so now take this sin upon your soul which is already burdened with treachery. I am a secret Judaist. Kill me!'

'O, if that is so,' screams Adelheid, 'then I am a secret Judaist. To the stake quickly! Let us be wed in death!'

'I understand everything,' interjects Kholmsky (it is good to know that someone's wits have been able to cope with this torrent of incident). However, like the good chap he really is at heart, he recognizes his own guilt, begs Adelheid's forgiveness, links her hand to Knyazhich's, abases himself further, falls prostrate, then scrambles up hurriedly as the Tsar's emissaries enter. The war with the Order is called off, Schlum-mermaus is led off to get his deserts, and Kholmsky's punishment turns out to be the gift of a sword from the Tsar. Under the strain of this unexpected turn of events, he confesses all.

'I must be punished on the place of execution,' he pleads.

'No. A childish prank does not merit punishment,' replies the boyars' spokesman. . . .

The only characters who emerge momentarily with any credibility from this farrago of nonsense are the Jewish household; the merchant Zachariah, kindly despite his part in the conspiracy, his daughter Rachel, and their gossipy, crotchety Russian housekeeper, Ilinishna. In the second scene of Act II, Ilinishna taunts Rachel by declaring that, while Russians can let themselves go in dance and song, Jews are incapable of real gaiety. Rachel forthwith seizes a bandura and tries to disabuse her, but after her song Ilinishna triumphantly declares that Rachel has proved her point for her, and goes on to demonstrate just what merry singing is. Glinka set both these songs, providing Rachel with a plangent little modal piece founded upon one of the studies he had composed in 1833 for his Berlin Jewess, Maria. Ilinishna may have claimed that her type of song yielded more enjoyment than Rachel's, but the Russian song Glinka gave her has less individuality, and it was Rachel's song that he used as the foundation of the orchestral prelude to the act, though he re-worked a good deal of it, and interjected two agitated semiquaver passages. The orchestral score gives no hint of the dramatic content of any of the entr'actes, but when Vladimir Stasov commented upon them in his biography of Glinka, he was probably speaking from a direct knowledge of the composer's intentions. Stasov stated that this first entr'acte was both a portrayal of the Jewish nationality in general, and of Rachel in particular. Glinka's rough-hewn presentation of diverse musical elements makes an excellent dramatic prelude. Likewise the entr'acte before Act III opposes brusque eruptions to a gently flowing $\frac{6}{8}$ tune, whose fragile charm could easily become insipid, were it not for the simple woodwind counterpoints that Glinka sets against it on its repetitions (Ex. 42). In the coda the two elements are nicely drawn together. In this entr'acte, wrote Stasov,

we meet for the first time the hero of the play, the young, ardent Prince Kholmsky himself, at that moment when he tells the cunning coquette, Baroness Adelheid, of his love. He does not sense that she is deceiving him, he believes her assurances, but his proud nature cannot remain solely in the rosy chains of love: constantly his ambitious designs awaken in him . . . In the present entr'acte these two elements comprise the whole content; after the sounds of passionate, amorous languor there follow gusts of grandeur and of proud expectations.[1]

[1] SG, p. 611.

The one remaining vocal movement, 'Rachel's Dream', occurs at the beginning of the second scene of Act III. Her astrologizing father is pensively surveying the stars when she enters, does not notice him, and recounts in song her nightmare of how her lover had responded to her embrace by pushing her into a river. As he did this he had laughed, but she still loved him, though she had perished. After a sombre introduction, Glinka set the narrative itself in tormented music (Ex. 43) whose quality Kukolnik for once nearly matched, for the scene which

(I saw him, my betrothed, in a quiet happy dream, somewhere in a heavenly land.)

follows is one of the few moments where the playwright actually achieves some genuine dramatic pathos. Zachariah guesses something at least of the significance of her song, and passionately tries to dissuade her from loving a Gentile: 'Love! Love! O my daughter, it is not for us to love, we tearful tribe of suffering mortals!' Glinka's two songs for Rachel are quite enough to establish her personality clearly.

The entr'acte before Act IV is a brisk march, not as individual as Chernomor's March, which Glinka had already prepared for *Ruslan and Lyudmila*, but still full of character. 'The music portrays that moment when the Russian warriors, commanded till then by Prince Kholmsky, have heard at the Assembly of Pskov from the Prince's lips of his intention to secede from his native land and create a new independent state,' recorded Stasov. 'His bodyguard flee in horror and indignation from their perfidious leader; trumpets and drums sound out their march; everywhere disordered, rather agitated activity is heard; a crowd of people whisper together gloomily and suspiciously about the unprecedented news (C minor trio) and the army leaves the Assembly to the fading sounds of the assembly bell (the measured strokes of the drums), the thunderous stroke of which opens the entr'acte.

'The fourth entr'acte . . . presents Kholmsky to us in, as it were, a final, last soliloquy. All his clear hopes have flown away like dust at the first contact with reality . . . each sound in Glinka's scene expresses cold horror and despair . . . But Glinka's nature could not finish with a dissonance, and he concluded his scene with something in the manner of an apotheosis of reconciliation . . . This entr'acte is one of Glinka's greatest compositions.'[1] Certainly the agitated brooding and dissonant hammering of the last entr'acte (Ex. 44a) throw into extra prominence the elegiac D major coda, which must surely have been in Tchaikovsky's mind when he composed his *Romeo and Juliet*. Tchaikovsky, like Stasov, had a great admiration for Glinka's *Kholmsky* music, even

Ex.44. **Allegro con spirito**

a)

judging that in this final entr'acte 'Glinka shows himself one of the most substantial symphonists of our time'.[1] This, like so many nineteenth century Russian pronouncements on Glinka, is an overstatement, but no more wrong than the judgement implicit in the music's complete neglect in the West. Admittedly the entr'actes are bound to sound less convincing in a concert performance, for they were conceived in relation to a particular theatrical context, and were intended to prepare succinctly for something larger that follows, rather than to offer a full and rounded experience in themselves; but the Overture would suffer less by such exposure. Glinka based it on two of the three vocal pieces of the production; 'Rachel's dream' (see Ex. 43) provided the first

[1] Quoted in LPG1, p. 400.

subject, and 'Ilinishna's song' the second. After a martial maestoso introduction (Ex. 44b), there follows a straightforward agitato vivace, in which the transition between the subjects (Ex. 44c) echoes the thematic shape of the introduction's motif, and foreshadows, too, the final entr'acte (see Ex. 44a). The Overture's coda also matches the coda of the same entr'acte, and the opening of the development presages the introduction to 'Rachel's dream'; such inter-relationships as these are obviously invaluable in establishing some sort of organic connection between the widely scattered movements of Glinka's score, as well as having a telling dramatic effect. Just before the Overture's coda Glinka neatly counterpoints the two subjects to each other, as well as drawing in the introduction's motif (see Ex. 44d). The Overture is a concise piece, lacking the sparkle and melodic distinction of its counterpart to *Ruslan and Lyudmila*, but still thoroughly effective, and very well worth a hearing.

The composition of the *Prince Kholmsky* music was not the only interruption to work on *Ruslan and Lyudmila* in 1840. In November Glinka again fell ill—dangerously so, he later recalled, vividly describing the spectacular rash that broke out all over him. Yet he had recovered sufficiently to accompany the great Pasta at a soirée on 2/14 December. It seems that since the separation from his wife he had been leading a much quieter life, but in his *Memoirs* there is to be detected a certain contentment with this more ordered existence. It is even more explicitly expressed in a letter to his mother written on 8/20 October: 'Despite my ailments I am leading a quiet and peaceful life—and, best of all, an untroubled one. Although my heart is somewhat empty, music gives me inexpressible comfort. I work almost the whole morning; in the evening the conversation of dear friends soothes me. If it goes on like this next year, the opera will be almost finished by the spring.'[1] Yakov looked after him faithfully; a relative of the Engelhardts, Pyotr Ruindin, often kept him company at home, while the Engelhardts themselves sent their fur-upholstered carriage for him, together with a fur coat, so that he might dine with them. Glinka expressed his gratitude by composing a romance, 'How sweet it is to be with you', on words by Ruindin. This is one of Glinka's relatively few minor key romances, and a piece whose yearning is strongly reinforced by the chromaticism of its solo piano passages. Among the others he visited were his married cousin, Sofiya Ivanovna, the companion of his music-making during

[1] GLN2, p. 146.

his school days, of whom he must have been very fond, for he was at one time to propose making over to her his share of the estate in the event of his death.

At about this time Pavel, the eldest of the Kukolnik brothers, arrived in St. Petersburg from Vilnius. Nestor wrote a verse of greeting which Glinka set and rehearsed. Late in 1840 he was afforded an opportunity to elicit royal gratitude when the Yekaterinsky Institute asked him to compose a chorus for their graduation ceremony. Early the next year Glinka attended some of the rehearsals, expressed himself well satisfied with the performance, and received from the Empress, who had been present at the première, yet another ring in token of imperial thanks. Having no wife to hand upon whom to bestow it, he sent it to his mother. The ring was well deserved. As with the Polonaise for the Smolensk nobility, Glinka could count upon a royal ear for his new work, and he discharged his commission excellently. He obviously took pains over the workmanship, organized his tonal scheme with some enterprise, and though a performance of it today would perhaps leave us quite unmoved, there can be little doubt that it would have stirred the hearts of the Institute's young ladies.

No sooner was this commission completed than a second, this time for a Tarantella to be performed at V. A. Karatygin's benefit concert at the Aleksandrinsky Theatre on 13/25 January 1841, briefly interrupted work on the opera yet again. Glinka composed a fairly elaborate work in a week at the turn of the year, designing it as a theatrical piece scored for reciter, chorus and orchestra. In addition to a purely instrumental tarantella to accompany the dancers, there are three choral-orchestral sections, and three places in which a 'declamation' is specified, in each of which, presumably, two stanzas of Ivan Myatlev's text were to be delivered. The piece achieved some success in Glinka's lifetime, and continued to be performed after his death. Today we would certainly find a performance of this Tarantella very odd, perhaps rather funny. Certainly it is a slight piece, but with some very nice scoring in the choral-orchestral sections which instils real charm into what is otherwise very slender material.

Before Easter 1841 Glinka moved in with the Stepanovs because, he said, they complained that he was favouring the Kukolniks too much. Again he found himself installed in the caricature-decorated room he had got to know so well immediately after leaving his wife. 'When, during the night, it happened that the lights of a passing carriage would momentarily illumine my room, strange figures appeared for an instant one after the other, and it seemed that the death's head on the stove grinned mockingly. It often appeared, to me at least, that it was laughing at my sufferings; then I would sleep badly, and often gave myself up to sad musings on my fate.'[1] Fortunately it seems that the bulldog had passed to higher service. He still pressed on with the opera, and Pyotr Stepanov described him at work at this time: 'Glinka would walk from room to room, completely absorbed in his creative work . . . Now he would go to the piano, pick out a few chords, hurry off to his room and write hurriedly on large music paper spread out over his table; again he would walk about, again write, often without the aid of an instrument.'[2] Yet, despite this work, his thoughts were constantly turning to the prospect of a trip abroad—or to the Ukraine. The preceding autumn he had declared to his mother that he would go abroad in April whether the opera was finished or not, and his mother had shown herself willing to make provision for the journey. He was still longing for Yekaterina, though he now acknowledged that his mother had been right to oppose the sort of relationship he had wished to establish with Yekaterina by travelling abroad with her. Now he was proposing to accompany his brother-in-law, Yakov Sobolevsky, to Paris during the spring. Sobolevsky's young son was half deaf, and Sobolevsky was taking him thither in hope of finding a cure. Glinka's sister, Yelizaveta, was going too. He was hoping for a meeting with Yekaterina before he left, and his inspiration with *Ruslan and Lyudmila* was fired. When, however, Anna Kern travelled to St. Petersburg on business, she left Yekaterina behind on the grounds that she was too ill to make the journey. Glinka's hopes were dashed, and his inspiration faded. In January Yekaterina's father, who had been the most determined opponent of Glinka's liaison with his daughter, had died, but there was still much family opposition on both sides. Perhaps in the desperate hope that a prolonged distant separation would cure him, Glinka proposed to his mother that he might stop abroad a whole year. His turbulent state at this time can well be imagined, and he poured out his heart in letters to Shirkov, who was in the Ukraine: 'Everything, as far as I was concerned, demanded that I should visit the Ukraine instead of Paris, but *her relatives* and the wishes of my mother (dear, but perhaps too cautious) dashed my hopes. I must go, sacrifice myself for my most dear mother. . . .'[3]

[1] GLN1, p. 211.   [2] StVG, p. 48.   [3] GLN2, p. 174.

Then suddenly a pressing matter arose which settled the matter for him. One evening when Glinka and Pyotr Stepanov were sitting quietly in Glinka's apartment, Yakov entered and shattered their calm with a bombshell.

'Mikhail Ivanovich, I have the honour to congratulate you,' [Yakov Ilyanovich addressed Glinka].

'For what, Ilyanich? This seems rather premature.'

'Mariya Petrovna has married.'[1]

Glinka was stunned: as Stepanov later remarked, there was something almost Shakespearian in Yakov's role at this moment. The marriage had indeed taken place on 15/27 March. Legally, of course, Mariya Petrovna was still tied to Glinka as firmly as ever, but her new 'husband', Nikolai Vasilchikov, being nephew to the chairman of the Council of Ministers, had influence in high places, and the divorce proceedings were not to go all that smoothly. The details of these need not concern us here. After refusing a proposal that he should take everything upon himself in return for Mariya Petrovna's renunciation of all claims to any part of the estate, Glinka instituted divorce proceedings that were to keep him based on St. Petersburg during the summer. The affair was to drag on for over five years before it was to be settled in his favour. He found the initial stages not only a trial but genuinely distasteful, with uncomfortable confrontations with his wife. In the autumn his sister and brother-in-law returned from Paris. No cure had been found for the boy, and Sobolevsky went home. Meanwhile Glinka and his sister, with their nephew, installed themselves in new lodgings, and his life once again became settled. Work on *Ruslan and Lyudmila* was resumed, and his muse, which had been dormant since the news of Mariya Petrovna's re-marriage, had now really awakened: 'At the end of the summer I was already feeling an unusual inclination to compose music, and this inclination did not alter.'[2] He began to study drawing, too, doing mainly landscapes, and was pleased with his own

---

[1] StVG, p. 52. Stepanov sketched a vivid little description of Yakov. It was he who kept Glinka in order, saw to his clothes, and managed the exchequer. When funds were running out, 'Yakov would sometimes come in and say: "Mikhail Ivanovich, you'll have to write to your mother. There's no money." He had so identified himself with his master that he never talked otherwise than about "our Novospasskoye, our opera, our sister". Along with this he was a great gossip; having loafed around the town most of the day, he would carry back and communicate to Mikhail Ivanovich everything he had heard that might interest him.' (StVG, pp. 51–2.) Yakov's references to *A Life for the Tsar* as 'our opera' had even led some people to suspect that he was a joint composer of the work!

[2] GLN1, p. 213.

progress. He made music with his sister who played the piano well; Glinka specially remembered playing Beethoven's 'Spring' sonata with her. These pleasant musical occupations were combined with less spiritual diversions with an eighteen-year-old serf in his sister's service. With such pleasures to hand, Glinka went out little, and the opera advanced so rapidly that he felt the tying-together process could not be long delayed. As usual he had worked unsystematically; now his librettist, Shirkov, was leaving for the Ukraine, and Glinka invited Nestor Kukolnik and Mikhail Gedeonov to dinner, and enlisted their services as supplementary librettists to patch up the holes in the opera—rather to Shirkov's annoyance.

By March 1842 *Ruslan and Lyudmila* was sufficiently near completion for Glinka to submit it to Gedeonov for acceptance. He took it without question. After the huge and lasting success of *A Life for the Tsar* Glinka was in a good position to bargain, and instead of a single payment of 4,000 roubles, he requested a royalty of six and two-thirds per cent of the takings. He proceeded with great tact in dealing with the ballet master, Titus, of whose talents he had in fact a rather poor opinion. Titus was noted for his love of good food, and Glinka entertained him lavishly to dinner in order to ensure that the wild oriental dance, the *lezghinka*, was done to his own liking. A certain Pavel Kamensky, a translator in the theatre director's office, was included among the guests since he was judged to be an excellent exponent of that dance. Titus was wined and dined, Kamensky demonstrated, and Titus, though he was not enamoured of what he saw, was sufficiently softened to agree to its being done as Glinka wanted.

Glinka was now entering what he described as one of the happiest phases of his life. The regular brotherhood had broken up, but he had other social compensations, for his mother had arrived in St. Petersburg before Easter, intending to stay a year so that her youngest daughter, Olga, might complete her education there. The Glinka family moved into new lodgings in order to be all together within the same building. Then, in February, Liszt had visited St. Petersburg, and though Glinka at this time had somewhat mixed feelings about him both as a person and as a pianist, he was very flattered by Liszt's interest in him. For the first time since his break with his wife he was drawn back into society—'and the Russian composer, whom almost all had forgotten, was forced to appear again in the salons of our capital at the recommendation of the famous foreign artist,' noted Glinka with a mixture of plaintiveness and pride.[1] He was highly pleased that Liszt often asked him to sing one or two of his favourite songs to him (Liszt's favourite was 'The fire of longing'), and he was very deeply impressed by Liszt's faultless sight-reading of several pieces from *Ruslan and Lyudmila*, in which the Hungarian showed a deep interest. As for the plans for production, Gedeonov gave Glinka a free hand in organizing it according to his own wishes. Karl Bryullov, who supervised the making of the main costumes, and Andrei Roller, the designer, were most diligent and co-operative. Titus returned Glinka's hospitality by entertaining him at his dacha on Krestov Island, and then forthwith set about preparing the dances. Glinka worked with him closely, and modified his music to suit Titus's requirements, regretting that he had to introduce a number of rather 'cheap' phrases into those of Act III so that they might be danced 'with passion'.[2] He recalled his daily routine in his *Memoirs*:

> At that time I was leading an extremely pleasant life. In the morning I would revise the dances and a few uncompleted parts of the opera, and at noon I would set off for the rehearsal in the theatre's hall or at the school, whence I was frequently conveyed home in the theatre's carriage with the pupils and actresses. I dined at my mother's, and spent the time after dinner with the family; in the evening I usually went to the theatre, where I remained nearly all the time behind the scenes. When I returned home in the evening, my sister Olga would meet me with a laugh, and to my question: 'What are you laughing at, Olga?' she would reply: 'You have come; that means there will be laughter.' And indeed a quarter of an hour had not passed before I would have my mother and sister laughing.[3]

Nor were these the only visits he paid after the theatre, for late on the night of 14/26 October, at his friend, Konstantin Bulgakov's, he dashed off the romance, 'I love you, dear rose',[4] a slight but most tender song in which he neatly takes the experience beyond the simple repetitions of its two strophes by allowing the voice to break into the piano coda unexpectedly at the very end, just as Beethoven had done so tellingly in his song, 'Andenken'.

The first rehearsal of the new opera (with strings only) took place on 13/25[5] August at his mother's apartment; there were no singers present, and Glinka supplied the wind parts on the piano. As before he rehearsed the principals separately. But when rehearsals began in earnest in the autumn, troubles started to arise. He found that many

---

[1] GLN1. p. 216.   [2] GLN1, p. 222.   [3] ibid.
[4] In his *Memoirs* Glinka assigned this song to 1843.
[5] In his *Memoirs* Glinka stated that this took place on 10/22 August.

adjustments and alterations were needed, and the final rehearsals were marred by tensions between Glinka and the performers. The trouble arose out of an article written by Bulgarin. Bulgarin had been the most outspoken critic of *A Life for the Tsar*, but since that time, he and Glinka seem to have established a surprisingly cordial relationship. Then, while preparations for *Ruslan and Lyudmila* were in progress, they quarrelled. Bulgarin appears, in fact, to have been a thoroughly unpleasant indivi-dual, and it was quite in character that he should, out of spite, have written an article in the *Northern Bee* three weeks before the première of *Ruslan and Lyudmila*, maligning the performers who were pre-paring the opera. The article was unsigned, and word got round that Glinka was the author. Naturally the artists were bitterly resentful, the goodwill went out of the rehearsals, and the level of performance declined. Glinka, instead of handling the situation tactfully, adopted a foolishly superior attitude, suggesting that sloppy performance was negligence, and hinting that he could have the musicians dis-missed for this. Despite all Glinka's disclaimers in his *Memoirs*, one wonders whether he had indeed made some unguarded remarks about the performers; to the end of her life Vorobyeva remained convinced that he had. Then, to add to these human problems, there were some unsatisfactory features about the stage designs. He was pleased with those for the first three acts, but Roller's sets for the last two were poor. Glinka was especially counting upon the visual impact of Chernomor's garden in Act IV to cover up the lack of dramatic movement in this scene. However 'the castle was like a barracks, the fantastic flowers on the sides of the forestage were ugly, and vilely daubed over with the very simplest colours, and speckled with gold leaf'.[1] Nor was there enough room for the actors. Glinka attributed Roller's feebleness in the last two acts to a wish to have his own back on Gedeonov, with whom he had quarrelled. Whatever the cause, the opera was badly handi-capped. Then Vorobyeva fell ill, and the part of Ratmir had to be sung by her understudy, Anfisa Petrova, who had just sung the part of Vanya when Glinka's earlier opera was given its Moscow première on 13/25 September. Unfortunately Petrova was not equal to the part of Ratmir; in addition, the elderly Italian, D. Tosi, who was to sing Farlaf, pro-nounced his Russian ludicrously, and Emiliya Lileyeva, who was cast as Gorislava, drove Glinka to despair at rehearsals through her in-ability to convey any warmth. The auspices for success were not good.

[1] GLN1, p. 224.

Glinka recalled only briefly the reception of the opera at its première:

The first act went quite well. Likewise the second act did not go badly, except for the chorus of the Head. In act three, in the scene 'Both warmth and ardour' [Ratmir's aria], the understudy, Petrova, proved exceedingly weak, and the audience noticeably cooled. The fourth act did not produce its expected effect. At the end of the fifth act the royal family left the theatre. When the curtain came down they began to call for me, but the applause was not warm, and there was some industrious hissing as well, especially from the stage and orchestra. I turned to General Dubelt, who was then in the director's box, and asked: 'They seem to be hissing; shall I take a bow?'

'Go on,' replied the General: "Christ suffered more than you!'[1]

Needless to say, the celebration party was not the joyous occasion that had been anticipated, though Glinka did his best to hide his disappointment. Bulgarin, of course, was triumphant. His correspondence reveals that he saw the *Northern Bee* as something of an official court organ, and he was most diligent to ensure that any views it expressed should not in any way conflict with those held in court circles. It was known that the royal family had expressed approval of the opera's staging, and the *Northern Bee* accordingly praised this lavishly; but there was no such royal approval for the music, and Bulgarin was free to let himself go. He did so with relish. 'The audience were quiet and waited for something,' he reported, 'waited, and having received nothing, dispersed in silence, in a certain despondency, filled with a feeling of sadness . . . But then, if the audience did not understand the opera, neither did the singers, nor the orchestra: in a word, we are all guilty.'[2] The opera's reputation for dullness was such that it caused the Tsar's brother, Mikhail, to prescribe attendance at a performance of *Ruslan and Lyudmila* as alternative punishment to confinement in the guardroom for guilty officers. However, the opera did have more success from the third performance, when Vorobyeva was well enough to sing. Gulak-Artemovsky also took over the role of Ruslan, and sang it better than Petrov. Vorobyeva sang her scene in the third act 'with such passion that she roused the audience to rapture. Loud and prolonged applause rang out, triumphantly calling first for me, then for Petrova [Vorobyeva],' Glinka recalled.

These calls continued throughout seventeen performances. In connection with this, Petrova was often angry with me. I did not listen to her during her scene,

---

[1] GLN1, pp. 227–8.   [2] Quoted in GLN1, p. 448.

but was whispering with one of the pretty understudies in a distant corner of the wings, and was often late for my call.[1]

Glinka's lack of consideration for his colleague was inexcusable, but as in his relations with his wife, he seems to have been incapable of seeing the deficiencies in his own behaviour.

Glinka was not the only one to record the changing attitude of the public to his new opera. On 5/17 December the *St. Petersburg Record* reported that 'Lyudmila's cavatina in the first act, Finn's ballad and Ruslan's aria in the second, Gorislava's and Ratmir's arias in the third, and the whole of the fourth act with its grotesque ballet at Chernomor's [castle] were greeted with loud applause; the audience demanded that the Lezghinka should be repeated, and at the end of the opera it was a long time before the fully merited demonstrations of general delight subsided.'[2] Koni, writing in the *Literary Gazette* ten days later, also reported this change. He was merciless to the libretto: 'There is absolutely no drama, of [real] characters there are even less . . . nor was there a trace of passions, spiritual conflict, and life.'[3] It was Glinka who had saved the situation: 'Glinka has covered up all the sins of the writer of the libretto . . . He has filled its meagre substance with such a wealth of music that it truly overflows in abundance. Indeed, he has performed miracles! But did this emerge from the opera? No!'[4] Nevertheless he saw a great future for the music itself: 'There was a time when everyone cried that *Ruslan and Lyudmila* was dull, exhausting; now almost everyone has become reconciled to it. A time will come when all will delight in it. Many have regretted that there aren't tunes in it, and that nothing embeds itself in the memory. Look! A month will not pass before people will be dancing quadrilles, mazurkas, galops and waltzes to these tunes. And within a year the ordinary Russian will be singing these rich tunes because street-organs will carry them throughout all Russia.'[5] This was over-optimistic, and Odoyevsky's partisan article is likewise over-enthusiastic in some parts, though its record of the growing appreciation of Glinka's work is probably accurate enough. Odoyevsky offered a direct riposte to Bulgarin: 'I read somewhere (I don't remember where) the declaration of one gentleman that the audience at the performance of *Ruslan and Lyudmila* was cold, and that neither this gentleman nor the audience understood this opera . . . But I can assure you that I have not missed a single

[1] GLN1, p. 228.   [2] Quoted in LPG1, p. 308.   [3] Quoted in LPOK, vol. 1, part 1, p. 274.
[4] LPOK, p. 275.   [5] Quoted in GLN1, pp. 448–9.

performance, and . . . as I have observed it, the audience with each performance discover new, at first unnoticed, beauties in the new opera.'[1] Obviously public utterances in the press by supporters of *Ruslan and Lyudmila* might be suspected of exaggerating the opera's success, but private, and therefore more reliable, evidence of the growing success of the opera is provided by a letter written shortly after the première by Osip Senkovsky, editor of the periodical, *The Reading Room*, to E. N. Akhmatova: 'I have just come from the theatre. After being a complete flop it is now a complete and raging success. Glinka got endless applause. Now he must be happy.'[2]

While *Ruslan and Lyudmila* was certainly not the huge success that *A Life for the Tsar* had been, it would certainly be wrong to consider it an unqualified failure. It was given thirty-two times during the first three months, and though the frequency of presentation dropped off radically after that, it still continued to receive a number of performances each year until 1848. It is difficult to believe that the changes in the casting of Ruslan and Ratmir on the third night accounted entirely for the change in the public's response. Glinka himself was the first to admit that the opera was deficient in dramatic movement, but clearly there was a significant body of Russian society which responded to the musical riches of the score, and which ensured that it continued in the repertoire for a number of seasons in St. Petersburg. Moscow heard it for the first time in 1846, when the Russian opera company transferred to Russia's second city. Since 1843 a re-formed Italian opera company had been challenging the native troupe in St. Petersburg, and had finally compelled it to move. By October 1848 Moscow had heard the opera eleven times; after this it was never again given complete in Glinka's lifetime.

[1] Quoted in GLN1, p. 449.   [2] Quoted in LPG2, p. 249.

9/*Ruslan and Lyudmila: Process of composition*

RUSLAN AND LYUDMILA was the work which established Pushkin's reputation. Completed in 1820 when its creator was scarcely out of his teens, it tells of how Lyudmila, daughter of the Prince of Kiev, is abducted by Chernomor, a wicked dwarf. This happens during the night after the feast celebrating her betrothal and marriage to Ruslan who, with her three unsuccessful suitors, forthwith sets out to rescue her. After defeating one of his rivals in combat and encountering a huge Head (which turns out to be Chernomor's brother changed into his present form by a trick of the dwarf), Ruslan reaches Chernomor's castle. The dwarf's source of strength lies in his immense beard, and after a struggle involving a three day aerial flight hanging on to the beard (an episode which, not surprisingly, exhausts Chernomor), Ruslan is able to cut it off with the magic sword given him by the Head. Thus he rescues Lyudmila, but not before Chernomor has put her into a charmed sleep. Ruslan sets out with her for Kiev along with the captured Chernomor, but on the way Farlaf, one of his rivals, kills Ruslan, steals Lyudmila away, and takes her to Kiev himself. Ruslan is restored to life and follows Farlaf, arriving in time to help deliver Kiev from a marauding army. Then with the aid of a magic ring given him by the friendly magician, Finn, he wakes Lyudmila amid general rejoicing.

Pushkin tells this romantic fairy story in verse which is filled with fantasy and enchantment, often sensuous, sometimes frightening, occasionally humorous, even satirical. It had a natural attraction for a reader of vivid imagination like Glinka, though there were clearly going to be problems when translating into a stage representation a piece whose narrative has the insubstantial fluidity of a tale recalled in a dream, and whose effect derives so much from powerful imaginative evocation. Pushkin himself would have found it difficult enough, and it was not among those of his own works which he suggested as possible subjects for the type of opera in which he had expressed an interest. As noted earlier, it was Shakhovsky and not Pushkin who suggested the subject to Glinka, and Pushkin's death thwarted Glinka's hope that the poet himself might have been persuaded to prepare the dramatic adaptation. In the end the basic scheme was worked out in circumstances which were scarcely ideal. Characteristically Glinka had already composed some pieces for the opera before ever this stage was reached. Then, early in the winter of 1837–8 he had performed some of these to a group of his friends, and he recorded what ensued: 'Konstantin Bakhturin was there among the visitors on that occasion; he took upon himself to work out the plan of the opera, and did it in a quarter of an hour while drunk, and—just imagine—the opera was written according to this plan. Bakhturin instead of Pushkin! How did this come about? I just cannot remember.'[1] In fact, Glinka's memory played him false in many particulars over the composition of *Ruslan and Lyudmila*.

In the opera the final layout of the plot is briefly as follows. Act I is set in Kiev. It is the feast before the wedding of Lyudmila to Ruslan. A minstrel (the Bayan) sings of trials in store for the bridegroom, though he predicts that true love will conquer all. Lyudmila nostalgically bids farewell to the happiness she has enjoyed in Kiev, and addresses her unsuccessful suitors, the Eastern prince, Ratmir, and the Varangian warrior, Farlaf (Rogdai, Pushkin's fourth suitor, has no part in the opera). But suddenly the scene grows dark, and when light is restored Lyudmila has disappeared. The Grand Prince promises her hand and half his kingdom to the man who shall rescue her. Act II opens with the good magician, Finn, telling Ruslan that it is Chernomor who has abducted Lyudmila, and warning him against the wiles of the wicked enchantress, Naina. It is this same Naina whom the frightened Farlaf now meets. She instructs him to wait at home, promising to help him defeat Ruslan and gain Lyudmila. The act ends on a battlefield where Ruslan encounters and subdues the gigantic Head, from beneath which he draws out a sword. The Head recounts how he had been turned into his present form, and how the sword is a magic one with which Chernomor may be defeated. The content of Act III has no place in the original poem, though Pushkin did dispose of Ratmir by exposing his susceptible Eastern temperament to enchantment (subsequently he set him up as a fisherman paired off with a beautiful girl). This act of the

[1] GLN1, p. 194.

opera is set in Naina's palace where a travel-weary Ratmir is succumbing to the charms of Naina's maidens, much to the distress of his slave, Gorislava, who loves him (Gorislava is also an invention of the opera). Ruslan arrives and, enchanted by the scene, falls for the beauty of an alarmed Gorislava. The situation is saved by the entry of Finn who breaks the seductive spell, brings Ratmir and Gorislava together, and sets the three of them on the way to rescue Lyudmila. Act IV takes place in Chernomor's palace. Lyudmila vents her despair and defiance, and indignantly rejects Chernomor's blandishments. Ruslan is seen approaching; Chernomor casts a spell over Lyudmila, plunging her into a deep sleep, and sets out to do battle with Ruslan. Chernomor's apprehensive followers witness the encounter and see Ruslan hanging on to Chernomor's beard. Ruslan enters victorious, having cut off the dwarf's beard and wrapped it round his helmet. But his elation turns to despair when he finds that Lyudmila cannot be wakened. He decides to take her back to Kiev. In Act V Lyudmila is stolen away by Farlaf who hurries ahead with her. Ruslan takes up the pursuit. Meanwhile Finn gives Ratmir the magic ring. In Kiev Farlaf is unable to waken Lyudmila, but when Ruslan arrives with Ratmir he breaks the spell with the aid of the ring, and the opera ends in general rejoicing.

Bakhturin's draft has disappeared, but there survives a scheme which Glinka wrote out before the end of 1837 in the notebook given to him by Nestor Kukolnik to be a repository of materials for the new opera. In its first three acts this *Initial Plan* is certainly much closer to the dramatic scheme of the final product than was the *Initial Plan* for *A Life for the Tsar*. In Act I Glinka was to expand the Introduction greatly (there is no provision for the Bayan's role in the original, for instance), but Lyudmila's cavatina and the finale remained essentially the same, except for the excision from the latter of a mysterious character called Ivan-Tsarevich, who had no part in Pushkin's poem, and whose role in the opera seems to have been to keep a watchful eye on the fortunes of the hero and heroine. He was quite unnecessary since this duty could equally well be fulfilled by Finn. Act II remained essentially the same, and the only change in Act III was the excision of a chorus of Maidens between Gorislava's[1] and Ratmir's solos, and the abandonment of the projected key scheme for the dances. However in Acts IV and V the revisions were more far-reaching, and will be discussed later. Vladimir Stasov considered that in general the magic element was much more

---

[1] In the *Initial Plan* Gorislava is called Milolika.

prominent in the *Initial Plan* than in the opera itself. The main value of this first draft lies in its inclusion of extracts from the music which Glinka had already composed for certain parts of the opera, and it reveals just how much had been written or at least sketched before the end of 1837. Most of the musical extracts present only the vocal line(s), but occasionally the accompaniment is added; most are wordless, though sometimes the opening phrase of a piece or section is texted.

As with *A Life for the Tsar,* Glinka already had a certain amount of material to hand before ever his thoughts fastened upon Pushkin's poem. The canon that follows Lyudmila's abduction in Act I was adapted from a baritone aria in A flat, composed in 1827, and the folk tunes which are the bases of Finn's Ballad and the Persian Chorus had been in store since 1829 (see above, pp. 47–8). The waltz theme which concludes Ratmir's aria in Act III seems to have been written at about this time, or while Glinka was in Italy. Glinka also found material in music rejected from *A Life for the Tsar,* taking two substantial chunks from the dance with oboe and cello obbligati which he had composed for the Polish act of his earlier opera. He acquired some extra folk material in 1837, for in his *Memoirs* he recalled that 'Gaivazovsky [the seascape painter, I. K. Aivazovsky], who visited Kulkolnik very frequently, communicated to me three Tartar melodies. Subsequently I employed two of them in the Lezghinka, and the third for the andante in Ratmir's scene in Act III.'[1] The *Initial Plan* reveals that by the end of 1837 the first two parts of Lyudmila's cavatina in Act I (the andante capriccioso and the allegro moderato) had already been sketched, and that Count Wielhorski had suggested that the as-yet-unwritten third section should be done 'more smoothly than the preceding'.[2] In Act II Glinka had prepared some music for Farlaf's aria, but the dozen bars quoted in the *Initial Plan* were subsequently rejected, though the final form of the aria still kept to the character originally envisaged: 'all allegro and buffo'.[3] Part of Ruslan's aria had been worked out very fully indeed. Later Glinka was to drop the idea with which he may have planned to open it, but in the *Initial Plan* he set out one hundred bars of the vocal part (starting from bar 159 of the final version; this includes the tune which was to become the second subject of the Overture), complete in places with accompaniment. The first part of Ratmir's aria in Act III was done too, though big changes were to be made in the latter half of this, and it shows that the fine demi-semiquaver ornamenta-

---

[1] GLN1, p. 180.　　[2] GLN1, p. 319.　　[3] GLN1, p. 320.

tion of the final version (Ex. 45b), which one might assume was genuinely oriental, is in fact Glinka's own invention; the original form in
the *Initial Plan* is much more commonplace (Ex. 45a). This section also

Ex.45.

appears here a major seventh above the final pitch,[1] which suggests that
it had not yet been decided to cast Vorobyeva in this role. As noted
earlier, Shakhovsky had proposed that she should sing the part of
Chernomor, and though this was later to become a mimed role, in the
Initial Plan it is conceived as a sung part, and presumably therefore was
still intended for Vorobyeva. The accompaniment was planned very
differently too; instead of the final scoring of cor anglais obbligato,
clarinets, and four horns, Glinka intended to use sustained violas, and
cellos playing slow arpeggios. He had also written the 'motif of
seduction' which the chorus sing after the dances in this act, though at
this stage he envisaged it as an instrumental piece. Act IV contains some
two dozen bars of Lyudmila's aria with the accompaniment written out
in full. Glinka had also sketched the music that was to be sung before
Chernomor's March while Lyudmila is falling asleep. After this he
intended to interpolate a duet for Lyudmila and Ivan-Tsarevich before
the March, and had done more than sixty bars of it. With the excision of
Ivan-Tsarevich this naturally became redundant, but Glinka did not
intend to waste his material, and adapted some of it for the E major
section of the duet for Ratmir and Finn in Act V. Lastly[2] he had also
sketched a 'final motif' for the very end of Act V, but this was later to
disappear in favour of the idea which was also used to launch the Overture.

What Glinka now urgently needed was a librettist, and he was
fortunate in meeting Shirkov at this time. Nevertheless he admitted

[1] A fragment of yet another version of the opening of this also exists (this is closer to
the *Initial Plan* version than to the final one); this is pitched in between the other two versions, in E major.

[2] At the end of the *Initial Plan* there is a sketch of some nineteen bars of Ruslan's 'distracted' scene at the end of Act IV, but this appears to have been added at some later stage.

that his own progress continued to be unsystematic: 'Instead of considering above all the whole and making a plan of the progress of the work,
I forthwith set about Lyudmila's and Gorislava's cavatinas, not caring
at all about dramatic movement and the progress of the plot, reckoning
that it would be possible to settle all this later.'[1] By 1854 Glinka had
clearly forgotten about the *Initial Plan*, but it is quite true that the work
went ahead very haphazardly. He completed Lyudmila's cavatina and
it was publicly performed with chorus and orchestra on 23 March/4
April 1838 (see above, p. 145). The Persian Chorus was perhaps already
done before he set off on his recruiting drive in the Ukraine in April,[2]
but both Chernomor's March and Finn's Ballad were certainly written
at Kachanovka, the latter during June.[3] Glinka had planned to write the
latter on Pushkin's own text, but this proved not completely suitable for
his purpose, and he enlisted the aid of his friend, Markevich: 'he
shortened it and produced as many imitation verses as were needed to
round off the piece. I well remember the time when I wrote Finn's
Ballad. It was warm, and Sternberg, Markevich, and I had met together.
While I wrote in the verses that had already been prepared, Markevich
gnawed at his pen; he found it difficult to imitate Pushkin in his additional verses.'[4]

On returning to St. Petersburg in September 1838, Glinka was
anxious to press ahead with the opera. He was delighted with the
progress of Shirkov, who had completed the libretto of Act I and had
started on that of Act II. His designer, Roller, had even done oil paintings
of some of the sets. But Glinka's own work on it was to be interrupted
for more than a year. First he had to compile the *Collection of musical
pieces* which he published in 1839 (see above, pp. 146–7); then he once
again became overwhelmed by his work at the Chapel and by his
deteriorating relationship with his wife. These distractions were so
great that he could remember only one tiny idea for *Ruslan and
Lyudmila* coming to him in the whole of 1839: 'I attended ex officio the
betrothal and marriage of H.R.H. the Grand Duchess Mariya Nikolay-

---

[1] GLN1, p. 194.

[2] In the preface to the full score of *Ruslan and Lyudmila* in GPSS14, the editor, G. V.
Kirkor, states that the Persian Chorus, Ratmir's romance in Act V, and Gorislava's
cavatina were all composed 'in the last months of 1837' (vol. 14A, p. xiii), but he offers no
evidence to support this.

[3] The original version of the ballad started with the tutti at bar 31 of the printed
edition.

[4] GLN1, p. 186.

evna. During dinner music was played, the court singers and the tenor Poggi . . . sang. I participated in the choruses, and the clatter of knives, forks and plates struck me, and gave me the idea of imitating it in the Introduction of *Ruslan*.'[1]

1840 saw the resumption of work on the opera. At the end of 1839 Glinka broke both with his wife and with the Chapel, and he spent the first part of the next year recovering from the strains of these experiences, and from the illness which had finally attended them. During early May, at a literary soirée attended by many prominent figures in St. Petersburg's cultural life, he performed extracts from his opera. Perhaps the great success of this occasion helped to re-awaken his active enthusiasm for the work; certainly by August, despite his separation from Yekaterina Kern, he was in high spirits about it. 'Circumstances were never more favourable,' he wrote to Shirkov. 'The theatre is entirely at my disposal, and I can practise and try out what I have written as I wish, and (what is better still) be assured of finding enthusiastic co-operation everywhere. Both the Petrovs are singing extremely well.'[2] He was still working as haphazardly as ever, and was anxious to have the whole libretto to hand as soon as possible. On 9/21 August he had sent Shirkov the scheme for Act IV, but thirteen days later he was asking him to press on with Act V instead, 'especially with the duet and finale. According to my calculations I have about two months' work to write out what I have already written—if you will send the fifth act by that time, then work will be in full swing.'[3] He also went ahead with new pieces, composing the Introduction to Act I in three weeks, and finishing Ruslan's aria in Act II at Novospasskoye on 1/13 September (though in December he was to write to Shirkov that he was still doing some work on it). While on the way back to St. Petersburg in late September he composed the final chorus of the opera, and despite having caught a chill on the journey, he set straight to work on Lyudmila's scene in Act IV, though he was to be distracted by other things. Still, he did finish the Chorus of Flowers, 'Do not lament, dear princess', in December, and during the four days following 14/26 January 1841, he added the adagio to Lyudmila's aria. The general public had had an opportunity to sample the new opera when Ratmir's romance from Act V was performed at a concert in December, and two months later the adagio with violin obbligato from Lyudmila's aria in Act IV was given at another concert in St. Petersburg. The Bayan's second song

---

[1] GLN1, p. 200.   [2] GLN2, p. 143.   [3] GLN2, p. 144.

from the Introduction to Act I had already been printed with different words as a romance.

It is clear, however, that work was slowing up, and there were difficulties that frustrated Glinka's optimistic prediction that the opera would be completed by the spring. During September and October his creative energies had been occupied by the composition of the incidental music to *Prince Kholmsky*; illness followed in November, and several more commissions interrupted in December and January. His unsettled emotional state over his relationship with Yekaterina Kern contributed to making his creative moods very fitful. In addition, the libretto was posing problems. Having consulted Nestor Kukolnik, Bryullov, and Roller, he wrote to Shirkov on 18/30 December 1840, requesting revisions to Act IV—'the result as much of scenic as of musical considerations'.[1] The plan which he had sent to Shirkov back in August had still been close to that which he had worked out at the end of 1837, except that it had clearly been decided that Chernomor should no longer be a singing role, which necessitated the excision of a recitative for him and Lyudmila which was to have followed the march (the duet for Lyudmila and Ivan-Tsarevich after her aria had also gone, of course). Now Glinka was requesting savage modifications to the first part of the act because, he said, the theatre had no actress good enough to play the part of Lyudmila as Shirkov envisaged it. The opening recitative would have to go completely, and Glinka wished Pushkin's own words to be fitted to the beginning of the aria, though in the end Shirkov provided all the text for this. The new scheme that Glinka now set out for Shirkov was that which was to go into the opera; all Shirkov had to do was to provide a few extra verses in accordance with the metres prescribed by Glinka. The march and dances were to follow as planned. But Glinka, as impulsive as ever, had had a bright idea; he was proposing to interpolate a quite new scene, adapted from Pushkin's poem, in which Lyudmila, by grabbing Chernomor's magic hat, putting it on and turning it round, made herself invisible. This would prompt a silly scene with a good deal of stage business and a 'playfully humorous' rondo for the heroine. Glinka considered that 'this new scene, besides its theatrical effect, would not hinder a greater revelation of Lyudmila's character'.[2] It is quite impossible to see how he really thought this could profitably add either to Lyudmila's character or to the opera; fortunately it was to be dropped. So, too, was the 'struggle'

[1] GLN2, p. 150.   [2] GLN2, p. 712.

between Chernomor and Ruslan which had been in the scheme from the very beginning. Shirkov had included a chorus for Chernomor's followers who were watching the struggle, and this was judged to be enough to cater for this part of the action. It certainly made production simpler. Shirkov, having had his work for the earlier part of the act thoroughly mauled, could console himself that the last part of his libretto for this act was considered splendid, and was used almost without modification.

As for Act V, it was clear that work on this had not progressed at all as Glinka had wished, and exactly two months later (18 February/2 March) he sent Shirkov his draft for this. This, too, was still close to that of the *Initial Plan*, and a good deal longer than that which finally went into the opera. In the *Initial Plan* after Ratmir's Romance there was to have been a duet for Farlaf and Naina who were to kill Ruslan and carry off Lyudmila. Ratmir and Ivan Tsarevich were to follow with an elaborate duet, during which Finn would be called up and restore Ruslan to life. A quintet would then precede the finale. Now Glinka was proposing to expand the first part even further, for the new scheme he sent to Shirkov interpolated a 'wordless' movement called 'Ruslan's Sleep' before Farlaf and Naina entered to kill him (though Glinka now intended to cut down their duet to a 'short two-stage recitative'). Since Ivan-Tsarevich had disappeared from the scheme, Ratmir was to be partnered by Gorislava in the duet. The quintet was dropped altogether. Even now Glinka confessed himself uncertain on several points in this new scheme, and in the end, though Shirkov did some of the libretto, this was to be the most heavily revised act of all, with Kukolnik writing most of it. In the final drastic surgery 'Ruslan's Sleep', the scene for Farlaf and Naina, and the duet for Ratmir and Gorislava were to go completely, and instead Chernomor's captured followers were simply to report the mysterious disappearance of both Lyudmila and Ruslan. Finn was now to be Ratmir's partner in the duet, during which he was to pass over the magic ring for Ratmir to give to Ruslan. The finale was to follow.

Glinka gave Shirkov a rough time with his various changes of plan. As can be seen from what has already been described, his revisions were prompted by a variety of sound and unsound motives—by dramatic and imaginative insights and practical commonsense on the one hand, and sheer impulse on the other. Thus practical considerations made him decide to cut the big duet Shirkov had written for Finn and Ruslan after Finn's Ballad in Act II because 'you won't find a tenor who would have the stamina to sing the duet pleasantly after such a difficult and exhausting piece'.[1] A few of Shirkov's lines for this duet were incorporated into the recitative before Finn's Ballad, and the text of the new brief recitative which follows the ballad was written by Gedeonov.[2] Dramatic considerations exercised Glinka in the handling of the section between Ruslan's aria and the Head's narrative in the same act. These two movements were the high points of the act, said Glinka; if the link were 'weaker, it will be flabby or, what is worse, laughable; if stronger, it will impair equally [Ruslan's] aria and the [Head's] narrative.'[3] Finally he decided upon a short orchestral storm and a bit of quick action. Unfortunately the dramatic implausibility of the whole situation made any salvage operation a lost cause.

Glinka's second burst of activity on *Ruslan and Lyudmila* was coming to an end, as the letter covering these proposed libretto revisions makes abundantly clear: 'the current [pre-Lenten] carnival has been more chaotic than all previous ones . . . Sadness of heart has drawn me away from the opera just as much as this distraction, and in Act V a great deal has still not become clear to me. Do what you can and as much as you can; our poor *Ruslan* will not only be incomplete by the Tsarevich's wedding, but if circumstances do not change for the better, then it will be necessary to work on it a lot longer.'[4] He reported his intention of going to Paris in April, and then took stock of the current position:

Everything of the opera so far written:

Act I	1.	Introduction
	2.	Lyudmila's aria
Act II	3.	Finn's Ballad
	4.	Ruslan's aria
Act III	5.	Persian Chorus
	6.	Gorislava's cavatina
Act IV	7.	Extracts from Lyudmila's scene, namely the Chorus of Flowers, 'Do not lament'; Andante, 'Ah, thou art my fate'
	8.	Chernomor's March
Act V	9.	Ratmir's romance; 'She is life to me'

[1] GLN2, p. 713.
[2] Shirkov's text for the longer duet is not printed in GLN1 or 2, but is given in PG, pp. 514–16.
[3] GLN2, p. 713.
[4] GLN2, p. 158.

In progress:

   a.   Finale to Act I
   b.   The scene of the Head (Act II)
   c.   The dances (Act III)
   d.   The scene of Lyudmila and dances (Act IV)
   e.   Final chorus of Act V

Not yet begun:

   1.   Scene of Farlaf and Naina (Act II)
   2.   Ratmir's aria ⎫
   3.   Finale   ⎬ (Act III)
   4.   The struggle and finale ⎫
   5.   The sleep scene   ⎬ (Act IV)
   6.   The murder scene ⎫
   7.   Duet   ⎬ (Act V)
   8.   Beginning of the finale ⎭

This is a detailed list. From it you will see that nine numbers are ready, five are in hand, and eight are not yet begun. The overture and entr'actes will be the last job.

I have now written nothing for about a month; my muse is sad and doesn't obey. She won't be coerced, and in addition unbroken rehearsals would not have allowed me to work, even if I had been capable of it. But always towards the end of the winter my nerves suffer sorely from the prolonged cold.[1]

Glinka still managed to do a little more, composing Ruslan's 'heart-searching' scene in the finale of Act IV ('Ruslan's song is very simple but expressive—the piece finishes with a march'[2]), and he wrote the first half of the scene of the Head which ends Act II. Then work on the opera remained at a standstill throughout the middle of 1841. Yet even during this tiresome period of his divorce petition, Glinka was looking ahead to a time when he might be able to start work again. On 22 July/ 3 August he wrote to Shirkov, who had moved to the Ukraine early in June: 'My muse has fallen completely silent. But if Valerian Fedorovich [i.e., Shirkov himself] has occasional moments free from cares, it would not inconvenience me to have the whole libretto by the winter. Who knows, perhaps my muse will awake unexpectedly.'[3] And so she did. Glinka recalled that by the end of the summer he was again feeling 'an unusual inclination for composing music, and this inclination did not change'.[4] In the settled domestic conditions which were restored by the return of his sister from Paris in the early autumn, he resumed intensive work. He finished the other half of the scene of the Head in Act II,

[1] GLN2, pp. 158–9.   [2] GLN2, p. 174.   [3] GLN2, p. 205.   [4] GLN1, p. 213.

Ratmir's aria in Act III, and towards the end of November the finale to Act V was done. During the ten days following the 18/30 December the scene of Lyudmila in Chernomor's Castle was at last completed.[1] 'Staying at home, I worked so assiduously that in a short time the greater part of the opera was ready. Looking over it, however, I found that an overall unity between the parts of the new opera was lacking. In order to help this, I invited Nestor [Kukolnik] and Misha Gedeonov to dinner . . . Because of Shirkov's departure for the Ukraine, Kukolnik and Gedeonov undertook to help in the difficult task of making a unity out of the heterogeneous separate parts of my opera. Kukolnik wrote verses for the finale of the opera,[2] and Ratmir's scene in Act III, "Both warmth and ardour",[3] Gedeonov wrote the little duet following upon Finn's Ballad between Ruslan and Finn, "I give you thanks, my glorious protector", Finn's recitative in Act III, "Knights! Cunning Naina", etc., and the prayer for four voices which ends the third act. And I myself wrote the scene of Farlaf and Naina, and Farlaf's rondo [in Act II], and also the beginning of the finale of the third act.'[4]

Inevitably Shirkov was resentful of this intrusion of others into his territory, and on 20 December/1 January Glinka wrote him a pacifying letter, including a frank assessment of Kukolnik's talents: 'Kukolnik throws off the verses hurriedly, paying no attention to the beauty of the verse, and everything that he has so far written for *Ruslan* is so untidy that it certainly requires alterations. Let me add that, however much I may value Kukolnik's gifts, yet I stand by my former opinion of him: he is a man of letters, not a poet. His verse is in general too ponderous and graceless after Pushkin's, Batyushkov's, and others'. Doubtless the metres will give you some difficulty, but the Bayan's Song, Gorislava's aria and other parts of your libretto vouch for your talents.'[5] It is in fact quite possible that Kukolnik's words were only intended to be temporary material giving Glinka a working basis, and that it was genuinely intended that Shirkov should replace them with more stylish ones. Yet in the end much of Kukolnik's and others' words remained. Besides the

---

[1] A good deal of this scene must have been done over a year earlier, for Glinka reported that he had often sung bits of it at the Engelhardts, during 1840. But, as has already been seen, his memory for dates is often fallible in his *Memoirs*.

[2] In fact, Kukolnik wrote the whole of Act V except for Ratmir's romance.

[3] There is conflicting evidence about this movement. On 7/19 November 1841 Glinka wrote to Shirkov enclosing what was clearly this aria for him to fit words to.

[4] GLN1, pp. 214–15.

[5] GLN2, p. 218.

movements just mentioned, Pushkin's own words were used for the Persian Chorus and for much of Finn's Ballad, Markevich supplying extra verses for the latter. In all, eight of the twenty-seven numbers in the opera were written by persons other than Shirkov.

During the winter of 1841–2 Glinka continued to work intensively, completing the finale of Act I, the duet of Ruslan and Finn, the scene for Farlaf and Naina, and Farlaf's Rondo from Act II, the finale of Act III, the chorus 'Let him perish!' from Act IV, and the recitative and chorus, and the duet for Ratmir and Finn from Act V. In the first two months of 1842 he composed the entr'actes, and had the score ready for submission to the theatre on 4/16 March.[1] Only the Overture still remained to be done, and this was put off until September to November when he 'wrote it straight out for orchestra, often in the producer's room during rehearsals'.[2]

While *Ruslan and Lyudmila* was being written, the tendency had been to expand; now, when rehearsals started, a drastic pruning began. Many of the cuts were made, it seems, by decision of Wielhorski, though Glinka evidently endorsed them, listing them very objectively in his *Memoirs*: 'From the Introduction [to Act I] it was necessary to cut the Bayan's second song, "There is a desert land",[3] and in like manner the whole concluding development (*développement et péroraison*) of the main theme

Lei- te pol - ne - ye ku-bok zla - toi

had to be subsequently deleted.

'In the finale to the first act the chorus to Lel in B major in $\frac{5}{4}$ was shortened . . . In Act III in place of the exceedingly difficult entr'acte which I had written, it was necessary to start straight off with the chorus, "The gloom of night lies over the field" [the Persian Chorus], the first verses of which are sung off-stage. In the finale the trio, "Why

---

[1] Not April, as stated in the *Memoirs*.

[2] GLN1, p. 224.

[3] This song, which tells of the 'young singer' whose work will one day immortalize Ruslan and Lyudmila, was a compliment to Pushkin, but it seems that the censor banned it because of its obvious reminder of Pushkin's exile. It had been published as a romance with other words in 1840, but it was still excluded from the first vocal score of *Ruslan and Lyudmila* which appeared in 1856.

love, why suffer", had to be cut because it slowed up the progress of the drama. In the fourth act Lyudmila's scene, for which Stepanova had thanked me during the rehearsals in the halls, completely failed on stage, and that very same Stepanova reproached me because I had calculated the scenic effect badly. In the finale of this and the last act it was necessary to shorten a lot.'[1]

It was the last act which was shortened most drastically of all. When Wielhorski heard the first part of this act at rehearsal, he bluntly told Glinka that it was 'bad'. Glinka retorted indignantly that though the music might be dramatically ineffective, it certainly was not bad; nevertheless the result was that 'the whole of that section of the fifth act was subsequently dropped'.[2] Thus much of the ruthless revision which produced the final form of this act was made during the rehearsals themselves. After the première further cuts were made at Cavos's suggestion.[3]

Most of the information we possess about the composition of *Ruslan and Lyudmila* is verbal. The manuscript remains of Glinka's second opera are more slender than those of *A Life for the Tsar*, and we have therefore much less information about musical revisions made during composition. Glinka's original score was destroyed in the fire at the theatre in St. Petersburg in 1859, and though there are autograph scores of a few movements of the opera, all published editions of the full score have had to rely upon a manuscript copy whose date is unknown, and about whose reliability nothing is certain. The theatre fire also destroyed the parts for

---

[1] GLN1, p. 223. The earliest surviving score of the opera, a manuscript copy (Glinka's manuscript score was burnt in 1859), shows the following cuts. Some could be those referred to in the *Memoirs;* whether the others were also made for the first performance is unknown:

Act I: Finale, bars 181–4.
Act II: Farlaf's Rondo, bars 175–264.
Act III: Persian Chorus, bars 25–48 (verse 2), and 97–116 (last verse). Naina's part is not included at all in this manuscript copy.
Act IV: Lyudmila's aria, bars 135–81, 209–19, 317–32. Chernomor's March, the second statement of the trio and return of first section.
         Chorus 'Let him perish', bars 34–77.
         Finale, bars 152–85, 193–219.
Act V: Entr'acte, bars 49–78.
         Finale, bars 29–44, 131–60, 234–58, 330–525.

[2] GLN1, p. 226.

[3] In the issue for December 1842 of the periodical, *The Reading Room*, Senkovsky extolled the beauties and originality of *Ruslan and Lyudmila* very enthusiastically in an article which is as intelligent as it is lengthy; yet he recommended the most drastic pruning which would have involved the excision of some of those pieces which had proved most successful. This article is quoted in LPG2, pp. 237–49.

the military band which plays on stage during certain movements of the opera. Since the instrumentation for this band is not included in the surviving copy of the full score, we shall never know exactly how it sounded at the first performances. In fact Glinka entrusted the scoring of the military band music to Fyodor Ral, who was on the music staff of the Imperial Theatres; the version now used is that made by Rimsky-Korsakov for the first publication of the full score in 1878. In this same edition Balakirev also provided arrangements for a single orchestra of those movements which involved the military band.[1] The one movement from *Ruslan and Lyudmila* which does still exist in a second version which may have been made by Glinka himself is Finn's Ballad. This alternative transposes the original down a tone, and revises the orchestration. It has been suggested that this may have been done for the first performance of the opera in Moscow in 1846, though it is equally possible that it was made in the course of the very first performances in St. Petersburg. It is quite certain that Glinka, at the theatre's request, transposed down a tone both Lyudmila's cavatina in Act I and her scena and aria in Act IV, and both these transpositions were retained in the first vocal score (1856); a note in the manuscript copy allows for both these transpositions. It is clear from some very fragmenatry sketches that have survived of the chorus, 'Let him perish', in Act IV that this was originally designed as a double fugue; a trace of one of the subjects survives in a very animated form in the first violin part in bars 13–14 (see Ex. 46k and l).

---

[1] Glinka himself scored Chernomor's March, which in the opera uses the military band, for single orchestra, and this version has survived. Curiously it includes no bell part in the trio, though Glinka's *Memoirs* make it clear that bells were intended from the very beginning.

10/*Ruslan and Lyudmila: The Music*

PARADOXICALLY one of the most favourable features of Pushkin's *Ruslan and Lyudmila*, as far as Glinka was concerned, was that it was not particularly Russian. The subject of *A Life for the Tsar* had been just that, and Glinka had drawn upon Russian folk-music characteristics in order to impart the requisite national flavour to an otherwise Western-based form. It had worked well, but there were limits to the possibilities within such a blend. If Pushkin's poem had been strongly Russian it might have tempted Glinka to concentrate again upon the same nationalizing processes as he had used in *A Life for the Tsar*. Now, however, he needed to go further, and to produce music which was Russian not simply because it had audible affinities with folk music, but because it reflected characteristic ways in which a Russian would devise and work his material when composing within a sophisticated musical language. There are, in fact, more folk melodies in *Ruslan and Lyudmila* than in the earlier opera, but they are mostly non-Russian, and in the case of the two most prominent (the themes used for Finn's Ballad and the Persian Chorus) the interest is less in the melodies themselves than in what Glinka does with them—in other words, they are no longer important simply because of their intrinsic regional character, but are now potent stimuli to Glinka's imagination. And it was just this imaginative stimulus which was also the most important property of Pushkin's poem. The fact that the subject was unreal, without many opportunities for the expression of deep or demonstrative human passions, did not really matter. Such things might have been essential to a composer of strong personality who cared deeply about these matters in life itself, and whose music was strongly marked by his own personality. It has been remarked earlier that Glinka himself was quite unexercised by anything beyond the events of his own existence, most of which were trivia. Just as his biography reveals how ordinary he was as a man, so his music never gives the impression of a marked personality. To feel intensely about things outside his own little life would have been beyond him, and the patriotism of *A Life for the Tsar*, real as it is, has nothing of the burning passion of Beethoven's idealism in *Fidelio*. Nor is the love music of *A Life for the Tsar* much more than perfunctory, for Glinka was incapable of experiencing in his own love-life a consuming passion such as fired Wagner in *Tristan und Isolde*. Glinka's best music is not the product of a vitally feeling personality but of a vivid and ready imagination. If it had reflected a personal view it would have been more consistent in style; being the product of a stimulated imagination, it turned out with the brilliance and unpredictability with which that imagination responded to stimulus. This is not the sort of situation which produces a work consistent in quality any more than in style, and *Ruslan and Lyudmila* is exasperatingly variable. Yet it was perhaps just this variability which made it so rich a source of ideas and inspiration for later Russian composers, for the range of ideas and manners is prodigious for a single work.

Dramatically it was doomed from the beginning. Pushkin's tale was full of scattered incidents, and needed pruning to become a satisfactory opera libretto. It would be unfair to put the blame for not doing this entirely on Bakhturin, since Glinka himself all too easily succumbed to the temptations of discursiveness. The great strength of the story of *A Life for the Tsar* had lain in its extreme simplicity, and Glinka had been compelled to supplement the basic incident with the love interest provided by Antonida and Sobinin in order to give it enough range and activity to make an acceptable opera plot. While composing it he had tended to expand, but fortunately the opera was completed largely in one creative burst so that there had been insufficient time for the discursiveness to get out of hand. In any case, Glinka made a very determined attempt to ensure a tight structure to the whole opera. The story had also offered splendid dramatic opportunities for which Glinka had evolved a new, flexible recitative manner which enabled him to treat scenes of developing dramatic action to continuous music. Yet he largely abandoned this recitative manner in *Ruslan and Lyudmila*, not because there were no contexts where he might have used it, fewer though they were, but because he chose to make little use of the opportunities that were offered. The trouble with *Ruslan and Lyudmila* was not so much that it was a tale that fitted uncomfortably within the ordered economy of the operatic plot, nor even that Bakhturin's scenario was a bad point of departure, for Glinka could have modified this as he went along: the real trouble was that Glinka took too long writing it, working spasmodically and unsystematically, composing what took his fancy with little concern for continuity or proportion, until he had written too much of the wrong sort of music, however good much of that music might be in itself. His letter to Shirkov early in 1841 makes this abundantly clear, though he himself was still unaware of it; of the nine movements already completed, eight were formal set pieces, and most of the pieces he was currently working on were essentially decorative (both sets of dances and the final chorus of Act V); some of the sections where something actually happened (the finale to Act III, the crucial encounter between Ruslan and Chernomor, and the abortive murder scene) had not even been started. Thus when he had at last got round to treating these incidents and the other smaller bits of action between the set pieces, he found them crowded out by the formal movements he had already composed. It was a fatal flaw which no amount of drastic pruning at rehearsals could conceal. *Ruslan and Lyudmila* still sounds like a series of self-contained set pieces, many of little or no relevance to the main thread of the plot, perfunctorily joined together, with occasional incidents which are inexplicable because some essential detail of Pushkin's poem has been overlooked. The result could not be other than a dramatic disaster.

Act I is the one exception to this. Glinka's liking for decorative spectacle could be a snare, but here it is apt, and Lyudmila's abduction is a splendidly treated climax. But the remaining four acts show all too clearly how he concentrated on the interstices of the drama, or on irrelevancies. Thus, of the five musical movements which make up Act II, two are narratives of past events of only marginal importance to the plot of the opera. The musical quality of Finn's Ballad at the beginning of the act might carry the audience through this static stage, but to treat so perfunctorily Ruslan's encounter with the Head (this is, after all, the moment of maximum tension, yet the climax is so feeble as to be ludicrous), and then to end with the extended non-drama of the Head's narrative was to kill the act completely. And how, one might ask, could Ruslan have been so improvident as to set out in search of Lyudmila without bothering to arm himself? The answer is that in Pushkin's poem his sword had been broken in his encounter with Rogdai, but this rival suitor and the combat are entirely omitted from the opera. Act III makes matters worse, since it is entirely superfluous, except that by finally pairing up Ratmir and Gorislava, it gives Ruslan a clear field as far as Lyudmila is concerned—though, in so doing, it deals a disastrous blow to Ratmir's image. Farlaf is only a comic suitor, but Ratmir should surely be considered a serious rival to Ruslan, and his transference of affection from Lyudmila to Gorislava would have been a process attended by some emotional crisis, unless he was the helpless victim of enchantment, as in Pushkin's poem; yet in the opera a few portentous words from Finn about destiny's intentions for the two couples is enough to effect this change of allegiance. A man who can so lightly change, even under the dictates of an 'immutable fate', is a mean man indeed. In Act IV we at last meet the villain Chernomor, who offers Lyudmila a ballet, is then summarily defeated by Ruslan, and disappears completely from the opera. Since there has already been a ballet in Act III, a second one is even less desirable. By this stage of the opera dramatic tension has utterly gone, and the drastic pruning which Glinka sanctioned in Act V was really a desperate attempt to ring down the curtain as quickly as possible on a situation which had become embarrassing.

Ruslan and Lyudmila is so flawed dramatically that there is no hope that it will ever become a repertoire piece outside Russia. Yet this impossible opera proved to be a work whose seminal influence in nineteenth century music was exceeded only by that of Beethoven's Ninth Symphony and Wagner's *Tristan und Isolde*. Without it the course of later nineteenth century Russian music would have been quite different. Here for the first time appeared that strain of orientalism and that 'magic' idiom which later Russians were to exploit.[1] More important still, here was established that heroic manner which is of such importance in certain works of later Russian composers—in Borodin's *Prince Igor,* Mussorgsky's *Khovanshchina,* Balakirev's *Russia,* to name but three. Here, in Ratmir's romance in Act V, was the source of a whole line of comparable compositions in later Russian music; here in several movements were fully demonstrated the possibilities of the changing-background tech-

[1] Senkovsky, the editor of *The Reading Room*, was quick to perceive the novelty of Glinka's treatment of operatic enchantment, and to recognize Glinka's eclecticism. 'In German "enchantment" the forms of the subjects are clothed in indefinable mystery, in gloom, in the mists of superstition and rapture; in a Russian fairy tale, on the other hand, all is light, happy, playful, distinct, diverse, out of the ordinary, amazing. And the music for a Russian fairy-tale subject must combine all these qualities—and these very qualities you will find here [in *Ruslan and Lyudmila*], developed to the highest degree, and with masterly art . . . Almost all music is joined together in it [*Ruslan and Lyudmila*]—eastern and western—Russian, Italian, German, Finnish, Tartar, Caucasian, Persian, Arabian—and all this forms the most artistic, truly picturesque whole.' (Issue of November 1842, quoted in LPG2, p. 233.)

nique which was to prove such a congenial method to the Russian when
building an extended structure. Above all, here was a work filled with
music which was non-Western not merely because it drew melodic life
from folk-song, but because it showed, for the first time in first-class
music, a character and characteristics which came from the Russian
nature itself, with which later Russian composers could readily identify,
and from which they could draw suggestions and inspiration for their
own works. Though as an opera it is a catastrophe, the quality of much
of the music is splendid, and some movements, taken by themselves,
are masterly dramatic conceptions.

The whole-tone scale, which is always associated with Chernomor,
is the one really clear Leitmotif in *Ruslan and Lyudmila*, but since it occurs
only three times during the opera, it has no all-pervasive importance,
striking as it may be. In its dearth of Leitmotif *Ruslan and Lyudmila* represents a retreat from *A Life for the Tsar*. Nevertheless there are certain pronounced affinities between a number of prominent themes in Glinka's
second opera which serve to give a marked consistency of character to
different parts of the work. The source theme appears to be the opening
of the allegro con spirito of Ruslan's aria in Act II (Ex. 46d), one of the

Ex. 46.

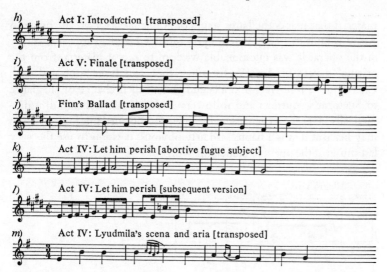

h) Act I: Introduction [transposed]

i) Act V: Finale [transposed]

j) Finn's Ballad [transposed]

k) Act IV: Let him perish [abortive fugue subject]

l) Act IV: Let him perish [subsequent version]

m) Act IV: Lyudmila's scena and aria [transposed]

earliest parts of the opera to be sketched, though its roots clearly go back beyond this to Russian folk music, perhaps to a folk-song like 'The snows are not white' (Ex. 46a). It proliferates effortlessly into new related shapes, even drawing close to the A minor chorus in the Act V finale (Ex. 46i) and the genuine folk tune of Finn's Ballad (Ex. 46j) through the lopped version of Ex. 46h, and exposing, as clearly as in *A Life for the Tsar*, the most tangible part of the secret of Glinka's melodic nationalism —the ability to write constant variations against the outline of some fundamental Russian prototype. The relationship between these melodies was a useful partner to Glinka's more deliberate efforts to impose an overall musical structure upon the whole opera.[1] Though in *Ruslan and Lyudmila* there is nothing like the intensive accumulation of familiar

[1] It is also worth noting the similarity of melodic contour between another two otherwise very different themes. Ex. 47a is the second subject of the allegro con spirito of Ruslan's aria in Act II (and of the Overture); Ex. 47b is a fragment from Lyudmila's part in Act V, sung after her awakening.

Ex. 47.

a) Ruslan's aria [transposed]

b) Lyudmila in Act V

material that marks the latter stages of *A Life for the Tsar*, the finale to Act V is built to a large extent upon music which had appeared earlier in the opera. It was questionable wisdom to repeat material from the oriental dances of Act IV, for there they had been associated with Chernomor's followers (Ex. 48a and c), and their change of allegiance to Svetozar's courtiers and followers in Act V (Ex. 48b and d) is dramatically inept, however acceptable their transformed musical condition may be. But it was a happy, if fairly obvious, decision to use the very last music of the opera to launch the work.

Ex. 48.

(The happiness and delights of pure love)

The neat and sparkling Overture is Glinka's most thoroughly satisfactory sonata structure. Like its counterpart in *A Life for the Tsar*, it sets out to presage the clash of opposing forces which is to follow. A substantial chunk of the allegro con spirito in Ruslan's aria provides the second subject, while the second of the pair of vigorous ideas from the Act V finale, which together make up the first subject, is a theme related to the very opening of the allegro con spirito of that aria (see Ex. 46d and e). In the Overture Chernomor is represented first by the chords which change round a single note during Lyudmila's abduction in Act I,[1] and then by the whole-tone scale, briefly used in the bass during the Overture's coda (Ex. 49) to produce an unusual structure of major triads

Ex.49. Presto

surmounted by fragments of Ruslan-related music. Thus Glinka graphically suggests his hero sliding rapidly up D major, B flat major and G flat major triads as the result of Chernomor's bass machinations, only to make an enharmonic leap back to D, regain his balance, and pin the dwarf down on to his dominant. It is a stroke as brilliant as it is brief.

The four entr'actes all serve the same function to the act they precede as the Overture does to the whole opera, in that each is founded largely or entirely upon music which comes at the end of the act. The last two entr'actes are no more than orchestral transcriptions of entire sections from the succeeding acts. In the case of Act V, the transcription of the lament of Svetozar's courtiers is preceded by a brusque derivative from an earlier chorus, but the Entr'acte to Act II aims at much greater independence by unfolding a series of abrupt alternations of elements from the Head's narrative and the Farlaf-Naina duet. The result, like that of the

[1] See Ex. 55, bars 13–21.

last entr'acte of the *Kholmsky* music, is as rough and effective[1] as that of the remaining entr'acte (to Act III) is smooth and ineffective. In the latter, Glinka wished to foreshadow the major dramatic incident of Finn's intervention, but since he had set this in recitative, the vocal part was unsuitable for use in the entr'acte. All that remained was a harmonic structure which Glinka decorated with semiquaver figuration to fashion the first half of the entr'acte. The result might almost be taken for the introduction to some early nineteenth century German symphony; here it is incongruous and rather dull.

Glinka had a pronounced liking for mediant relationships, particularly chromatic ones, and especially when they involved a bass move of a major third. This characteristic shift is a significant factor in making Act I of *Ruslan and Lyudmila*, like its counterpart in *A Life for the Tsar*, the most satisfactory in the opera. A chromatic mediant shift had produced the unexpected key for the second subject in the Overture's exposition (F major against a D tonic), a relationship which may have been designed as a preparation for the opposition of D major to a B flat tonic which is the main tonal feature of the Introduction to Act I. This act is as notable for its clear planning of dramatic events as for its satisfying tonal structure. It surrounds a predominantly solo centre with two solo-choral flanks, both of which are marked by a basic tension between keys whose roots are a major third apart, deployed in such a way that the scheme for the second turns out to be almost an inversion of that for the first (Ex. 50). Between these two chunks, founded upon B flat and E flat respectively, is set Lyudmila's cavatina in G major. Ex. 50 also shows material relationships which reinforce this lucid tonal structure;[2] to these should be added the tonic-dominant invocation to Lel which is heard in the choral interjections in Lyudmila's cavatina, and which recurs in the C flat major (written B major) section of the second flank. Had Glinka maintained the dramatic and structural level of this act, *Ruslan and Lyudmila* would have been a masterpiece.

Glinka's archaic-heroic vein, which is prominent in much of the music of this act, was far from being a re-writing of genuine old music.

[1] Tchaikovsky rated this entr'acte very highly, just as he did the last of the Kholmsky entr'actes: 'If Glinka had written nothing but this brief piece, a judge of music would still have, on the strength of this alone, to number him along with the most first-rate musical talents.' (Quoted in LPG1, p. 372.)

[2] It is perhaps worth noting the cadential passage which concludes the first E flat section of Flank II, which is recalled in bars 405–9 of the very last E flat section. The final cadence of the act is an assertion of the chromatic mediant relationship.

Ex.50.

FLANK I

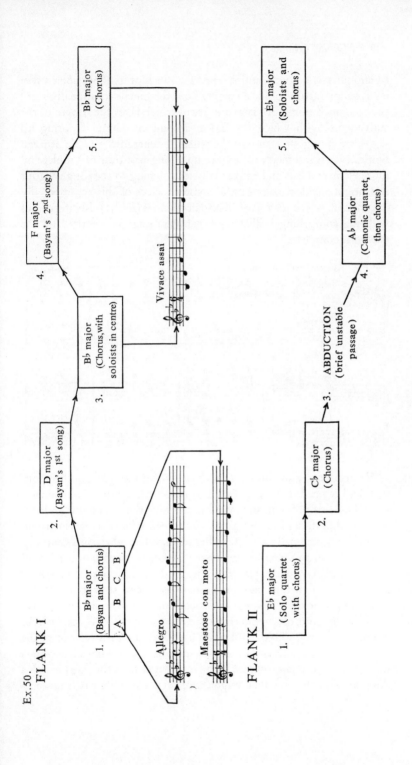

| 1. Bb major (Bayan and chorus) | 2. D major (Bayan's 1st song) | 3. Bb major (Chorus, with soloists in centre) | 4. F major (Bayan's 2nd song) | 5. Bb major (Chorus) |

A B C B

Allegro

Maestoso con moto

Vivace assai

FLANK II

| 1. Eb major (Solo quartet with chorus) | 2. Cb major (Chorus) | 3. ABDUCTION (brief unstable passage) | 4. Ab major (Canonic quartet, then chorus) | 5. Eb major (Soloists and chorus) |

Its antiquity was bogus, and it relied for much of its effect upon a few clear, simple strokes of local colour. Thus the touches of modalism and the combined sound of piano and harp, which fakes the timbre of the native gusli with which the Bayan accompanies himself during his songs, are enough to transport the willing listener into 'ye olde' Russian world. Nor is it difficult to conjure up a long-past time of simpler and more elemental acts and emotions when listening to the rough vigour and bright, strident colouring of some choruses of this act, especially the one in $\frac{5}{4}$, which may have Georgian affinities (Ex. 51). Reinforce this with the compelling brilliance of elaborate stage pageantry, and the illusion is complete.

Yet it is largely an illusion. Detach the Bayan's songs from their context, and it needs little perception to detect the sentimental romance behind the first of them, and even more behind the second. In this latter one, could anything be more typical of a romance (or of a drawing room ballad), or more un-Russian (whether medieval or nineteenth-century), than the accompaniment figure, or the dominant seventh in bar five of Ex. 52, which opposes blatantly the local colour so selfconsciously sought in the first four bars? Yet listen to the bass shift to a flattened seventh in bar eleven before it twists back on to E natural in bar twelve —and, even more, observe the unexpected breadth of the second melodic phrase which spans itself out for six bars over the firm descent of the bass to its plagal cadence in the relative minor: such things it is which move the piece away to something far stronger than the short-winded domestic pleasantries which might have been feared after bars seven to

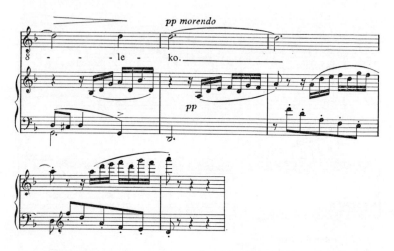

(There is a desert country, a desolate shore; it is a far place at midnight.)

eleven. Note also the melodic expansiveness of bars five to nine of the Bayan's first song (Ex. 53), the terse strong phrases of bars ten to thirteen with their underpinning of forceful appoggiaturas and powerful minor-chord plagal progressions on to the supertonic (B minor after A major); note, too, the laconic fatalism of the abrupt and bare final phrase. Through these factors the music gains that strength which is an indispensable element in the evocation of this romantic world of past heroes and deeds of long ago—a strength which may come from melodic breadth, rhythmic virility, or harmonic sturdiness.

Lyudmila's cavatina in the centre of the act is consistent neither in style nor in quality. The brief choral interjection in $\frac{5}{4}$ is as lovely as it is un-Western, but the first part of the aria, despite its very Russian opening phrase, is overburdened with Italianate coloratura of a type Glinka might have been expected to scorn. It is likewise Italianate in its allegro moderato, though there are one or two tiny touches which betray Glinka at work.[1] But the third section, addressed to Ratmir, borrows a little of that character's orientalism to present a few bars which Borodin could have comfortably incorporated in his *Polovtsian Dances*. The dominant major ninth of Ex. 54a, chromatically flattening in bar two to

---

[1] Like the passing flattened sixth in bar 92, for instance.

(With the dawn the flower of love, of spring adorns itself
with luxurious beauty: and suddenly, beneath the vault of
azure itself, the leaves are scattered by the gust of a tempest.)

Ex. 54. **L'istesso tempo [Allegro moderato]**

a)

Mech u - kro - - yet— pod— tsve - ta - mi,

(She conceals the sword beneath flowers.)

b) **Andantino [transposed]**

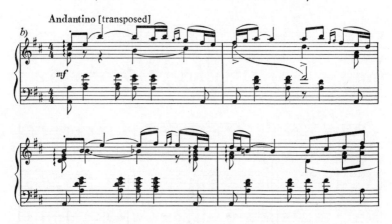

c) **Allegro non troppo, ma con fuoco**

resolve on to a second inversion tonic, prefigures other moments in later Russian music where orientalism appears either avowedly or simply by suggestion. Ex. 54a could have been the nucleus of the first of Borodin's dances (Ex. 54b); similarly it could have been the source of the second subject in the finale of Balakirev's Piano Sonata (Ex. 54c). Both Borodin and Balakirev had eastern blood in them, yet it was from Glinka, whose ancestry was rooted in the western bounds of Russia, that they caught the first suggestions for their own oriental music. It is a pity that this cavatina is not more consistent, for it is an effective piece, dramatically enlivened by choral interjections, though in no way matching the theatrical impact and musico-dramatic mastery of the following scene in which Lyudmila is abducted. Here the sudden intrusion of Chernomor's whole-tone scale (Ex. 55) ensures a tonal disruption matching the dramatic one, and the dwarf's presence is confirmed by his characteristic device of otherwise unrelated chords suspended upon a single note they have in common (Ex. 55, bars 13–21). The hypnotic power of the spell

Ex. 55.

with which he binds the assembled guests is brilliantly suggested by the prolongation of the E flat on the horns through a further forty-six bars of adagio music. It was also an apt idea to chain the principals into a hushed vocal canon, and later the nervous little flute flutter above the awestruck music for the chorus is like a last lingering flicker of the magic which holds all in stunned subjection. For dramatic ends achieved through musical means this is not only the finest scene Glinka ever wrote, but as impressive as any in nineteenth century music.

The problems of extended musical structure were among the most difficult the Russian composer had to solve. Composers of the central European tradition had learned to generate movements through tonal argument and thematic development, but these evolving techniques did not come at all easily to the Russian. We have already observed in this book how Glinka was repeatedly drawn towards variation procedures as a means of extending a movement. As early as the Symphony in B flat he had treated folk-tunes to simple variations, and the technique had been consolidated in the Symphony on two Russian themes and the Capriccio on Russian themes, both composed in Berlin in 1834. So, too, we have noted the part played by variation procedures in *A Life for the Tsar*. Yet it was not until *Ruslan and Lyudmila* that the trend shown in all these earlier pieces reached its complete fulfilment. The earliest movement to embody the changing-background technique fully formed was the Persian Chorus in Act III of *Ruslan and Lyudmila*, where Glinka used a borrowed tune[1] to set lines taken from Pushkin's poem. The result is

---

[1] There is considerable doubt about whether the tune upon which Glinka founded this chorus is genuinely Persian, since it was widely disseminated in various forms in many of the S.E. regions of Russia.

certainly one of the most perfect pieces in the opera, with unstrained variety of background, especially notable perhaps for the chromatic flute arabesques set against a warm cello line in the third verse (Ex. 56a), followed by a darker fourth verse which views the tune from the relative minor and exploits the clash of flattened and sharpened leading notes (Ex. 56b).

Two of the five movements of Act II employ the changing-background principle. The Head's narrative, which ends the act, is a

(With us you will find a swarm of beauties.)

(For you from the dawn of morning [we will fill a farewell cup].)

similar type of strophic piece to the Persian Chorus, though less inventive in background than that sensuous music of dusky houris. Clearly the changing-background method was one which, if constantly used in its simplest repetitive form, could soon prove monotonous. The Head's narrative has interjections for Ruslan after each of its first two verses, and Glinka uses the method with even greater freedom in the D minor opening section to the finale of Act V, where he allows his theme to hover between soprano and alto, to migrate to the bass for two verses, to be seen from a different key point (F major), while against the five statements of the theme he unfolds a scene, just as he had done against less systematic repetitions in the middle of Act III of *A Life for the Tsar* (see above, p. 126). In Finn's Ballad, which opens Act II, he combines changing background procedures with rondo features, for though the piece is monothematic, it twice breaks away from straightforward thematic repetition to interpolate passages which include rising modulations, and which have the effect of episodes in a rondo structure. To have held rigidly in this context to some eight or nine unvaried reiterations would have been to court monotony; in any case Finn's narrative has dramatic implications not possessed by the completely decorative Persian Chorus. The virtuoso pursuit of unrelenting repetition had to wait until *Kamarinskaya*.

While Act II has nothing like the dramatic sweep of Act I, and while its climax is feeble, its actual music is perhaps more consistently fine. The Head's narrative, dramatically inept as it is, is worthwhile in itself, and Finn's Ballad is splendid. The following duet for Farlaf and Naina proved to be the precedent for a type of 'magic' music which was to recur a good deal in later Russian scores. Farlaf's introductory recitative

Glinka and his servant, Jakov. Drawing by N. A. Stepanov

PLATE III

proclaims clearly that there is an Italian root to this style, and the duet continues to use the quaver patter of opera buffa in its vocal lines. The novelty of this music lies in the orchestral part which is light-textured, with sharp, clear colours, taut, pert rhythms, and with much use of diminished triads and intervals, and constant very tiny chromatic details (Ex. 57). Glinka has here deftly caught something of the playful side of Pushkin's

Ex.57. L'istesso tempo [Allegro]   NAINA

Po - ver, na-pras-no tui khlo-po-chesh

i strakh i mu-ku pe-re - no-sish:

Lyud-mi - lu mu-dre-no sui-skat!

O - na da - le-ko za-be-zha-la.

Stu-pai do- moi   i zhdi me-nya,

(Believe me, you are agitating yourself and enduring fear and torture in vain. To search for Lyudmila is hard; she has fled a long way. Go home and wait for me.)

poem, for this Naina is no frightening ogress but the fantasy figure of a child's fairy story, and her encounter with Farlaf is more than half humorous. Naina is seen too little in this opera for any sharply defined personality to be projected, but Glinka neatly catches her image in a few economical strokes. The witch who conjures up such tritone-related sevenths to substantiate her identity is no import from Western opera (Ex. 58). Mussorgsky was to use this seventh progression as an important

Ex. 58. Allegro

NAINA: I tak, uz-nai: vol-sheb-ni-tsa Na-i-na ya!

FARLAF: O u-zhas!

(*Naina*: And thus know: I am the enchantress Naina!
Farlaf: O horror!)

motif in *Boris Godunov*. Farlaf, the cowardly braggart, is a much more conventional type, as his rondo, good as it is of its kind, is less interesting. He is a Russian-naturalized opera buffa figure, and it is only necessary to recall, say, the B flat 'champagne' aria for the hero in Act I of Mozart's *Don Giovanni* to realize that Farlaf's rondo is almost all purely Italian in style. Not so Ruslan's aria, which is the most impressive solo movement in the whole opera, and which, as has been shown, cast its influence over much other music in the work. Its three parts—a recitative, a largo, and an allegro con spirito—each start with a variant of the same theme as a kind of headmotif (see Ex. 46b, c and d). This is noble heroic music of Beethovenian strength—though thoroughly un-Beethovenian in other respects.[1] After the richly dark orchestral colouring in the recitative, it unfolds with sombre firmness through the largo, in which the brooding chromaticism of bar seven of Ex. 60 seems to draw the music down into even darker shadow, and ends with powerful resolution in the allegro con spirito, a movement which has the outlines of a sonata structure, and in which the second subject appears in the same chromatic mediant relationship to the first subject as it had in the overture, though this time

Ex.60. Largo

Vre - myon ot vech - noi tem - no - tui, buit

[1] Except, perhaps, for the end of the orchestral prelude which is curiously redolent of the Offertory from Beethoven's *Missa solemnis* (Ex. 59), which Glinka must surely have heard at its first complete performance in St. Petersburg in 1824.

Ex. 59.

a) Moderato   GLINKA

b) Sostenuto ma non troppo   BEETHOVEN

(Perhaps there is no salvation for me from the eternal darkness of time. Perhaps on some silent hill they will set the
quiet grave of Ruslan.)

the relationship is the more surprising for occurring in the recapitulation, not in the exposition. Yet despite its sonata patterning, the allegro
con spirito is essentially a melodic conception demonstrating Glinka's
masterly ability to invent melody which is strong enough in itself to
sustain the broad span of the movement. As in the Overture, the coda of
this aria provides a deft musical anticipation of the forthcoming struggle
of Ruslan and Chernomor, for at the words 'in vain the enchanted
strength of a cloud moves over us', Ruslan's tune is briefly thrown off
course by a succession of chords which has strong whole-tone implications in its bass relationships (Ex. 61).

(In vain the enchanted strength of a cloud moves over us.)

Much of the characterization of this opera is admirable, thanks not to Glinka's handling of the actual actions engineered by the plot, for at these moments the actors often seem no more than puppets, but thanks to the music which he devised for each character. Fortunately Ruslan's main scenes in the opera place him in varied situations, and Glinka's music is therefore able to portray him with considerable roundness, revealing him resolute without arrogance in danger, capable of deep but manly distress in sorrow, and tender but unsentimental in love. Avoidance of sentimentality also marks Glinka's portrayal of Gorislava's distress in Act III. This Act opens with the Persian Chorus and continues with Gorislava's cavatina, in which Glinka's rich diatonic harmony, abounding in seventh chords and suspensions, and enhanced by the use of pedals, is a splendid support to the singer's full-throated lament. The tormented sequence of Ex. 62a might possibly have suggested to Tchaikovsky the opening of the Prelude to *Yevgeny Onegin* (Ex. 62b),

(Is it really possible for me, in the prime of life and love, to say: 'Farewell for ever!'?)

though Glinka's phrase is stronger and his chromaticism is less fundamental to the progress of the phrase than is Tchaikovsky's. The latter's
is far more emotional, too, proceeding in four brief, panting phrases
which always return to the same sighing cadence, and culminating in a
long-drawn span of subsiding emotion when the sequences of Ex. 62b
are drawn out over four and a half bars. Tchaikovsky's throbbing, soft-
centred chromaticism contrasts sharply with Glinka's which, even when
used expressively, still has a firmness which prevents it becoming over-
ripe. There is pathos in plenty in the coda of Gorislava's cavatina (Ex.
62c), but not a trace of sentimentality.

The fact is that for Glinka, chromaticism served colouristic more than
emotional ends. True, it could be used to enrich pathos (as in Gorislava's
cavatina,) but he also applied it to dazzle with uncompromising brazen-
ness (as in the trombone bass to the Arabian Dance in Act IV (Ex. 63)),
and most often of all, to enrich a diatonic background with a patch or
perhaps only a tiny touch of colour, often associated with seventh or
ninth chords and with sustained or pedal bass parts. Not infrequently a
chromatic passage in the coda sets the expressive seal upon a piece.
Chromaticism was, of course, a particularly useful source of variety in
movements founded upon the changing-background technique. Since
any extended passage of ascending chromaticism tends to raise tension
and serve emotional ends, Glinka's is almost always descending. His
favourite chromatic note was the flattened sixth which is found dozens of
times throughout his work, becoming not only a fingerprint of his style

Ex.63. Allegro con spirito

but also of later Russian music. Pictorial chromaticism, as in the tempestuous gusts which represent the Head's blowing in Act II,[1] is untypical of Glinka, and he makes no use of chromaticism to suggest sexual passion. Surprisingly this commodity is notably absent from *Ruslan and Lyudmila*, for even the seductive dances of Naina's maidens in Act III are quite unerotic; the Cornish night of *Tristan und Isolde* is infinitely less temperate than these scented Persian airs. The dances through which Ratmir was to be seduced are even prim, could mostly have been taken straight from a formal French ballet, and have nothing that might credibly induce even the most susceptible to sexual abandon. It is difficult to believe that Gorislava had much to fear from such competition. It seems, indeed, that Glinka was simply unable to express real physical passion in music, a failing which may account for the disastrous end to the aria which Ratmir sings just before these dances. It starts beautifully enough with its Tartar theme, and, with its languid echoes of the singer's phrases by obbligato cor anglais, it conjures up all the dark romance of the East. Likewise its second borrowed tune (of Arab origin) is turned by Glinka's treatment into a characteristic piece of Russian orientalism (Ex. 64), which emphasizes devastatingly the stylistic non-sequitur of the concluding section, where the languishing oriental, approaching the height of passion, is converted into a waltzing Westerner. Glinka betrayed Ratmir badly in *Ruslan and Lyudmila*.

There is much that is beautiful and characteristic in the solo/choral

---

[1] It was this passage Glinka had in mind when he told Serov that the opera had 'a storm, only not at all like those in *The Barber* [*of Seville, William*] *Tell*, and various other operas: this will be the wind moaning, as it does in a Russian stove chimney.' (SVG, p. 150.)

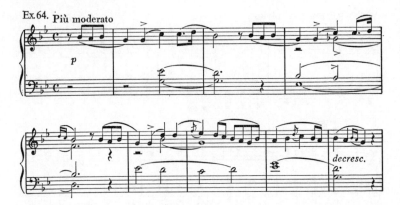

Ex. 64. Più moderato

ensemble of seduction which opens the finale to Act III. The choral parts
in particular are captivating, and Gorislava's two solo outbursts are
quite heart-rending. At first sight it may seem that Glinka has underplayed
Finn's intervention, but the use of simple accompanied recitative brings
just the right note of plain reality to break the elaborate enchantment
which is alleged to have woven itself around Ruslan and Ratmir. It is
to be regretted that the concluding quartet is so stiff and formal, despite
the attractive warmth of the accompaniment passages for cellos *divisi a 4*
and double bass.

The general level of Act IV is much higher both musically and dramatically. Lyudmila's aria, with which it opens, is punctuated by choral
interjections, thus creating a constant tension between the tempting
words of Chernomor's rusalkas and Lyudmila's resistance. She had also
been served with choral interludes in her cavatina in Act I, which had
again afforded her an active situation in which more facets of her character might be revealed than in the straightforward soliloquy aria. The
result is that it is perhaps she who emerges as the most vivid personality
in the whole opera—vivacious, mischievous, and a bit of an exhibitionist
in Act I, but in Act IV facing trials and torments with the same spirit
which carries her from despair through sorrow to bold defiance. Glinka's
music for female chorus in this opera is always very appealing, but none
of the choral interjections in Lyudmila's aria quite equals the exquisite
sounds of the little lullaby which follows, in which women's voices,
accompanied by harp, musical glasses, and the soft sounds of the wind,
weave a spell of delicate enchantment which Glinka never surpassed
(Ex. 65). Chernomor's brilliantly original march (Ex. 66), which makes

(Peaceful dream, calm the heart of a maid! Let sadness and melancholy fly away from her! Having forgotten her betrothed, let the princess live here.)

Ex.66.[Tempo di marcia]

use of the dwarf's characteristic musical trait of otherwise unrelated chords suspended upon the one note they have in common (see also Ex. 55, bars 13–21), catches the grotesque little sorcerer most vividly, and is a truly marvellous example of that Russian gift for creative caricature which manages to be bizarre without becoming ridiculous. Glinka may have written pieces that are bolder in sound than this, but never one that was more utterly new in character; it is the first of those brilliantly grotesque studies which are to be found in Russian music— like Mussorgsky's Gnome or his two Jews in the *Pictures from an Exhibition,* for instance. Indeed, Mussorgsky seems to have borrowed the trio of Chernomor's March for another piece in this set, the ballet of the chicks in their shells (Ex. 66b and c).

The Turkish Dance (see Ex. 48c) is beautiful, especially in the delicate chromatic tinting at the end, but the Arabian Dance is less consistent, striking as is the brazen chromatic tread of the trombones (see Ex. 63), for an incident like the little bell theme converts the piece momentarily into a polite, if playful waltz. The Lezghinka, on the other hand, matches Chernomor's March in sheer brilliant originality. This wild dance with its elemental rhythms, brilliant colours, harsh counterpoints, and daemonic end, must surely have been the most advanced piece of European music of its time. The brusque chromatic phrase of the opening serves as an abrasive bass to both the main themes (Ex. 67a), and Glinka's favoured major-third bass shift is found both in the main modulation of the piece (D major to B flat) and in a tight rotation of chords (Ex. 67b). The deliri-

Ex.67.

ous coda, which makes much use of a chord of superimposed fifths
founded upon violin tuning (Ex. 67c), incorporates the rhythmic jab of
a descending octave (bars two, four, six, and eight of Ex. 67c) which had
been associated with Chernomor's descending whole-tone scale in the
abduction scene in Act I (see Ex. 55), and this prepares for its prominent
part in the following chorus, where Ruslan does battle with the sorcerer.
Though the battle chorus is easily overshadowed by the imaginative
brilliance and masterly execution of the Lezghinka, yet it is a no less
remarkable achievement. Glinka's first intention had been to present a
clash of materials in a double fugue on one quite new subject and another
related to Ruslan's music (see Ex. 46k). Slender fragments of this have
survived, enough to show that it would have been too academic for the
context. Having abandoned this, Glinka resolved not to engage materials
representing the two protagonists contrapuntally, as in the coda of the
Overture, but instead to oppose Chernomor's unstable whole-tone
manoeuvres with a firm E major from Ruslan (the key of his aria in
Act II). The dwarf brings to the battle not only the big guns of his full
whole-tone scale but also an armoury of smaller whole-tone reinforce-
ments—chordal, as in the three-note chord of bars two and three of Ex.
68, and contrapuntal, as in the series of vocal entries in bars five to nine,
which appear each a whole tone higher than the preceding, only to be
firmly wrenched back by Ruslan into E major. The hushed E minor conclusion confirms Ruslan's hard-won victory.

The rest of Act IV is concerned with Ruslan's despair at finding
Lyudmila in a charmed sleep, a sorrow presented through manfully sad
music with the singer's passion reinforced by an eloquent clarinet obbligato; it ends with Ruslan's urgent resolution to bear her back to her

Ex.68. Vivace

(Before the terrible stronghold of the enchanted castle many warriors have perished.)

native city. As for Act V, it has much of the inconsistency of Act III. It is not surprising that Ratmir's romance should have become a particularly popular piece, for it manages to blend the sultry world of the romantic East with a manner fostered in the drawing rooms of St. Petersburg, and has therefore the attraction of being both exotic and familiar (Ex. 69). The centre of this ternary structure is related tonally to

Ex.69.

(She is life and happiness to me! She has given me back my
lost youth.)

its flanks by Glinka's favoured bass shift of a major third. The recitative and chorus that follow are short, probably because this was composed at a very late stage to fill a gap left by last-minute surgery. The recitative is in fact a little gem, but the extensive duet for Ratmir and Finn which follows is amiable music which would have graced a salon admirably, but which completes the debasement of Finn into a faceless fairy god-father, and reduces Ratmir to a limp cipher. Finn, like Ratmir, diminishes in interest as the opera proceeds, for he is never really caught up in the plot in a way that might expose further the facets of his character suggested by the recital of his past sufferings in his Ballad. His role becomes that of *deus ex machina* whose over-easy interventions (for he seems to have unfailing resources for thwarting the powers of evil) make one wonder why he did not personally settle Chernomor and Naina in Act II—except, of course, that then there would have been no opera. This duet is open to the very sort of criticism that Glinka made of the typical Italian operatic duet, which only shows how far his theory and practice might diverge when the impulse—and the wish to find employment for material which had become redundant in another context—took hold of him.

The three-part structure of the Finale works well. The first part is mainly taken up by choruses of grief over Lyudmila, the first section being a set of five variations upon the sixteen-bar theme initiated by the Lezghinka motive, in which the last variation, which accompanies Farlaf, involves some thoroughly characteristic chromaticism. The second part is the plaintive chorus that had provided the entr'acte. This is one of Glinka's most exquisitely decorated inventions, with delicate chromatic enrichment and short strands of semiquavers affording gently animating counterpoint (Ex. 70). Its key, rhythm, and character make this chorus sound like an extension of Gorislava's cavatina in Act III, an impression strengthened by the similarity of the soprano phrase in Ex. 70 (bars 3–4 and 5–6) to an idea in the Cavatina (see Ex. 62a). In the centre of the finale Ruslan awakes Lyudmila with a phrase which blends strength with tenderness, and there follow the universal expressions of joy in the music which had opened the Overture.

The saddest thing for the Western student of Glinka is that he knows, for all his commendations of the riches in *Ruslan and Lyudmila*, that what he writes is less likely to prove a testimonial that will gain the work admission to the opera houses of the West than an obituary. The opera's best moments are superb. Had the dramatic level of Act I been consistently maintained in the succeeding acts, and had the whole opera been compounded consistently of music as right as the Overture, Ruslan's aria, the Persian Chorus, Chernomor's March, the *Lezghinka* and the A minor chorus in the finale to Act V, and had the crisis moments all been treated in as masterly a fashion as in Lyudmila's abduction and in

Ex. 70.

(Ah, Lyudmila, the tomb must not take you, dear princess.)

the struggle between Ruslan and Chernomor, then it would have been one of the masterpieces of nineteenth century opera. There is much music that is only a little less perfect than these movements—such pieces as Finn's Ballad, Gorislava's cavatina, Lyudmila's aria in Act IV, and some passages in the finales of the last two acts. There are other movements that are very unequal, but whose best music is of the highest quality—Ratmir's aria or the finale to Act III, for instance. And even in other less interesting stretches of the work there may suddenly appear a passage or a moment as fine as the best that the opera has to offer. Singers might search with profit through the score, for Glinka was a master of vocal writing, and some movements would make splendid concert pieces, even though such formal presentation must inevitably deprive them of the stage aura which their composer envisaged as an essential part of their impact. Meanwhile it would still be worth while for enterprising opera companies from time to time to apply their resources to staging this work; then we might experience some of Glinka's finest music in its proper setting, and recapture a little of the excitement with which the next generation of Russian composers received this music.

Although he had another fifteen years to live, Glinka never again composed anything as ambitious as either *A Life for the Tsar* or *Ruslan and Lyudmila*. Set beside the manifold splendours of contemporary Russian literature, his achievement seems pitiful. Many of the reasons for this have become abundantly clear in the preceding narrative, but there were other causes too. Paradoxically early nineteenth century Russian letters were aided not only by the many currents of deep dissatisfaction with the state of Russian society—a dissatisfaction which encouraged vigorous debate and afforded writers a wealth of material (and the involvement of Russian authors with the problems of their own society has been the source of some of the finest Russian novels), but also by the official censorship which, by obstructing the direct voicing of discontent through the press, diverted it into imaginative literature. And in addition to the multitude of pressing subjects to excite the writer, there was the unique challenge of evolving the Russian literary language. To the Westerner it must come as a surprise to learn that the use for literary purposes of ordinary Russian, as opposed to old Church Slavonic, first dates from the latter half of the seventeenth century. In addition, the subsequent development of Russian literary prose was frustrated by the Russian practice of using French as the language of polite and cultivated society, a domination so strong that even Pushkin admitted that, when he was concerned with something more than the description of fact, he could express himself more readily in French. Small wonder, then, that with the stimulus of so many ideas and subjects and with so many basic possibilities of the Russian language still unexplored, Russian literature thrived during Glinka's lifetime. But these incentives were denied to the musician unless the presence of a text or of some avowed extra-musical association made them a part of the musician's inspiration; nor was there such a thing as a Russian musical language, as distinct from the Western musical language as Russian speech was from French, for him to exploit. Only in *A Life for the Tsar* does Glinka seem to have been at all fired with something of the same idealism as contemporary writers, and the sustained stimulus of the themes of patriotism and heroic sacrifice undoubtedly was an important factor in aiding Glinka to maintain the comparative consistency of that opera.

Nor must we underestimate the disadvantage to Glinka of being an isolated figure without the company of other composers with whom he could exchange ideas, and from whom he could gain moral support in the way his contemporaries in literature could—or as Balakirev and his group were able to do later in Russian music. In view of his passive character, his isolation, and the absence of outer pressures to goad him into creative activity, the wonder is that he achieved as much as he did. And, despite his small output after *Ruslan and Lyudmila*, his subsequent achievement as a composer was far from unimportant. First he was to seek inspiration away from Russia and from non-Russian material; then he was to return and present his compatriots with, among other things, a little work for orchestra called *Kamarinskaya*, which Tchaikovsky was later to describe as the acorn from which the oak of the whole Russian symphonic school sprang. Few works in music history have ever had an influence so disproportionate to their size and their expressive ambition.

11/*Paris and Spain*

EARLY in 1843 Liszt paid a second visit to Russia and attended a performance of *Ruslan and Lyudmila*. Of all favourable critical reactions to his second opera, it was Liszt's above all that Glinka prized, for this great figure of European music not only perceived the very qualities in it which Glinka wished to be recognized, but also offered a counterblast to those who, like Wielhorski, pronounced it to be an '*opéra manqué*'. Glinka recalled Liszt's verdict on this point: 'according to him, not only in St. Petersburg but also in Paris, my opera, having survived only thirty-two performances in the course of one winter, could be considered a success. Rossini's *William Tell* was given only sixteen times during its first winter.'[1] Liszt gave concrete proof of his admiration for Chernomor's March by transcribing it for piano. Glinka also found great stimulus in discussing art and music with Liszt, but his own life still centred upon aimless social activities, with all-night parties at Mikhail Gedeonov's featuring prominently. There is no doubt that these provided an escape from the inner discontent which came in the aftermath to the production of *Ruslan and Lyudmila*. Despite Liszt's reassurances, Glinka was bitterly disappointed with the reception of his opera. The atmosphere in the theatre was still uncomfortable, and the re-birth of an Italian opera company in St. Petersburg in 1843 did nothing to help the fortunes of *Ruslan and Lyudmila*. Glinka freely admitted that some of his carousings came out of sheer boredom. His passion for Yekaterina Kern had cooled, though he continued to be on friendly terms with her. His wife had given birth to a daughter by her second husband, but he

---

[1] GLN1, p. 230. It is possible that Glinka did think briefly in February 1843 of writing an opera on *Hamlet*. The sole source of this information (a letter written by N. Polevoi to Verstovsky) is not very reliable, and Glinka certainly took no active steps to initiate the project.

felt no wish to harass her further, despite his mother's promptings. His dejection became worse when his mother went back to Novospasskoye in the spring. His spirits rose again a little in the winter when she returned to St. Petersburg for the wedding of Glinka's sister, Yelizaveta, to Viktor Fleri, though Glinka had the distress of seeing his mother struck down by an affliction which necessitated a painful operation. He took his share in trying to distract her from her sufferings. When she left for the country in March 1844 his apathy returned. He had ailed for several months during the preceding year; now he alleged that he was chilled when seeing his mother off, and suffered from rheumatism in consequence. He recalled his condition at this period:

after my mother's departure I would play the violin until dinner out of boredom in order to rouse my birds to song. I had up to sixteen of them . . . After dinne r I often visited the Fleris; there the fire was lit for me, and when I had warmed myself I would set about playing cards with Viktor Ivanovich's children by his first wife. Anyuta, his eldest daughter, a ten-year-old girl, constantly cheated, and I got very angry about this.[1]

Nor were his musical pleasures unalloyed. Some gave him great delight, for Serov remembered that at this time Glinka had close contact with the Warsaw pianist, V. M. Kazhinsky, who 'played from memory a great number of Chopin's mazurkas to which Glinka always listened with especial pleasure'.[2] Glinka's later piano music and songs were to reveal just how deep an impression these pieces of Chopin had made upon him. At this time, too, the distinguished amateur scholar, Aleksandr Uluibuishev, who was later to play such an important part in the early musical life of Balakirev, sent Glinka his new three-volume book on Mozart, which stimulated him to a re-investigation of that composer's operas. But Glinka recalled with revulsion a performance of *Don Giovanni* ('that masterly but not perfect work'[3]), obtusely directed and for the most part badly sung. Rubini, who was cast as Don Ottavio, was the prime offender. Glinka knew him, of course, from his years in Italy, and had found little attraction in his voice even then. Now, he said, Rubini had become excessively mannered and his voice was failing, though the St. Petersburg public evidently received him with that uncritical fervour still habitually accorded to declining singers of legendary repute. He composed a little, including a romance, 'To her', where the adoption of tempo di mazurka may have been a self-conscious effort to

[1] GLNi, pp. 234–5.   [2] SVG, p. 156.   [3] GLNi, p. 233.

achieve a correct Polish character for this Mickiewicz setting, but which seems hardly more appropriate to the ecstatic tone of the lyric than the similar Polish 'characterization' accorded the Poles in *A Life for the Tsar*. He also wrote a Tarantella for piano, a vigorous little piece based upon the folk-song, 'In a field there stood a birch tree', which both Balakirev and Tchaikovsky were later to use. The interest of this piece stems not from the treatment of the tune, whose three-bar phrases are strait-jacketed into a gay four-bar tarantella manner, but in the sharp confrontation between F minor and A minor which occurs half-way through the piece. (Ex. 71). Though essentially a salon piece, and doing little service to the

Ex. 71.

folk tune, it is more characterful than most of Glinka's compositions of this type.

It is not surprising that, in this bored, dispirited condition, beset by the personal strains of the relations within the theatre and of his divorce proceedings, Glinka wished to escape from Russia. The urge to visit Paris reawakened. He was free to leave, and his mother approved. Glinka's dependence upon his mother, not only financially but also personally, is very marked during the next few years. When he received three thousand roubles from the Imperial Theatre in payment for *Ruslan and Lyudmila*, he promptly sent it to her for safe keeping, and later, when he was in Europe, he still sought his mother's approval before acting upon some new intention. He had to do this because he was financially dependent upon her, but she also provided him with stability, and her approval gave him the assurance which his own immature personality was incapable of achieving. He could submit to her in a way he could have done to no other woman, and all his subsequent love affairs were trivial and transitory. After his mother's death the only other woman with whom he managed to establish some sort of stable relationship was his sister, Lyudmila.

Nor did he feel equal to facing foreign travel alone, and he persuaded his sister Natalya's brother-in-law, Fyodor Gedeonov, who had once lived in Paris, to go with him. Various matters conspired to delay their departure until June when, after spending a few days in Novospasskoye, Glinka joined Gedeonov—and the latter's companion, a young French girl called Adèle Rossignol. Their journey took them through Smolensk, Warsaw, and Posnan to Berlin, where Glinka enjoyed a few days with his old teacher, Dehn, who in turn had the pleasure of studying the achievements of his erstwhile pupil. Glinka had brought along the full scores of his operas in the hope of arranging productions in Paris, and Dehn took particular delight in the trio from *A Life for the Tsar*. The journey to Paris was completed via Cologne, Aachen, and Brussels. They arrived in the French capital in the latter half of July, in time to experience the boisterous celebrations of the 'July days' of 1830. Glinka enjoyed the bustle of Paris, though his own existence was relaxed and wholesome. He assured his mother that she need have no fear that any French mademoiselle had turned his heart; if only his mother would join him in Paris his happiness would be complete. He went sightseeing, visiting Versailles, but finding his greatest pleasure in the Jardin des Plantes with its menagerie. He was deeply impressed by French courtesy, though he discovered another side to this strict observance of social proprieties, for the stiff formality of Paris salons and soirées repelled him. Most of his social pleasure was found in the company of his compatriots who were

in Paris, especially since the most notable members of the native popula-
tion had left for the country or were travelling during the summer
months. Later, when the French winter closed in and Paris became a
less idyllic place, he found a different kind of delight in the company of
young French actresses from the Chantereine Theatre, and the noisy
parties which he and Gedeonov arranged for them at their flat aroused
protests from the other tenants. The other participants at these parties
were mostly Russians, and one of the guests at their New Year's Eve
party was Dargomuizhsky. Before 1844 was out Glinka had arranged a
closer relationship with a certain Adelina, whose dramatic talents he
endeavoured to supplement with vocal ones. The result was a disaster:
'When Adelina made her début at the Théâtre des Variétés I was in one
of the theatre's boxes with her mother and brothers. From fright—or
from habit—she sang so off pitch that our neighbours constantly cried
out: "What is the matter with the woman?" We blushed, but there was
nothing to be done about it.'[1]

Among the notables Glinka met in Paris were Auber (the director of
the Conservatoire) and Victor Hugo. Yet by far the most important
events of his whole Paris visit were his meetings with Berlioz, and the
two concerts, one promoted by Berlioz himself, in which some of
Glinka's works were performed. Paris had already been prepared a little
for Glinka's work by another Frenchman, whose appreciation had
delighted him. In 1840 Henri Merimée, the cousin of Prosper, who was
visiting Russia, attended a performance of *A Life for the Tsar*; he was
deeply impressed by it, and four years later he published his reactions in
the *Revue de Paris*. Glinka received a copy of this just before leaving for
Paris. Merimée had noted the opera's unprecedented Russianness, its
range and directness: 'it is more than an opera: it is a national epic,' he
declared.[2] Glinka was thrilled; 'up till then none of my compatriots had
written about me in such flattering terms,' he wrote.[3] He had first hoped
to introduce himself to the French public through his songs, translations
of which were undertaken by Prince Elim Meshchersky, but the project
foundered through Meshchersky's death in November. In any case,
Glinka felt that his music lost something when provided with a French
text. But a far grander *entrée* into French musical life was now planned,
for one of the greatest musicians in Europe was to introduce his work
and to write about him in the French press.[4] Initially Berlioz had re-

---

[1] GLNi, p. 243.   [2] Quoted in GLNi, p. 237.
[3] GLNi, p. 235.   [4] Berlioz's article is included in full in the Appendix.

ceived Glinka coolly, but the Frenchman was planning a trip to Russia at this time, and Glinka realized that the change in attitude towards him might have been prompted by Berlioz' calculation that patronage of a noted Russian musician in Paris could increase his own success in Russia. Some years later the truth of Glinka's suspicions was confirmed, for though he was to live in Paris from 1852 to 1854, he saw Berlioz only once during all that time. 'I am no longer necessary to him, and in consequence our friendship is at an end,' he reported to Nestor Kukolnik.[1] Still, Berlioz had already been impressed by Glinka's melodic gift when they had met some thirteen years earlier in Rome, and it was quite natural that Glinka's imaginative originality should have had a very real appeal to this vividly imaginative Frenchman. While in Paris Glinka met Berlioz several times a week, talking about music in general and Berlioz' own works in particular, and enjoying the Frenchman's lively and mordant conversation. He wrote home to Nestor Kukolnik about these meetings. 'For me the most notable contact is quite certainly that with Berlioz. It was one of my musical intentions in Paris to study his compositions, so lauded by some and so censured by others, and the event has been completely beneficial to me. Not only have I heard Berlioz' music at concerts and *at rehearsals*, but I have got to know this *first* (in my opinion) composer of our time (within his own province, of course), as far as one can get to know a man who is so extremely eccentric. And this is my opinion: in the realm of fantasy in art no-one has approached these colossal and, in addition, always new conceptions [of his]. The scope of the whole, the development of the details, the consistency, the harmonic texture, finally the powerful and ever new orchestration—here is the essence of Berlioz' music. In drama, being attracted by the fantastic side of the situation, he is unnatural and consequently false. Of the pieces I have heard, the *Francs Juges* overture, The Pilgrims' March from the symphony, *Harold in Italy*, the Queen Mab scherzo [from *Romeo and Juliet*], and likewise the 'Dies irae' and 'Tuba mirum' from the *Requiem* have made an indescribable impression on me. I have now several of Berlioz' unpublished manuscripts which I am studying with inexpressible delight.'[2]

This study was to have a profound effect upon Glinka's creative intentions. Shortly after arriving in Paris he had toyed with the idea of writing a comic opera for the Italian opera company there, which he rated as the best in the world. The project had even been reported both

[1] GLN2, p. 503.   [2] GLN2, pp. 274–5.

in the French and the Russian press, but nothing came of it. Though he wrote no music during his Paris visit, his creative future became clear to him through his contact with Berlioz and Parisian musical tastes. Later in the above-quoted letter he wrote: 'In the realm of art the study of Berlioz' music and of the audiences has had very important results for me. I have decided to enrich my repertoire with a few (and, if my strength allows, with many) concert pieces for orchestra under the title of *fantaisies pittoresques*. Up to now instrumental music has been divided into two opposing categories: [on the one hand] quartets and symphonies, valued by a few, alienate the mass of listeners with their deep and complicated conceptions; and [on the other] what are properly called concertos, variations, and such-like weary the ear with their disjointedness and difficulties. It seems to me that it is possible to unite the demands of art and the demands of the time and, employing perfect instruments and perfect performing technique, to compose pieces which communicate equally with connoisseurs and the ordinary public. I have already started on the project. I am devising a coda for Chernomor's March; it has been much enjoyed here, but without a coda it cannot satisfy an audience.[1] In Spain I shall set about these proposed *fantaisies*. The originality of the indigenous melodies will be a significant aid to me, the more so since up till now no-one has studied this field. And, in addition to something original, my unbridled fantasy needs a text or some positive data [to guide and control it]. We'll see when we get there whether I can undertake an opera in a Spanish vein; in any case, I shall endeavour to translate my impressions into sounds.'[2]

But this is leaping ahead. What Glinka currently desired was to be known in France, but he realized there was no hope of having either of his operas produced, and he discovered that French concert life was organized in circles into which it was very difficult to break—though, paradoxically, it was easier for him simply because he was only a bird of passage, and so not likely to make a permanent challenge to the musical establishment. Berlioz' interest was therefore particularly valuable. Not surprisingly Berlioz liked the Lezghinka from *Ruslan and Lyudmila*, and he included this, together with Antonida's cavatina from *A Life for the Tsar*, in one of his 'monster' concerts at the Cirque Olympique of the Champs Elysées on 4/16 March 1845. The soloist in

[1] This coda has not survived. Berlioz commented adversely upon the abrupt termination of the March in his article on Glinka (see the Appendix).
[2] GLN2, p. 276.

the cavatina was Aleksandra Solovyeva, who had sung the role in St. Petersburg, and whom Glinka well remembered because of the time it had taken her to learn the part. Glinka found the standard of discipline among French orchestral players to be very low. During rehearsals 'they liked to chat with their neighbours. I noticed also that sometimes, especially in difficult passages, they resorted to their snuff boxes and their handkerchiefs,' he recalled.[1] The wind, particularly the horns and clarinets, were unreliable. Glinka, evidently in consultation with Berlioz himself, had arranged the Lezghinka for a single orchestra which, he admitted, destroyed a good deal of its effectiveness. In addition, Berlioz' one hundred and fifty musicians were so spread out that it was impossible to get any balanced impression of the whole effect. Solovyeva, despite a false start through an attack of nerves, sang the cavatina well, but one critic complained of the piece that 'one constantly hears one and the same note (*on entend toujours la même note*). At the time I was very indignant about this,' wrote Glinka in his *Memoirs*, 'but now I see that the critic was completely right; in the cavatina's allegro, "In the village beyond the river", the dominant occurs too often and too strongly, which is very national, but tiresomely monotonous.'[2] However, another critic, Maurice Bourge, writing in the *Revue et gazette musicale*, commented upon the freshness and melodic tenderness of the Rondo, and recorded that the Lezghinka was well received.

Nearly a month later, on 29 March/10 April, Glinka himself promoted a concert in the Salle Herz including, along with a variety of other compositions played by other performers, a number of his own pieces—the Krakowiak from *A Life for the Tsar*, Chernomor's March, and the Valse-Fantaisie. The orchestra was that of the Théâtre Royal Italien which Glinka so much admired. Solovyeva was to have sung the romance, 'Doubt', and Lyudmila's cavatina, but she was taken ill during the concert, and the only vocal piece by Glinka that was included was the early Italian-texted piece, 'Il desiderio', sung by an excellent tenor called Marras. Glinka himself played the piano. It was an expensive affair, and Glinka recorded his gratitude to Prince Vasily Golitsuin who was in Paris and who helped with the finances. The concert suffered a loss, though Russian society in Paris turned out in force to support their compatriot (the pageantry of the ladies' dresses made one

---

[1] GLNi, p. 244. This brings to mind Berlioz' allegations concerning Habeneck's behaviour.

[2] GLNi, p. 246.

critic observe that it was 'like a flower garden'), and the hall was full. Glinka enjoyed a *succès d'estime*; the press was kind and his pleasure was crowned by Berlioz' article in the *Journal des débats*.[1] Berlioz started with a brief biographical sketch for which Melgunov, who was also in Paris, provided the data.[2] He then quoted and fully endorsed Merimée's verdict on *A Life for the Tsar*, but added that he considered *Ruslan and Lyudmila* so different 'that one would believe that it had been written by another composer. The talent of the author here appears more mature and more powerful. *Ruslan* is indubitably a step forward, a new phase in Glinka's musical development . . . Glinka's talent is essentially supple and varied; his style has the rare distinction of changing itself at the composer's will according to the requirements and character of the subject he is treating. He can be simple and even naïve without ever stooping to use a single vulgar idea. His melodies have unexpected accents and phrases of a charming quaintness; he is a master of harmony, and writes for instruments with a care and knowledge of their more secret depths which transforms his orchestra into one of the newest and most exciting modern orchestras that one could hear.' After commenting upon Glinka's melodic originality as displayed in the Valse-Fantaisie, the Krakowiak from *A Life for the Tsar*, and Chernomor's March, Berlioz concluded: 'This talent is very rare, and when the composer adds to it that of a refined harmonic sense and of a fine, clean orchestration, flawless and full of colour, he may with good reason claim a place among the outstanding composers of his time. The composer of *Ruslan* is certainly in this category.'

Praise like this was enough to make Glinka's ten months in Paris thoroughly worthwhile. In general it had been a happy time, despite the weather, the increased prices during the winter, the strained relations with Gedeonov after the latter had quarrelled with Adèle, the failure of his mother to come to Paris, and some pressures from her that he should return to Russia. Yet only two months after arriving in the French capital he had already turned his thoughts towards Spain. Liszt was going there, and this roused an urge in Glinka to go too. He took Spanish lessons, but his mother was against the project. Nevertheless he continued to hope, and even engaged a certain Don Santiago Hernandes

[1] See Appendix.

[2] Berlioz had in fact first approached Glinka himself for these biographical details. Perhaps Glinka felt that modesty would prevent him presenting himself as flatteringly as Melgunov could do it. However, he was so pleased by the comments Berlioz made that he forthwith sent the article to St. Petersburg where it appeared in the press.

as a servant in anticipation of his departure. In every letter home he bombarded his mother with good reasons why he should go: the warm weather would be better for his health, it would be cheaper, etc.—and he would find there new artistic stimulus. '[Spanish folk tunes] somewhat resemble Russian ones, and will (I hope) make it possible for me to undertake a big new work,' he declared to her, having in mind the opera on Italian words.[1] Finally she relented. Glinka stayed in Paris until his concerts were over; then in May, with Berlioz' plaudits and Adelina's sobbings ringing in his ears, he left Paris for the south in the company of Don Santiago and the latter's nine-year-old daughter. Travelling through Orléans, they reached Pau in the Pyrenees three days later, only to discover that Glinka's passport had been mislaid. Here Berlioz' article proved of unforeseen use, for it was among the pieces of evidence to his worthiness with which Glinka induced the local authorities to issue him with a temporary passport. He decided to avoid the coast road because of the injurious effects sea air had upon him, and they crossed the Pyrenees with pack mules, reaching the Spanish frontier on 20 May/1 June, and heading via Pamplona and Burgos to Valladolid, where they installed themselves with Don Santiago's sister. They had already decided to spend the summer there, since the heat in Madrid would be intolerable.

Glinka and Don Santiago had arrived in Spain well armed with letters of introduction, and Glinka was to find these very useful. 'Spaniards are honourable, straightforward in their speech, unaffected, and not full of ceremony like the French,' he informed his mother. 'On the other hand they are exceedingly proud, and it would be considered a great insult not to esteem the letter of a relative or friend.'[2] In Valladolid, however, Don Santiago's family could provide him with friends in plenty, and Glinka had soon established a pleasant social life for himself. One of the acquaintances he made rendered him considerable musical service. This was a local merchant and a good guitarist, Felix Castilla, from whom Glinka heard the *jota aragonesa* and its variations. He stored these in his memory, and a month or two later used them as the basis of his First Spanish Overture. However, he admitted that at this stage he was still not applying himself seriously to the study of Spanish music.

Glinka was delighted with Spain. His letters home were filled with his enthusiasm, and he reassured his mother about the people: 'the

[1] GLN2, p. 254.   [2] GLN2, p. 300.

Spaniards are good people and not at all such as they are represented by those who know them only by hearsay. It is true that they are quick-tempered, but it doesn't last.'[1] He made expeditions to see the sights, visiting Segovia and the fountains of St. Ildefonso. In mid-September he and Don Santiago set off for Madrid, and settled themselves near the centre of the city. Glinka's initial reaction to the Spanish capital was unfavourable, not because the sights of the city did not attract him, but probably because he found it difficult to establish the sort of social life he had enjoyed in Valladolid. This lack of social distraction proved a blessing in disguise, for Glinka applied himself to composition, using the *jota aragonesa* as his basis. Thus was born the first of the *fantaisies pittoresques* which he had projected in France. Later Odoyevsky suggested the title of First Spanish Overture, but at this stage the piece was called *Capriccio brillante on the jota aragonesa*. Though Glinka deployed the piece as a sonata movement, his primary purpose was not to create an organic structure but to record musically his impressions of Spain. Thus the *jota* dominates the entire piece; the whole theme is used for the first subject, while the second subject is a series of six new melodic

Ex.72. Allegro

[outline harmonization]

variations based upon the easily recognizable tonic-dominant-tonic harmonic progression which accompanies the first part of the *jota* theme at the beginning of the exposition (Ex. 72). Each variation usually involves two lines in counterpoint, and though Glinka had heard many variations played by Castilla, there can be little doubt that those in his Overture are essentially his own work. The extended introduction, which Glinka added only after he had completed the rest of the piece, is portentous and in no way Spanish; the most memorable single incident here is the striking succession of four differently scored chords (Ex. 73)

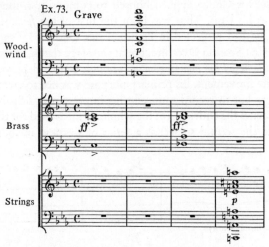

Ex.73. Grave

which, though they recur in the coda, are less important than the broken arpeggios on the brass that precede them, and which reappear in combination with particles of the *jota* theme in the development and coda. The recapitulation simply repeats the *jota* material, following it with further variations based upon the harmonic foundation of Ex. 72. The sonata scheme has provided Glinka with a useful determinant of the sequence of musical events, but the crude carpentry of the transition in the exposition, and the rudimentary, though effective, procedures of the development only serve to emphasize that the real virtues of the piece do not lie here, but rather in Glinka's inventiveness in devising melodic combinations, and in the sound of his orchestration[1],

[1] While in Warsaw at the end of 1849 Glinka, following Odoyevsky's suggestion, revised the orchestration of the first thirty-two bars of the vivace. As with most of his revisions of orchestration in *A Life for the Tsar*, Glinka's changes in the First Spanish Overture consisted of filling out the sound.

Glinka and his sister Lyudmila Shestakova in 1852. Daguerreotype

PLATE IV

which is quite individual, even though he has obviously profited from his recent study of Berlioz' scores. The wit of Glinka's contrapuntal imagination is often captivating. Could anything be more infectious than the sparkling line of quavers with which he matches the juvenile two-note second subject—a line of quavers which, in the next variation, itself acquires a new flowing line as a counterpoint, which in its turn is served with a fresh quaver companion? And note, too, the irresistible bubbling of the lively quaver lines in the variations towards the end of the recapitulation.

The sound of the Overture is quite new, and to this the orchestration contributes much. The harp and pizzicato strings are clearly intended to suggest guitars, and the percussion includes castanets, but it would be wrong to attribute the special character of the sound solely to the search for local colour. Despite the large orchestra, the scoring is as notable for its economy as for its range of sound. There is never any filling-out for the sake of textural roundness. Thus the harp and string pizzicati are considered enough to relieve a little the severity of the two-part counterpoint in Ex. 74a; likewise the more complex web of lines in Ex. 74b is clearer and brighter for having only the lightest of support. Even the most cursory glance at the different dynamic levels assigned to the various instruments in Ex. 74 must reveal Glinka's fastidious attention to balance within the group of instruments being used at any one moment. Since the ear is never sated with opulently rich sounds, it is the more sensitive to the numerous contrasts in timbre. The piece is a true *fantaisie pittoresque*, structurally naïve, simple in thought, but completely effective.

Having composed this delightfully characterful piece, Glinka naturally wished to hear it played—and to find out what the Spaniards would think of it. The orchestra of the principal theatre in Madrid was excellent, and he decided upon a concert of his own music. Unfortunately, however, the time of the Madrid copyists was being absorbed by a new ballet, and Glinka began to have doubts about whether the interest of the performers and public would make the event worthwhile. He also admitted that his own knowledge of Spanish music was still slender, and may have wondered whether this would be all too apparent to a Spanish audience. And so the Overture remained unperformed, and Glinka applied himself more systematically to the study of indigenous Spanish music. While in Valladolid he had already discovered that this would be difficult: 'it is not easy to root out these folk-songs, and even more

Ex.74. Allegro (più animato)
a)

difficult to catch the national character of Spanish music,' he had reported to his mother.[1] French and, in particular, Italian music was popular, and in Madrid he found a strong predominance of Italian music in the theatres. It was difficult to find folk singers who did not contaminate their songs with Italianisms. Still, he did run to earth some singers and guitarists who dealt in the genuine article; 'in the evenings they come to play and sing, and I note down their songs,' he recorded.[2] He also wrote down folk tunes from a mule carriage driver who visited him, and from this source he obtained the two *seguidillas manchegas* which he later used in his Second Spanish Overture. Yet it is perfectly clear that Glinka's investigations had nothing of scholarly thoroughness in them. All he really wanted from Spain was new impressions and experiences, as broad and varied as he could find. Thus he not only saw the sights, but visited the Teatro del Principe, where he was deeply impressed by the performances. He also experienced the bullfight. 'My first impression was somewhat wild and strange,' he wrote, 'but afterwards I became accustomed to it, and subsequently found entertainment in this bloody drama where each participant finds himself in constant danger.'[3] He met a Russian architect, Karl Beine, who recorded Glinka's mode of living at this period. 'He lives quietly but very purposefully. There is often a gathering at his home. There they play and dance the *jota*. When by himself he talks to me about the black keys, about the relationship of sounds, about instruments, about drama in music, and about Bortnyansky. There is talk about Verdi and so on, endlessly, eloquently, and eruditely.'[4] With Beine, Glinka visited the Art Gallery. His enjoyment may have been enriched by Beine's company on these occasions, but he was also responsible for an experience which Glinka found less to his taste, for he compelled him to sit through a performance of Verdi's *Ernani*. Glinka never liked Verdi's music, and he enjoyed infinitely more the Spanish dancing at the Circo Theatre, though the authentic national character was compromised since the composer was the theatre's conductor, who was Czech. Another of Glinka's visitors was Wilhelm von Lenz, who was to be the author of important studies of Beethoven.

Glinka made various expeditions from Madrid, including one to Toledo, whose situation he greatly admired. He liked the cathedral, too,

---

[1] GLN2, p. 302.   [2] GLN2, p. 319.   [3] GLN1, p. 252.
[4] Quoted in LPG2, p. 25. The talk about the black keys may refer to the pentatonic scale which is used in some Spanish folk tunes.

and was allowed to play the organ. At first he rated much less highly the Escorial. 'That eighth wonder of the world (as it is called here) made no impact upon me. It is a sad building and in bad taste,' he concluded,[1] though he was to revise his opinion drastically when he visited it again the next year. Then in early December, with Don Santiago still in attendance, he left Madrid for Granada with its milder winter climate. The vistas on the journey delighted him; so, too, did Granada itself, with its splendid situation and, above all, its Alhambra ('the halls, galleries, baths and other parts of this building are finished off so skilfully and with such taste that this palace seems like an enchanted castle,' he wrote[2]). He was also delighted with a young Andalusian folksinger, Dolores Garcia, to whom he paid court, and who also broadened his acquaintance with Spanish folk music, as did a certain Don Murciano, an innkeeper who was a brilliant natural guitarist. The other local personality Glinka specially recalled was Don Francisco Bueno y Moreno, a smuggler-turned-glove-maker and dealer in skins, who introduced him to Dolores and to other ladies with whom he could find 'refuge'. Near the Alhambra Glinka and Don Santiago moved into a pleasant two-storey house with a terraced garden, little fountains, numerous fruit trees, and flowers all the year round. 'It was so fine and warm that, except for three weeks out of the three months, we dined daily in the garden, and often in our summer clothes. Don Santiago reared geese, ducks, and other domestic animals which came up to us during dinner and ate out of our hands . . . In the evenings I went down to the town where I passed the time pleasantly with friends of Don Francisco. There was singing, dancing, and amusements of various kinds.' Beine and his English companion, an architect called Robertson, arrived and joined in these activities. 'I would go to the Alhambra when they were sketching, and they in their turn would visit me and sometimes breakfast with me,' Glinka recalled.[3] With the help of his local acquaintances Glinka was able to witness all manner of regional festivities and customs. He tried to note down folk tunes, but found it difficult because of the constant variants the singers made upon each repetition of the melody. He also perceived how inseparable music and dancing seemed to be in this part of Spain, and consequently took some lessons in Spanish dancing, but with only moderate success: 'My legs obeyed, but I could not master the castanets,' he lamented.[4]

It had been agreed that he should remain in Spain for one year, but

[1] GLN2, p. 321.   [2] GLN2, p. 328.   [3] GLN1, p. 254.   [4] GLN1, p. 255.

within a month of his arrival he had started to prepare his family for a longer stay. While in Granada the hints turned into positive pleading; he had not finished his studies, it would be unwise to leave a hot country and arrive in Russia in the autumn when the cold season was setting in, it would bring back all the strains and worries associated with his divorce suit, and Don Santiago would not be able to leave, as unavoidable business was demanding his presence in Spain. 'I need at least one more year to study that which I have in mind,' he claimed, 'and by a natural process I shall probably become accustomed to Spain, and having satisfied my curiosity, I shall return to my native land joyfully, no matter how unpleasant everything may be.

'My self-respect of necessity demands on the one hand that I should make a name for myself, and on the other that I should show my St. Petersburg friends that I can exist without them—and exceedingly pleasantly!'[1] It is not clear exactly why he needed to demonstrate this independence of his St. Petersburg friends, but when Glinka wanted something he would write anything that suited his purpose, and he accompanied this plea with extravagant accounts of the glories of Spain, the incomparable worthiness of the Spaniards, and the unspeakable benefits of the Spanish climate to his health—all of which contrasts sharply with his comments in a letter to Viktor Fleri, where he characterizes the Andalusians as vain, garrulous, and dishonest (the very opposite of the people of Castille with whom he had stayed when he had first entered Spain), and where he admits that life in Granada has become monotonous. The fact is that, however much he might wish to extend his stay in Spain, he had had enough of Granada and had decided to return to Madrid a month earlier than originally planned. And so in March 1846 he went back to the Spanish capital, still not knowing whether his mother would let him extend his stay. He settled into his former quarters with Dolores, but this relationship did not last long, for he soon realized that her musical aptitudes were limited, and in June he returned her to her mother.

However, another and much more important relationship was just beginning for him. During the month before Dolores' departure, he had occasionally been visited by a young music student from Valencia, Don Pedro Fernandez. Don Santiago was becoming more involved in his own family affairs, and he and Glinka parted company amicably after returning to Madrid. Don Pedro's visits became yet more frequent

[1] GLN2, p. 338.

after Dolores' departure. The two men must have taken to each other very much, for after Glinka had returned from a visit to Segovia and La Granja at the end of June, he and Don Pedro moved into a new flat together. It was the beginning of a companionship that lasted nine years, during which Don Pedro acted as a friend, a servant, and a secretary to Glinka. The latter set Don Pedro to study Cramer's piano studies, and the Spaniard learned them by heart. When Glinka returned to Russia, Don Pedro was to go with him.

Glinka stayed in Spain another year. In August he was invited to Murcia where there was a fair and a children's theatre which presented Bellini's *Norma*. Glinka attended a rehearsal and was quite impressed by the performers, though by this time Bellini and all Italian opera composers had become distasteful to him. They had thoroughly captured the Spanish musical taste, and his renewed plans to promote a concert of his own music, for which he intended to write some special pieces in a Spanish idiom, came to nothing. In Murcia he no doubt enjoyed the local gipsy dancing more than *Norma*, and he was delighted with the town and its fertile valley. His return journey to Madrid proved less comfortable than the outward one, for the best transport had been commandeered by Spaniards swarming to the capital for the double wedding of Queen Isabella II and her sister. When he arrived he witnessed the celebrations that attended this event. He decided to spend the winter in Seville, where Don Pedro had friends. They set out in November, found a small villa, and Glinka enjoyed a pleasant winter, with social gatherings in general and a closer relationship with an 'inconsolable widow' in particular. In the spring he indulged in his old hobby of keeping birds. 'Of all the cities I have so far seen in Spain, none is more cheerful,' he wrote to his mother, '. . . and nothing I have so far seen . . . can compare with the local dancers.'[1] He wrote in more detail of these in his *Memoirs*, recalling the complexity of some of the rhythms. 'During the dances the best local folk-singers burst into song in an eastern manner while the dancers danced on skilfully, and it seemed that you heard three different rhythms. The singing went along of its own accord, the guitar went separately, while the dancer clapped her hands and stamped quite independently (so it seemed) from the music.'[2] An elderly but eminent folk-singer called Planeta visited them and sang for them, while in the spring the distinguished Norwegian violinist, Ole Bull, arrived in Seville, spent some six weeks there, and had frequent

[1] GLN2, pp. 368–9.　　[2] GLN1, p. 260.

contact with Glinka. Glinka had reservations about Bull's musicianship: 'his playing was powerful and exceedingly clear; but, as with the majority of virtuosi, his musicianship was not too strong.'[1] Glinka's pleasures in Seville were augmented by the news that his divorce proceedings had been completed, and this weight and worry were at last lifted from him.

In May 1847, with mutual regrets, Glinka and Don Pedro parted from their friends in Seville, and returned to Madrid. Glinka's stay in Spain was drawing to a close. For two years he had enjoyed the varied impressions the country had afforded him, always accompanying these pleasures of the spirit with a full measure of varied physical gratification. But the musical fruits of these years were (so far, at least) disappointing. While in Spain he had completed only one piece, the First Spanish Overture. Spanish translations had been made of several of his pieces, but it seems that the only important performance of his music in Spain was of the Trio from *A Life for the Tsar*, which was given at a court concert in November 1846. The opera which he was projecting before he entered the country had vanished without trace. Much as he had enjoyed these two years, he had now had his fill of the country. On their return from Seville, Glinka and Don Pedro spent three weeks in Madrid, and then headed for the French frontier. Their journey again took Glinka through Pau. During a three-week stay in Paris he heard that Pyotr Stepanov was in Kissingen and wished to see him, and Glinka set out thither, travelling through Cologne and then up the Rhine to Frankfurt. Stepanov had news for Glinka; Vasilchikov had died and left his wife well provided. 'Although I did not love Mariya Petrovna, yet I confess it would have pained me to see her in poverty,' he decided.[2]

It happened that the Tsarevich, the future Aleksandr II, was also in Kissingen, and Glinka was greatly flattered by the kindness with which he and his wife received him. Glinka did not delay there long, however, but set out with Don Pedro to Regensburg, and proceeded thence along the Danube to Vienna, where he was splendidly entertained by a counsellor and a secretary from the Russian embassy. Warsaw was his next destination. He stopped there for six days, and then set out on the final stage of his journey to Novospasskoye. On 28 July/9 August he arrived home.

[1] ibid.   [2] GLN1, p. 261.

12/Smolensk and Warsaw

G LINKA was glad to be back, to see his relatives and friends, and to join in the visits and expeditions which were a regular part of this life. He could also engage in undemanding musical activities from which he clearly derived much pleasure, though they were very different from, and far humbler than those in which he participated with the professionals and cultivated amateurs of St. Petersburg. When in Novospasskoye, he liked to assemble a choir of about a dozen from the estate to which he would teach some pieces of church music, training the boys with the aid of a violin. Then he would conduct or accompany this choir in the local church services, playing one part on the violin while simultaneously singing another. There was now also a wind band of twelve players at Novospasskoye. 'When there was a holiday,' some of Glinka's peasants later recalled, 'Mikhail Ivanovich would summon Stepan, the assistant gardner, and say to him: "Stepanushka, today is a holiday. There is no work in the fields. Collect together my musicians on to the balcony, and tell the head man of the estate to summon the girls and boys from the village. Let them make merry!" . . . Half an hour later music rang out on the balcony, and Mikhail Ivanovich himself simply waved his baton, or sometimes took his violin and himself played with the musicians. And when the maidens and swains had gathered together from the village, then the musicians would play a jolly Russian piece, to which there was dancing.'[1] During the 1840s Glinka regularly participated in such diversions when he returned to Novospasskoye, and doubtless there were such activities during the present visit. If so, it was the last time he was ever to engage in them, for after this visit Glinka was never again to see his birthplace and home.

Unfortunately the period of untroubled enjoyment and good health did not last for more than a couple of months. Being afflicted with loss of

[1] Quoted in GG, p. 366.

appetite, Glinka recklessly ventured upon physical exercise as a remedy, and tried his hand at chopping down trees. The result could not be anything other than a catastrophe, and with alarming symptoms manifesting themselves, he fled to his doctor in St. Petersburg. He did not reach the capital; the illness forced him to delay in Smolensk, and the result was that he spent the winter from September to March in that city. Though his health was not good, his life was quiet and pleasant, and he once again set about composing in the mornings, and directing the studies of Don Pedro, which included practising Clementi's *Gradus ad parnassum*. The evenings were passed relaxedly in the company of his friends. It would have been surprising if any really major composition had issued from this indolent and undirected existence, but there are clear signs of a more enterprising approach, especially to harmony, than is generally to be found in similar works from earlier in his life. For the Smolensk Chief Constable, who was an amateur composer and who had lent Glinka his piano, he wrote 'Recollection of a mazurka' and a Barcarolle as tokens of gratitude, and a further piano piece, a set of variations on a 'Scottish' theme, for Yelizaveta Ushakova, to whom he had felt strongly attracted over twenty years before. These three pieces, together with a fourth piano piece, 'Prayer', were later published under the title of *A Greeting to my native land*. Serov stated that Glinka originally intended to subtitle the mazurka 'Hommage à Chopin', but decided against it on the grounds that there were too many 'hommages' to Chopin around already. There is no doubt, however, of Chopin's very beneficent presence in this piece, which is harmonically and tonally richer than Glinka's earlier efforts at solo piano dances—and thematically more memorable, too (Ex. 75). Even in the Barcarolle,

Ex. 75. Moderato

where Glinka had few precedents as distinguished as Chopin's mazurkas upon which to found his piece, the harmonic range is broader than in his earlier Italianate compositions. Glinka's national identification was wrong in the set of variations, for the tune itself, 'The last rose of summer', is Irish. Not that this misattribution mattered as far as Glinka's treatment was concerned; the first variation has all the pianistic sparkle of the earlier sets, though the craftsmanship is more fastidious, with chromatic touches which add an extra sophistication to a basically tinselly piano style. The next variation shows the same increasing harmonic enterprise (Ex. 76); Vladimir Stasov was particularly enthusiastic about it, describing it as 'a perfect little piece of its kind, not unworthy of Beethoven'.[1] The rest of the piece is on a much lower

---

[1] SG, p. 663. Beethoven himself had also arranged the tune.

level—an extended finale in which the listener will be hard put most of the time to detect any trace of the original tune, except for its left-hand appearance (now in ⁴⁄₄) under mighty arpeggio washes in the right hand —the sort of thing that might make an Englishman giggle and the Irish-man reach for his cudgel.

There can be no doubt that Glinka wrote these variations affection-ately, and to judge from the dedication, he had his earlier romantic interlude with Yelizaveta in mind. But it was for his sister, Lyudmila, that on 17/29 November he composed the romance, 'Darling', based on a Spanish *jota* theme, though, as in the piano variations, there is not a trace of any national style. Glinka also recalled writing another romance, 'Soon you will forget me', which he described as 'a melan-choly product of my sick fantasy'.[1] Certainly the despairing sentiments of the text elicited a strong response from him; as in the piano pieces, expressive chromaticism is now playing a larger, though controlled role in his work. There is some in 'Darling' too, but in 'Soon you will forget me' a dragging, constricted chromatic line twists tormentedly beneath the whole of verse two (Ex. 77), and re-emerges in the

Ex.77. Andante con moto

Tui no-vui-ye li-tsa u-vi-dish i

no-vuikh dru-zei iz-be-ryosh; tui

(You will see new faces and choose new friends.)

[1] GLN2, p. 372.

extended vocal-piano coda. The structure of this song is close to the extended ternary scheme of 'I recall a wonderful moment'. 'Soon you will forget me' seems to reflect something of the same sort of personal involvement that had produced 'A voice from the other world' twenty years earlier. It is certainly a far better composition than the remaining piano piece from this phase, 'Prayer', which Glinka had composed on 28 September/10 October, and had dedicated to Don Pedro. Glinka especially recalled the circumstances under which the first version of this piece had been composed:

Pedro was away, and being left alone in the twilight, I felt such a deep sadness that, weeping, I prayed inwardly and improvised a wordless 'Prayer' for piano.[1]

One fears the worst, and the piece fulfils all expectations, with pseudo-drama in its lame tremolando opening, and with a gushingly sequential main theme and empty chordal episode. Yet Glinka seems to have been oddly attached to this rather horrid piece—or perhaps he simply sensed that it could become popular if its fulsome platitudes were pressed. A year later in Warsaw he supervised an arrangement of the piece for solo trombone and orchestra (made by a Warsaw musician, Aleksandr Pohlens), and in 1855 he himself made a version of it for alto solo, chorus, and orchestra, using Lermontov's poem, 'In a difficult moment of life'.[2]

Despite such a tearful episode, Glinka's mode of living was in general congenial, and remained thus until early in 1848, when he finally had to capitulate to persistent pressure from an uncle of Nikolai Izmailov, who had very recently married Glinka's youngest sister, Olga. This uncle was anxious to give a grand dinner in Glinka's honour, mainly, Glinka asserted drily, to inflate his own self-importance. The affair took place on 23 January/4 February. The Governor attended, and an orchestra played the Polonaise from *A Life for the Tsar* while Glinka was introduced. The whole event was considered worthy of a report in the *Northern Bee*. Obviously Glinka revelled in this event in his honour, but the consequence was that he found himself drawn into the social life of the city, and was constantly asked to perform at balls and

[1] GLN1, p. 262.
[2] It is good to know that Glinka himself, at the prompting of some of his friends, had doubts about the piece, repeatedly asking Vladimir Stasov whether there was 'enough nobility' in the tune. Later, however, Glinka lapsed, and when he made the vocal version, he opined that he had caught something of 'the simplicity and breadth of Gluck'. (SG, pp. 682 and 683.)

parties. The strain finally began to tell, and such events became distasteful. The only way in which he could hope to break this round of engagements was to leave Smolensk. He felt an urge to return to Warsaw with the intention of going, it seems, on to France, despite the news of revolution in Paris. In March he set out with his brother-in-law, Vasily Shestakov, and Don Pedro. When they reached Warsaw, however, Glinka heard that his application for a passport had been refused. He could not go on.

And so Glinka settled down in Warsaw. He and Don Pedro installed themselves in a comfortable apartment, and Glinka acquired some sixteen birds of various species, and also two rabbits which were given a free run of the place at some hazard to the legs of guests. His health improved, and in June he added to his menagerie a pretty girl called Angélique, whom he had first met in a café. He went for walks, had sociable evenings at home at which there was sometimes dancing, and composed. Among his projects was a piece on the subject of Ilya Muromets, the legendary Russian medieval warrior hero, but nothing came of it. He made friends with the Warsaw censor, Pavel Dubrovsky, who was responsible for drawing Glinka's attention to some verses that he might use for songs. The results were settings of Lermontov's 'When I hear your voice', Pushkin's 'The toasting cup', and Gretchen's song from Goethe's *Faust* (in a Russian translation), all composed, according to Glinka, during September while he was remaining strictly indoors to avoid catching cholera, which was raging in Warsaw.[1] He remembered how during the epidemic he had each day watched the funeral processions of victims pass the window, and the seriousness of his frame of mind at this time is reflected in the quality, if not always in the manner, of these settings. All three confirm his greater preoccupation with harmonic richness and dynamic tonal schemes. The latter feature is less apparent in the Lermontov setting because of its relative brevity, though the sudden shift from F major to D flat to set the final couplet is a type of effect Glinka had rarely sought in his earlier songs. Its use here is primarily expressive, but the tonal course pursued in the successive verses of the rumbustious Pushkin setting (A flat–E flat–E major [F flat]–A flat) achieves a powerful series of thrusts to a new level in each

---

[1] Dubrovsky, however, gave a different account of how the first of these came to be written, asserting that Glinka conceived it on an outing with friends in May, and that he forthwith performed it on his return home, just as though it were a thoroughly finished composition.

verse—a sense of progress that is reinforced by the new material which appears in the first part of each of the two central verses. This urge to keep the musical organism in constant evolution is also apparent in Glinka's other five songs written in Warsaw between 1848 and 1850. Each of them is cast in a large ternary structure, but in each case the song leads off in a new direction soon after the reappearance of the original material, or else is furnished with a coda more substantial than is required for a formal rounding of the piece. This is the fulfilment of the practice for which 'I recall a wonderful moment' is the precedent (though it is foreshadowed even earlier in the strophic 'Tell me why'). In the case of 'I recall a wonderful moment' it could be argued that the song was really through-composed, but that since there was a verbal repetition from the first stanza during the course of the lyric, Glinka decided to match the verbal repetition with a musical one. In one of the Warsaw songs, too (the Goethe setting), a similar verbal repetition could have produced the musical scheme, but the appearance of this same pattern in the other songs shows that Glinka had used it for itself alone. Perhaps it was Chopin's mazurkas that fostered it, just as they were obviously a crucial source for Glinka's new harmonic practices, for the Polish master had made a point of providing many of his finest mazurkas with a very substantial coda, sometimes using quite new material. The influence of the text upon the musical structure in the Goethe setting has just been remarked, but the substantial final section, which uses material from the middle of the song, is also worth noting. In this song the key sequence is a powerful agent in propelling the music forward. Starting in B minor, Glinka moves via D major to B flat for Gretchen's climactic words—

the rapture of his embraces and kisses

—and then employs an abrupt confrontation of B flat major and B minor to suggest Gretchen's return from blissful dreams to harsh reality (Ex. 78), as the text and music revert to the opening. When Serov expressed his own rapture at this moment in the song, Glinka readily acknowledged his debt to Chopin: 'such modulations are also frequent in Chopin. It is a native fibre that he and I have in common.'[1] The recitative at the end proclaims the operatic composer, and the whole piece

[1] SVG, p. 163.

Ex.78. Andante

vo - storg___ ob - ya - ty i po - tse -

- lui! ___ Tyazh -

-ka pe - chal i gru - sten svet. Ni

sna, ni po - ko - ya mne, bed - -noi, net. O

(the rapture of his embrace and kiss. My sadness is grievous,
and my world is full of sorrow. I, poor wretch, have neither
sleep nor peace.)

suggests a revisiting of the world of Gorislava's cavatina from *Ruslan and Lyudmila*. Its quality is comparable, too; only, perhaps, in the major-key conclusion, does the song suggest a fulfilment less convincing than the hopeless longing into which Schubert's Gretchen finally sinks in his famous setting (though it must be remembered that Schubert made this possible by taking the liberty of repeating Goethe's opening line at the end). Most musicians will feel that Schubert has caught all the burden of Gretchen's words once and for all, and it is useless to pretend that Glinka has matched the level of the Austrian composer's first master-piece, for his music has melancholy rather than pathos. Yet Glinka's Gretchen is far from negligible; forget Schubert (perhaps, too, forget Goethe's play), take Glinka's setting on its own terms, and it shows itself to be a very fine song.

Yet the nine months spent in Warsaw were more notable still for two other compositions, this time for orchestra, which Glinka had completed a little before these songs. The first was *Recollections of Castille*, which Glinka rewrote three years later and re-named *Recollection of a summer night in Madrid*, and which became the Second Spanish Overture; the other was *Kamarinskaya*. The chain of events which led to their composition had started with a rough encounter. One day soon after Glinka had arrived in Warsaw, he had met the Governor, Prince Paskevich, while out walking. Glinka had removed his hat but Don Pedro, being unaware of the exalted rank of the Prince, had kept his firmly in place. The Prince was enraged at this and, galloping up to the pair, had nearly knocked Glinka over. Glinka was so upset that he wished to leave Warsaw immediately, but this was impossible. Mean-while the Prince had second thoughts about his own behaviour, and to smooth things over, promptly invited Glinka to dinner, an invitation frequently repeated. The Prince had an orchestra which Glinka found could be of use to him, though it was not faultless. He rehearsed with them the Chorus of Furies from Act II of Gluck's *Iphigénie en Tauride*; this was the first time he had ever heard any of Gluck's music per-formed, and he was so impressed that Gluck became an object for study during the remaining years of his life. He was also able at last to hear his First Spanish Overture, though Pohlens, the orchestra's director, had to reduce Glinka's scoring to accommodate his resources. In addition Glinka composed his *Recollections of Castille* especially for the orchestra. The piece, which Glinka himself described as a pot-pourri, was based upon four Spanish melodies. Two were parts of *seguidillas manchegas* which he had noted down from a Spanish mule-carriage driver in Madrid; both versions have a rondo-type structure, and the ritornello is common to both, though the episodes are quite different. Glinka employed the common ritornello and two episodes taken from different versions. The sources of the other two tunes, a *jota* and a *punto moreno*, are not known. The title of Glinka's piece makes it clear that the tunes must have been of North Spanish provenance. In any case, Glinka found material from the south of Spain generally intractable: 'my repeated attempts to make something out of Andalusian melodies remained quite unsuccessful. The majority of them are founded upon an eastern scale completely different from ours.'[1]

Glinka's use of abrupt movement from one section to another in *Recollections of Castille* was not just an attempt to avoid the problem of constructing transitions. Though no programme is specified, the piece is to a certain degree programmatic, for the entries of the second and third Spanish tunes are both made in mid-course, and have the effect of suggesting that the listener has just passed straight into the middle of another scene in the panorama of Spain's night life as the preceding scene fades away. Mozart had used the same device in the finale to Act I of *Don Giovanni*, where the minuet is first introduced by a final phrase, thus suggesting that the dance had already been in progress, though the listener has only just become aware of it. Perhaps this is where Glinka caught the idea. In *Recollections of Castille* he abandoned completely the sonata patterning of the First Spanish Overture in favour of a freer structure which bluntly juxtaposes the four tunes upon which it is based, and in which each section is extended by simple variational procedures. Certainly it was a far less developed piece than the earlier Spanish stylization, and it is not surprising that Glinka felt he could do better with the material. Two years later it was to be performed in St. Petersburg in Glinka's absence, and he was not at all pleased when he heard about it. 'I give the Overture *Jota* [First Spanish Overture] and *Kamarinskaya* to the concerts of the Philharmonic Society with pleasure,' he wrote to Vasily Engelhardt. '. . . As for the *Recollections of Castille*, this piece is only a trial run, and I intend to take two themes from it for the Second Spanish Overture, *Recollection of a summer night in Madrid*. Therefore I ask you not to perform this latter piece [*Recollections of Castille*] anywhere or to give it to anyone.'[2] A year later (1851), when

---

[1] GLN1, p. 266.   [2] GLN2, p. 387.

visiting Warsaw again, he made the full revision.[1] First he greatly expanded the introduction, retaining the first eight bars of *Recollections of Castille*, but replacing the next eight bars by fifty-six bars of exquisitely scored hints of themes to come. There can be no two minds about the improvement effected by this expansion. After this, *Recollections of Castille* had presented the four tunes, each with very simple variations, and in the new version Glinka retained all of these (not just two, as had been his original intention). It was after this that the expansion really started. In the earlier version, after theme four, Glinka had been content simply to repeat the introduction, passing on to the *jota* in the tonic (A major), followed by the coda. Now he halved the length of the original section 5 (see the plan below), and inserted sections 6 and 7, which traced their way through the themes in reverse order, thus producing a mirror structure in their deployment, though not in their tonal scheme. He also tacked an extra nine bars on to the coda. The first and the final schemes appear thus:

Recollections of Castille

Recollection of a summer night in Madrid (Second Spanish Overture)

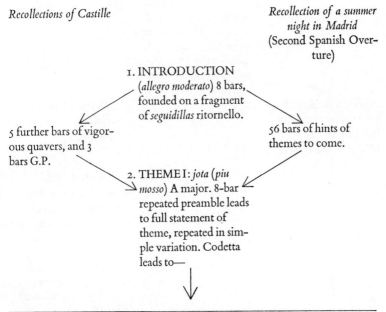

1. INTRODUCTION (*allegro moderato*) 8 bars, founded on a fragment of *seguidillas* ritornello.

5 further bars of vigorous quavers, and 3 bars G.P.

56 bars of hints of themes to come.

2. THEME I: *jota (piu mosso)* A major. 8-bar repeated preamble leads to full statement of theme, repeated in simple variation. Codetta leads to—

---

[1] It was thought that *Recollections of Castille* was irrecoverably lost until 1954, when the orchestral parts of the piece were discovered in the Soviet Union. The comparisons between the two versions made here deal with only the major differences; the reader who wants to know more should consult the scores of the two works printed in GPSS2.

3. THEME II: *punto moreno* (*piu lento*) D minor. Theme enters in middle. Full statement, almost all in 'heterophonic unison', repeated in simple variant. Rudimentary link leads to—
↓

4. THEME III: *seguidillas manchega I* [*piu mosso*] E major. Theme enters with an episode, followed by ritornello, all twice repeated in simple variant. Codetta leads to—
↓

5. THEME IV: *seguidillas manchega II* (*meno mosso*) C major. Theme enters in middle of an episode, followed by ritornello, still all at unison. Episode and ritornello repeated.

Further repetition of last 14 bars; then 8-bar link leads to return of INTRODUCTION, less first 4 bars.

Link leads to brief recollection of overture's opening, then—
↓

6. THEME IV [*piu mosso*] A major. Full statement of episode, followed by 2 variants of it, then ritornello. Link comprising sequential passage founded upon episode from THEME III, followed by a derivative from the ritornello, leads to—
↓

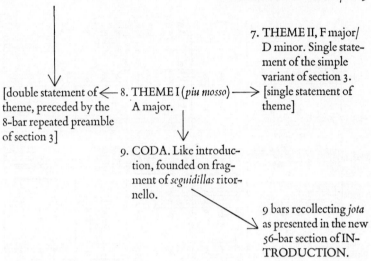

7. THEME II, F major/ D minor. Single statement of the simple variant of section 3.

[double statement of ←— 8. THEME I (*piu mosso*) ——→ [single statement of theme, preceded by the   A major.   theme]
8-bar repeated preamble
of section 3]

9. CODA. Like introduction, founded on fragment of *seguidillas* ritornello.

9 bars recollecting *jota* as presented in the new 56-bar section of INTRODUCTION.

As in the First Spanish Overture, it is the sheer attractiveness of the material and of Glinka's presentation of it, both in his decorative variations and in his instrumentation, that wins the listener to the piece and retains his attention. The scintillating violin quavers and the new harmonic structure of Ex. 79b add a fresh exhilaration to the already buoyant invention of Ex. 79a, and though the tune of Ex. 80 may be Spanish, the treatment is thoroughly Glinkaesque. Glinka's Spanish Overtures are relaxed pieces which make no attempt to scale the heights; they offer entertainment and diversion in the best sense of the words, requiring no condescension from the listener.

Ex.80. [Allegro moderato]

Glinka started work on *Kamarinskaya* in mid-August, immediately after completing *Recollections of Castille*, and finished it on 19 September/ 1 October. Eight years earlier he had attempted a piano piece on the *Kamarinskaya* tune, but it had been a failure; now, however, another factor came into the composition and really fired his imagination:

by chance I discovered a relationship between the wedding song, 'From behind the mountains, the high mountains', which I had heard in the country, and the dance tune, 'Kamarinskaya', which everyone knows. And suddenly my fantasy ran high, and instead of a piano piece I wrote an orchestral piece called *Wedding tune and dance tune*.[1]

Immediately after Glinka's death Dubrovsky wrote a fascinating sketch of Glinka at work on the piece. In the early stages Glinka made frequent use of Prince Paskevich's orchestra, often arranging for the players to assemble at his own home to try over parts of it. Then followed a period during which he simply pondered the work without reference either to the orchestra or even the piano. Finally he committed it to paper, and Dubrovsky recalled visiting Glinka during this phase. 'He [Glinka] was sitting at a small table in the middle of the room, in front of his birds, and was writing something on a big sheet of paper . . . This was *Kamarinskaya*. It was all prepared in his imagination; he was writing it out, like an ordinary mortal jotting down hasty notes, and at the same time he talked and joked with me. Soon afterwards two or three friends arrived, but he carried on through loud laughter and conversation, in no way hindered by this; and during this he was noting down one of his most remarkable compositions.'[2]

And remarkable it certainly is—less aggressively original than the Lezghinka from *Ruslan and Lyudmila*, but quite as bold as the chorus, 'Let him perish', in its juxtaposition of opposing elements. In *Kamarinskaya* the opposition is between two tunes, outwardly quite dissimilar, but which, as Glinka perceived, could be drawn into one. The work is based entirely upon variation procedures without a trace of sonata thinking, and the scheme has a simplicity which can easily deceive the casual listener into thinking it simple-minded:

1. INTRODUCTION: very brief, founded upon a fragment from the middle of the WEDDING TUNE
2. WEDDING TUNE stated; repeated three times with different backgrounds (D minor/F major)
3. DANCE TUNE (*Kamarinskaya*) (Ex. 81a): thirteen variations (D major), which slide seamlessly (see Ex. 81b) into—
4. WEDDING TUNE: repetition of the first one and a half variations (F major). Very brief transition leads to—
5. DANCE TUNE: twenty-one further variations (initially B flat, then D major).

[1] GLN1, p. 267.   [2] Quoted in GLN1, p. 458.

Ex.81.

Nor is the casual listener's respect likely to be increased by the juvenile quality of the *Kamarinskaya* tune. Yet to judge this composition by the worth of its basic material would be as rash as to fault Mozart for using the clichés and trivialities of opera buffa, to reprove Haydn for some stroke of musical humour in the high-minded world of the quartet or symphony, or to deny the devastating emotional force of some of Mahler's self-conscious banalities. Glinka knew perfectly well what he was about, and the insistent triviality of the dance tune ensures that it remains subservient to the seemingly inexhaustible variety of the treatment that Glinka's fertile imagination accords it.[1] First he matches it boldly with a lively counterpoint, then affords it a happy quaver accompaniment, fragments it into a sparkling line of semiquavers, refashions its contours and rhythms with hints of the wedding song, and then, with consummate ease, completes the transformation: the cheeky urchin has become the handsome boy, and we have hardly noticed how it was done. But Glinka's invention is not yet exhausted, and he skips back to the dance tune to dazzle with further fantasy, pirouetting round it, couching it in a soft cushion of string lines with a hint of the wedding tune in the bass, and then smiting it with a naked little pedal (Ex. 82). A little later the tune is again afflicted with an even more obstinate 'wrong note' pedal, only to be effortlessly returned to the comforts of the sustained string sound (Ex. 83). It speaks volumes for Glinka's quite prodigious variety of invention that he is able to make the seventy or so repetitions of a tawdry little four-bar phrase not only tolerable but enjoyable.

---

[1] 'Inexhaustible' is very much the word, for Vladimir Stasov, who did not meet Glinka until after *Kamarinskaya* was finished, recalled that Glinka's variational inventiveness was by no means played out. In the spring of 1849 Stasov heard Glinka improvise more variations on the tune. 'I [Stasov] would keep on playing the tune for him at the top of the piano, and often asked him ro repeat this or that variation (the last or next to last) which he had played to us. But often he had already forgotten them, and instead of these, his fantasy invented still more new ones—without end.' (Quoted in LPG2, pp. 54–55.)

Ex.82. **Allegro moderato [poco meno mosso]**

Ex.83.

Nor, while delighting in the wit of Glinka's treatment of the dance tune, should we overlook the beauty in his treatment of the wedding song. Organic counterpoint may have been difficult for most nineteenth century Russian composers, and their fugues may in general be dull, but decorative counterpoint was quite a different matter for them. Glinka had already displayed his skill in this field in many of his earlier pieces, and in *Kamarinskaya* the lovely contrapuntal backgrounds to the wedding song, so different from the sparkling and frothy sounds of the First Spanish Overture, show, in their gentle sustained lines and telling chromatic decoration, an equally complete mastery of decorative counterpoint. Dubrovsky's account of Glinka's compositional practices is enough to show that he was a 'thoughtful' composer, and the fact that some of his inspirations seem to have come to him involuntarily and effortlessly should not be allowed to obscure the fact that he was capable of giving extended and concentrated thought to a compositional problem when this was demanded—and when, of course, his imagination and interest were aroused.

The orchestration of *Kamarinskaya* is less immediately arresting than that of the First Spanish Overture, but this is simply because it was not intended self-consciously to reflect a Russian milieu, whereas his earlier work had deliberately sought to evoke the sounds of native Spanish music in its instrumentation. Yet the same characteristic crispness of colour and texture is to be found in the later piece. Take, for instance, the woodwind chord in bar ten, and contrast it with B flat chords as scored for wind by Beethoven and Wagner (Ex. 84). The German composers aim at a blended sound, with consistency and closeness in spacing,

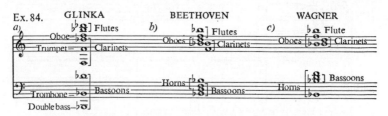

Ex. 84.

a) *Kamarinskaya*, bar 10
b) 'Pastoral' symphony, end of slow movement
c) *Die Meistersinger*, Act III (Sachs' solo before the Quintet)

and horns fusing with bassoons to ensure that the components from top to bottom coalesce. Glinka dispenses with the softer sound of horns, using instead the clear notes of trumpet and trombone, wide separation of the two clarinets and the two bassoons, a more spare texture at the bottom end of the sound—all of which ensures a brighter, harder timbre, a monolithic starkness, even, which could be the embryo of the sound world of a work like Stravinsky's *Symphonies of wind instruments*.

Kamarinskaya had a great success with Glinka's contemporaries, and deservedly so, for it is arguably his most remarkable single achievement. The Overture to *Ruslan and Lyudmila* is his most accomplished piece of instrumental music based on sonata thinking. Good as it is, it is really a less notable achievement than most of his subsequent orchestral works. The *First Spanish Overture* proved to be a transitional work in which the shift to variational procedures is pronounced, but in which the periodic scheme of the sonata remains. *Recollections of Castille* and *Recollection of a summer night in Madrid* are deliberately evocative pieces, their liberal fund of themes and blunt sectionalization dictated by the wish to suggest a wide variety of impressions in kaleidoscopic succession. *Kamarinskaya* is the very opposite in character: 'I can say definitely that while writing this piece I was guided solely by inner musical feeling, not thinking of anything that happened at a wedding,' wrote Glinka,[1] recording how Feofil Tolstoi had told the Dowager Empress Aleksandra Fedorovna that the pedal F sharp and pedal C (see Exs. 82 and 83) represented a drunken man knocking at the door of a peasant's hut. That sort of friendly help was, Glinka remarked bitterly, the sort of thing he had had to suffer more than once in his life. *Kamarinskaya* was a musical conception without outside associations, the fruit of his fertile fantasy, completely original in structure, and utterly new in effect. Tchaikovsky was later to write that the Russian symphonic school 'is all in *Kamarinskaya*, just as the whole oak is in the acorn'.[2] Yet, for all its great legacy to later Russian symphonic music, it remains to this day unique, simply because it was unrepeatable. And as far as Glinka was concerned, it proved to be his last really major work.

[1] GLN1, p. 267.   [2] See footnote on p. 1.

13/Last Years

There is no point in wearying the reader with a detailed account of the last nine years of Glinka's life. By this time the triviality of many of the events recorded in the *Memoirs* must have become tedious. There is something unutterably depressing about a composer who already had two remarkable operas and some striking orchestral works behind him, and who could presumably have written more if only he could have stirred himself to work, and yet who could count carousings and dalliances as the things that were really worthy of record. Who could he think was really interested in his alcoholic orgies with the hussars' regiment that was stationed near Warsaw when he stayed in that city for a second time? Was it really worth describing how he was invited to a reception of the Empress when she was visiting Warsaw, simply in order to be able to record her memorable greeting: 'Hello, Glinka. What are you doing here?' and her dazzling rejoinder when he replied that he found the Warsaw climate better for him than that of St. Petersburg: 'The difference is small, but I'm glad, very glad to see you.'[1] And who is interested in Emilia of Warsaw, Léonie of Paris, or Amalia from Bordeaux, who were among the successors to Angélique of Warsaw and Dolores of Granada? Let us take such things for granted in Glinka's life, and say no more about them.

There were, however, some new friends and acquaintances who were to be of real significance. In Berlin in 1852 he met Meyerbeer. Glinka had a poor opinion of Meyerbeer as a composer: 'I do not respect charlatans,' he had once replied caustically when Serov had asked him for his opinion of the German-Jewish composer.[2] Meyerbeer's view of Glinka was more kindly, and a year earlier he had written to Glinka, asking to see scores of his operas. Glinka was very flattered by this re-

[1] GLN1, pp. 272 and 275. [2] SVG, p. 141.

quest, and when they met he found that Meyerbeer was affable and easy to get on with. Glinka's personal fame had spread, but his compositions remained unknown, and Meyerbeer asked him why this was so. 'It is very natural,' Glinka replied. 'I am not in the habit of peddling my products.'[1] Glinka delighted in preserving his *bons mots,* and he recorded another which he vouchsafed when he and Meyerbeer met again in Paris the following year. This time Glinka had expressed his views on art to Meyerbeer, and the latter felt that they were exceedingly critical. ' "But you are very exacting," Meyerbeer said to me. "I have every right to be," I replied. "I start with my own works, with which I am rarely satisfied." '[2] On this occasion Meyerbeer was at last introduced to the scores of *A Life for the Tsar* and *Ruslan and Lyudmila*. 'The talk turned to Gluck,' Glinka recalled, 'and to my question about whether his music would be effective on the stage, Meyerbeer replied that it was precisely on the stage that Gluck became great (grandiose). He promised me that when I left he would let Berlin know in time, and try to arrange that one of Gluck's operas would be given for me.'[3] Later, indeed, Glinka did see his first Gluck opera on the Berlin stage, though in fact Meyerbeer was to have no hand in arranging it. During the last year of his life Glinka was to have close contact with Meyerbeer who conducted the last public performance Glinka ever heard of one of his own works. Meyerbeer was one of the mourners at Glinka's funeral.

Of even more importance, perhaps, was his meeting early in 1849 with the young Vladimir Stasov, 'an extremely sound musician, a lover of fine art, and a very educated man'.[4] Stasov was to be Glinka's first biographer, and was to play a very important role in the activities of the next generation of Russian composers. Late in 1851 Glinka came to know Vladimir's equally distinguished brother, Dmitri. But far more important still for Russian music was his meeting late in 1855 with an eighteen-year-old mathematics student from Kazan University. This was Mily Balakirev. He was introduced to Glinka by Uluibuishev, and was to become not only the leader of the next generation of Russian composers but also, with Lyudmila Shestakova, the great apostle of Glinka in Russia and abroad in the second half of the nineteenth century. The reverence of this obstinate, despotic young man for Glinka was unbounded, and Glinka was quick to recognize Balakirev's talents. Lyudmila recalled the first meeting between the two men. 'Glinka asked Balakirev to play something. He performed his arrangement of the

[1] GLN1, p. 283.   [2] GLN1, p. 291.   [3] GLN1, pp. 290–1.   [4] GLN1, p. 269.

trio from *A Life for the Tsar*, "Do not torment me, dear father". My brother listened very attentively, and afterwards talked about music with him for a long time . . . He was very often with us afterwards at my brother's constant invitation, and each time he appeared, he had to play his fantasia on the Trio.'[1] Before he left for Berlin in 1856, Glinka instructed his sister to entrust the musical education of his young niece to Balakirev if he himself were unable to undertake it. 'He is the first man in whom I have found views so closely resembling my own on everything concerning music . . . He will in time become a second Glinka.'[2]

Such new contacts were important and fruitful; yet, in general, the very absence in the *Memoirs* of information of compelling interest to the student of music is a sign of the futility of much of Glinka's life during these last nine years. He had intended to visit Moscow, but when he left Warsaw in November 1848 he returned to St. Petersburg instead. One noteworthy social event at which he was present was the party given on 19/31 January 1849 by Prince Vyazemsky for Zhukovsky to celebrate the latter's fifty years of literary activity. Glinka also mixed with some of the new generation of Russian writers, including the young Dostoyevsky, who was deeply impressed by Glinka's performance of his own songs.[3] But Glinka did not find life in St. Petersburg conducive to work, and on 9/21 May he returned to Warsaw in the hope of combining composition with a pleasant stay. However, despite a delightful journey, he was disappointed when he got there. Melancholy descended upon him, and he was drawn into 'violent orgies'[4] in an attempt to dispel his despondency. Yet there were more positive occupations, too. His growing interest in earlier music was fostered by the performances of Bach preludes and fugues by the organist, August Freyer, whom Glinka rated as the foremost musician in Warsaw. Then, in the autumn, he broke away from his riotous companions, and in this quieter existence com-

[1] Quoted in GVS, p. 291.
[2] ibid.
[3] Dostoyevsky was especially impressed by Glinka's performance of 'To her', and it seems certain that it was his recollection of Glinka's singing that he incorporated into the story, *The eternal husband*. The account is put into the mind of his hero, Velchaninov: 'He [Glinka] had by then no voice left, but Velchaninov remembered the extraordinary impression which was made then by this very romance. No adept salon singer could ever have achieved such an effect . . . To sing this tiny but unusual trifle, it was absolutely essential to have truthfulness, real full inspiration, real passion, or a full poetic command of it [passion] . . . Truth and artlessness redeemed all.'
[4] GLN2, p. 376.

Glinka in 1853. Caricature by V. Samoilov

PLATE V

posed three worthy songs. These were 'Adèle' and 'Mary' on texts by Pushkin, and 'Conversation' on a text by Mickiewicz; this last one was inspired by Emilia Ohm, who was the lady of his life at that moment, and who taught him to say the words in Polish. Like the three songs he had composed in Warsaw a year earlier, these new pieces reveal the same increased harmonic range, and a continuing inclination to get away from the simple strophic song and to produce an altogether more substantial composition. Mickiewicz's Polish text prompted Glinka to turn again to the mazurka, and Chopin's influence is clear, especially in things like the enharmonic switch and subsequent succession of sevenths above a circle of fifths in Ex. 85. 'Adèle' shows a broadening tonal range. In this

Ex.85. Tempo di mazurka

-dra- biać na sło-wa, któ-re, nim słuch twój i ser-ce do-

-ścig-ną, w us-tach wie-trze-ją, na po-wie-trzu styg-ną?

(Why must I break my soul into words which, chilling and
dissipating in the air, will penetrate to your heart before they
touch your ear?)

song Glinka reverses the poet's and composer's roles, repeating the same words to new music—or, rather, to music whose tonal course has been modified, for at line seven of the verbal repetition he moves not to the relative minor (C sharp minor) as he had done the first time round, but to C major instead. Pushkin's final couplet is reserved for an extensive coda. 'Adèle' has a delicacy of texture not surpassed anywhere in Glinka's songs; it is, indeed, one of the tenderest of his compositions, as fresh as the fourteen-year-old girl to whom Pushkin had devoted his verse. For 'Mary', however, the poet had turned to Barry Cornwall as a model. This time the sweet girl is seen through the eyes of a solitary man draining his cups to her, and Glinka's setting is aptly celebrational, but economical with some effective irregular phrasing. He could have set it as three strophes, but chose not to; verse two has new music, and while the opening of verse three returns to the music of verse one to establish the ternary structure, it quickly moves on to new material.

Early in 1850 Glinka was delighted to hear of the first public performances of his First Spanish Overture and of *Kamarinskaya*, both of which had taken place in St. Petersburg. He, of course, had not been present, and his disapproval of further public exhibition of *Recollections of Castille*, which was also played in the same concert, has already been noted: but the success of the other two works gave him deep satisfaction. *Kamarinskaya* was encored. However, his next work was to be far less well received. Over a year earlier, while he was still in St. Petersburg, he had been asked to write a graduation chorus for the girls' school at the Smolny Monastery. Glinka had misgivings, since the choruses supplied in previous years had been notable failures. The Inspector at the Smolny Monastery, and the man who was to conduct Glinka's chorus, was Ivan Cavos, son of Catterino who had conducted the first performance of *A Life for the Tsar*. Ivan Cavos wanted Glinka to use a small accompaniment—piano, harp, and a few wind instruments—but Glinka, who had a poor opinion of the young ladies' abilities, used a full orchestra instead of wind alone. He himself did not attend the first performance in April 1851, and he alleged that it was Cavos' disregard of his instructions for placing the orchestra which accounted for the work's failure. The Tsar was present, and Cavos reported the monarch's views: 'His Majesty the Emperor found the instrumentation of the chorus to be feeble, and I completely share His Majesty's view.' 'Cavos shares His Majesty's opinion!' snorted Glinka.[1] Yet His Majesty was not altogether wrong. Glinka had obviously done his best to satisfy Cavos' requirements for instrumental colour, and had used the full orchestra sparingly —too sparingly, perhaps, for when it is used, its presence only emphasizes the barer textures of the wind or piano/harp passages; it would not be altogether surprising if the royal ears did find the sound rather starved. But this is not all, for the real trouble is that the musical invention is less

[1] GLN1, pp. 275–6.

appealing. Not that Glinka's earlier commissions of this sort had produced music distinguished in itself. Nevertheless, having gauged the undemanding level on which he had to work, he had unfolded fabrics which were always attractive and sometimes woven with a finer craftsmanship than the material or the occasion really merited. Captivating textures and timbres, nice contrasts, and an effective tonal scheme had made his graduation chorus of ten years earlier a winner, but in this one the scoring is less graceful, the invention sometimes frankly dull, and the endless $\frac{3}{4}$ becomes monotonous. Glinka has tried, but the music sounds tired and unwilling.

On 8/20 October 1850 Glinka completed a setting of Obodovsky's 'Palermo' which he had tried unsuccessfully to compose with Vladimir Stasov's help the preceding year. This was to be published with the title, 'The Gulf of Finland'. The poet watches the sunset over the Gulf of Finland, and his thoughts fly to the crystal skies and turquoise waters of distant Palermo. The sea vistas of the poem prompted Glinka to set it as a barcarolle, though this time he confidently transmutes its Italian character so that the music, like the poem, hovers between northern and Mediterranean worlds. The pastel chromaticism is thoroughly typical of Glinka, and the delicate piano figuration of the middle section provides a happy contrast to the gentle, rocking chords of its flanking passages. As in so many of Glinka's other late songs, the coda is of great importance. 'The Gulf of Finland' proved to be his last composition of any real quality, and otherwise Glinka's two-year stay in the Polish capital was almost barren of new music. He did not particularly enjoy Warsaw society, and he constantly hinted that his mother and sister Lyudmila should join him to keep him company. The one favourable feature was the climate. Then in June 1851 he suffered a cruel blow in his mother's death. The shock caused a nervous reaction, which made it difficult for him to write: 'It cost me less labour to write notes than to sign my name,' he remembered.[1] Lyudmila hastened to Warsaw to nurse him, and when she left in August, he set about revising the *Recollections of Castille* to turn it into *Recollection of a summer night in Madrid*.

In September Glinka left for St. Petersburg to expedite the issue of a passport, and he lost no time in involving himself in the musical life of the Russian capital. On 3/15 October Serov was writing to Vladimir Stasov: 'What pleases me exceedingly is Glinka's lively enthusiasm for

[1] GLN1, p. 277.

everything that is outstanding in art. It is as though he has grown young, has grown fresh in this respect . . . He told me he wants to have an influence upon the St. Petersburg concerts of Lvov and the Philharmonic. "Do you remember, sir, the chorus in Gluck's *Armide*, 'The birds speak of love in their singing' ['*C'est l'amour qui retient*']? Let's have Lvov give that to us—and at the Philharmonic I'll order the fourth and eighth symphonies of Beethoven. Both works are miracles!" He himself has not yet heard *Kamarinskaya* played by an orchestra—in consequence they will certainly perform it here, and more than once. Likewise the *Jota* [First Spanish Overture]. A day or two ago Glinka told Konstantin Lvov to put on [Méhul's] *Joseph* and [Cherubini's] *Les deux journées* likewise. Lvov will also give the third, "Pastoral", and the ninth symphonies [of Beethoven]: Engelhardt has also arranged good quartet sessions for Glinka, where they will perform mainly Haydn quartets.'[1] Glinka was soon enjoying regular Friday evenings of music with his friends, events which included performances of extracts from his operas, arranged for three pianos, twelve hands! Then his health began to decline. He begged Lyudmila to come to St. Petersburg, and we may gather something of the strength of his attachment to her by the manner of his greeting when at last she appeared. She arrived in St. Petersburg late one evening, and found her brother entertaining the Engelhardts and other guests—'but, despite everything, when he saw me,' Lyudmila recorded, 'my brother threw himself on his knees and wept like a child'.[2] Lyudmila liked to emphasize her closeness to her famous brother and his dependence upon her, but there is no doubt that Glinka was now desperately needing both her love and her care, and these she lavished upon him. As Lyubov Karmalina, one of his singing pupils and partners in musical activities, observed: 'Lyudmila Ivanovna . . . looked after M[ikhail] I[vanovich] as a mother looks after her child . . . Rarely, indeed, have I met such another tender sister and marvellous woman.'[3] Yet, despite her devoted nursing, his health continued to deteriorate, and by early 1852 he was really ill. He recovered sufficiently to be able to prepare, at the composer's request, the singers for Lvov's *Stabat Mater* which was to be performed in March at the concert celebrating the fiftieth anniversary of the Philharmonic Society. Glinka was not represented as a composer at this event, but he had the compensation of a second Philharmonic Society concert on 2/14 April, in which Mariya Shilovskaya, who was reckoned one of the finest interpreters of his

[1] Quoted in GLN2, p. 779.   [2] SGVES, p. 596.   [3] KVos, pp. 268-9.

music, sang several of his songs, and in which he heard for the first time both his Second Spanish Overture and *Kamarinskaya* (as at its first performance, the latter was encored). He had already had proof of the esteem in which his fellow musicians held him in the ovation he had received at the final rehearsal for the concert, and this esteem was confirmed when, later in April, the Philharmonic Society elected him an honorary member. In the same month he committed to paper a Polka for piano duet which he had carried in his head for twelve years, expanding it into a fairly lengthy piece, and dedicating it to his little niece, Olga, daughter of his beloved Lyudmila. Glinka was greatly attached to Olga, 'for whom at this time,' Stasov wrote, 'he would improvise dances and songs for whole days, often himself playing and dancing with her with the simplicity and carefree joy of a child'.[1] Glinka also reported that his understanding of Gluck's music had been advanced by hearing during February Dmitri Stasov's arrangements of some arias from *Armide* and *Iphigénie en Tauride*.

Other things gave him less pleasure, however. In May he attended a performance of *A Life for the Tsar* at the Aleksandrinsky Theatre. This was the first time he had seen his opera since its initial performances of 1836 and 1837, and he was dismayed by what he found. 'For eighteen years[2] nothing had been refurbished,' wrote Lyudmila, 'the costumes and sets were the very same ones, and the Polish ball was lit by only four lights. Concerning this, my brother observed to me that soon it would be lit with the stumps of two tallow candles. But the sound produced by the orchestra, and the tempi that were set were frightful. I can understand what a great sacrifice my brother made on my behalf by not quickly leaving the theatre.'[3] As it was, he fled before the end of the performance. Even worse, his health continued to be poor and this kept his spirits low. As Dargomuizhsky had reported back in February: 'At the beginning of the season he was quite well and in most wonderful spirits; but he is finishing badly. His health is worse than before, and his state of mind, as you know, is always inseparable from his state of health.'[1]

---

[1] SG, p. 681.

[2] Lyudmila mistakenly assigned this visit to 1854. Darya Leonova, who sang the role of Vanya in this performance, to Glinka's great approval, is also confused in her dates, implying that it took place in 1853 (elsewhere she asserted that Glinka saw her off to Berlin in 1858, a year after his death!). She reported that the performance was very successful with the audience, however.

[3] SPGG, p. 614.   [4] DM, p. 570.

It is not surprising, therefore, that Glinka should have thought of travelling abroad again, and on 23 May/4 June he and Don Pedro set out again for Western Europe. An attractive woman in the coach to Warsaw inspired Glinka to compose a little sixteen-bar mazurka in the style of Chopin. In Berlin he had his first meeting with Meyerbeer, and had the pleasure of seeing Dehn again. From Berlin he travelled to Paris by way of Cologne and Strasbourg, intending finally to go on to Seville. Ever since he had left Spain five years before, his thoughts had constantly returned to Andalusia where it was 'warm, gay, and where life is four times cheaper than here [in Warsaw] or in Russia.'[1] He was delighted to be back in Paris, that 'wonderful town! marvellous town!', as he ecstatically wrote to his sister.[2] He enormously enjoyed his fortnight there, and his reunion with Henri Merimée who acted as his guide in further explorations of the city. On 2/14 July he left for the south, intending to approach Spain by an indirect route that would take him down the Rhone valley. The Spanish trip was to prove abortive. Soon after leaving Paris, Glinka felt ill. He reached Avignon, where he was greatly impressed by the panorama, but where his physical condition persuaded him to hurry on to Spain without delay. By the time he reached Toulouse he was too ill to proceed further, and after passing a fortnight of continuous suffering there, he abandoned any idea of reaching Spain. Instead he set out north through Poitiers to Tours, then along the Loire valley to Orléans, and thence to Paris. He felt too apathetic even to make the short detour to visit the chateaux of Chenonceau and Chambord.

Nevertheless, within four days of his return he had recovered sufficiently to feel like composing, and on 19/31 August he resumed work on his Ukrainian Symphony, *Taras Bulba,* based upon the colourful Cossack hero of Gogol's historical novel on the seventeenth-century Cossack-Polish wars. Although Glinka's *Memoirs* strongly suggest that this was the date on which he actually started work on the project, he had already played material for it to Vladimir Stasov before leaving St. Petersburg, and Dubrovsky recalled that Glinka 'had long thought of it, and while still in Warsaw had improvised several bits of it for me'.[3] Now he worked on it hard and successfully for a week or two; then doubts and difficulties arose, and by the end of October he had abandoned it. 'I wrote the first part of the first allegro (C minor), and the beginning of the second part, but, not having the strength or the

[1] GLN2, p. 397.   [2] GLN2, p. 418.   [3] Quoted in LPG2, p. 96.

disposition to get out of the German rut in the development, I rejected the labour I had already begun, and Don Pedro subsequently destroyed it.'[1] Commenting on his failure to complete the work successfully, Glinka observed to his sister that he had written very little of his music abroad. 'And now I feel quite positively that only in my homeland can I still be any good for anything. Somehow I am clumsy here.'[2] He passed the winter quietly in Paris, revelling in the Louvre, teaching a little singing, and reading Homer, Sophocles, Ovid, Ariosto's *Orlando furioso*—and putting on a lot of weight. He visited the theatre very little because he found the Parisiennes' liberal use of scent made the atmosphere intolerable, though he went to see Méhul's *Joseph* twice, and was deeply moved by it. However, he was disappointed by Auber's *Marco Spada*, whose première he attended, and he found the manner of performance of Beethoven symphonies by the Conservatoire orchestra was still as affected as when he had last heard it. By the beginning of 1853 he wanted to return home, for he was tired of Paris, and the deteriorating political situation worried him. He had already planned to return by way of Italy, visiting Milan, Florence, and Rome, but Don Pedro was very reluctant to leave, and their departure was delayed. In the end Glinka remained in Paris another year. In April he had acquired an excellent Indian cook called Zoë, and her culinary ministrations helped to make his stay pleasant. At the beginning of July he had his second meeting with Meyerbeer, and he was able to marvel at the new hippopotamus and chimpanzee acquired by the menagerie at the Jardin des Plantes. These botanical gardens were one of Glinka's favourite haunts in Paris. He went for walks, entertained (especially liking to welcome any of his compatriots who had just arrived in Paris), and read Boccaccio's *Decameron* and the *Arabian Nights*: 'What a pity I did not read these fairy stories before composing my opera *Ruslan*!' he exclaimed of the latter.[3] He confessed that none of his reading was serious like that of the preceding winter, but he felt disinclined to undertake weightier matter. Nevertheless, he did tackle Rousseau's *Émile*. His interest in this book clearly sprang from his concern for his niece, Olga, since *Émile* deals with Rousseau's ideas on education. Glinka judged it to be 'a long and boring book, though some happy ideas are encountered in it. I

---

[1] GLN1, p. 286. None of Glinka's materials for *Taras Bulba* survive in his own manuscripts, but in 1886 Vasily Engelhardt and Balakirev noted down, at the request of Vladimir Stasov, three snippets from the symphony that they could remember hearing Glinka play.

[2] GLN2, p. 435.

[3] GLN1, p. 292.

agree with him [Rousseau] about the education of young children, that in the initial upbringing no-one can replace the mother. When we meet,' he informed Lyudmila, 'I'll tell you all I know and think about the further direction of education.'[1]

When the weather deteriorated his health declined also, and he admitted that he smoked too heavily. As during the previous winter, he had a stove placed in his bedroom, thus re-creating the atmosphere in which he had lived the first few years of his life with his grandmother, and some of his friends had to shed even their jackets and ties when they visited him on account of the heat. Pedro observed that oranges could have ripened in it. It was well that Glinka planned to leave France that spring, for on 16/28 March 1854 war erupted between France and Russia. Seven days later Glinka left Paris as planned. He travelled through Brussels, Cologne, and Hanover, making the journey by rail, which he hated, and arriving in Berlin the worse for wear. Here Dehn revived him with quartets by Haydn and Beethoven (the former was Glinka's favourite composer of chamber music), and arranged for him to hear organ music by Bach. In addition, through an approach to the Superintendent of Theatres, the King gave permission for Gluck's *Armide* to be presented. At last Glinka could hear Gluck in the proper context, and he was deeply impressed not only by the music but by the performance. On the other hand, Graun's *Tod Jesu*, which he heard on Good Friday, pleased him not at all. His next stop was Warsaw, where he delayed a week because of a swelling on his leg. On 11/23 May he left by carriage for St. Petersburg, arrived five days later, and settled in with Lyudmila.

It is only necessary to read the letters that Glinka had written to his sister while he was in Paris to see that a great change had come over him. His letters should rarely be taken quite at their face value, for his expressions of longing for his homeland and the company of his family were often at their strongest when he was preparing excuses for remaining abroad. Yet there is no doubt that he and Lyudmila had drawn very close together, and when he made his will he left everything to her in gratitude for 'her love and sisterly friendship towards me'.[1] The letters written during his last winter in Paris are those of a man who realizes that his youth is passed. He is fifty next birthday, has put on weight, is having trouble with his eyesight; his passions have cooled, and he knows that his best years are gone. Now all he wants is a house with a garden at the back where he can enjoy seclusion. It is to be on the outskirts of

[1] GLN2, p. 464.   [2] From Glinka's will, quoted in GLN2, p. 673.

St. Petersburg where he can easily visit his friends and the city. He wants a room for birds next to his bedroom—and this room is to be between his and Pedro's bedroom so that he may be spared the disturbance caused by Pedro's inclination to vigorous physical activity in the mornings. Although Glinka was still to plan a new opera and undertake a study of church music, nothing came of the former project and little from the latter. Nor did anything come of the hoped-for house and garden—only the birds were to materialize. 'My muse is silent,' he wrote to Nestor Kukolnik in November 1854, 'partly, I suppose, from the fact that I have changed a great deal, have become more serious and quieter, am very rarely in a rapturous state, above all because, little by little, I have become more critical about art—and now the only music I can listen to without boredom is *classical* music. As for this last point, if I am critical of others, then I am even more critical of myself.'[1] Two months later he elaborated further on this to Kukolnik:

I was never a Hercules in art. I wrote by my feelings, and I loved and still love it [art] sincerely . . . What can I do if, comparing myself with masters of genius, I am attracted by them to such a degree that I am no longer able or inclined to write with conviction? If my muse should awaken unexpectedly, I shall write for orchestra without a text, renouncing Russian music like a Russian winter. I do not want a Russian play—I have had enough to do with that.[2]

He was soon to change his mind on this last point, but the hindrance of other music to his own creative processes continued. A month or two later he was even more specific on this point: 'When I settle down to work I involuntarily hear the music of others, and this distracts me from my work.'[3] The composers who particularly commanded his veneration and attention in these last years were Gluck, Bach, and Handel. Towards the end of 1855 he wrote to a friend, deriding his attraction to Spohr and Bortnyansky, and making some assessment of the particular merits of his own favourites:

No. 1. For dramatic music:
  Gluck, first and last, scandalously pillaged by Mozart, Beethoven, etc., etc.

[1] GLN2, p. 502.
[2] GLN2, p. 509.
[3] GLN2, p. 521. It is worth recalling that, while composing *A Life for the Tsar,* he had deliberately refrained from going to the opera in St. Petersburg, presumably to avoid having his own independence compromised by the influence of other operatic music.

No. 2. For Church and organ:
Bach, Seb.
B minor Mass and Passion Music.
No. 3. For concert music:
Handel, Handel, and Handel.
. . . Of Handel I recommend:
Messiah
Samson (in this there is an aria in B minor for soprano and chorus where
Delilah lulls Samson asleep to deceive him, which is like my aria, 'O my
Ratmir, love and peace', from *Ruslan*, except that it is a hundred times
fresher, more intelligent, and more pointed).
Jephtha.[1]

There is no reason to doubt the genuineness of Glinka's reservations
about his own powers, for when the young Anton Rubinstein ventured into print with an article in which he praised Glinka to the skies, he
was to be disconcerted at the reception Glinka gave him when they met
later in Berlin. 'I knew him [Glinka] in St. Petersburg, always esteemed
him highly, and he always behaved very cordially towards me . . .
But this time he was in Berlin, ill, fretful; I visited him there . . . he
received me distantly, and heaped upon me reproaches and admonitions
about that very article,' lamented Rubinstein.[2]

Glinka's last three years were largely spent in reviewing the past and
putting his musical affairs in order. It was immediately after his return
from Paris that, under pressure from Lyudmila and Dmitri Stasov, he
started to write his *Memoirs*. According to Vladimir Stasov, Glinka once
again took up *Taras Bulba*.

For whole days he devoted himself to it, thought over the further developments of the work, and nearly every day played ever new details of this new
creation to his young friends and admirers. Glinka had given Russia the first
Russian opera; now he was filled with the idea of writing the first Russian
symphony . . . Glinka already felt himself to be a complete, equipped, mature
symphonist. And *Taras Bulba* went ahead strongly.[1]

Stasov's unbounded admiration for Glinka often led him to overstatement, and it is difficult to believe that Glinka, except in a burst of
optimism after a good day's work, would ever have uttered such a bold
assessment of his own mastery. If he did feel the way ahead was clear,

---

[1] GLN2, pp. 557–8.   [2] RVos, p. 551.   [3] SNM, p. 387.

he was soon to discover insuperable difficulties, and *Taras Bulba* foundered again and sank for the last time.

During September and October Glinka orchestrated Weber's *Invitation to the dance* and Hummel's Nocturne in F, Op. 99, expressing himself particularly satisfied with the latter. He also revised the score of *Ruslan and Lyudmila*, and worked over his songs and other earlier pieces, writing out from memory some pieces that had been lost or destroyed. Just how close all these remembered reconstructions were to the originals is, of course, impossible to say. Nevertheless, among the pieces which Glinka wrote out from memory was 'Venetian night', a song which he had composed in Milan in 1832. What he had completely forgotten was that his friend, Melgunov, had published this song in the first issue of a new periodical, *The Moscow Observer*, which had appeared in March 1835. A comparison of this version with Glinka's later reconstruction reveals some differences, but they are marginal enough to show that Glinka's memory of his first invention was essentially accurate. At the beginning of 1855 he helped Nestor Kukolnik with the music Kukolnik had written for his own play, *The session at Azov,* correcting it and making suggestions for instrumentation. Later Glinka orchestrated three of his own songs ('Call her not heavenly', 'Soon you will forget me', and 'The midnight review'), as well as re-orchestrating and adding chorus parts to his piano 'Prayer'. These were all made for a concert to be given by his singing pupil, Darya Leonova. The event had originally been planned for February, but it had to be postponed until May because of the death of the Tsar. The coronation of the next Tsar elicited from Glinka a Polonaise on the theme of a Spanish bolero, chosen, Glinka stated, because 'I could not offer a Polish gesture to a White Russian Tsar'.[1] Glinka was very anxious that the Tsar should be aware of his loyalty and that he should accept the dedication of the work. The piece is undistinguished. He also projected a vocal work for the coronation, but in the end nothing came of this. Despite the views expressed in the letter to Kukolnik, he even planned a third opera. This was to have been based on *The Bigamist* (or *The Brigands of the Volga*) by Shakhovsky, which was currently enjoying a great success at the Aleksandrinsky Theatre. According to Leonova, Glinka was moved to undertake this work by her performances of his music, and the main role was to be written for her. A librettist had been found in the person of Vasily Vasilko-Petrov, who was a teacher at the Theatre School. Glinka spent

[1] GLN2, p. 521.

a good deal of time with Petrov working on the libretto. He planned to incorporate into it materials from the abortive *Taras Bulba*, and he prepared enough music to be able to improvise some of it for his friends. Indeed, Vladimir Stasov recalled that Glinka had celebrated his fifty-first birthday by improvising bits of the opera until four in the morning. But before 1855 was out he had abandoned the work. '*The Bigamist* has long since been broken off . . . I am glad, because it is tricky and almost impossible to write an opera in a Russian manner without borrowing at least the character of my old woman [*A Life for the Tsar*].'[1] By the middle of 1855 he was tired of St. Petersburg, and was scheming to go to Warsaw again, but when the autumn arrived he was not well enough to travel, and he resigned himself to a further winter in St. Petersburg. Early in 1856 he made his second orchestral version of the Valse-Fantaisie, and in March he composed his last romance—a setting, made after urgent pleading from the poet, of Nikolai Pavlov's 'Say not that it grieves the heart'. It would be nice to be able to report that this romance was a worthy culmination of his work in this genre—or even that it equalled his earlier setting of words by Pavlov, 'Call her not heavenly'; unfortunately it is an undistinguished specimen. Looking to the future, he wrote a few morsels of church music which were performed that Easter at the Sergiyevsky Hermitage near St. Petersburg. He was also able to follow the progress of Dargomuizhsky's *Rusalka* when extracts from it were performed that winter at Glinka's home. In general his life was by now very quiet, for his health was genuinely declining, and he rarely went out, even to hear his own compositions performed.

On 27 April/9 May Glinka set out on what was to be his last journey abroad. His ultimate objective was Paris, but initially he wished to spend a period in Berlin. For some time now his interests had been shifting to earlier music. During the winter of 1851–2 Glinka, along with Serov, Dmitri Stasov, and Vasily Engelhardt, who now formed a new and more worthy Brotherhood, had explored a good deal of 'classical' music, in which category Glinka included the works of Bach and Handel, his enthusiasm for whom has already been noted. Then in 1853 Vladimir Stasov had visited Italy and enthused to Glinka about Italian Renaissance church music. Glinka was in Paris at the time, but he had begged Stasov to bring or send a selection of these pieces to St. Petersburg so that he might be able to study and perform them when he himself arrived home. Subsequently Glinka became increasingly interested in this music; now

[1] GLN2, p. 560.

he believed that, just as Dehn had clarified and set in order his musical technique a quarter of a century before, so he could help him in his new study of the modes and of the contrapuntal techniques of church music. 'It is a difficult matter, but . . . very useful to Russian music,' Glinka decided.[1] These studies proved taxing, but Glinka remained convinced of their value. 'My studies with Dehn go along slowly but surely,' he reported. 'We are struggling with fugue; I am almost convinced that it is possible to unite Western fugue with the requirements of our music in the bonds of a legitimate marriage.'[2] The models that Dehn set before Glinka were Palestrina and Lassus, and Glinka's own intention was 'to write a trial piece (but not a model) for three and two voices in the Russian Slavonic Orthodox manner on the liturgy of St. John Chrysostom, not for a choir but for churchmen. I have brought along with me materials for this, namely, a collection of old tunes.'[3] In the end nothing came of this intention, and the only results to issue from Glinka's studies were a large quantity of fugal exercises. Despite Glinka's disclosure of his models, there are no signs whatsoever of the styles of either Lassus or Palestrina in any of these, for their technique is a sort of anonymous sixteenth century one, thoroughly corrupted by later contrapuntal practices. An attempt to work a Russian tune in stretto was a syntactical disaster, and Glinka's numerous efforts to use the same tune for what, presumably, he fondly imagined to be two-part compositions like Lassus' *Bicinia* are at best arid, at worst ungrammatical. Looking through this mound of two-, three-, and four-part fugues, double fugues, fugal expositions, episodes, canons, exercises in invertible counterpoint, and so on, one marvels at the dullness, clumsiness, and sometimes outright unmusicality of the composer of *A Life for the Tsar*, *Ruslan and Lyudmila*, *Kamarinskaya*, and so many other splendid works. The only clue to where Glinka thought these studies might lead him is one of his 'experimental pieces', a setting of the Resurrection Hymn, which he first wrote out 'as it was usually sung by the deacons and the people', and which he then treated 'as I thought of setting it for the deacons and the people (Ex. 86)'.[4] It is not apparent why such a mountain of contrapuntal study was necessary to produce such a compositional molehill, and it is quite impossible to believe that any more ambitious creative results of any real value could have issued from these labours with Dehn. Apart from these exercises and an arrangement for small orchestra of Alyab-

[1] GLN2, p. 594.   [2] GLN2, p. 636.
[3] GLN2, pp. 596–7.   [4] GPSS17, p. 112.

Russian Hymn of the Resurrection as it is normally sung by the deacons and the people:

The same hymn as I have thought of setting it out for the deacons and the people:

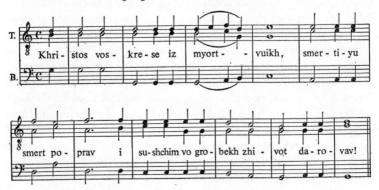

(Christ is risen from the dead, having amended death by death and having given life to those who were in their graves.)

yev's 'The nightingale' for the use of an Italian singer in Berlin, Glinka's own practical work was at an end.

There was, however, one other small product of his time in Berlin. This was 'A School of Singing', a series of exercises which he devised for his pupil, Adèle Kashperova, and it affords us some interesting glimpses of Glinka's musical values, as well as drawing attention to his lifelong pre-occupation with this art. We have noted before that, from all accounts, Glinka was a splendid singer. Serov's testimony may be added to those already cited, for he recalled hearing Glinka on many occasions at soirées in St. Petersburg. 'Glinka's voice was a tenor, not particularly high (though he did go up to high A, sometimes also to B flat), not particularly beautiful in tone, but purely a resonant chest voice, sometimes rough and metallic on high notes, and unusually adaptable throughout its whole range to passionate dramatic expression. Of contemporary singers there is only one [Tichatschek] who clearly recalls both Glinka's manner of singing and his declamation . . . His pronunciation was of the clearest, his declamation most true and excellent. Glinka "minted" every word when he sang.'[1] His singing of his own songs was unrivalled, and Serov devoted a substantial part of his own reminiscences of Glinka to trying to pin down those qualities in his performances of individual songs that made them so unforgettable. Glinka was a master at varying the mood from verse to verse in strophic songs. Apart from Mikhail Wielhorski's romance, 'I love', he sang only his own songs, but he could hold an audience for two whole hours on end with his performances of these, always singing from memory. The passage of time had certainly over-idealized Serov's memories of Glinka's singing, but he also faithfully recorded Glinka's disenchanting comment upon the way his own performances, which seemed so passionately spontaneous, were achieved. 'This is not as difficult as you imagine,' Glinka had said. 'Sometime or other, in a particularly inspired moment, it happens that I sing a piece in a way which completely accords with my ideal. I catch all the shades of that happy occasion, of that happy (if you like) "print" or "specimen performance", and I *stereotype* all these details once and for all. Thereafter I merely turn out the performance each time in its pre-prepared form. Because of this I can appear to be in the highest ecstasy when inwardly I am not at all animated.'[2]

It is apparent from this just how clearheaded Glinka was in his approach to performance, and there is no doubt that he could have built himself a great reputation as a teacher of singing, had he wished. As it was, he taught singing during most of his adult life. His first pupil was Ivanov, whom he took in hand before the two of them left for Italy in 1830, and subsequently he coached the principals for the performances of his operas, was in charge of the Imperial Chapel Choir for three years, and numbered among his pupils some of the finest singers in Russia. There have survived five sets of vocal studies composed at

[1] SVG, p. 133.   [2] SVG, p. 141.

different times of his life, and this set written in Berlin reflects his values at the end of a lifetime of experience. There is no virtuosity in them; mostly they are full of stepwise movement, and the instructions show clearly that the aim was evenness and clearness of line, and good intonation. 'All these studies must be sung slowly, being careful not to make any grimaces or to strain, not opening the mouth too wide, but keeping it in the natural, half-open position as in conversation. Attack the notes as accurately as possible, for accuracy and not power is the main thing in music.'[1] Fatigue was to be avoided at all costs because it was harmful, and attentiveness was required at all times when practising. The values reflected in 'A School of Singing' were those which appeared in Glinka's assessment of performers in his *Memoirs* and letters, where it was the artist who sang or played clearly and without affectation who won his approval. Every singer who performs Glinka's music today would do well to treat the evidence of his writings, and the accounts of his own performances, with the utmost seriousness and respect.

Likewise, it was this same clarity and cleanness without artifice that Glinka sought in his use of the orchestra. His creative approach to this craft—and the word 'creative' is used deliberately, because Glinka was an original in matters concerning the actual sound through which his musical thought was presented—is shown in the fragment of what appears to be a concerto for orchestra. There is absolutely no further documentary evidence about this piece, no indication of when it was composed, and little can be deduced from internal evidence, for the music, though capably written (and therefore not very early), has no marked individuality, nor any Russian character. It could have been started at almost any time in his life. The piece is simply headed 'Concerto', but there is no sign of any single solo instrument, and the way in which Glinka deploys his orchestra in the surviving seventy-one bars of the allegro risoluto suggests that his aim was to set off three groups (woodwind plus horns, trumpets plus trombones, and strings) against one another.[2] Thus the first four bars are scored for trumpets and trom-

---

[1] Printed in GPSS11, p. 66. Lyubov Karmalina recorded his views on contemporary Russian singers during the last years of his life. 'He disapproved of the manner of singing of Russian singers, finding in it a mixture of the Italian and the ecclesiastical, together with a gipsy [manner of] singing. He could not bear a constant vibrato, portamento, the gipsy [manner of] breathing with an "akh" [sound], the imprecise attack on the note after the church fashion (he did not like Bortnyansky). In singing Glinka liked to hear every word uttered clearly, cleanly, and correctly.' (KVos, p. 270.)

[2] Findeizen described this work as a concerto for brass instruments (i.e. the trumpets and trombones), and the fact that Glinka placed these instruments at the top of the score gives

bones, the next four for strings, then four for trumpets and trombones, followed by eight for woodwind and horns. A similar antiphony between strings and woodwind on the one hand, and trumpets and trombones on the other, is employed in the second subject before the score breaks off. It appears that Glinka was embarking on an experiment in which orchestration was one of the principles actually determining the composition; had he finished it, it might have proved one of his most fascinating, if not one of his best compositions. The craft of orchestration, like that of singing, was obviously a life-long preoccupation with him, and in 1852 Serov took down from Glinka's dictation his observations on the use of the orchestra. Glinka's precise comments on the potentialities, limitations, and quality of intonation of the individual instruments come as no surprise to anyone familiar with his lucid, carefully calculated scoring, He emphasizes the virtues of moderation in tuttis, and refers briefly but appositely to the peculiar problems of writing for the acoustics of the theatre as opposed to the church or concert hall. He roundly berates his *bête noire* of orchestral abuse, Verdi, and will not exempt Meyerbeer or Rossini from guilt in this matter. In Rossini's case he attributes his faults to composing at the piano. While commending Beethoven's orchestration, it is clear that Bach, Handel, and, above all, Gluck are the composers whose intrumentation really appeals to him. 'Instrumentation stems directly from the composer's music itself. Beauty of musical thought elicits beauty from the orchestra,' he concluded.[1]

Glinka's last months were generally contented ones, for the life in Berlin suited him well. Constantly in his letters he speaks of the calm and quiet of his existence, and of the benefits which his capricious health derived from this untroubled life. He read much, and there were plenty of musical riches to fill his time. When the season started in the autumn he was able to enjoy (among other things) Beethoven's *Fidelio*, Mozart's *La Clemenza di Tito, Le Nozze di Figaro,* and *Die Zauberflöte,* and Bach's B minor Mass, the *Crucifixus* of which he considered to be 'divine'. Above all, he was able to acquaint himself further with the operas of Gluck, and he was especially overwhelmed by the performances of *Iphigénie en Aulide* and *Iphigénie en Tauride*. There was talk of putting on

---

some support to this view of the work. Vladimir Stasov described it as a concerto for orchestra; certainly Glinka's handling of the brass group in the extant fragment does not suggest that this was *the* solo section.

[1] GLNi, p. 349.

A Life for the Tsar, but this was not to happen. Nevertheless, the trio from this opera was performed at a court concert on 9/21 January 1857 through the initiative of Meyerbeer, who was a frequent visitor to Glinka's home. Glinka considered this performance a great honour; 'in order to understand the importance of this event for me, you must know that it is the only concert of the year that is *tout en grand gala* . . . Unless I am mistaken, I think I am the first Russian to have been accorded this honour.'[1] Meyerbeer conducted ('he is a most outstanding Kapell-meister in all respects,' Glinka enthused[2]). It was well that he was happy about the occasion, for it proved fateful for him, and within a month he was dead. He caught a cold after the concert, and though the baths pre-scribed by his doctor had a favourable effect, he had a relapse and the final decline set in. On 23 January/4 February Odoyevsky visited him, and Glinka got out of bed, 'asserting that he was only slightly ill, and played his new little piece in the strict church style'.[3] It is ironic that when Glinka was at last desperately ill, he should have played it down. On 1/13 February, when Dehn visited him, he was still able to talk about his own fugues, but the next day Dehn realized that the situation was critical. Later he wrote to Lyudmila Shestakova that Glinka became 'indifferent to everything . . . The doctor said that his illness had suddenly taken another course, and that the patient's life was in danger', but added that 'the sick man would not die immediately because of his unusually strong [sic!] bodily frame'.[4] It was not to be. Suddenly, at five o'clock the next morning, Glinka died peacefully. The post-mortem, which Glinka had specially requested should be carried out, revealed that his stomach had shrunk and that his liver was grossly enlarged. It seems he had died of carcinoma of the stomach. There is no evidence for the more sensational diagnosis of syphilis.

Russia was full of tributes. 'Russia bewails a great native artist, the founder of the Russian school in music, one of the first-rank creators of the art of music in general,' wrote Serov,[5] and the cry was echoed through all the Russian press. The great Ivan Turgenev conveyed his feelings more privately in a letter to Vladimir Kashperov, the husband of Adèle, Glinka's singing pupil in Berlin: 'His [Glinka's] name will not be forgotten in the history of Russian music—and if it is decreed that it [Russian music] should at some time develop, it will take its origin from

[1] GLN2, pp. 646 and 648.   [2] GLN2, p. 646.   [3] Quoted in GLN1, p. 465.
[4] SPGG, p. 628.   [5] Quoted in GLN1, p. 466.

him.'[1] On 3/15 March the Konyushennaya Church in St. Petersburg was filled to overflowing for the memorial service, and five days later the Philharmonic Society presented a memorial concert of Glinka's works. In May, Vasily Engelhardt, who had undertaken during Glinka's lifetime to be the custodian of his manuscripts, travelled to Berlin to bring back to Russia the body of their creator. On 24 May/5 June, surrounded by a little group of relatives and close friends, Glinka was buried in the Tikhvinsky Cemetery.

[1] Quoted in LPG2, p. 148.

14/Conclusion

THE final chapter of a book like the present one usually serves one (or both) of two purposes. Either it will attempt a summary of the composer's musical personality and style, or else an assessment of his influence upon later music. It would be quite impracticable to embark here upon a study of Glinka's influence, for a proper account would expand this book beyond all reasonable limits. But when we turn to look at the composer himself, the problem is to find any substance at all to the figure that cast such a gigantic shadow across the musical future of Russia. What is the personality behind the musical style? Indeed, is there such a thing as a Glinka style? The answer is: no. We may point to certain features like the chromaticism and orchestration of Glinka's works, but neither these nor any of the other new features which appear in his work in any way constitute a style, either singly or in aggregate. So, too, Glinka's use of a procedure like the whole-tone scale is utterly novel, but the music which comes from it is in no way personal. Thus Stasov was quite wrong when, near the conclusion of his biography of Glinka, he observed that 'art was for him a means to the embodiment of that with which his soul constantly burned, for the embodiment of his own life, his joys and sorrows, its delights, triumphs, and downfalls', adding that 'he set out his whole life on the pages of his own compositions'.[1] Music of this sort can only be written by a thoroughly defined, positive personality who subjects the musical materials to the full force of his own unique complex of expressive impulses, which shape these musical materials in a particular, individual way, so that the resulting music has a quite different character from that of other composers, even though basic techniques may be held in common. The trouble with Glinka was that, for all his charm, sociability, and intelligence, he had no strong personality which could break through in his music, giving everything

[1] SG, p. 694.

he wrote an individual stamp. Thus, despite some features which have earlier been described as 'characteristic' because they recurred in his work, Glinka's music remains paradoxically anonymous. The only compositions in which something of the composer himself is to be found are certain of the romances, but their passions and plaints are those of a little man, and their music rarely even attempts to break out of the drawing room world. When he did compose a purely instrumental piece under the pressures of his own personal feelings, what emerged was that nasty effusion, 'Prayer'.

Because of the essential anonymity of Glinka's music, the only way in which the various stages of his creative life can be defined is through the influences that successively dominated or were incorporated into his music. Certain elements were constantly cropping up. One such was folk-music, with which he had engaged intermittently in the 1820s, and which he fully and finally digested into his own musical processes in the 1830s with *A Life for the Tsar*. So, too, the world of the St. Petersburg drawing rooms, in which he shone so brilliantly as a performer, constantly claimed a part of him, making the more striking a song like 'The midnight review', where he suddenly burst into another expressive realm, or songs where he sublimated salon sentiment (as in, for example, 'A voice from another world', 'Where is our rose?', or 'I recall a wonderful moment') in music which required more than the light dewy-eyed response of fashionable gentility. Of the successive influences to appear in Glinka's music, the first was the classical one to be seen in the chamber and orchestral works of the 1820s, where he was attempting a type of composition following in the wake of the classical masters, Haydn, Mozart, and Beethoven. None of the works of this classical phase was successful. This was not simply because Glinka's craftsmanship was still imperfect, for he could never have fitted into this line of evolution at any time in his career, and he had virtually abandoned this type of composition before leaving for Italy in 1830. During the next twelve years he used sonata structures only rarely (notably in his operatic and *Prince Kholmsky* overtures), and passed subsequently through the transitional sonata-cum-variation procedures of the First Spanish Overture to the independent form of instrumental thinking of the Second Spanish Overture and *Kamarinskaya*, founded upon variation techniques, especially that of the changing background. Even before 1830 Italian operatic manners had replaced classical pastiche, and these were to be a persisting ingredient in his subsequent work. The one remaining composer to

exert a deep influence upon him was Chopin. His presence is first felt in
the mid-1840s, and is especially apparent in Glinka's harmonic language,
but can also be detected, one suspects, in the more complex structural
organisms of Glinka's later songs. It is obvious, too, that Berlioz influ-
enced Glinka in the mid-1840s, more, however, in directing Glinka's
creative impulses towards the sort of material and attitudes of his
fantaisies pittoresques than as an actual presence in the music itself—though
one may wonder whether the sound of the First Spanish Overture would
have been quite the same if Glinka had not intensively studied Berlioz'
scores in Paris. It must remain a matter for speculation whether Gluck,
who made such a powerful impression upon Glinka in his later years,
could have proved as potent an influence upon his music.

The musical decline of Glinka's last years was clearly tied up with
psychological causes and, to a certain extent at least, with physical ones.
Glinka had aged. But Vladimir Stasov was probably right in perceiving
another factor: 'time and death had separated him from the majority
of his contemporaries, friends, and companions . . . [until] finally even
that small circle of enthusiastic supporters of his talent which remained
around him in the last years of his life . . . was not in a condition to
satisfy those demands for general sympathy which were one of the
fundamental traits of his character.'[1] Earlier in this book there have been
recorded specific instances of the extraordinarily public way in which
Glinka liked to create. In one respect at least he was the very opposite of
his arch-romantic contemporaries of Western Europe; he was a supreme
musical extrovert, reacting strongly to the world around him, and re-
sponding to its stimuli strongly but erratically—as has been written earlier,
a brilliant musical imagination rather than a personality. 'My brother,'
recorded Lyudmila, 'wrote only when something strong and pleasant
acted upon him, be it a woman, nature, the climate, or an outstanding
work of art. Then he was inspired.'[2] And he constantly needed new
stimuli, as Vladimir Stasov was really observing when he wrote: 'There
are natures which from the very beginning repeat themselves, while
others never repeat themselves, and cannot repeat themselves. Glinka
belonged among the latter.'[3] In his search for broader musical fields he
went not only to his own native folk music, but to Eastern and Spanish
music as well. All these fertilized his creative processes, and issued in
works which were not mere pastiches of the original inspiration, but
genuinely fresh, creative, and of great variety. Glinka's investigation of

[1] SG, p. 665.   [2] SPGG, p. 616.   [3] SG, p. 670.

Western church music in the last year of his life was a forlorn hunt for yet another other-musical stimulus which might have fanned the flames to their former brilliance and heat.

The two most important stimuli which aroused Glinka's creativity were poetry and drama. Admittedly only a very few of his songs could make any claim to a place in an anthology of the finest nineteenth-century examples of the genre, but the best moments in the operas are as good as any to be found in the work of contemporary Western composers. Allied to this dramatic sense was a natural flair for musical characterization which was doubtless aided by his very precise observation of the people who filled the world about him. We have seen the very alert ear he applied to performers, especially singers, and we have noted the almost cold-blooded way in which he created some of his own most moving performances. When it came to compositional problems he brought just the same clear-headed approach when seeking solutions, however disorderly his actual organization of his composing activities may have been. Without the support of his sharp-eared intelligence, his imagination might have floundered inarticulately, instead of finding its brilliant utterance in forms which were not only apt and new, but completely lucid.

It was Glinka's creative freshness and variety which were of such value to later Russian composers. A defined musical personality could only have been of use to any of them if the later composer could have identified with it. On the other hand, musical attitudes and procedures may be freely traded, and these Glinka afforded in abundance. They were taken up avidly by his successors, starting with Balakirev, who knew Glinka well and who, after Glinka's death, went on not only to plough his own personal furrow in the field of Russian music, but also to form and direct the cultivation of other parts of this virgin soil by Mussorgsky, Borodin, and Rimsky-Korsakov. Through his attitude to his art Glinka gave these composers the confidence to pursue creative independence for themselves; in his music he bequeathed to them an heroic manner, a magic idiom, and a narrative style for opera, and showed them how to elevate the sentimental romance, and incorporate eastern and Spanish manners into sophisticated music. He showed them how Russian folk melody might generate a whole melodic world, how the harmonic spectrum might be broadened with bold new sounds, how the vitality of rhythm might be intensified, how variation procedures might be substituted for organic development in extended pieces, and how such procedures might be compounded with sonata structure. He showed, too, the possibilities of caricature in music. Rarely can an individual, so insignificant in himself, have had such a wide and long-lasting influence. Tchaikovsky, whose debt to Glinka was really as great as that of his more obvious nationalist contemporaries, realized this disparity between personality and achievement. Granted Tchaikovsky's effusive comparisons of Glinka with Mozart and Beethoven are wild: the fact remains that in some other respects he was very perceptive, though not quite right either about Glinka's impatience of criticism or about the ownership of the bulldog. 'What an exceptional phoneme-mon Glinka is! When you read his *Memoirs,* which reveal a good, amiable, but empty and rather commonplace man: when you play his slighter compositions, it is just not possible to believe that all these were written by the very same man who created, for example, . . . the *Slavsya* Chorus! And how many other surprising beauties are there in his operas [and] overtures! What a stunningly original piece is *Karaminskaya,* from which all later Russian composers to the present day (and I, of course, among them) draw, in the most obvious fashion, contrapuntal and harmonic combinations as soon as they have to develop a Russian dance tune . . . And suddenly this very same man, now in his full maturity, composes such a flat, disgraceful banality as the Coronation Polonaise (written a year before his death) or the Children's Polka about which he speaks with such self-satisfaction and in such detail in his *Memoirs,* as though it were some masterpiece . . . Glinka is a talented Russian gentleman of his time, pettily proud, little developed, full of vanity and self-adoration, intolerant and pathologically touchy as soon as it comes to the evaluation of his own compositions. All these qualities usually belong to mediocrity, but how they could find their place in a man who, it would seem, ought to have been calm and to have recognized his own strength with proud modesty—that I emphatically do not understand! In one place in his *Memoirs* Glinka tells how he had a *bull-dog* which *did not behave itself,* and how his servant had to clean out the room because of its dirty deeds. Kukolnik, to whom he gave his *Memoirs* to look over, put in the margin: "Why put this in?" Glinka replied in pencil in the same place: "But why not?" Is this not very characteristic?

'But all the same he wrote the *Slavsya* Chorus.'[1]

[1] P. Tchaikovsky, *Perepiska s N.F. von Meck,* vol. 2 (Moscow/Leningrad, 1935), pp. 369–70.

Appendix
GLINKA: *Biographical Note*

[Glinka's *Biographical Note* was written at the end of 1854 for Fétis' *Biographie universelle des musiciens*. Glinka gave it to Vladimir Stasov for his comments, and the latter judged it to be inadequate since it was neither precise enough nor sufficiently comprehensive, and in any case omitted many important matters concerning Glinka himself and the impact of his work upon Russian society. As a result of this criticism the *Biographical Note* was never sent to Fétis. It is reprinted here not for the factual information it contains, which is not always correct, but because its terms and tone reveal a good deal about Glinka's attitude to, and assessment of, his own achievement. From certain phrases in it, it would seem that Glinka had just re-read Berlioz' article about him before writing this article. The *Biographical Note*'s style is rough and sometimes ungrammatical. The following translation endeavours to purge the worst of these features.]

Mikhail Glinka, a Russian composer enjoying a fully merited fame in his own country and in the musical world, was born on 20 May/1 June 1804 on the estate of his father, a Russian gentleman of the Smolensk province.

Being of a weak and nervous constitution, he was educated at home under the supervision of his parents, and from his earliest childhood manifested an inclination to the sciences and the arts. His favourite occupations were drawing, reading about travels, and the study of geographical maps. His musical instinct had not as yet revealed itself in any way, unless account is taken of the genuine passion with which he listened to the sound of bells. But when, at the age of ten, he heard a performance of a clarinet quintet[1] by Crusell, at once a craving for music blazed up fiercely in him.

[1] In his *Memoirs* Glinka described this as a quartet.

Remaining at home with his parents until he was thirteen, he zealously set about learning to play the piano and the violin. In 1817 he was sent to St. Petersburg and enrolled in the University's boarding school. While diligently attending his teachers' lessons there, he found no less time to devote himself enthusiastically to his musical occupations. First he took piano lessons with the celebrated Field, subsequently with one of his pupils, Aumann, and later still with Zeuner, who taught him the theory of intervals with their inversions and figurings. Zeuner's extreme pedantry compelled him to turn to the then celebrated pianist, Charles Mayer. At the same time he took violin lessons with Boehm, at that time the leading concert violinist in St. Petersburg; but here he was less successful than with the piano because Boehm, an excellent player himself, had no talent for teaching. This did not in any way hinder Glinka, each time he returned to his parents' home, from making a fundamental study of musical scores, performing them himself, and directing his uncle's orchestra which could play adequately overtures and symphonies of classical composers.

Glinka's first attempts at musical composition date from 1822. Being attached in 1824 to the office of the Council of Communications, it became possible for him to strike up an acquaintance with many households where excellent music was performed. But his first composition to attract the attention of the public was a romance which he composed in 1825 to Russian words. Between this time and 1830 he wrote about seventeen romances which people still enjoy singing today. Also during these five years he studied harmony and counterpoint, and tried out his powers in all genres, even in dramatic music for voices and orchestra. More than to anyone else Glinka was indebted to Charles Mayer for his counsels. Mayer was not so much a teacher as a friend to him.

In 1830 Glinka undertook a trip to Germany and Italy along with the court singer, Ivanov, the possessor of an excellent tenor voice. As his teacher of composition, he [Glinka] chose the director of the Milan conservatoire who, wishing to refine his musical faculties, quickly discouraged him by the aridity of his academic exercises for four voices. Having withdrawn from his [the director's] lessons, Glinka set about writing for the piano either as a solo instrument or as accompaniment in an endeavour to maintain the fame he had gained as a good pianist; the pieces he wrote in Italy were carefully published by Giovanni Ricordi. Having occasion at the same time to observe the style Ivanov had acquired in his singing lessons, he himself applied all his efforts to studying the difficult and capricious art of controlling the voice and writing in accordance with the characteristics of different voices. To this end he listened very attentively to the most celebrated singers, professional and amateur; Nozzari and Signora Fodor[-Mainvielle] were his greatest helpers in this respect.

In Naples in 1832 he left Ivanov who soon afterwards had to make his début at the San Carlino Theatre. Having lived a further year in Milan, Glinka set off in the spring of 1833 for Venice, where he endured a cruel illness, as a result of which a strong and high tenor voice manifested itself in him in place of the dull and undefined voice he had possessed up to that time. On the other hand a real longing for his own country seized him, finally convincing him that he was travelling a wrong road and that he could not sincerely create after the pattern of contemporary Italians. In June of that year he left for Vienna, and in October for Berlin.

Throughout the whole winter which he spent in the latter city he took lessons from Siegfried Dehn, now the curator of the music section of the Royal Library in Berlin. Gifted with great insight, Dehn divined the inclinations of his pupil, and having discarded all kinds of pedantry and unnecessary aridity from his teaching, he set him [Glinka] to exercise himself in the writing of three- and four-voice fugues after having accelerated the development of his taste, and put in order his musico-theoretical knowledge. Here, as in Italy, Glinka wrote a few more Russian romances and small pieces for piano, continuing to devote himself entirely to studying the spirit of Russian music, a thing which had become an *idée fixe* for him.

On his return to Russia in 1834 this idea gained still more strength. He then conceived the idea of writing a Russian opera, but did not yet have a definite subject. In the winter of that same year the celebrated Russian poet, Zhukovsky, suggested to him a subject taken from an historical event of 1612.

The subject completely answered Glinka's wishes, so that in a very short time he had drawn up a plan of the opera, and from the beginning of 1835 he set about composing it; Baron Rosen wrote the libretto in accordance with the composer's plan. This opera in four large acts with an epilogue was completed at the end of 1835[1] and was first presented on the stage of the Bolshoi Theatre in St. Petersburg on 27 November

---

[1] The opera was not finished until 1836.

1836 with the title of *A Life for the Tsar*. It had a brilliant success, and is still given to this day, to great public satisfaction.

In January 1837 the Tsar appointed him Kapellmeister of the choir of the Imperial Chapel. However, this appointment in no way distracted him from his main occupation, and while fulfilling his new duties he continued to compose romances and started upon a new opera of a fantastic or magical kind, the subject for which he took from the poem *Ruslan and Lyudmila* by the famous Russian poet, Pushkin.

Many unfavourable circumstances prevented the composer from occupying himself with the new composition with as much ardour or consistency as with his first opera; in addition the subject, rich in magnificent detail, did not as a whole possess any dramatic interest. Glinka yielded to its charm and, not restricting himself to his own inspiration, introduced into the opera several Circassian and Crimean tunes which had struck him by their originality—even going as far as using a Finnish melody upon which he composed the magician's [Finn's] ballad. Incidentally, in his first opera, which had become popular because of its prevailing purely Russian character, there is only one Russian song which is not the composer's own—and which, moreover, was not known at all up to that time by anyone.

The opera, *Ruslan and Lyudmila*, was first given on 27 November 1842 on the stage of that same Bolshoi Theatre. The first two performances were only moderately successful because of the illness of the principal contralto (Miss Petrova). At its third performance, in which this singer participated, the opera was enthusiastically received, and lasted for forty-five[1] performances in the course of that winter.

At the end of 1839 Glinka retired because of illness, and up to 1843 wrote, in addition to the above-mentioned fantastic opera, a large number of Russian romances and several other compositions for orchestra and for piano.

In 1844 he went to Paris where he made the acquaintance of Berlioz, who wanted several numbers from Glinka's operas to be performed at the concerts which he gave in the hall of the Cirque Olympique in the Champs-Elysées. At the insistence of his own compatriots, Glinka in his turn gave a concert in the Salle Herz in April 1845 in aid of a charitable society. On the occasion of this event, Berlioz wrote in the *Journal des Débats* a big article about the composer, his compositions, and the concert that had just taken place.

---

[1] *Ruslan and Lyudmila* was in fact performed thirty-two times in the first winter.

Having left for Spain at the end of the spring, Glinka set about a careful study of the national music of that country. In Madrid in the autumn of the same year he wrote a piece on the theme of the *jota aragonesa*, which subsequently received the title of [First] Spanish Overture. On his return from Spain in 1847 he wrote several more romances and piano pieces in Smolensk. After this he spent about three months in Warsaw where, in addition to romances, he composed a second Spanish Overture[1] and a national scherzo known by the name of *Kamarinskaya*.

'Glinka has never treated his art in a mercenary way,' it is stated in Berlioz' article. That is why he never writes except when he has felt real inspiration. Now in St. Petersburg he is preparing as complete an edition as possible of his compositions and, incidentally, is writing his recollections of his artistic life.

[1] *Recollections of Castille*, not *Recollection of a Summer night in Madrid*.

A Life for the Tsar [and] Ruslan and Lyudmila
by HECTOR BERLIOZ

[Berlioz' article appeared in Paris in the *Journal des débats* of 16 April 1845. Melgunov provided Berlioz with the biographical data which, it will be noted, is not always flawlessly accurate. The article is reprinted here since it affords the clearest extant indication of Berlioz' real attitude to Glinka and his music.]

In France, especially in Paris, we are rather inclined to base our conduct with regard to foreign composers, as yet unknown, on a kind of preconceived notion, the injustice of which becomes evident through experience—alas, always too late and always to no avail. One's opinion about them, favourable or hostile, is decided in advance according to one's social class, habits, and expressed ideas, and one conforms to this opinion right from the start before knowing anything that might justify it, though one may perhaps abandon it later if absolutely necessary. Thus, should one speak about a new Italian composer in front of the great majority of Parisian artists, they will think, even if they do not say so, that this must be some mediocre scribbler of cavatinas, hardly able to write three chords according to the rules, a servile copyist of copyists who imitates the imitators of Rossini, and is unaware of what is happening in the main-stream of music—such as what is being sung in the Juggernaut pagoda, the frequenting of which is to be dreaded by whoever is not bent on passing for a blockhead. This means that the greatest Italian masters might have incurred amongst us this unjust stigma if they had come to make their first appearance here *ex abrupto*. On the other hand, in the fashionable world, the world of musical soirées, where the title *concert* is given to the more or less grotesque performance of half a dozen airs, some undistinguished Italian duos and trios with piano accompaniment, the newcomer will be presumed, on the contrary, to be a delightful composer, abounding in easy melodies, worthy of the encouragement and support of all those who love and honour the arts. Then, if by chance he manages to get one of his scores heard by the general public and the work falls flat, you are allowed to drop it without fuss, and the author returns to his oblivion.

A German composer would find in these two courts of judgement a quite different attitude towards himself. The artists will show themselves, if not biased in his favour, at least ready to listen to him, to study him seriously, whilst people in high society, especially the ladies, will dread in him the learned musician who composes quartets, sonatas, and Lieder, *in which there is no tune at all*. Weber would have been treated by these latter people as a cold contrapuntalist, and Albrechtsberger would have been welcomed by the first group almost with the respect due to a genius.

As far as a French composer is concerned, he will find in the salons the most icy indifference, and in the orchestras a terrible lack of interest. This is perfectly proper; the proverb, 'No-one is a prophet in his own land', must not be shown to be wrong.

But we have never taken it into our heads to consider what the people of the North might produce in the way of noteworthy musical composition, and we are unaware even that they might be superior to us in certain aspects of performance. I know, however, of Danish works of exquisite refinement, full of poetry, and written with a truly rare purity and stylistic assurance. The appearance of the symphonies of Gade, a Danish musician made known by Mendelssohn two years ago in Leipzig, created a sensation in Germany, and now we have M. de Glinka, a Russian composer with a talent notable for its style, its harmonic skill, and above all for the freshness and novelty of its ideas.

No doubt you will be very grateful to have a few details concerning him.

Michel de Glinka [sic!], whose two pieces that we have recently performed at the Cirque Olympique have revealed for the first time his name and talent to Parisians, has nevertheless already gained in Russia a well-deserved fame. Born of a noble, affluent family, he was not destined at first for a musical career. He studied at St. Petersburg University, but the success he achieved there in all branches of learning, in science, in modern and ancient languages, did not at all deter him from his favourite study, that of the art of music. Nevertheless, he never thought of becoming completely devoted to music. His tastes, essentially free of all inclination towards theory and calculation, prevented him from doing so, as much as his social status. So the young musician found himself situated in the most favourable conditions for developing carefully and by all possible means the fortunate gifts bestowed on him by nature. It is under similar circumstances that masters like Meyerbeer, Mendelssohn and Onslow were brought up. Glinka, in the midst of his labours in composition, did not in the least neglect his instrumental practice, and in a few years became a powerful pianist, and was well versed in the violin, thanks to the excellent lessons of Charles Mayer and Boehm, artists of great talent from St. Petersburg. Being soon obliged, as was the custom in Russia, to go into the civil service, he still never forgot for one moment his true vocation, and in spite of his youth, his name rapidly became well known on account of his compositions, which were full of grace and unaffected originality. But when he wanted to engage in a higher and more serious type of work, he felt the need to travel and, by a succession of new impressions, to give to his talent the strength and breadth which it still lacked. He left the civil service and set off for Italy with the tenor, Ivanov, who owes to his [Glinka's] enlightened friendship a part of his musical education. At this time, sometimes living in Milan, on the shores of Lake Como, sometimes travelling through the rest of Italy, Glinka was writing primarily for his favourite instrument, the piano, and the catalogues of Ricordi, his Milan publisher, are there as a witness to the activity of the young Russian master and to the variety of his ideas. Nevertheless, the main object of his stay beyond the Alps was to study the theory of singing and the mysteries of the human voice, a study which he later turned to very good account. In 1831 I met him in Rome and had the pleasure of hearing at one of M. Vernet's, our director's, soirées several Russian songs he had composed, delightfully sung by Ivanov, which struck me greatly with their ravishing melodic turn of phrase, so completely different from what I had heard up to then.

After stopping in Italy for three years he arrived in Germany. It was mainly in Berlin, under the direction of the learned theorist, Dehn, at that time Music Librarian of the Royal Library, that he delved into the study of harmony and counterpoint. The strict and painstaking studies undertaken during his travels finally made him master of all the resources of his art, and he came back to Russia filled with the idea of a Russian opera written in the style of national folk-song, an idea he had nurtured for a long time. He began, therefore, to work enthusiastically at a score whose libretto, written under his guidance, was of a kind to emphasise the characteristic traits of the Russians' musical feeling. This

Glinka in 1856

PLATE VI

score, of which just lately we have heard another charming cavatina, is called *A Life for the Tsar*.

The subject of the piece is taken from the story of the wars of independence at the beginning of the seventeenth century. This truly national work was a dazzling success; but, quite apart from all patriotic bias, its worth is manifest, and M. Mérimée was quite right in saying in one of his letters on Russia, published a year ago, that the composer had grasped and realized perfectly the poetry in this both simple and moving composition. *A Life for the Tsar* had as great a success in Moscow as in St. Petersburg. Then, to set the seal on this double success and to ratify it by a favour to which a musician of Glinka's years could not [normally] aspire, the Emperor named him *maître de chappelle* of the court singers.

One must point out that the choir of the Emperor of Russia is a wonderful institution of which, if one is to believe all the Italian, German, and French artists who have heard it, one can form only a very imperfect idea. Indeed, last year, Adam, on his return from St. Petersburg, published an account of the extraordinary impression made on him by this magnificent vocal ensemble. Other artists as well, perfectly capable of adequately judging such an establishment, likewise agree with one another when referring to it. And one cannot doubt that if today the instrumental ensemble of the Paris Conservatoire is superior to all known orchestras, the choir of the Russian court should be placed higher still above all choirs existing at the moment anywhere in the world. It is composed of about one hundred men's and boys' voices, singing unaccompanied; the Russian church, like the Eastern church in general, forbids the use of female voices, organs, or any other instrument. These singers are recruited primarily from the provinces in the middle of the Empire; their voices are of an exquisite timbre, and their range, especially in the bass, almost unbelievable. Ivanov belongs to it, and I remember him in Rome replying modestly to the compliment paid him on the beauty of his voice, that several tenors of the Imperial Chapel had voices greatly superior to his own in range, strength, and purity. The deep voices are divided into basses and contra-basses, these last mentioned going down effortlessly and with a quite astonishing fullness of sound to the low A flat (a third below the cello's bottom C), allowing the bass of the harmony to be doubled at the octave. This gives to the ensemble this velvet quality which we do not meet in our vocal groups, and transforms this choir into an expressive human organ whose majesty and whose effect on the nervous system of impressionable listeners cannot be described. Glinka travelled through the Ukraine, seeking for the choir those children's voices, those seraphs's voices, as he calls them, which this half-wild land alone seems to possess. And a strange point or, at least, a little known point—these children are at the same time gifted with a musical skill so fine that he failed to confuse them by playing to them on the violin the strangest intervals, and the most unusual and difficult progressions for the voice.

At the end of three or four years Glinka, seeing his health beginning to break up, decided to give up conducting the court singers and once again to leave Russia. Nevertheless, this choir, which he left in a splendid state, has improved even more latterly under the wise leadership of General Lvov, a very worthy composer and violinist, one of those musical enthusiasts—one might say one of the most distinguished artists—which Russia possesses, and whose works I often heard praised during my stay in Berlin.

Before leaving, M. Glinka gave to the Russian stage a second opera (*Ruslan and Lyudmila*) whose subject is taken from a poem by Pushkin. This work, of a fantastic and half-oriental character—as if it were inspired both by Hoffmann and the *Tales of a Thousand and one Nights*—is so different from *A Life for the Tsar* that one would believe that it had been written by another composer. The talent of the author here appears more mature and more powerful. *Ruslan* is indubitably a step foward, a new phase in Glinka's musical development.

In his first opera the dominant influence of Italy is felt throughout the melodies, stamped though they are with such fresh and true national colours; in the second, on the contrary, one feels the predominant influence of Germany in the importance of the role played by the orchestra, in the beauty of the harmonic texture, in the skill of the instrumentation. The numerous performances of *Ruslan* confirm that it had a real success, even after the complete popular success of *A Life for the Tsar*. And among the artists who were the first to do brilliant justice to the beauties of the new score, one must mention Liszt and Henselt, who transcribed and wrote variations on some of the most outstanding themes. Glinka's talent is essentially supple and varied; his style has the rare distinction of changing itself at the composer's will according to the requirements and character of the subject he is treating. He can be simple and even naïve without ever stooping to use a single vulgar idea. His melodies have unexpected accents and phrases of a charming quaintness; he is a master of harmony, and writes for instruments with a care and knowledge of their more secret depths which transforms his orchestra into one of the newest and most exciting modern orchestras that one could hear. The public seemed to share this opinion wholeheartedly at the concert given last Thursday in the Salle Herz by M. Glinka. The indisposition of Mme. Solovyeva, a singer from St. Petersburg who has performed all the principal roles of the Russian composer's operas, prevented us from hearing the vocal excerpts announced on the programme; but his scherzo in waltz form [the Valse-Fantaisie] and his Krakowiak [from *A Life for the Tsar*] were warmly applauded by the glittering audience; and if his fantastic march from *Ruslan and Lyudmila* created less of a sensation, that is only because of the abrupt conclusion to this piece, whose coda changes direction sharply and finishes in such an unexpected and laconic fashion that one must see the orchestra stop playing to believe that the composer finishes at that point. The scherzo is full of spirit and of exceedingly piquant rhythmic *coquetteries* which are really new and superbly developed. The Krakowiak and the march are also outstanding, especially on account of the originality of the melodic style. This talent is very rare, and when the composer adds to it that of a refined harmonic sense and of a fine, clean orchestration, flawless and full of colour, he may with good reason claim a place among the outstanding composers of his time. The composer of *Ruslan* is certainly in this category.

[Translated by ELIZABETH BROWN]

Bibliographical Note and Selected Bibliography

A splendidly comprehensive bibliography of Glinka, listing nearly 3,500 Russian-language titles published up to 1956, was printed in *M. I. Glinka: sbornik statei*, edited by E. Gordeyeva (Moscow, 1958). The specialist should consult this; as for the average English reader, he will find little use in this present book for a long string of Russian titles, however impressive it might appear. The bibliography below is therefore restricted to the first publications of Glinka's *Memoirs*, of his writings on the craft of orchestration, and of his collected letters, to certain of the most important reminiscences of him, and to landmarks in Glinka scholarship, both in Russia and the West. The other titles are of fundamental Soviet sources used in this study (including the complete edition of his music), and of a few other books that have provided incidental but valuable material on Glinka and his work, or on his historical and cultural background. Other sources which have provided snippets of information are not included here, but are listed in footnotes in the appropriate places in the main body of this book. To save space in footnotes, abbreviations have been devised for those sources from which direct quotations have been made in the course of this book.

AORM   ABRAHAM (G.), *On Russian music*. pp. 279. (London, [1939])

ABRAHAM (G.), *Studies in Russian music*. pp. vi + 355. (London, [1935])

ANDERSON (W. R.), 'Michel Ivanovitch Glinka' (*The Music Masters*, edit. A. L. Bacharach, vol. 2 (London, 1950), pp. 131–7)

ASAFYEV (B. V.), *M. I. Glinka*. pp. 306. (Moscow, 1947)

ASAFYEV (B. V)., *Russian music from the beginning of the*

nineteenth century. Translated by A. Swan. pp. viii + 329. (Michigan, 1953)

CALVOCORESSI (M. D.), *Glinka: biographie critique*. pp. 126. (Paris, [1911])

CALVOCORESSI (M. D.) and ABRAHAM (G.), *Masters of Russian music*. pp. 511. (London, 1936)

DM   DARGOMUIZHSKY (A. S.), 'Materialui dlya yevo biografy' [Autobiography and a selection of letters]. (Seven parts in *Russkaya starina*, vols. 12 and 13 (1875))

DKO   DRUSKIN (M. S.) and KELDUISH (Y. V.) [editors], *Ocherki po istory russkoi muzuiki, 1790–1825*. pp. 455. (Leningrad, 1956)

FINDEIZEN (N. F.), *Katalog notnuikh rukopisei, pisem i portretov M. I. Glinki, khranyashchikhsya v Rukopisnom Otdeleny Imperatorskoi Publichnoi Biblioteki v S-Peterburge*. pp. 133. (St. Petersburg, 1898)

FINDEIZEN (N. F.), *Mikhail Ivanovich Glinka: yevo zhizn i tvorchestkaya deyatelnost*. Vol. 1, [part 1 only published]. (St. Petersburg, 1896)

FOUQUE (O.), *Michel Ivanovitch Glinka d'après ses mémoires et sa correspondance*. pp. 105. (Paris, 1880)

GLN1 and GLN2   GLINKA (M. I.), *Literaturnoye naslediye*. 2 vols. 1 Avtobiograficheskiye i tvorcheskiye materialui. 2. Pisma i dokumentui. Edited by V. Bogdanov-Berezovsky. (Leningrad, 1952–3)

GLINKA (M. I.), *Polnoye sobraniye pisem*. Collected and published by N. F. Findeizen. pp. ii + 566. (St. Petersburg, [1907])

GPSS1 to GPSS18   GLINKA (M. I.), *Polnoye sobraniye sochineny* [Complete edition of his compositions]. 18 vols. (Moscow, 1955–68)

GLINKA (M. I.), 'Zametki ob instrumentovke' and 'Prilozheniye instrumentovki k muzuikalnomu sochineniyu' (*Muzuikalnuy i teatralnuy vestnik*(1856), No. 2, pp. 21–23 and No. 6, pp. 99–101)

GLINKA (M. I.), 'Zapiski' [*Memoirs*]. (Seven parts in *Russkaya starina*, vols. 1 and 2 (1870))

GLINKA (M. I.), *Zapiski M. I. Glinki i perepiska yevo s rodnuimi i druzyami*. pp. iv + 456 + iv. (St. Petersburg, 1887)

GLINKA (M. I.), *Zapiski*. Edited by A. N. Rimsky-Korsakov. pp. 568 (Moscow/Leningrad, 1930)

GZ   GLINKA (M. I.), *Zapiski*. Edited by V. Bogdanov-Berezovsky. pp. 281. (Leningrad, 1953)

GLINKA (M. I.), *Memoirs*. Translated from the Russian by R. B. Mudge. pp. xi + 264. (Norman: Oklahoma, 1963)

GOLAVACHEVA (PANAYEVA) (A. Y.), 'Vospominaniya' (*Istorichesky vestnik*, vol. 35 (1889), pp. 291–333)

GG   GORDEYEVA (E.) [editor], *M. I. Glinka: sbornik statei*. pp. 817. (Moscow, 1958)

KNG1   KANN-NOVIKOVA (E.), *M. I. Glinka: novuiye materialui i*
KNG2   *dokumentui*. 3 vols. (Moscow, 1950–55)
KNG3

KVOS   KARMALINA (L. I.), 'Vospominaniya . . .: Glinka i Dargomuizhsky' (*Russkaya starina*, vol. 13 (1875), pp. 267–71)

PG   KISELEV (V. A.), LIVANOVA (T. N.) and PROTOPOPOV (V.V.) [editors], *Pamyati Glinki, 1857–1957: issledovaniya i materialui*. pp. 598. (Moscow, 1958)

LV   LEONOVA (D. M.), 'Vospominaniya artistki imperatorskikh teatrov' (*Istorichesky vestnik*, vol. 43 (1891), pp. 120–44, 326–51)

LIVANOVA (T. N.), *M. I. Glinka: sbornik materialov i statei*. pp. 391. (Moscow, 1950)

LPG1   LIVANOVA (T. N.) and PROTOPOPOV (V. V.), *Glinka:*
LPG2   *tvorchesky put*. 2 vols. (Moscow, 1955)

LPOK   LIVANOVA (T. N.) and PROTOPOPOV (V. V.), *Opernaya kritika v Rossii*. Vol. 1 [issued in 2 parts]. (Moscow, 1966–7)

MG MELGUNOV (N. A.), 'Glinka i yevo muzuikalnuiye sochineniya' (*Russkaya starina*, vol. 9 (1874), pp. 713–23, where it is incorporated in Strugovshchikov's reminiscences)
MIRSKY (D.), *A History of Russian literature*. Edited and abridged by F. J. Whitfield. pp. xi + 518 + xxiv. (London, 1949)
MONTAGU-NATHAN (M.),*Glinka*. pp. 85. (London, 1916)

GVS ORLOVA (A. A.) [editor], *Glinka v vospominaniyakh sovremennikov*. pp. 431. (Moscow, 1955)

GLZ ORLOVA (A.A.) and ASAFYEV (B. V.) [editors], *Letopis zhizni i tvorchestva Glinki*. pp. 540. (Moscow, 1952)

OG OSSOVSKY (A. V.) [editor], *M. I. Glinka: issledovaniya i materialui*. pp. 272. (Leningrad/Moscow, 1950)
PARES (Sir B.), *A History of Russia* [revised edition]. pp. ix + 674. (London, 1955)

PISG PROTOPOPOV (V. V.), '*Ivan Susanin' Glinki*. pp. 419. (Moscow, 1961)

RVOS RUBINSTEIN (A. G.), 'Vospominaniya' (*Russkaya starina*, vol. 64 (1889), pp. 518–600)
SEAMAN (G.), *History of Russian music*. Vol. 1. (Oxford, 1967)

SVG SEROV (A. N.), 'Vospominaniya o M. I. Glinke' (*Iskusstva* (1860), Nos. 1–5). [Reprinted in Serov (A. N.), *Izbrannuiye stati*, Vol. 1. (Moscow/Leningrad, 1950), pp. 129–63. All references are to this edition.]

SB SHESTAKOVA (L. I.), 'Builoye M. I. Glinki i yevo roditelei' (*Yezhegodnik imperatorskikh teatrov* (1892–3), pp. 427–57)
SHESTAKOVA (L. I.), 'Iz neizdannuikh vospominany "Moi vechera"' (*Russkaya muzuikalnaya gazeta*, No. 41 (9 October 1910), pp. 862–7)
SHESTAKOVA (L. I.), 'Iz neizdannuikh vospominany o novoi russkoi shkole' (*Russkaya muzuikalnaya*

gazeta, Nos. 51 and 52 (22 and 29 December 1913), pp. 1180–1, 1185)

SGVES   SHESTAKOVA (L. I.), 'M. I. Glinka v vospominaniyakh yevo sestrui' (*Russkaya starina*, vol. 44 (1884), pp. 593–604)
SHESTAKOVA (L. I.), 'Moi vechera' (*Yezhegodnik imperatorskikh teatrov* (1893–4), pp. 119–140)

SPGG   SHESTAKOVA (L. I.), 'Poslednuiye godui zhizni i konchina M. I. Glinki . . . (1854–7)' (*Russkaya starina*, vol. 2 (1870), pp. 610–32)

SVOS   SOLOGUB (V. A.), 'Vospominaniya' (*Istorichesky vestnik*, vol. 23 (February 1886), pp. 321–42)

SG   STASOV (V. V.), 'M. I. Glinka' (Four parts in *Russky vestnik* (1857). [Reprinted in Stasov (V. V.), *Sobraniye sochineny*, vol. 3 (St. Petersburg, 1894). All references are to this edition.]

SNM   STASOV (V. V.), 'M. I. Glinka: novuiye materialui dlya yevo biografy' (*Russkaya starina*, vol. 61 (1889), pp. 387–400)

StVG   STEPANOV (P. A.), 'Vospominaniya o M. I. Glinke' (*Russkaya starina*, vol. 4 (1871), pp. 39–58)

SGV   STRUGOVSHCHIKOV (A. N.), 'M. I. Glinka: vospominaniya' (*Russkaya starina*, vol. 9 (1874), pp. 697–725)

TVG   TOLSTOI (F. M.), 'Vospominaniya po povodu "Zapisok" M. I. Glinki' (*Russkaya starina*, vol. 3 (1871), pp. 421–54)

VVG   VOROBYEVA (A. Y. PETROVA-), 'Vospominaniya' (*Russkaya starina*, vol. 27 (1880), pp. 611–17)

List and Index of Works

In categories 1–10 are included not only pieces which Glinka completed but also other compositions of which some movements are complete (e.g. quartets, symphonies), or of which the greater part of the composition appears to have survived. Works of which only a small fragment is extant are listed in a single category of FRAGMENTARY AND LOST WORKS. It is possible that a few of the works in this last division are not by Glinka, but are copies of other compositions made by him.

Where works with Russian titles are mentioned in the main body of this book English translations of these titles are provided, and in the list below the English titles are used.

Each of the following categories is arranged in chronological order. Where no date can be assigned even tentatively to a work, it is listed at the end of its category.

1. OPERAS AND STAGE MUSIC:

Aria with chorus for the play, *The Moldavian girl and gipsy girl* (or *Gold and the dagger*), by Bakhturin (1836), 81

A Life for the Tsar (Ivan Susanin): opera in four acts and an epilogue, by Rosen and others (1834–6), 3, 7, 23–4, 26, 41, 43–4, 49, 62, 68, 73–6, 78–81, 85–9, 91–136 passim, 137–8, 140–1, 144–5, 155, 177, 179, 185–6, 196, 198–9, 202–6, 214, 216, 235, 240–1, 243–5, 248, 256, 261, 279–80, 282, 285, 289, 292–3, 298, 301, 304, 307–8, 313–15

Scene at the gates of the monastery: additional scene to Act IV of *A Life for the Tsar*, by N. Kukolnik (1837), 98, 106, 141

Incidental music to *Prince Kholmsky*, by N. Kukolnik (1840), 2, 68, 159, 164–73 passim, 190, 206, 301

Tarantella for reciter, chorus, and orchestra (Myatlev) (1840–1), 174

Ruslan and Lyudmila: opera in five acts, by Shirkov and others, after Pushkin (1837–42), 2, 4, 30, 39, 43, 47–8, 81, 89, 105, 116–17, 119, 126, 130–1, 136, 143–7, 149, 154–5, 158, 164, 169, 173, 175–82,

183–236 passim, 237, 240, 243–5, 265, 271, 279, 287, 290–1, 293, 301, 308, 314–15

2. ORCHESTRAL WORKS:
Andante cantabile and *Rondo* (*c.* 1823), 32–3
Symphony in B flat (*c.* 1824). Incomplete, 33, 62, 214
Overture in D (between 1822 and 1826), 32
Overture in G minor (between 1822 and 1826), 32
Symphony on two Russian themes (1834). Incomplete, 62, 69–71, 214
Valse-fantaisie (1839: orchestrated by Glinka in 1856. [See also WORKS FOR PIANO SOLO and FRAGMENTARY AND LOST WORKS], 2, 155, 158, 162–3, 244–5, 292, 315
Capriccio brillante on the Jota aragonesa (*First Spanish Overture*) (1845), 2, 246–51, 256, 265–6, 275–6, 282, 284, 301–2, 309
Kamarinskaya: scherzo for orchestra (1848), 1, 2, 70, 157, 216, 236, 265, 270–7, 282, 284–5, 293, 301, 304, 309
Recuerdos de Castilla (*Recollections of Castille*) (1848), 265–8, 276, 282–3, 309
Recollection of a summer night in Madrid: fantasia for orchestra (*Second Spanish Overture*) (1851), 2, 148, 252, 265–70, 276, 283, 285, 301
Polonaise on a Spanish bolero theme (1855), 291, 304

3. CHAMBER WORKS:
Septet in E flat, for oboe, bassoon, horn, 2 violins, cello, and double bass (*c.* 1823). Incomplete, 32
String quartet in D (1824). Incomplete, 34, 53
Sonata for piano and viola (or violin) (1825–8). Incomplete, 34–5, 45, 49
String quartet in F (1830), 52–3
Divertimento brillante on themes from the opera, *Sonnambula*, by Bellini, for piano, 2 violins, viola, cello, and double bass (1832), 61, 65
Serenade on themes from the opera, *Anna Bolena*, by Donizetti, for piano, harp, bassoon, horn, viola, cello, or double bass (1832), 61, 63
Gran sestetto originale in E flat, for piano, 2 violins, viola, cello, and double bass (1832), 61, 65
Trio pathétique in D minor, for piano, clarinet, and bassoon (1832), 63, 65–7

4. WORKS FOR SOLO PIANO:

Variations on a theme of Mozart, for harp or piano (1822), 22

Variations on an original theme (*c.* 1824), 34

Variations on the Russian song, 'Among the gentle valleys' (1826), 38, 147

Variations on a theme from the opera, *Faniska*, by Cherubini (1826 or 1827), 147

Variations on the romance, 'Benedetta sia la madre' (1826), 38

[5] nouvelles quadrilles françaises (1826(?))

Cotillon in B flat (by 1828), 49

Mazurka in G (by 1828), 49

[4] nouvelles contredanses (by 1828) [also known as French quadrille or Première contredanse], 49

Nocturne in E flat, for piano or harp (1828)

Finnish song (1829), 47–8

Farewell waltz in G (1831)

Rondino brillante on a theme from the opera, *I Capuletti e i Montecchi*, by Bellini (1831)

Variations on a theme from the opera, *Anna Bolena*, by Donizetti (1831), 58

Variations on two themes from the ballet, *Chao-Kang* (1831), 58–9

Variations on a theme from the opera, *I Capuletti e i Montecchi*, by Bellini (1832), 59

Variations on the romance, 'The nightingale', by Alyabyev (1833), 26, 69

Fugue in A minor (1833 or 1834), 68

Fugue in D (1833 or 1834), 68

Fugue in E flat (1833 or 1834), 68

Mazurka in A flat (1833 or 1834)

Mazurka in F (1833 or 1834)

Motif de chant national (1834(?)–1836(?))

Mazurka in F (1835(?))

[5] contredanse[s] (1838), 147

Waltz in E flat (1838), 147

Waltz in B flat (1838(?)), 147

La couventine: new contredanse[s] (1839) [See also FRAGMEN-TARY AND LOST WORKS], 150–1

Grande valse in G (1839) [See also FRAGMENTARY AND LOST WORKS], 150

Polonaise in E (1839) [See also FRAGMENTARY AND LOST WORKS]

Nocturne in F minor (*La séparation*) (1839), 157

Valse-fantaisie in B minor (1839) [See also ORCHESTRAL WORKS and FRAGMENTARY AND LOST WORKS]

Galopade in E flat (1838 or 1839), 147

Bolero (1840) [See also SONGS WITH PIANO ACCOMPANIMENT: 'O my beautiful maid', 158

Tarantella in A minor (1843), 239

Mazurka in C minor (1843(?))

A greeting to my native land: (1847)

    1. 'Recollection of a mazurka', 258

    2. 'Barcarolle', 258

    3. 'Prayer' [See also WORKS FOR TWO OR MORE VOICES], 258, 261, 291, 301

    4. Variations on a Scottish [in fact, Irish] theme, 258–60

Polka in D minor (1849)

Mazurka in C (1852), 286

Excerpt from the Epilogue to *A Life for the Tsar* (1852)

Excerpt from Finn's Ballad from *Ruslan and Lyudmila* (1852)

Excerpt from Lyudmila's scene in Act IV of *Ruslan and Lyudmila* (1852)

Children's polka in B flat (1854), 34, 304

Las Mollares: Andalusian dance transcribed for piano (1855(?))

Leggieramente in E major (?)

5. WORKS FOR PIANO DUET:

2 trots de cavalerie (1829–30)

Impromptu en galop on the barcarolle from *L'elisir d'amore* by Donizetti (1832)

Capriccio on Russian themes (1834), 62, 69, 71–2, 118, 214

Polka (conceived 1840: written down 1852), 285

6. SONGS WITH PIANO ACCOMPANIMENT:

'My harp' (Sir W. Scott, translated Bakhturin. Original lost: written down from memory in 1855) (1824), 36

'Do not tempt me needlessly' (Baratuinsky) (1825) [See also WORKS FOR TWO OR MORE VOICES], 36

'Ah, my sweetheart, thou art a beautiful maiden' (folk text) (1826)
'Consolation' (Uhland, translated Zhukovsky) (1826), 39, 49
'The poor singer' (Zhukovsky) (1826), 39–40, 49, 75
'Le baiser' [See '"I love," was your assurance']
'Bitter, bitter it is for me' (Rimsky-Korsakov) (1827)
'Heart's memory' (Batyushkov) (1827), 46, 48–50
'"I love," was your assurance' (Rimsky-Korsakov; French text, 'Le baiser', by S. Golitsuin) (1827), 41, 49
'Only for one moment' [See 'Pour un moment']
'Why do you cry, young beauty?' (Delvig) (1827)
'Pour un moment' (S. Golitsuin) (1827 or 1828), 46, 49
'Tell me why' (S. Golitsuin) (1827 or 1828), 49, 75, 263
'I love the shady garden' [See 'Mio ben, ricordati']
'Mio ben, ricordati', for soprano (1827 or 1828) [See also WORKS FOR TWO OR MORE VOICES]
Due canzonette italiane: (1828)
    1. 'Ah, rammenta, o bella Irene'
    2. 'Alla cetra'
'Dovunque il guardo giro', for bass (1828)
'Ho perduto il mio tesoro', for tenor (1828)
'Mi sento il cor trafiggere', for tenor (1828)
'O Dafni che di quest'anima amabile diletto', for soprano (1828)
'Pensa che questo istante', for alto (1828)
'Piangendo ancora rinascer suole,' for soprano (1828)
'Pur nel sonno', for soprano (1828)
'Tu sei figlia', for soprano (1828)
'Disenchantment' (S. Golitsuin) (1828), 49–50, 75
'The maids once told me, grandfather' (Delvig) (1828), 47
'O thou black night' (Delvig) (1828), 47, 50, 52
'Shall I forget?' (S. Golitsuin) (1828), 50
'Sing not, thou beauty, in my presence' (Pushkin) (1828), 47, 50
'Beloved autumn night' (Rimsky-Korsakov) (1829), 49, 52–3
'A voice from the other world' (Schiller, translated Zhukovsky) (1829), 50–2, 261, 301
'Il desiderio' (Romani) (1832), 61, 65, 244
'Desire' [See 'Il desiderio']
'L'iniquo voto': cavatina, *Beatrice di Tenda* (Pini) (1832), 64–5
'The conqueror' (Uhland, translated Zhukovsky) (1832), 65, 159
'Venetian night' (Kozlov) (1832), 65, 292

'Call her not heavenly' (Pavlov) (1834). Later orchestrated by Glinka, 75, 291–2

'I am here, Inezilla' (Pushkin, after Barry Cornwall) (1834), 77

'I had but recognized you' (Delvig) (1834), 77

'The leafy grove howls' (Schiller, translated Zhukovsky) (1834), 69

'Say not that love will pass' (Delvig) (1834), 69

'The midnight review' (Sedlitz, translated Zhukovsky) (1836). Twice orchestrated by Glinka, 82–4, 291, 301

Stanzas: 'Here is the place of secret meeting' (N. Kukolnik) (1837)

'Where is our rose?' (Pushkin) (1837), 141, 148–9, 301

'Always, everywhere thou art with me' (Rimsky-Korsakov) [See also 'The fire of longing burns in my blood']

'Doubt' (N. Kukolnik) (1838) [Also exists with accompaniment for violin and harp], 139, 147, 244

'The fire of longing burns in my blood' (Pushkin) (1838), 142, 147, 178

'The night zephyr' (Pushkin) (1838), 141, 147–8

'Sing not, O nightingale' (Zabella) (1838), 144, 148

'The wind blows' (Zabella) (1838), 144, 148

'The bird-cherry tree is blossoming' (Rostopchina) (1839), 157–8

'Declaration' (Pushkin) (1839)

'If I shall meet you' (Koltsov) (1839), 157

'The North star' [See 'Wedding song']

'Wedding song' (Rostopchina) (1839), 157

A farewell to St. Petersburg: cycle of 12 romances (N. Kukolnik) (1840)

  1. Romance from David Rizzio, 159–60

  2. 'Hebrew song' from the tragedy, Prince Kholmsky, 159

  3. Bolero: 'O my beautiful maid', 158–9

  4. Cavatina: 'Long since thou didst blossom gloriously like a rose', 159

  5. Cradle song. Later arranged for voice and strings by Glinka [See also WORKS FOR TWO OR MORE VOICES], 159–60

  6. 'Travelling song', 159

  7. Fantasia: 'Stand, my true, tempestuous steed', 159

  8. Barcarolle, 159

  9. 'Virtus antiqua', 159–60

  10. 'The lark' [See also WORKS FOR TWO OR MORE VOICES], 159

  11. 'To Molly', 157, 159

  12. 'Song of farewell', 159–62

'How sweet it is to be with you!' (Ruindin) (1840), 173

'I recall a wonderful moment' (Pushkin) (1840), 155–8, 261, 263, 301

'I love you, dear rose' (Samarin) (1842), 178

'To her' (Mickiewicz, translated S. Golitsuin) (1843), 238–9, 280

'Darling' (author unknown) (1847), 260

'Soon you will forget me' (Zhadovsky) (1847). Later orchestrated by Glinka, 260–1, 291

Gretchen's song from Goethe's *Faust* (translated Huber) (1848), 262–5

'The toasting cup' (Pushkin) (1848), 262–3

'When I hear your voice' (Lermontov) (1848), 262

'Adèle' (Pushkin) (1849), 281

'Conversation' (Mickiewicz) (1849), 281

'Mary' (Pushkin, after Barry Cornwall) (1849), 281–2

'O dear maid' [See 'Conversation']

'The Gulf of Finland' (Obodovsky) (1850), 283

'Palermo' [see 'The Gulf of Finland']

'Say not that it grieves the heart' (Pavlov) (1856), 292

7. WORKS FOR TWO OR MORE VOICES:

'Do not tempt me needlessly', for two voices and piano (1825) [See also SONGS WITH PIANO ACCOMPANIMENT]

Prologue on the death of the Emperor Aleksandr I and the accession of Nikolai I: cantata for tenor solo, chorus, piano, and double bass (Olidor) (1826), 39

'Mio ben, ricordati': duet for alto, tenor, and piano (1827 or 1828) [See also SONGS WITH PIANO ACCOMPANIMENT], 49

'O God, preserve our strength in the days of confusion': trio for alto, tenor, bass, and piano (1827 or 1828)

'Come di gloria al nome': quartet for soprano, alto, tenor, bass, and strings (1828 or 1829). Incomplete, 46

'A, ignobil core': aria for bass, men's chorus, and orchestra (1828 or 1834). Incomplete

'Sogna chi crede d'esser felice': quartet for alto, 2 tenors, bass, and strings (1828), 46

Vocal quartet in B flat ('Prayer'), with piano accompaniment (1828). Incomplete

'Drinking song', for tenor, men's chorus, and piano (Delvig) (1829(?)). Incomplete

'Not the frequent autumn shower', for tenor, men's chorus, and piano (Delvig) (1829), 49

Comic canon (Pushkin, Zhukovsky, Vyazemsky, and Wielhorski) [Music in collaboration with V. F. Odoyevsky] (1836)

Polonaise: 'Our God is great', for chorus and orchestra (Sollogub) (1837), 140

'Adieu, petit réduit': duet with piano accompaniment (1837), 141

'Hymn to the master': cantata for voice and orchestra (Markevich) (1838). Incomplete, 144

'You will not return again': duet for 2 sopranos and piano (1837 or 1838)

Farewell song of the pupils of the Yekaterinsky Institute, for soprano, female chorus, and orchestra (Obodovsky) (1840), 174, 283

Cradle song, arranged for soprano, tenor, and piano by K. Villebois under Glinka's supervision (1840) [See also SONGS WITH PIANO ACCOMPANIMENT]

'The lark', arranged for soprano, tenor, and piano by K. Villebois under Glinka's supervision (1840) [See also SONGS WITH PIANO ACCOMPANIMENT]

'Toasting song', for solo and chorus (1847)

Farewell song for the pupils of the Society of Genteel Maidens [at the Smolny Monastery], for women's chorus and orchestra (Timayev) (1850), 282–3

'The tress': gipsy song for voice, chorus, and orchestra (Rimsky-Korsakov (1854)

'Prayer: In a difficult moment of life', for solo, chorus, and orchestra (Lermontov) (1855) [See also WORKS FOR PIANO SOLO (1847)]

8. CHURCH MUSIC:

'Cherubims' song' in C, for 6 voices unaccompanied (1837), 142

First Litany, for 4 voices unaccompanied (1856)

'Let my prayer be fulfilled', for 2 tenors and bass unaccompanied (1856)

'Resurrection hymn', for 2 tenors and bass unaccompanied (1856 or 1857), 293–4

9. VOCAL STUDIES:

7 studies for alto and piano (1829 or 1830), 54
6 studies for soprano and piano (1833), 68, 159
Exercises for smoothing and perfecting the voice (1835 or 1836)
4 exercises for voice (1840 or 1841)
A school of singing (1856 or 1857), 294, 296

10. ARRANGEMENTS OF MUSIC BY OTHER COMPOSERS:

SHTERICH, Waltz on a theme from Weber's *Oberon*, arranged for orchestra (1829)

YAKOVLEV, 'When, my soul, you asked': elegy (Delvig), transcribed for alto, bass, and piano (1838: revised 1855)

BOIKOV, 'John's couplets', arranged for piano (1854)

HUMMEL, Nocturne: 'Souvenir d'amitié', Op. 99, orchestrated (1854), 291

HANDEL, 3 arias from *Jephtha*, realized and/or arranged for voice and piano:

1. 'The smiling dawn of happy days' (1854)
2. Recit. and aria: 'Tune the soft melodious lute' (1854)
3. 'Welcome as the cheerful light' (1855)

'Ah, would that I had known before': old gipsy song arranged for voice and piano (1855)

DARGOMUIZHSKY, 'Fever': song (folk text), orchestrated (1855)

FEDOROV, 'Forgive me, forgive': romance (Bulgakov), transcribed for alto, tenor, and piano (1855)

GLUCK, Act IV, scene II of *Armide*, arranged for piano (1855)

GLUCK, Sacrificial chorus, Act III, scene IV, of *Iphigénie en Tauride*, arranged for piano (1855)

LEONOVA, 'The tear': romance (Vasilko-Petrov), arranged for voice and piano (1855)

MEHUL, Duet from Act III of *Joseph*, arranged for piano (1856)

ALYABYEV, 'The nightingale': romance (Delvig), orchestrated (1856)

PAER, Duet from Act I of *Sargino*, arranged for voices and piano (?)

CHERUBINI, Romanza from the opening of Act I of *Les deux journées*, arranged for voice and piano (?)

MOZART, Tamino's aria from *Die Zauberflöte*, arranged for voice and piano (?)

11. FRAGMENTARY AND LOST WORKS:

Variations on a theme in C from the opera, *The Swiss family*, by Weigl, for piano or harp (1822). Lost, 22

Waltz in F, for piano. Lost, 22

Rokeby: opera after Sir W. Scott (1824). Tiny fragments, 36

Rondo in G, for piano (1824–5). 2 fragments

Rondo brillante for piano and orchestra (1824–5 or 1827–8). Fragmentary

French quadrille, for orchestra (1825). Lost, 36

Aria in A flat, for baritone (1827). Lost, except for what may be 8 bars from the middle, 43, 186

Chorus in C minor on the death of a hero (1827). Lost, 43

Prayer (for the theatre): 'O God, by thy mighty right hand' (1827 (?)). Fragmentary, 43

Recitative and duet, for tenor and bass (1827). Lost, 42

Cotillon, for orchestra (1827–8). First violin part

'O mia dolce, mia carina': serenade for voice and piano (1827 or 1828). Lost, 46

Rondo in D, for string quartet (1827–8). Fragmentary

String quartet in C (1827 or 1828—or early 1830s). Fragmentary

String quartet in E flat (1827–8 (?)). Fragmentary

'Let us lift up all things unto the Tsar', for 4 voices unaccompanied (1828). Fragmentary

'We in this sacred cloister': canon (S. Golitsuin) (1828). Lost

Barcarolle in A flat, for tenor and piano (1828). Lost

'Lila in the black mantle': couplets with chorus (S. Golitsuin) (1828). Lost, 41

Aria in D, for alto and piano. (1828). Fragmentary

Quartet: 'La notte omai s'appressa', for soloists, chorus, and strings (1828). Fragmentary

Aria to be included in Donizetti's *Faust* (1832). Lost, 62

'A hundred bright-eyed beauties': romance (1832). Bass part only

Marina Grove: opera after Zhukovsky (1834). Fragments, later incorporated into *A Life for the Tsar*, 75, 99

'Romance', without text, for soprano and piano (?) (between 1835 and 1844). Music complete, but authenticity questionable

GENISHTA, 'The day's light has died': elegy (Pushkin), orchestrated by Glinka (1838). Sketch

La couventine: contredanse[s] for orchestra (1839). Lost. [See also WORKS FOR SOLO PIANO], 150–1

Grande valse in G, for orchestra (1839). Lost. [See also WORKS FOR SOLO PIANO], 150

Polonaise in E, for orchestra (1839). Lost. [See also WORKS FOR SOLO PIANO], 150

Valse-fantaisie, for piano (1839), orchestrated by Glinka in 1845. Lost. [See also ORCHESTRAL WORKS and WORKS FOR SOLO PIANO]

HALEVY, Aria from *Guido e Ginevra*, orchestrated by Glinka (1839). Lost

LABITSKY, Waltz: 'Souvenir du Palais d'Anitshkoff', orchestrated by Glinka (1839). Fragmentary

Nocturne, for piano (*Le regret*) (1839). Lost, 157, 159

Chorus to Pavel Vasilyevich, for tenor and chorus (N. Kukolnik) (1840). Lost, 174

Kamarinskaya: piece for piano, three hands (1840). Lost, 158, 270

Waltz in B flat, for orchestra (1840). Lost, 155

Vaudeville couplets, for voice and piano (1842). Lost

Jaleo de Xerés, for orchestra (1845). Lost

Ukrainian symphony: *Taras Bulba* (1848(?)–1852). Three tiny fragments remembered by V. Engelhardt and Balakirev, 286–7, 290–1

Tarantella: fantasia for orchestra (1850). Lost

WEBER, *Aufforderung zum Tanz*, orchestrated by Glinka (1854). Lost, 291

The Bigamist (or *The brigands of the Volga*): uncompleted opera (Shakhovsky) (1855). Lost, 291

Mirror waltz for piano (1856). Lost

Concerto [for orchestra] (?). Fragmentary, 296–7

Fugue: 'Cum sancto spiritu', for unaccompanied choir. (?) Fragmentary

'Funesti pensieri d'un alma dolente': aria for soprano and piano (?). Fragmentary

'Incline thine ear, O Lord, and hear me', for four voices unaccompanied (?). Fragmentary

Fugue for the concerto, 'I shall invoke God', for four voices un-accompanied (?). Fragmentary

Subject for the fugue for the third concerto, 'Who shall proclaim the strength of God?' (?)

12. OTHER MUSIC NOTED DOWN BY GLINKA:

17 Spanish folksongs (1845–6)

Spanish march theme [used by Balakirev in his *Overture on a Spanish march theme*] (1845 or 1846)

Index of Persons

Index of Persons

(Dates of birth and death are given, when known)

Abraham, Gerald (b. 1904), 5, 111, 136
Adam, Adolphe (1803–56), 314
Adelaide [Didina of Milan], 58, 61, 63
Adelina [of Paris], 241, 246
Aivazovsky [Gaivazovsky], I. K., 186
Akhmatova, E. N., 181
Albrechtsberger, Johann (1736–1809), 311
Aleksandr I (1777–1825), 37, 39, 145
Aleksandr II (1818–81), 78, 140, 256, 291
Aleksandra Fyodorovna, Dowager Empress, 277
Alyabyev, Aleksandr Aleksandrovich (1787–1851), 26, 69, 147, 294–5
Amalia [of Bordeaux], 278
Angélique [of Warsaw], 262
Apukhtin, General, 38
Ariosto, Lodovico (1474–1533), 287
Auber, Daniel (1782–1871), 241, 287
Aumann, V., 20, 21, 306
Avdotya Ivanovna [nurse], 12

Bach, Johann Sebastian (1685–1750), 46, 52, 153, 288–90, 292, 297
Bakhturin, Konstantin Aleksandrovich (1809–41), 36, 38, 81, 145, 184–5, 199
Balakirev, Mily Alekseyevich (1837–1910), 1, 96, 105, 110, 197, 201, 212–13, 236, 238, 239, 279–80, 287, 303
Barteneva, Praskovya Arsenevna (1811–72), 81
Basili, Francesco (1767–1850), 57, 306
Batyushkov, Konstantin Nikolayevich (1787–1855), 194
Beethoven, Ludwig van (1770–1827), 26–7, 31–2, 34, 56, 77, 144, 177–8, 199, 201, 219, 252, 259, 276, 284, 287–9, 297, 301, 304
Beine, Karl Andreyevich (1816–58), 252–3
Bellini, Vincenzo (1801–35), 46, 58–9, 61, 63, 87, 139, 159, 255

Belloli [singing teacher], 36
Berlioz, Hector (1803–69), 5, 60, 241–6, 249, 302, 305, 308, 310–15
Bitton, Mr., 19
Boccaccio, Giovanni (1313–75), 287
Boehm, Franz (1789–1846), 21, 28, 94, 103, 306, 312
Boïeldieu, François (1775–1834), 17, 25–6, 41, 59
Borodin, Aleksandr Porfirevich (1833–87), 2, 110, 201, 210, 212, 303
Bortnyansky, Dmitri Stepanovich (1752–1825), 252, 289, 296
Bourge, Maurice, 244
Brailov, Dr., 42
Branca, Dr., 61, 64, 67
Branca, Emilia, 61
Bryullov, Karl Pavlovich (1799–1852), 178, 190
Bueno y Moreno, Francisco, 253
Bulgakov, Konstantin Aleksandrovich (1812–62), 178
Bulgarin, Faddei Benediktovich (1789–1859), 87, 179–81
Bull, Ole (1810–80), 255–6

Castilla, Felix, 246, 248
Cavos, Catterino Albertovich (1776–1840), 19, 26, 28, 84, 88, 91, 105–6, 196, 282
Cavos, Ivan Catterinovich (1805–61), 86, 282
Cherubini, Luigi (1760–1842), 21, 25–6, 31–2, 34, 56, 78, 284
Chirkov, N., 68, 74
Chopin, Frederic (1810–49), 135, 162, 238, 258–9, 263, 281, 286, 302
Clementi, Muzio (1752–1832), 258
Colombi, [a dancer], 58–9
Columbus, Christopher (1451–1506), 17
Cornwall, Barry (1787–1874), 77, 282

Cramer, Johann Baptist (1771–1858), 52, 255
Crusell, Bernhard (1775–1838), 15–6, 305
Cui, Cesar Antonovich (1835–1918), 111, 114

Dargomuizhsky, Aleksandr Sergeyevich (1813–69), 77–8, 136, 147, 241, 285, 292
Davuidov, Stepan Ivanovich (1777–1825), 26, 28
Dehn, Siegfried (1799–1858), 2, 68, 72–3, 78, 240, 286, 288, 293, 298, 307, 312
Delvig, Anton Antonovich (1798–1831), 24, 47
Dever, Count, 43
Didina [*see* Adelaide]
Donizetti, Gaetano (1797–1848), 46, 58, 60–3
Dostoyevsky, Fyodor Mikhailovich (1821–81), 280
Dubelt, General, 180
Dubrovsky, Pavel Petrovich (1812–82), 141, 144, 262, 271, 275, 286

Engelhardt, Pavel Vasilevich (d.1849), 68, 99, 173, 194
Engelhardt, Sofiya Grigorevna (d.1875), 68
Engelhardt, Vasily Pavlovich (1828–1915), 53, 99, 266, 285, 287, 292, 299

Fernandez Nolasko Sandino, Pedro (d.1885), 254–6, 258, 261–2, 265, 286–9
Fétis, François (1784–1871), 305
Field, John (1782–1837), 20, 85, 306
Filippi, Dr. de, 61, 64
Findeizen, Nikolai Fyodorovich (1868–1928), 4, 296
Fioravanti, Valentino (1764–1837), 57
Fleri, Anyuta Viktorevna, 238
Fleri, Viktor Ivanovich, 10, 238, 254
Fodor-Mainvielle, Joséphine (1789–1870), 60, 61, 307
Freyer, August (b.1803), 280
Fuchs, J. L., 28

Gade, Niels (1817–90), 311
Gaivazovsky [*see* Aivazovsky]
Garcia, Dolores, 253–4, 278
Gasovsky, Dr., 46–7
Gedeon, Bishop, 142–3

Gedeonov, Aleksandr Mikhailovich (1791–1867), 80–1, 84–6, 137, 141, 177–9
Gedeonov, Fyodor Dmitriyevich (b.1797), 68, 240, 245
Gedeonov, Mikhail Aleksandrovich (b.1814), 177, 192, 194, 237
Gedeonov, Nikolai Dmitriyevich, 10, 64, 68, 74, 76
Giulini, Luiggia, 64
Glebov, Mikhail Nikolayevich (1804–51), 37
Glinka, Afanasy Andreyevich (1772–1827), 9, 15, 20
Glinka, Aleksei Ivanovich (b.1803: died in infancy), 10–11
Glinka, Andrei Ivanovich (1823–39), 10, 151
Glinka, Boris Grigorevich (1810–95), 38
Glinka, Dmitri Grigorevich (1808–83), 38
Glinka, Fekla Aleksandrovna (d.1810), 10–13
Glinka, Fyodor Nikolayevich (1786–1880), 9
Glinka, Grigory Andreyevich (1776–1818), 9
Glinka, Ivan Andreyevich (1777–1849), 20–1, 28
Glinka, Ivan Nikolayevich (1777–1834), 9–10, 12, 22–3, 28, 33, 40, 45, 54, 74, 76, 138
Glinka, Lyudmila Ivanovna [*see* Shestakova]
Glinka (*later* Stuneyeva), Mariya Ivanovna (b.1813), 10, 46, 76, 150, 158
Glinka, Mariya Petrovna (*née* Ivanova), 46, 76–81, 85–7, 138–40, 150–5, 162, 173, 176–7, 188, 237, 256
Glinka (*later* Gedeonova), Natalya Ivanovna (b.1809), 10, 52, 54, 64, 68, 74, 76, 240
Glinka, Nikolai Alekseyevich (1735–1806), 11–12
Glinka (*later* Ismailova), Olga Ivanovna (1825–60), 10, 177–8, 261
Glinka, (*later* Sobolevskaya), Pelageya Ivanovna (1805–28), 10, 38, 44, 50
Glinka, Sergei Nikolayevich (1776–1847), 9
Glinka, Sofya Ivanovna (b.1804), 21, 173
Glinka, Vladimir Andreyevich (1790–1862), 9
Glinka, Yakov Yakovlevich, 8
Glinka (*later* Fleri), Yelizaveta Ivanovna (1810–50), 10, 76, 175–7, 193, 238

Glinka, Yevgeniya Andreyevna (1784/5–1851), 9–10, 13, 52, 76, 79, 85–6, 89, 137–8, 145–6, 152–3, 173–5, 177–8, 238, 240, 245–6, 252, 255, 283
Glinka, Yevgeny Ivanovich (1815–34), 10, 76
Gluck, Christoph (1714–87), 39, 261, 265, 279, 284–5, 288–9, 297, 302
Goethe, Johann (1749–1832), 18, 262–3, 265
Gogol, Mariya Ivanovna, 29
Gogol, Nikolai Vasilevich (1809–52), 29, 78, 88, 286
Golitsuin, Sergei Grigorevich (1806–68), 41, 48
Golitsuin, Vasily Petrovich (1800–63), 41, 244
Gorgoli, I. S., 45
Gorgoli, Poliksena I., 45
Gorodetsky, S., 98
Graun, Karl (1704–59), 288
Griboyedov, Aleksandr Sergeyevich (1795–1829), 24, 47–8
Gulak-Artemovsky, Semyon Stepanovich (1817–73), 143, 180

Habeneck, François (1781–1849), 244
Handel, George Frederick (1685–1759), 289–90, 292, 297
Haydn, Joseph (1732–1809), 18, 26–7, 29, 141, 273, 284, 288, 301
Hempel, Karl Fyodorovich, 21, 39, 80, 158
Henselt, Adolf von (1814–89), 314
Herman [a conductor], 158
Hoffmann, E. T. A. (1776–1822), 314
Homer, 286
Hugo, Victor (1802–85), 241
Hummel, Johann Nepomuk (1778–1833), 20, 32, 34, 52

Isabella II (1830–1904), 255
Isouard, Nicolo (1775–1818), 25
Ivanov, Nikolai Kuzmich (1810–80), 41, 54, 56–61, 295, 306–7, 312–13
Ivanova [see Glinka, Mariya Petrovna]
Izmailov, Nikolai Aleksandrovich, 10, 261

Johannes, Ivan Ivanovich, 88

Kamensky, Pavel Pavlovich (1810–75), 177
Karatuigin, V. A., 174
Karmalina, Lyubov Ivanovna, 284, 296

Kashin, Daniel Nikitich (1769–1841), 9
Kashperov, Vladimir Nikitich (1827–94), 298
Kashperova, Adèle Nikolayevna, 294, 298
Katinka [of St. Petersburg], 40
Kauer, Ferdinand (1751–1830), 28
Kazhinsky, V. M., 238
Kern, Anna Petrovna (1800–79), 47, 151, 155, 175
Kern, Yekaterina Yermolayevna (1818–1904), 47, 151, 155, 157, 162, 164, 175, 189, 190, 237
Khovanskaya, Princess E. A., 36
Khosrev-Mirza [grandson of Shah of Persia], 48
Kipriyanov, Aleksandr Ivanovich (1780–1872), 14
Klammer, Varvara Fyodorovna, 16
Kochubei, V. P., 41
Kolkovskaya, Karolina Iosifovna (1823–57), 139, 142, 147, 151
Kolmakov, Ivan Yekimovich, 44
Koltsov, Aleksei Vasilevich (1809–42), 157
Koni, Fyodor Alekseyevich (1809–79), 89, 113, 181
Konstantin [brother of Aleksandr I], 37
Kozlowski, Jósef (1757–1831), 26
Krasovsky, Afanasy Ivanovich (1785–1843), 146
Kreutzer, Rudolph (1766–1831), 17
Küchelbecker, Wilhelm Karlovich (1797–1846), 17–18, 24, 38
Kukolnik, Nestor Vasilevich (1809–68), 4, 7, 78, 87, 97, 109, 140–1, 158–60, 164, 174, 177, 185–6, 191, 194, 241, 289, 291, 304
Kukolnik, Pavel Vasilevich (1795–1884), 174
Kukolnik, Platon Vasilevich (d.1849), 158

Lanner, Joseph (1801–43), 67, 99
Lassus, Rolande de (1532–94), 293
Lenz, Wilhelm von (1809–83), 252
Léonie [of Paris], 278
Leonov, L. I. (1815–after 1862), 85
Leonova, Darya Mikhailovna (1835–96), 100, 112, 285, 291
Ligle [of Vienna], 36
Lileyeva, Emiliya Avgustinovna (1823–92), 179
Lindquist, Andrei Andreyevich (1762–1831), 22, 37

Lipinski, Karol Jósef (1790–1861), 140, 145
Liszt, Franz (1811–86), 59, 66, 147, 177–8, 237, 245, 314
Luisa [German servant], 74, 76
Lukyanovich, Nikolai, 44
Lvov, Aleksei Fyodorovich (1793–1870), 21, 137–8, 140–2, 147, 153–4, 284, 314
Lvov, Fyodor Petrovich (1766–1836), 54, 137
Lvov, Konstantin, 284

Mahler, Gustav (1860–1911), 273
Maria [Berlin Jewess], 68, 74, 76–7, 159
Mariya Nikolayevna, Grand Duchess, 141, 157, 188–9
Markevich, Nikolai Andreyevich (1808–60), 18, 144, 146, 188, 195
Marochetti [teacher of Italian], 46
Marras, 244
Maurer, Ludwig (1789–1878), 31
Mayer, Charles (1799–1862), 21, 28, 31–2, 34, 38, 41, 105, 306, 312
Méhul, Etienne (1763–1817), 17, 21, 25–6, 31, 74, 284, 287
Melgunov, Nikolai Aleksandrovich (1804–67), 19, 39, 44–5, 75–6, 88–9, 112, 245, 291, 310
Mendelssohn, Felix (1809–47), 59, 67, 77, 311–12
Mérimée, Henri, 241, 245, 286, 313
Mérimée, Prosper (1803–70), 241
Meshchersky, Elim Petrovich (1803–44), 241
Meyerbeer, Giacomo (1791–1864), 58, 87, 278–9, 286–7, 297–8, 312
Mickiewicz, Adam (1798–1855), 47, 239, 281
Mikhail [brother of Nikolai I], 180
Montagu-Nathan, Montague (1877–1958), 2
Moscheles, Ignaz (1794–1870), 52
Mozart, Wolfgang (1756–91), 1, 21–2, 25–7, 31–2, 34, 41, 59, 141, 218, 238, 266, 273, 289, 297, 301, 304
Müller, Heinrich, 32
Müller, Ivan, 42
Murciano, Francisco-Roderigo, 253
Mussorgsky, Modest Petrovich (1839–81), 2, 84, 110, 121, 133, 148, 201, 218, 228, 303

Napoleon I (1769–1820), 9, 14–15, 18, 91

Netoyev, Yakov Ilyanovich, 99, 176
Neverov, Yanuary Mikhailovich, 88–9, 112–13, 121
Nikolai I (1796–1855), 37, 39, 61, 84–7, 97, 138, 140, 145–6, 153, 282, 291, 308, 313
Nolde [*see* Glinka, Sofya Ivanovna]
Nozzari, Andrea (1775–1832), 60–1, 307

Obodovsky, Platon Grigorevich (1805–64), 283
Odoyevskaya, Princess O. S., 140
Odoyevsky, Vladimir Fyodorovich (1804–69), 81, 86, 88–9, 92–3, 95–8, 107, 109, 112, 157, 181, 247–8, 298
Ohm, Emiliya, 278
Olga Nikolayevna, Grand Duchess, 141
Olidor [French tutor], 39
Onslow, George (1784–1853), 312

Paër, Ferdinando (1771–1839), 21
Palestrina, Giovanni da (1525–94), 293
Paskevich, Ivan Fyodorovich (1782–1856), 265, 271
Pasta, Giuditta (1798–1865), 58, 173
Pavlischchev, Nikolai Ivanovich (1802–79), 49
Pavlischcheva, Olga Sergeyevna, 79
Pavlov, Nikolai Filippovich (1805–64), 75, 292
Pedro, Don [*see* Fernandez Nolasko Sandino]
Petrov, Osip Afanasevich (1807–78), 80, 85–7, 109, 139, 141, 180, 189
Petrova, Anfisa, 179, 180
Petrova-Vorobyeva [*see* Vorobyeva]
Planeta [Spanish folk-singer], 255
Poggi [tenor], 189
Pogodin, V. V., 40
Pohlens, Aleksandr, 261, 265
Polevoi, Nikolai Alekseyevich (1796–1846), 237
Pollini, Francesco (1763–1846), 59, 63
Prokofiev, Sergei Sergeyevich (1891–1953), 131
Protopopov, Vladimir Vasilevich, 111
Pushkin, Aleksandr Sergeyevich (1799–1837), 9, 18, 24, 28, 39, 47, 49, 77–9, 82, 89, 142, 144–5, 148, 150, 155, 183–6, 188, 195, 198–201, 214, 217, 235, 262, 281–2, 308, 314
Pushkin, Lev Sergeyevich, 18, 22, 40
Pyotr I [Peter the Great] (1672–1725), 113

Raimondi, Pietro (1786–1853), 60

Ral, Fyodor Aleksandrovich (1802–48), 197

Rémi [violinist], 43

Ricordi, Giovanni (1785–1853), 63, 306, 312

Righini, Vincenzo (1756–1812), 21

Rimsky-Korsakov, Aleksandr Yakovlevich (b.1804), 40, 44, 142

Rimsky-Korsakov, Nikolai Andreyevich (1844–1908), 2, 197, 303

Robertson [English architect], 253

Rolla, Alessandro (1757–1841), 63

Roller, Andrei Adamovich (1805–91), 84, 178–9, 188, 190

Romberg, Bernhard (1767–1841), 31

Rosen, Georgy Fyodorovich (1800–60), 78, 97–8, 105–6, 108, 125, 307

Rossignol, Adèle, 240, 245

Rossini, Gioacchino (1792–1868), 21, 25–6, 31, 41, 46, 58–60, 63, 80, 87, 223 237, 297, 310

Rousseau, Jean Jacques (1712–78), 287–8

Rubini, Giovanni (1795–1854), 58, 60, 238

Rubinstein, Anton Grigorevich (1830–94), 290

Ruileyev, Kondraty Fyodorovich (1795–1826), 91–2

Ruindin, Pyotr P., 68, 173

Ruindina, Natalya Ivanovna, 68

Santiago Hernandes, Don, 245–7, 253–4

Sarti, Giuseppe (1729–1802), 142

Schiller, Friedrich (1759–1805), 50, 68

Schubert, Franz (1797–1828), 265

Schumann, Robert (1810–56), 34, 49

Schuppanzigh, Ignaz (1776–1830), 27

Scott, Walter (1771–1832), 36

Sedlitz, J. C. von, 82

Senkovsky, Osip Ivanovich (1800–59), 182, 196, 201

Serov, Aleksandr Nikolayevich (1820–71), 4, 43, 125, 139, 223, 238, 258, 263, 278, 283, 292, 295, 297–8

Shakespeare, William (1564–1616), 237

Shakhovsky, Aleksandr Aleksandrovich (1777–1846), 91, 144, 184, 187, 291

Shestakov, Vasily Illarionovich (d.1857), 10, 262

Shestakova, Lyudmila Ivanovna (1816–1906), 4, 7, 10, 17, 22–3, 50, 54, 240, 260, 279, 283–8, 290, 298, 302

Shestakova, Olga Vasilevna (1853–63), 280, 285, 287

Shilovskaya, Mariya Vasilevna (1830–79), 284

Shirkov, Valerian Fyodorovich (1805–56), 145, 154, 158, 164, 175, 177, 186, 189–95, 200

Shterich, Yevgeny Petrovich (1809–33), 47, 56–9

Sivers, Count, 33

Skoropadsky, Pyotr Petrovich, 146

Snegirev, L., 87

Sobolevsky, Sergei Aleksandrovich (1803–70), 57, 62, 73, 146

Sobolevsky, Yakov Mikhailovich (d.1844), 10, 38, 50, 151, 162, 175–6

Sokolovsky, Vladimir Ignatevich (1808–39), 145

Soliva, Carlo-Evazio (1792–1853), 141

Sollogub, Vladimir Aleksandrovich (1813–82), 43–4, 78, 97, 140

Solovyeva, Aleksandra Frantsevna, 244, 315

Spindler, Dr., 54

Spohr, Ludwig (1784–1859), 26, 56, 289

Spontini, Gasparo (1774–1851), 21, 59

Stabrovsky, Ivan, 14

Stasov, Dmitri Vasilevich (1828–1918), 279, 285, 290

Stasov, Vladimir Vasilevich (1824–1906), 3, 8, 10, 92, 98, 125, 134, 159, 167–70, 172, 185, 259, 261, 273, 279, 283, 285–7, 290, 292, 297, 300, 302, 305

Steibelt, Daniel (1765–1823), 17

Stepan [sub-gardener at Novospasskoye], 257

Stepanov, Nikolai Aleksandrovich (1807–77), 152–3, 174

Stepanov, Pyotr Aleksandrovich (1805–91), 4, 81, 153, 174–6, 256

Stepanova, M. M. (1815–1903), 196

Sternberg, Vasily Ivanovich (1818–45), 144, 188

Strauss, Johann (1804–49), 67, 99

Stravinsky, Igor Fyodorovich (1882–1971), 114, 131, 276

Stroyev, Pavel Mikhailovich (1796–1876), 92

Strugovshchikov, A. N., 4, 19, 89, 158

Stuneyev, Aleksei Stepanovich, 46, 76–7, 140

Stuneyev, Dmitri Stepanovich, 10, 46, 150

Stuneyeva, Sofya Petrovna, 76
Sumarokov [senator], 152
Swan, Alfred (1890–1970), 13
Szymanowskaya, Maria (1790–1831), 47

Tarnovsky, Grigory Stepanovich (d.1854), 142–4, 146
Tchaikovsky, Pyotr Ilich (1840–93), 1–2, 162, 170, 172, 206, 221–2, 236, 239, 277, 304
Tichatschek, Joseph (1807–86), 295
Titov, Aleksei Nikolayevich (1769–1827), 26
Titus, Antoine, 84, 177
Todi [Italian singing teacher], 21
Tolstoi, Feofil Matveyevich ['Rostislav'] (1809–81), 4, 44, 46, 62, 73, 125, 136, 277
Tosi [prima donna], 62
Tosi, D., 179
Turgenev, Ivan Sergeyevich (1818–83), 298

Uluibuishev, Aleksandr Dmitriyevich (1784–1858), 238, 279
Ushakov, Aleksei Andreyevich, 38
Ushakova, Yelizaveta Alekseyevna, 38, 258

Varlamov, Aleksandr Yegorovich (1801–48), 43
Vasilchikov, Nikolai Nikolayevich, 176, 237, 256
Vasilko-Petrov, Vasily Petrovich (1824–64), 291–2
Verdi, Giuseppe (1813–1901), 57, 160, 252, 297
Vernet, Horace (1789–1863), 312
Verstovsky, Aleksei Nikolayevich (1799–1862), 18, 26, 44, 112–13, 147, 238
Vigel, Filipp Filippovich (1786–1856), 89
Vitkovsky, Ivan Matveyevich, 29

Volkonskaya, Zinaida Aleksandrovna (1792–1862), 59
Volkonsky, Grigory Petrovich (1808–82), 137
Volkov, Nikolai Stepanovich, 81
Vorobyeva, Anna Yakovlevna (1816–1901), 80–1, 85–7, 105, 119, 124, 139, 141, 144, 179–80, 187, 189, 308
Vorontsov-Dashkov, Count, 58
Vyazemsky, Pyotr Andreyevich (1792–1878), 24, 87
Vyazemsky, Vladimir Andreyevich, 280

Wagner, Richard (1813–83), 119, 201, 223, 276
Weber, Carl Maria von (1786–1826), 25, 56, 74, 311
Weigl, Joseph (1766–1846), 22
Wielhorski, Mikhail Yurevich (1788–1856), 81, 94, 137, 186, 195–6, 237, 295

Yekaterina [Catherine] II (1729–96), 14
Yushkov, Pyotr Ivanovich (1771–1847), 21
Yusupov, Nikolai Borisovich, 80

Zabella, Viktor Nikolayevich (1808–69), 144, 146, 148
Zagoskin, Mikhail Nikolayevich (1789–1852), 91
Zamboni, Luigi (1767–1837), 46
Zampo, Ninetta, 63
Zeuner, Karl (1775–1841), 21, 306
Zherebtsov [landowner], 28
Zhukovsky, Vasily Andreyevich (1783–1852), 10, 24, 39, 50, 65, 75, 78, 82, 84, 89, 91, 96–8, 109, 140, 280, 307
Zingarelli, Niccolo (1752–1837), 58
Zoë [Indian cook], 287

45375

n, David
ail Glinka

DATE DUE
